GHOST URN 04

SHIROW MASAMUNE
RIKUDOU KOUSHI

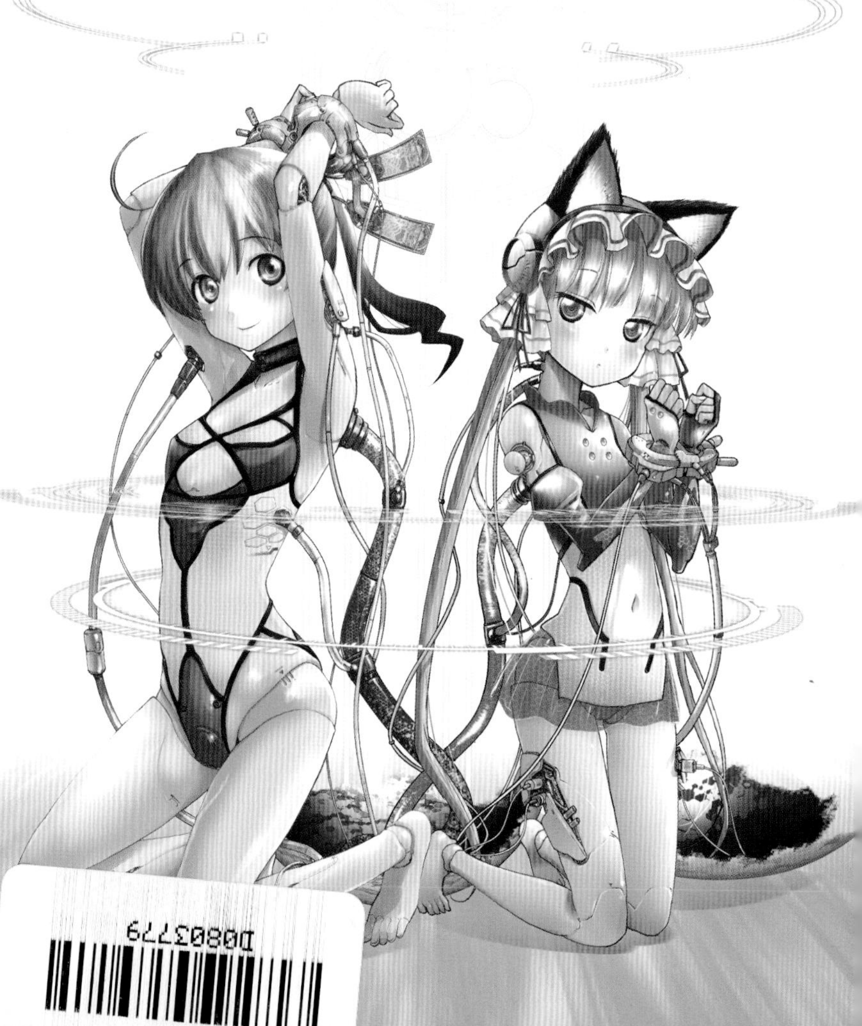

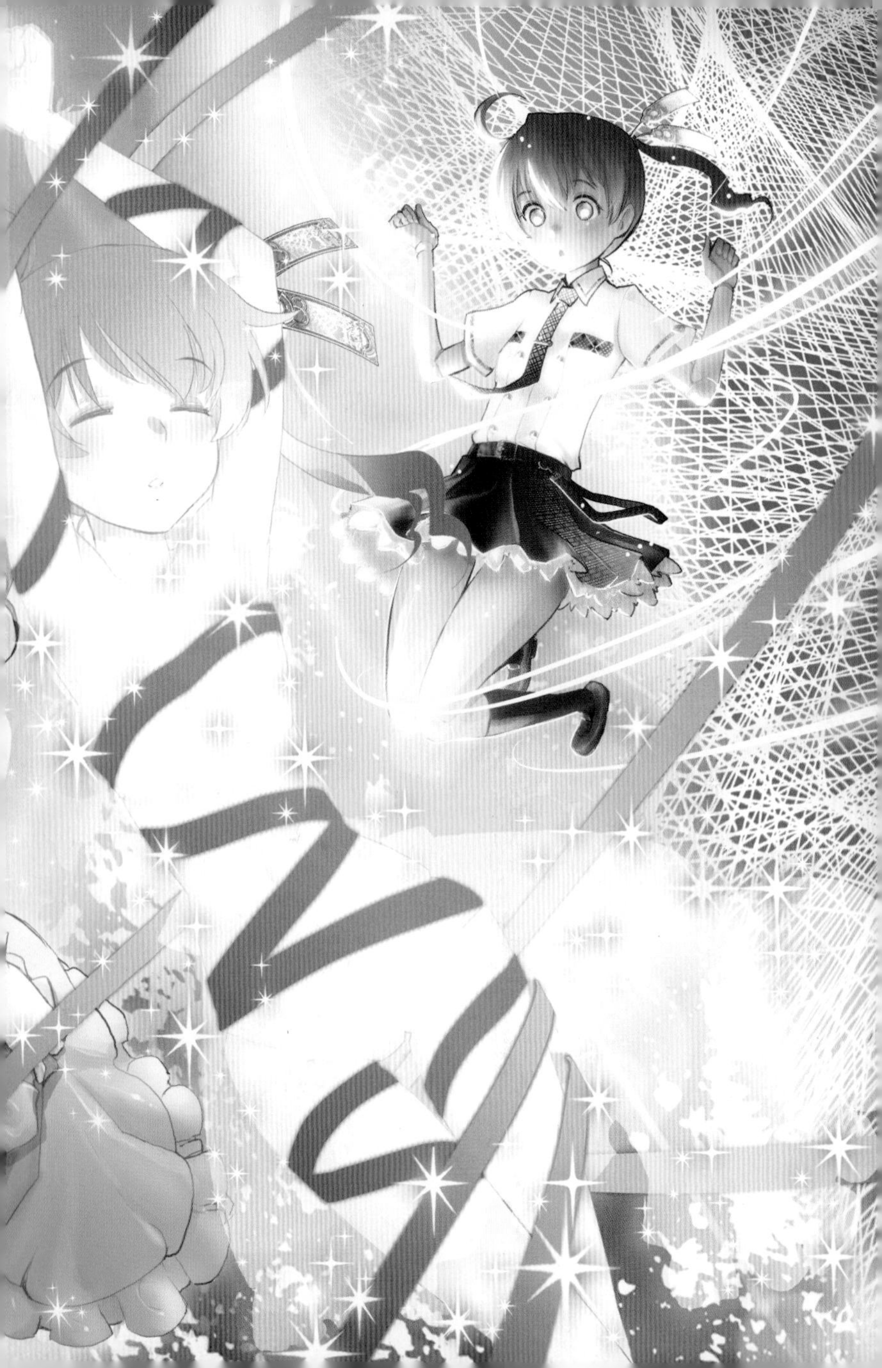

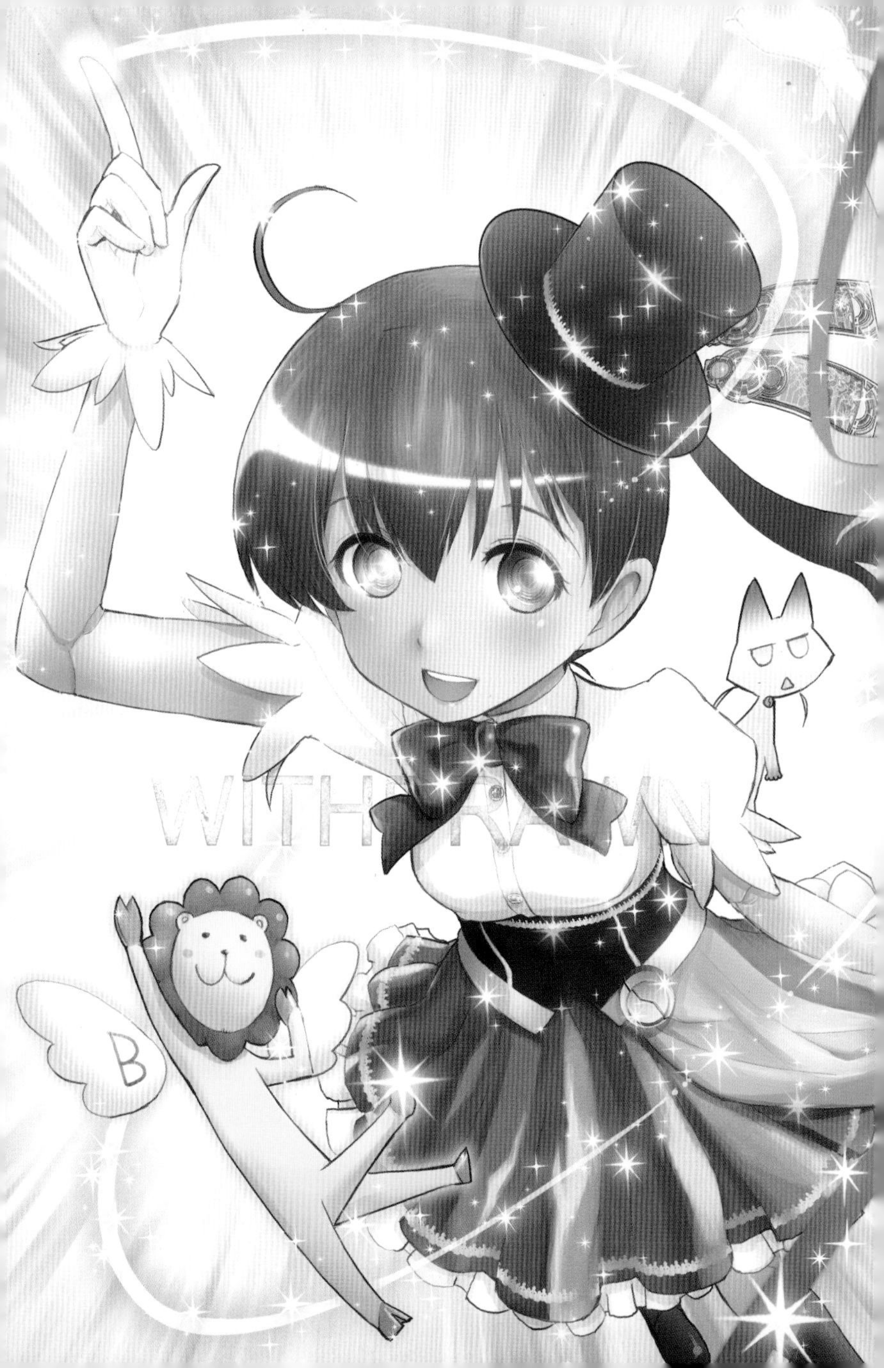

CLARION

row Ma

udou Koushi   Rikudou Kou

GHOST URN 04

PANDORA IN THE CRIMSON SHELL

STORY BY
SHIROW MASAMUNE

ART BY
RIKUDOU KOUSHI

rrow Masamune Shirow Masamune Shirow Masamune Shirow Masa

GHOST URN-EPISODE.log——The story so far!

Nanakorobi Nene, a girl who uses a full-body prosthetic, has a special ability: with help from her partner Clarion, an android, she's able to control the Pandora Device and install an endless variety of temporary abilities!

Nene and Clarion are settling into a routine on the artificial resort island of Cenancle, but the island itself is at risk as Colonel Kurtz and his followers from the American Empire move forward with their plot to unearth the massive boring machine Buer from deep underground...

udou Koushi Rikudou Koushi Rikudou Koushi Rikudou Koushi Rikudo

GHOST URN-CHARACTERS —— Main Characters

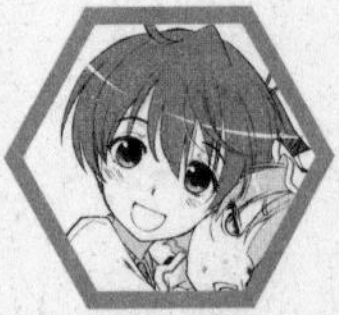

■Nanakorobi Nene

A girl whose brain was implanted into an entirely artificial body after an accident when she was young. Nene has one of the few full-body prosthetics in the world!

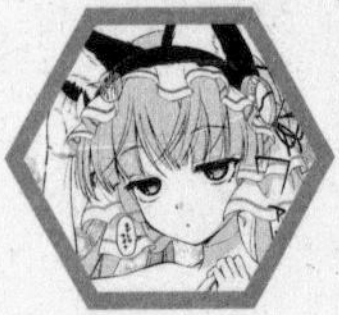

■Clarion

A combat android owned by Uzal. Clarion has many top-secret, illegal programs tucked away inside her.

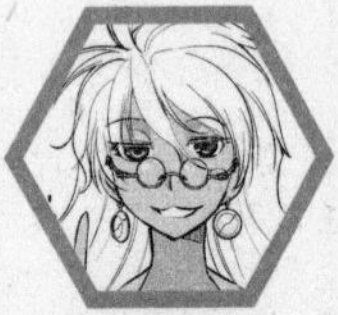

■Uzal Delilah

The mysterious Uzal, also known as Sahar Schehera, is a well-known international businesswoman, but she has plenty of secrets. She's responsible for the recent uproar on the island. At the moment, no one knows where she is.

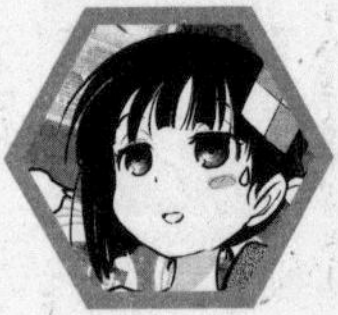

■Korobase Takumi

Age unknown. She heads up the Korobase Foundation, which controls cybrain marketing, but has a pathological fear of people.

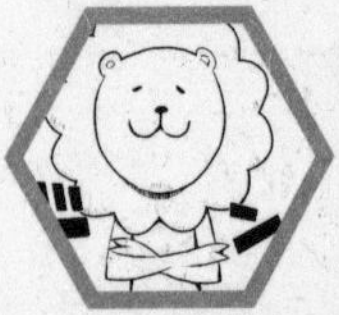

■Massive boring machine Buer: Central Nervous Unit

The central control unit for the large multi-legged boring machine, Buer. The unit speaks pompously, and is often subjected to abuse from Clarion. Buer's actual body is currently dormant and hidden deep underground.

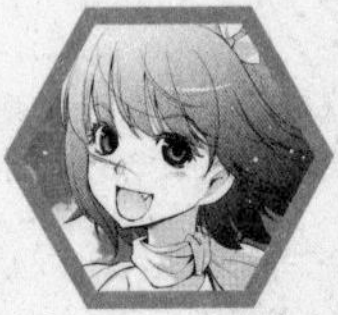

■Vlind——————

A perky, enthusiastic new Titan TV reporter who happened to be on the scene when the terrorist incident occurred. She miraculously survived! She currently has a part-time job, but she's working hard to move up in the world.

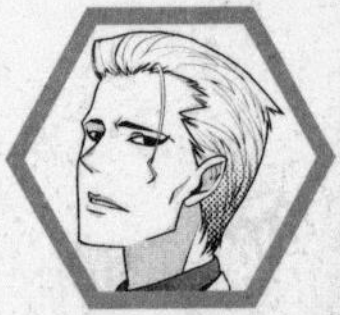

■Kurtz

A member of the American Imperial army. He's aiming to seize control of Buer, the machine Uzal left behind.

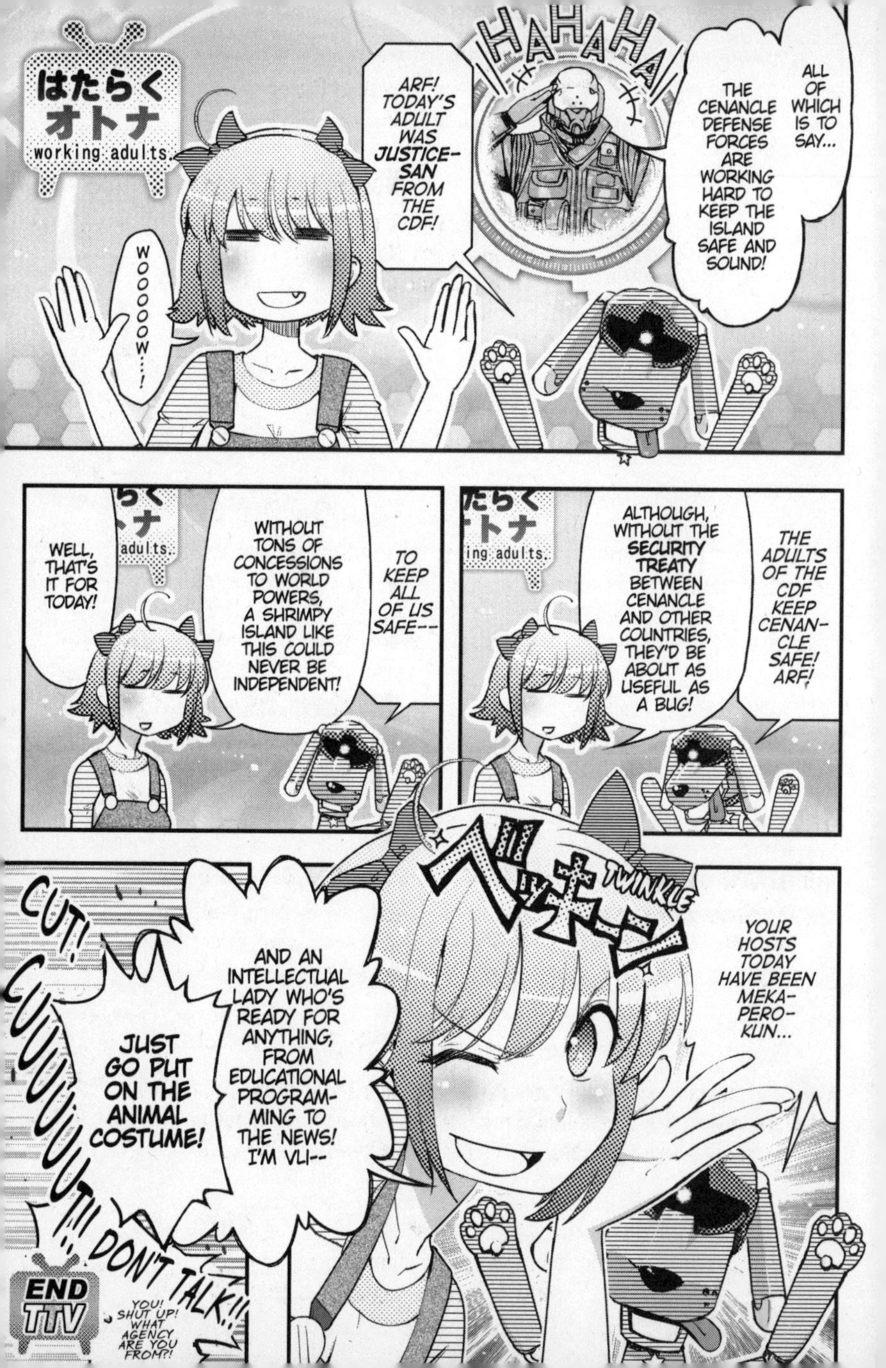
ALL OF WHICH IS TO SAY...
THE CENANCLE DEFENSE FORCES ARE WORKING HARD TO KEEP THE ISLAND SAFE AND SOUND!
HAHAHA
ARF! TODAY'S ADULT WAS JUSTICE-SAN FROM THE CDF!
WOOOOOOW...!
はたらくオトナ
working adults.
THE ADULTS OF THE CDF KEEP CENAN-CLE SAFE! ARF!
ALTHOUGH, WITHOUT THE SECURITY TREATY BETWEEN CENANCLE AND OTHER COUNTRIES, THEY'D BE ABOUT AS USEFUL AS A BUG!
ing adults.
TO KEEP ALL OF US SAFE--
WITHOUT TONS OF CONCESSIONS TO WORLD POWERS, A SHRIMPY ISLAND LIKE THIS COULD NEVER BE INDEPENDENT!
WELL, THAT'S IT FOR TODAY!
adults.
YOUR HOSTS TODAY HAVE BEEN MEKA-PERO-KUN...
TWINKLE
AND AN INTELLECTUAL LADY WHO'S READY FOR ANYTHING, FROM EDUCATIONAL PROGRAM-MING TO THE NEWS! I'M VLI--
JUST GO PUT ON THE ANIMAL COSTUME!
CUT! CUUUUUUUT!!! DON'T TALK!!!
YOU! SHUT UP! WHAT AGENCY ARE YOU FROM?!
END TTV

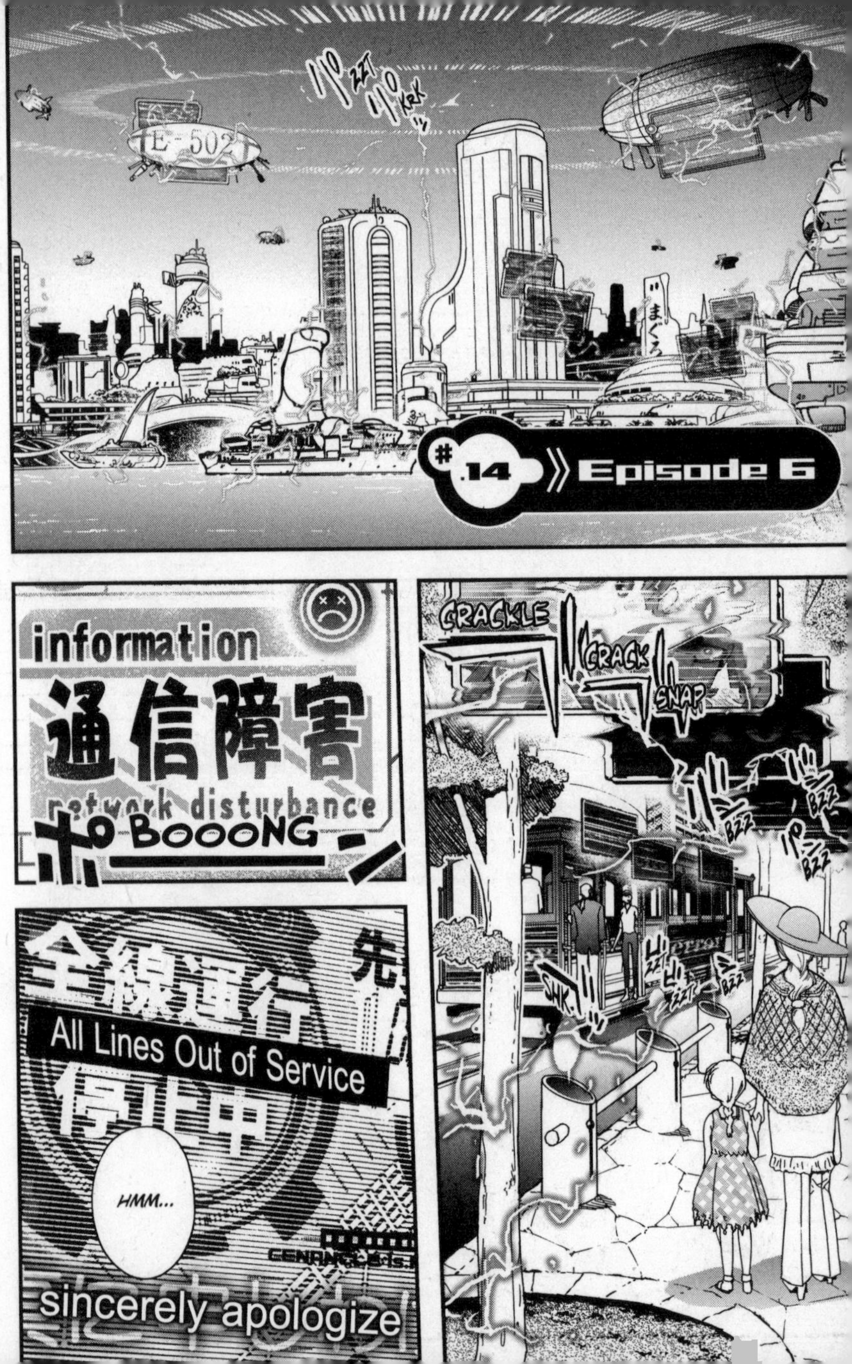
ZZT
KRK
E-502
まぐろ
#.14
Episode 6
CRACKLE
CRACK
SNAP
BZZ
BZZ
BZZ
SHK
ZZT
ZZT
BZZ
information
通信障害
network disturbance
BOOONG
全線運行
All Lines Out of Service
停止中
HMM...
sincerely apologize

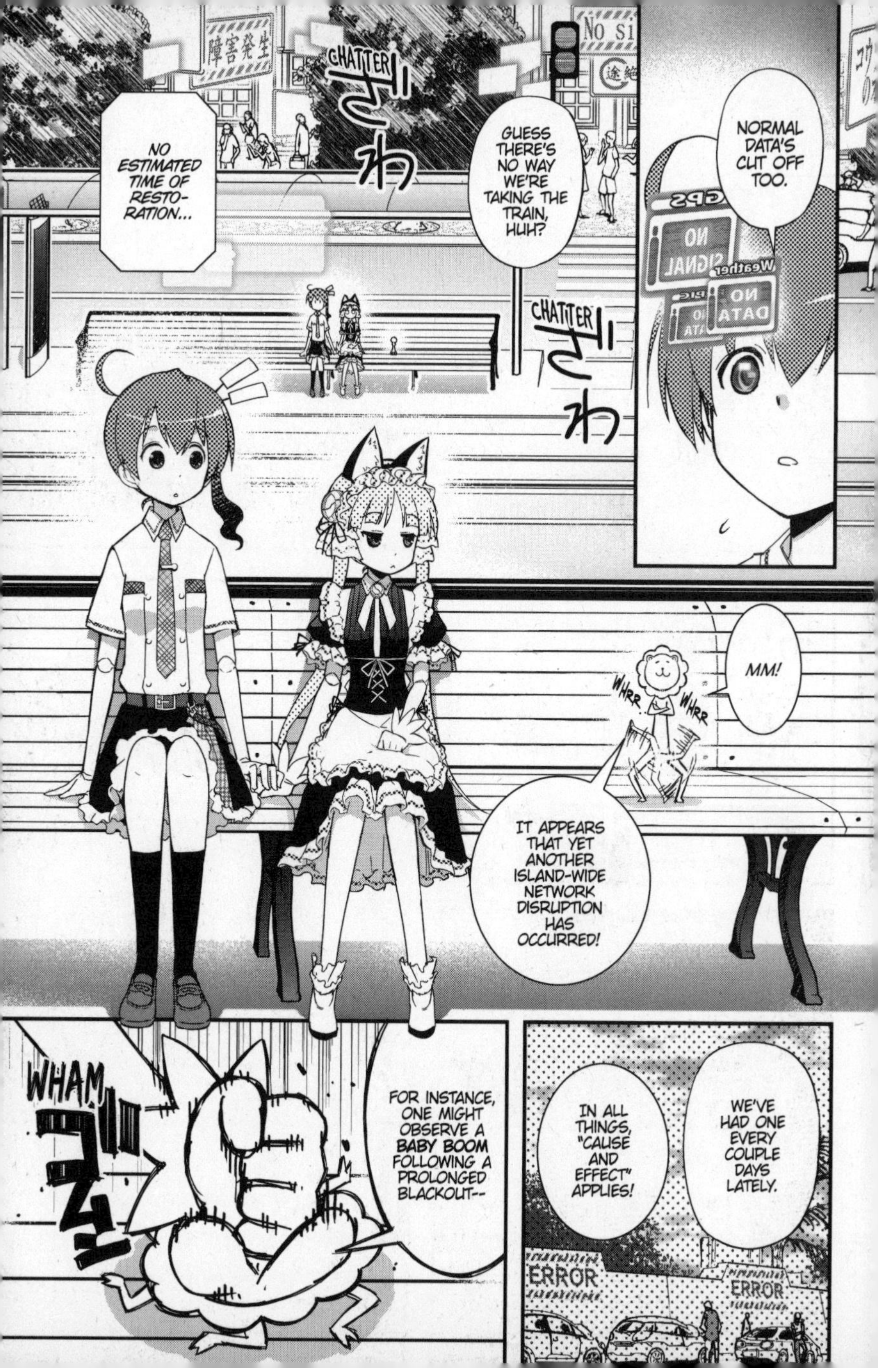

NORMAL DATA'S CUT OFF TOO.
GPS
NO SIGNAL
Weather
NO DATA
障害発生
CHATTER ざわ
GUESS THERE'S NO WAY WE'RE TAKING THE TRAIN, HUH?
NO ESTIMATED TIME OF RESTO-RATION...
CHATTER ざわ
MM!
WHRR WHRR
IT APPEARS THAT YET ANOTHER ISLAND-WIDE NETWORK DISRUPTION HAS OCCURRED!
WE'VE HAD ONE EVERY COUPLE DAYS LATELY.
IN ALL THINGS, "CAUSE AND EFFECT" APPLIES!
ERROR
ERROR
FOR INSTANCE, ONE MIGHT OBSERVE A **BABY BOOM** FOLLOWING A PROLONGED BLACKOUT--
WHAM ゴッ

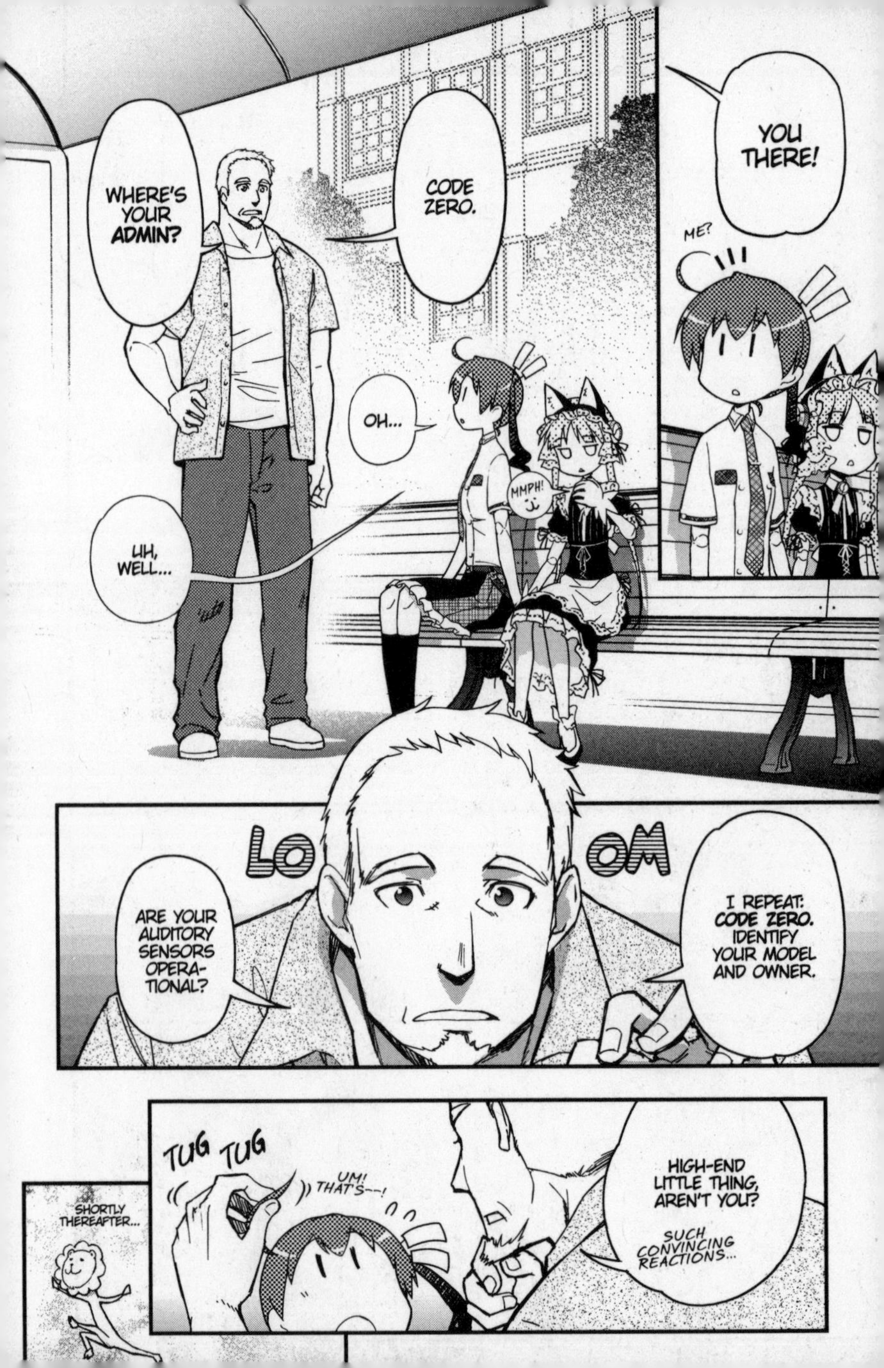

YOU THERE!
ME?
CODE ZERO.
WHERE'S YOUR ADMIN?
OH...
MMPH!
UH, WELL...
LO OM
I REPEAT: CODE ZERO. IDENTIFY YOUR MODEL AND OWNER.
ARE YOUR AUDITORY SENSORS OPERA-TIONAL?
HIGH-END LITTLE THING, AREN'T YOU?
SUCH CONVINCING REACTIONS...
UM! THAT'S--!
TUG TUG
SHORTLY THEREAFTER...

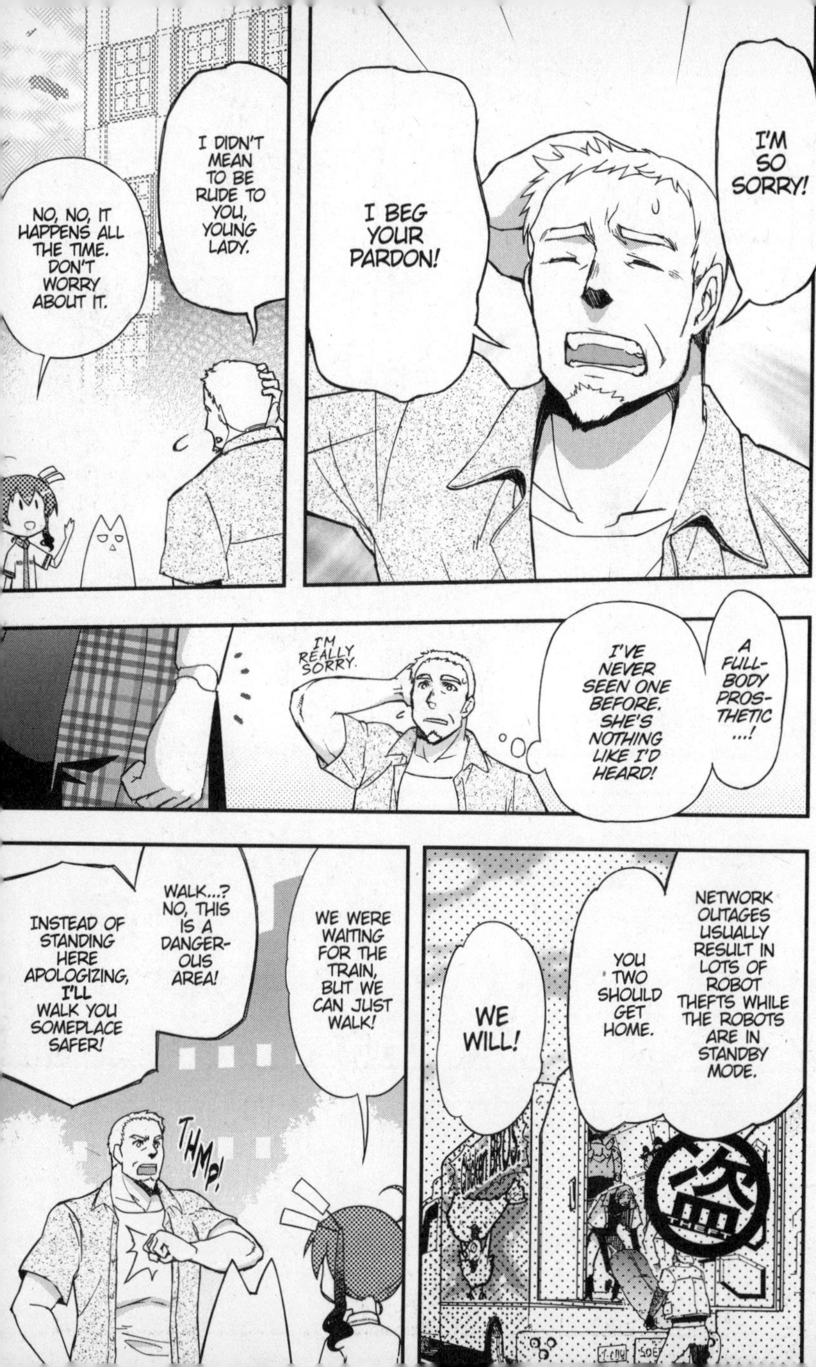
I'M SO SORRY!
I BEG YOUR PARDON!
I DIDN'T MEAN TO BE RUDE TO YOU, YOUNG LADY.
NO, NO, IT HAPPENS ALL THE TIME. DON'T WORRY ABOUT IT.
A FULL-BODY PROS-THETIC...!
I'VE NEVER SEEN ONE BEFORE. SHE'S NOTHING LIKE I'D HEARD!
I'M REALLY SORRY.
NETWORK OUTAGES USUALLY RESULT IN LOTS OF ROBOT THEFTS WHILE THE ROBOTS ARE IN STANDBY MODE.
YOU TWO SHOULD GET HOME.
WE WILL!
WE WERE WAITING FOR THE TRAIN, BUT WE CAN JUST WALK!
WALK...? NO, THIS IS A DANGER-OUS AREA!
INSTEAD OF STANDING HERE APOLOGIZING, **I'LL** WALK YOU SOMEPLACE SAFER!
THMP!

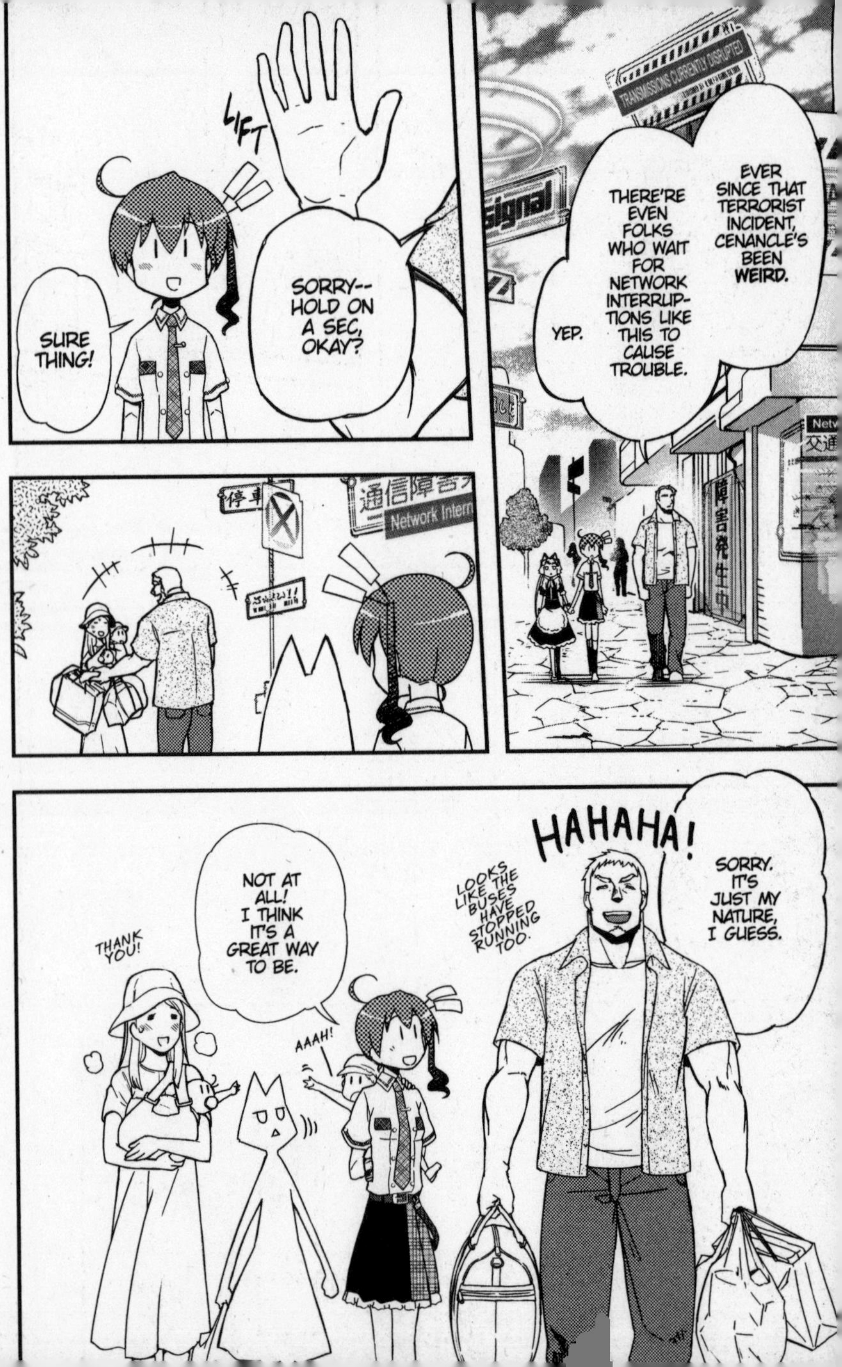
TRANSMISSIONS CURRENTLY DISRUPTED
signal
EVER SINCE THAT TERRORIST INCIDENT, CENANCLE'S BEEN WEIRD.
THERE'RE EVEN FOLKS WHO WAIT FOR NETWORK INTERRUP-TIONS LIKE THIS TO CAUSE TROUBLE.
YEP.
障害発生中
LIFT
SORRY-- HOLD ON A SEC, OKAY?
SURE THING!
HAHAHA!
SORRY. IT'S JUST MY NATURE, I GUESS.
LOOKS LIKE THE BUSES HAVE STOPPED RUNNING TOO.
NOT AT ALL! I THINK IT'S A GREAT WAY TO BE.
AAAH!
THANK YOU!

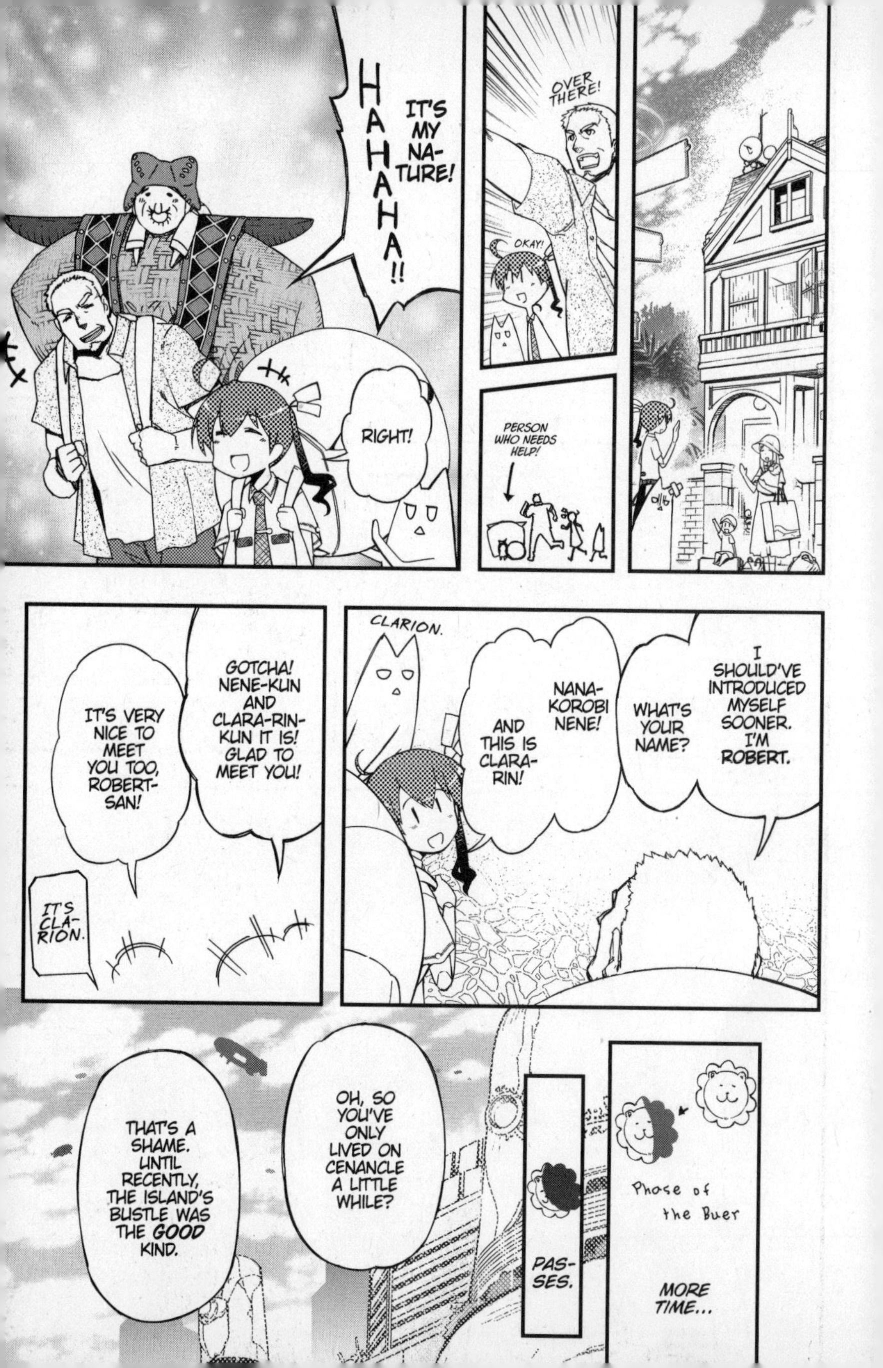
OVER THERE!
OKAY!
PERSON WHO NEEDS HELP!
IT'S MY NA-TURE!
HAHAHA!!
RIGHT!
I SHOULD'VE INTRODUCED MYSELF SOONER. I'M ROBERT.
WHAT'S YOUR NAME?
NANA-KOROBI NENE!
AND THIS IS CLARA-RIN!
CLARION.
GOTCHA! NENE-KUN AND CLARA-RIN-KUN IT IS! GLAD TO MEET YOU!
IT'S VERY NICE TO MEET YOU TOO, ROBERT-SAN!
IT'S CLA-RION.
Phose of the Buer
MORE TIME...
PAS-SES.
OH, SO YOU'VE ONLY LIVED ON CENANCLE A LITTLE WHILE?
THAT'S A SHAME. UNTIL RECENTLY, THE ISLAND'S BUSTLE WAS THE GOOD KIND.

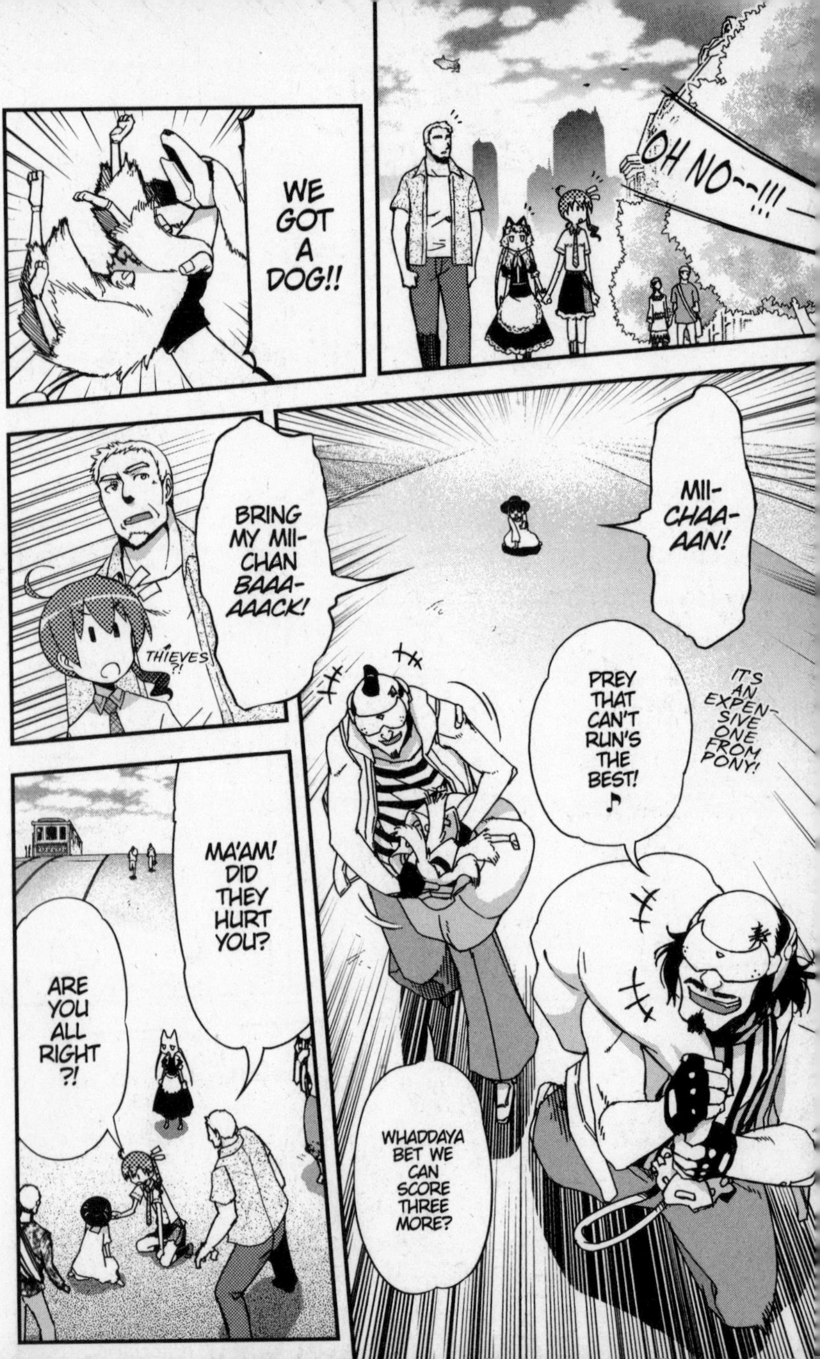
OH NO~~!!!
WE GOT A DOG!!
MII-CHAAA-AAN!
PREY THAT CAN'T RUN'S THE BEST! ♪
IT'S AN EXPEN-SIVE ONE FROM PONY!
WHADDAYA BET WE CAN SCORE THREE MORE?
BRING MY MII-CHAN BAAAA-AAACK!
THIEVES ?!
MA'AM! DID THEY HURT YOU?
ARE YOU ALL RIGHT ?!

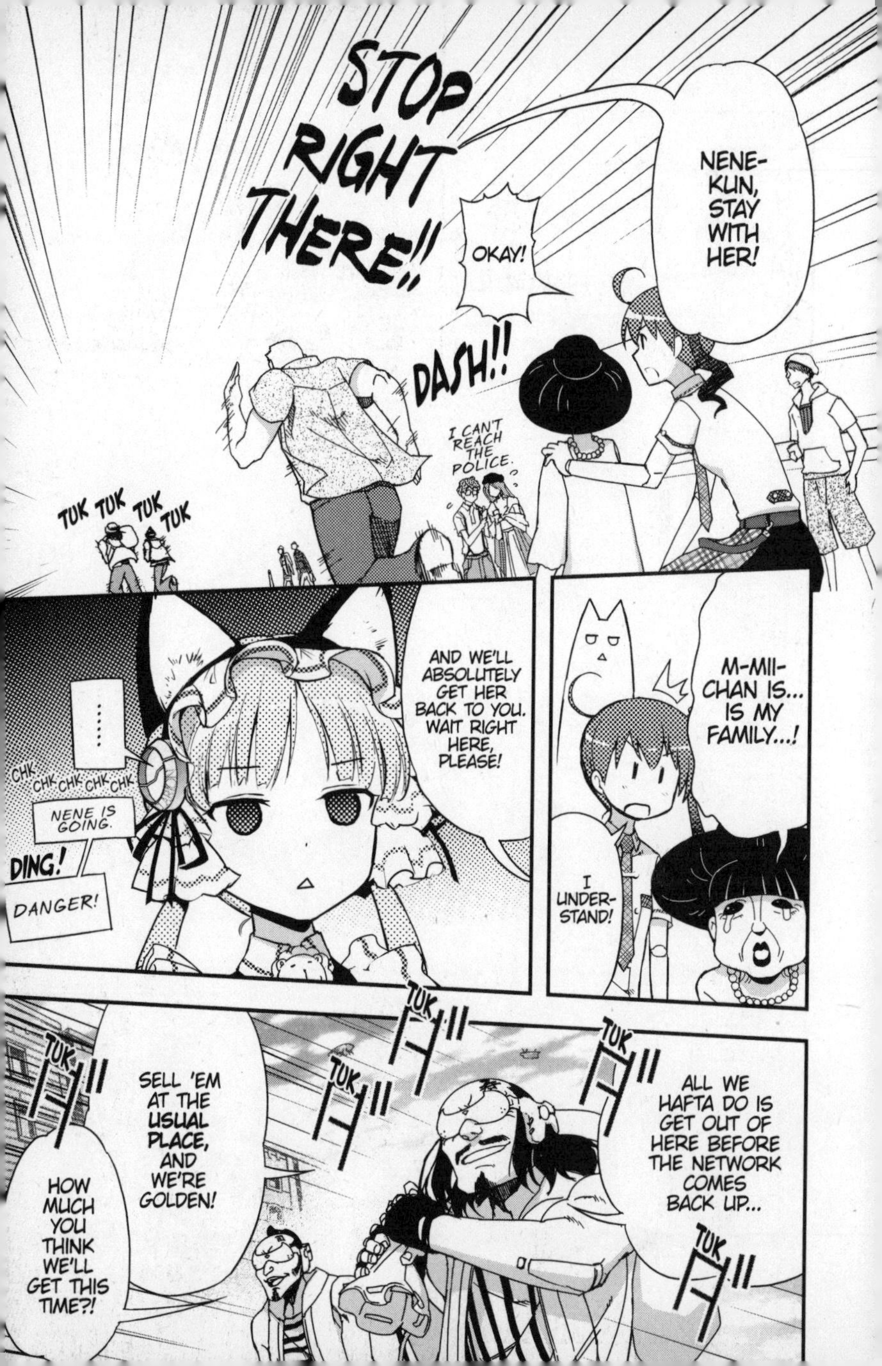
NENE-KUN, STAY WITH HER!
OKAY!
STOP RIGHT THERE!!
DASH!!
I CAN'T REACH THE POLICE.
TUK TUK TUK TUK
M-MII-CHAN IS... IS MY FAMILY...!
I UNDERSTAND!
AND WE'LL ABSOLUTELY GET HER BACK TO YOU. WAIT RIGHT HERE, PLEASE!
......
CHK CHK CHK CHK CHK
NENE IS GOING.
DING!
DANGER!
TUK TUK
ALL WE HAFTA DO IS GET OUT OF HERE BEFORE THE NETWORK COMES BACK UP...
TUK
SELL 'EM AT THE USUAL PLACE, AND WE'RE GOLDEN!
TUK
HOW MUCH YOU THINK WE'LL GET THIS TIME?!
TUK

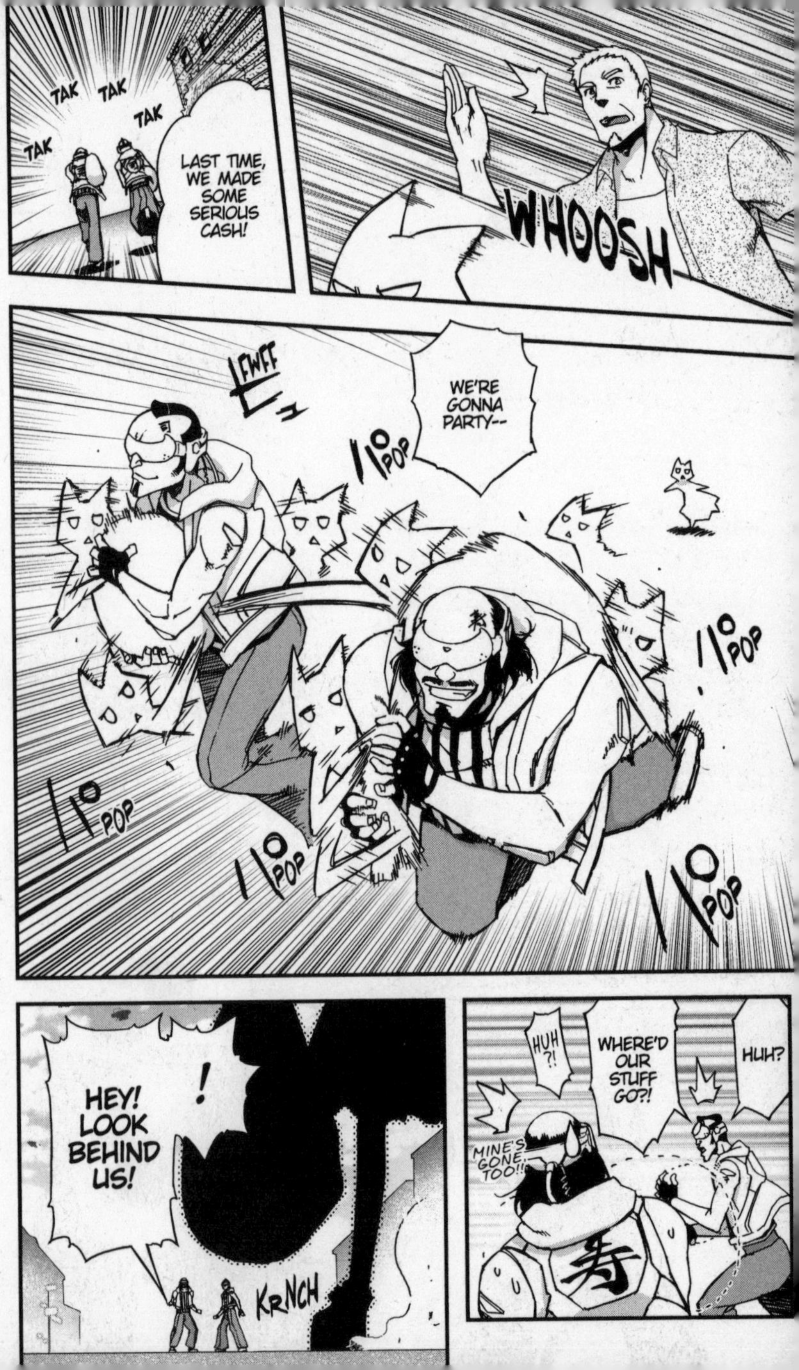
WHOOSH
TAK
TAK
TAK
TAK
LAST TIME, WE MADE SOME SERIOUS CASH!
WE'RE GONNA PARTY--
FWFF
POP
POP
POP
POP
POP
HUH?
WHERE'D OUR STUFF GO?!
HUH ?!
MINE'S GONE, TOO!!
!
HEY! LOOK BEHIND US!
KRNCH

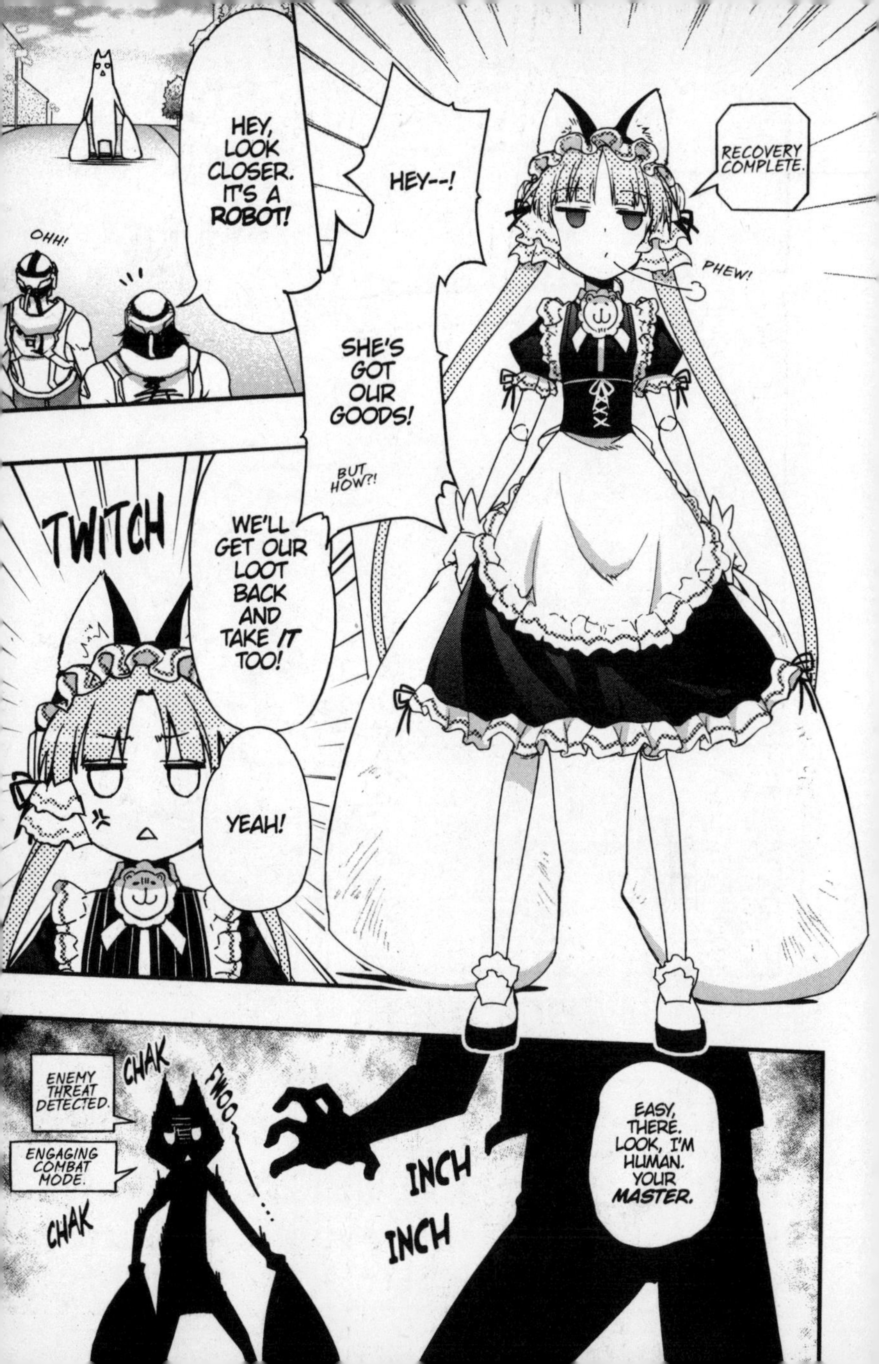
RECOVERY COMPLETE.
PHEW!
HEY--!
SHE'S GOT OUR GOODS!
BUT HOW?!
HEY, LOOK CLOSER. IT'S A ROBOT!
OHH!
WE'LL GET OUR LOOT BACK AND TAKE *IT* TOO!
YEAH!
TWITCH
EASY, THERE. LOOK, I'M HUMAN. YOUR **MASTER.**
INCH
INCH
FWOO-
CHAK
ENEMY THREAT DETECTED.
ENGAGING COMBAT MODE.
CHAK

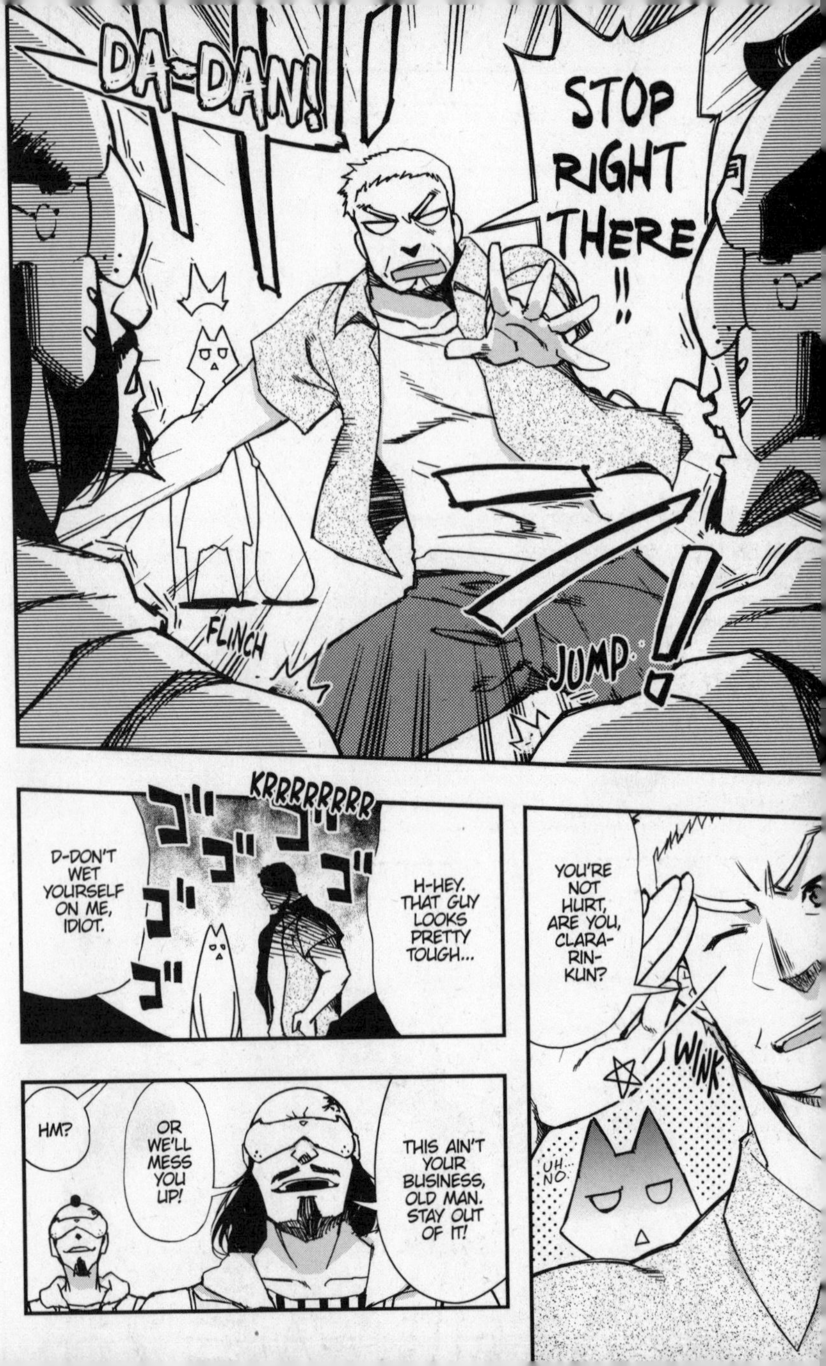
STOP RIGHT THERE!!
DA-DAN!
JUMP!
FLINCH
YOU'RE NOT HURT, ARE YOU, CLARA-RIN-KUN?
WINK
UH... NO.
KRRRRRRRR
H-HEY. THAT GUY LOOKS PRETTY TOUGH...
D-DON'T WET YOURSELF ON ME, IDIOT.
THIS AIN'T YOUR BUSINESS, OLD MAN. STAY OUT OF IT!
OR WE'LL MESS YOU UP!
HM?

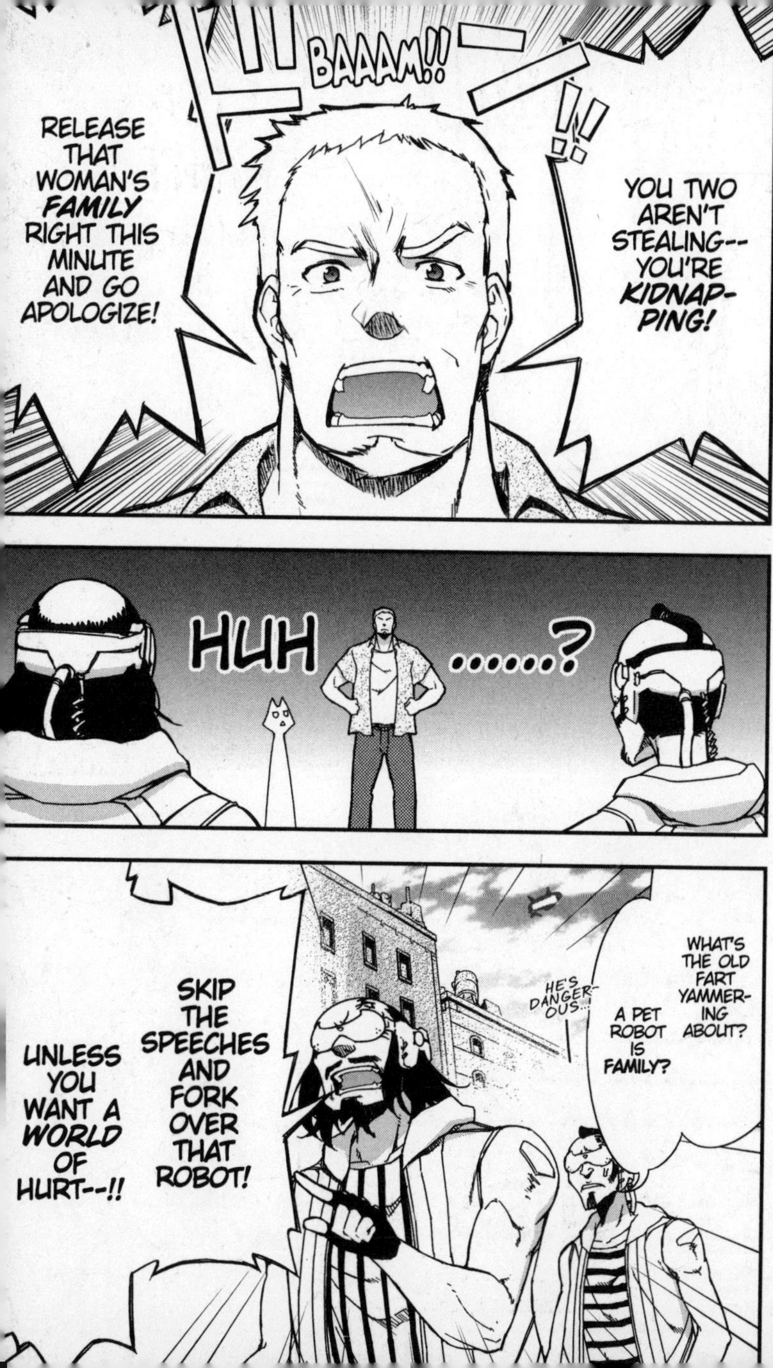
BAAAM!!
YOU TWO AREN'T STEALING-- YOU'RE *KIDNAPPING!*
RELEASE THAT WOMAN'S *FAMILY* RIGHT THIS MINUTE AND GO APOLOGIZE!
HUH ......?
WHAT'S THE OLD FART YAMMERING ABOUT?
A PET ROBOT IS FAMILY?
HE'S DANGEROUS...
SKIP THE SPEECHES AND FORK OVER THAT ROBOT!
UNLESS YOU WANT A *WORLD* OF HURT--!!

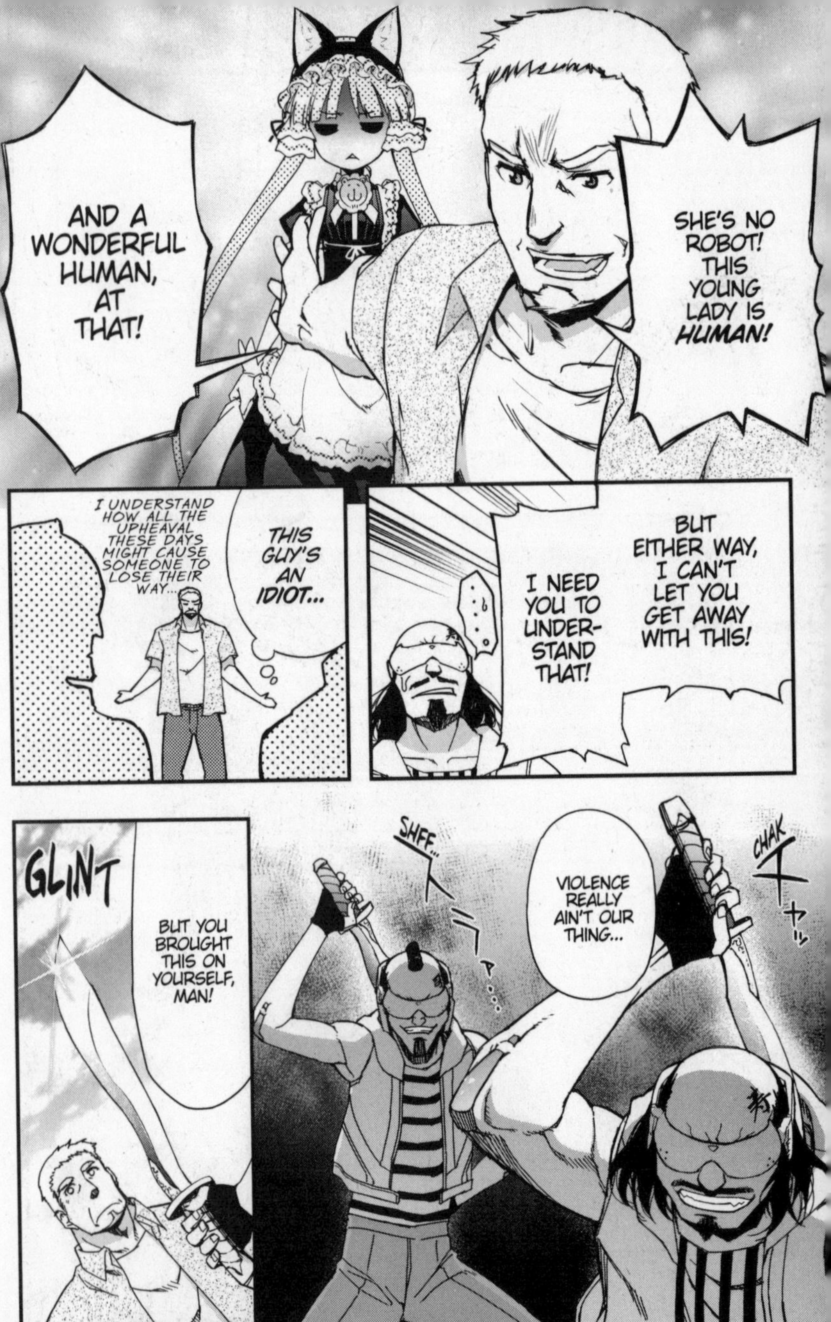
SHE'S NO ROBOT! THIS YOUNG LADY IS HUMAN!
AND A WONDERFUL HUMAN, AT THAT!
BUT EITHER WAY, I CAN'T LET YOU GET AWAY WITH THIS!
I NEED YOU TO UNDER-STAND THAT!
THIS GUY'S AN IDIOT...
I UNDERSTAND HOW ALL THE UPHEAVAL THESE DAYS MIGHT CAUSE SOMEONE TO LOSE THEIR WAY...
CHAK
VIOLENCE REALLY AIN'T OUR THING...
SHFF...
GLINT
BUT YOU BROUGHT THIS ON YOURSELF, MAN!

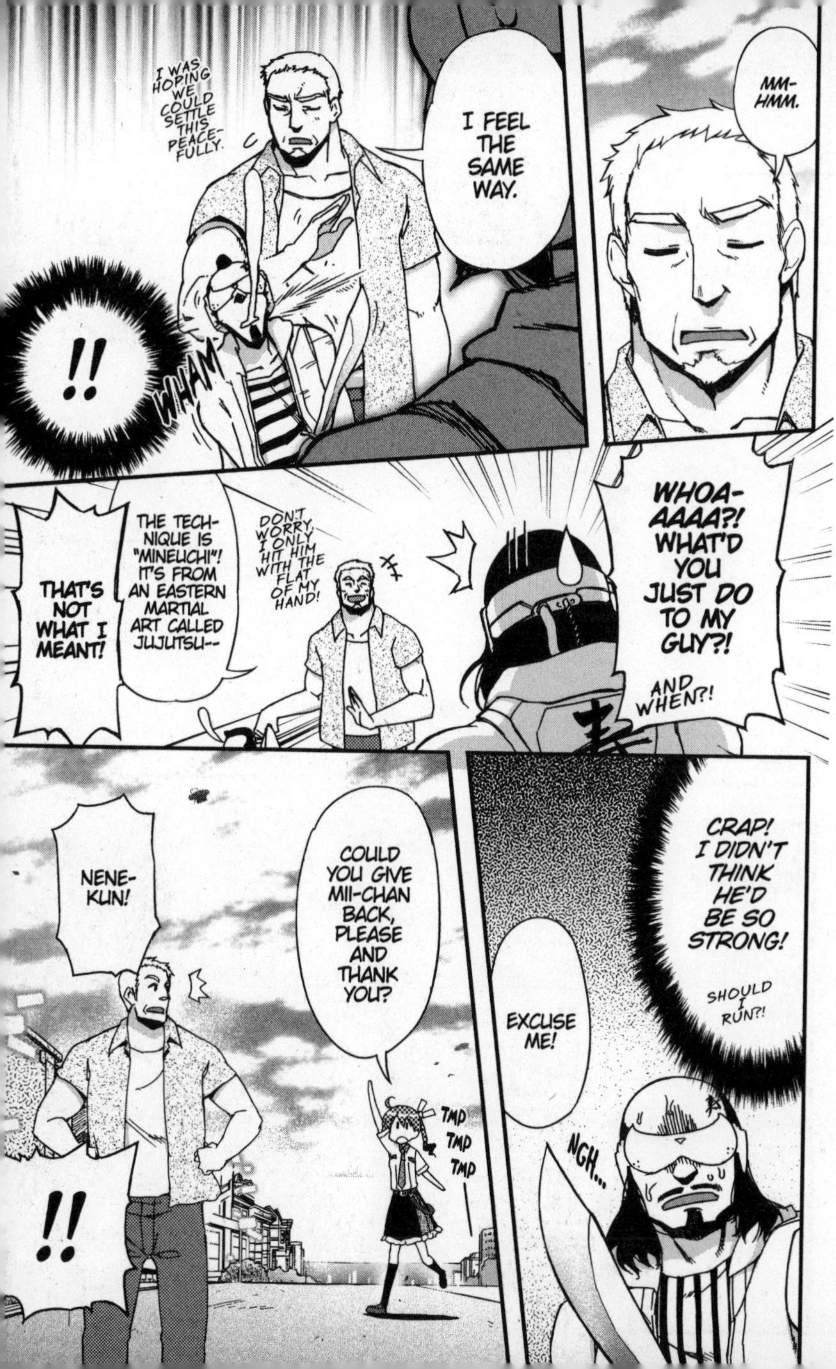
MM-HMM.
I FEEL THE SAME WAY.
I WAS HOPING WE COULD SETTLE THIS PEACE-FULLY.
WHAM
!!
WHOA-AAAA?! WHAT'D YOU JUST DO TO MY GUY?!
AND WHEN?!
DON'T WORRY, I ONLY HIT HIM WITH THE FLAT OF MY HAND!
THE TECH-NIQUE IS "MINEUCHI"! IT'S FROM AN EASTERN MARTIAL ART CALLED JUJUTSU--
THAT'S NOT WHAT I MEANT!
CRAP! I DIDN'T THINK HE'D BE SO STRONG!
SHOULD I RUN?!
EXCUSE ME!
NGH...
COULD YOU GIVE MII-CHAN BACK, PLEASE AND THANK YOU?
TMP TMP TMP
NENE-KUN!
!!

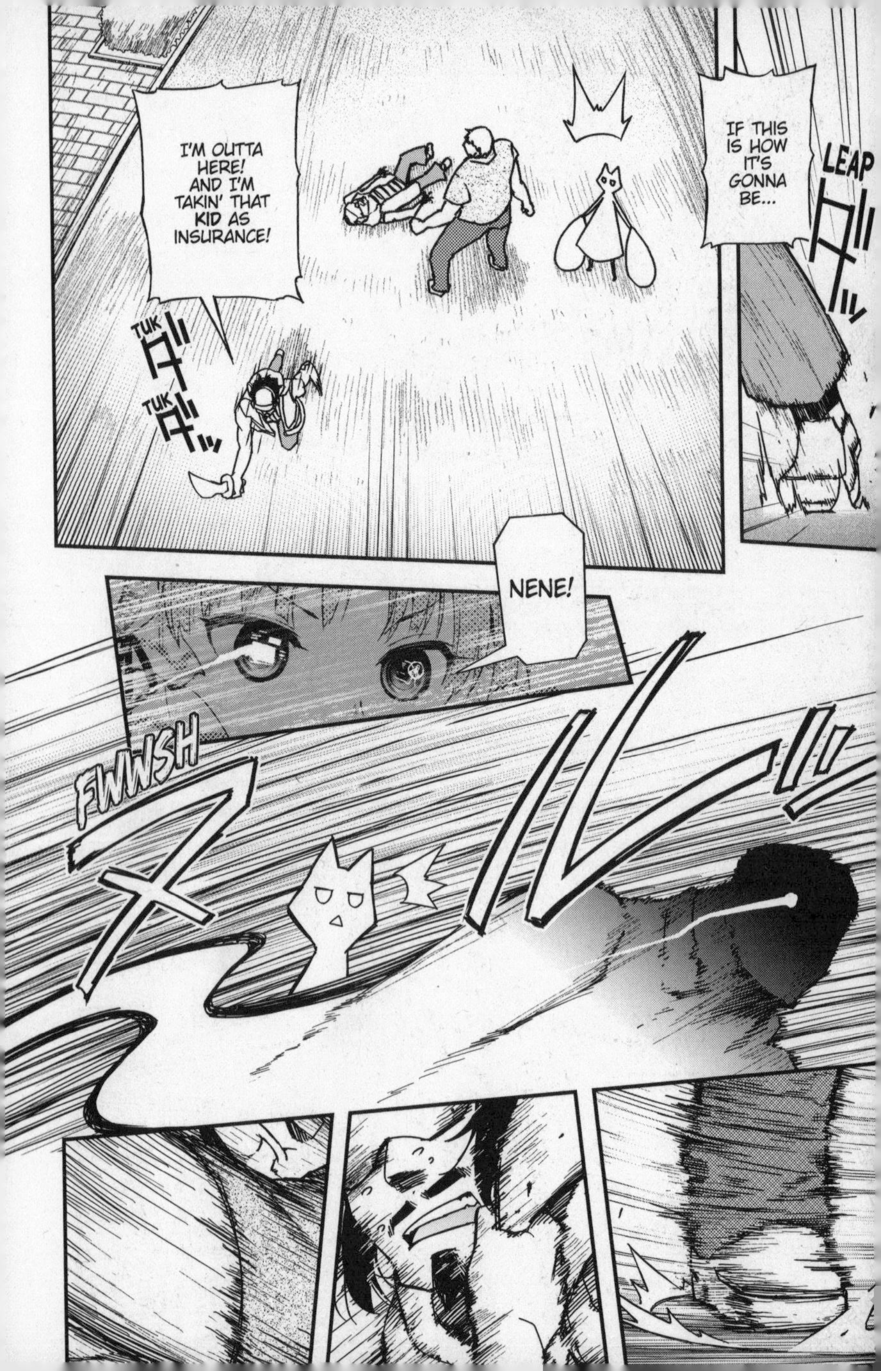
IF THIS IS HOW IT'S GONNA BE...
LEAP
I'M OUTTA HERE! AND I'M TAKIN' THAT KID AS INSURANCE!
TUK
TUK
NENE!
FWWSH

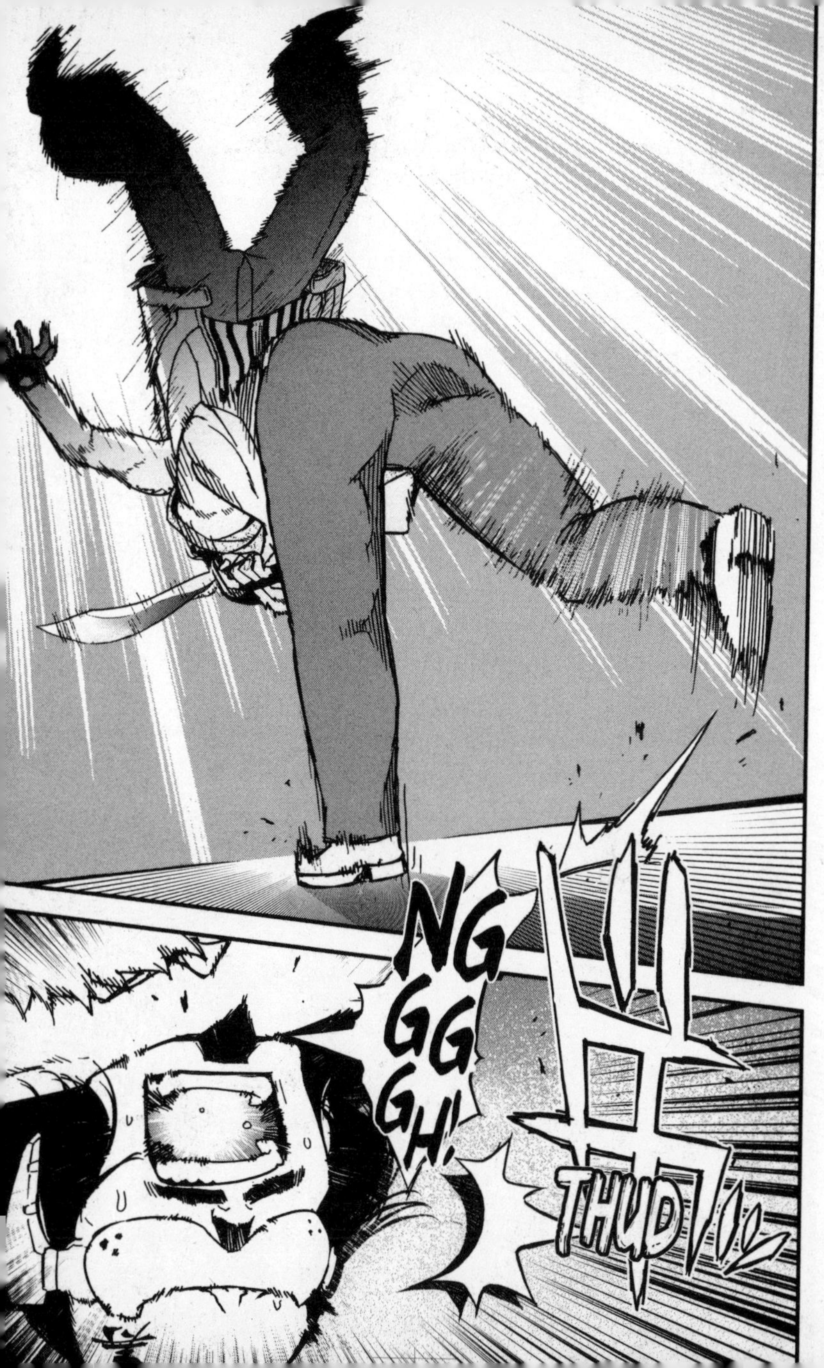
NGGGGH!
THUD

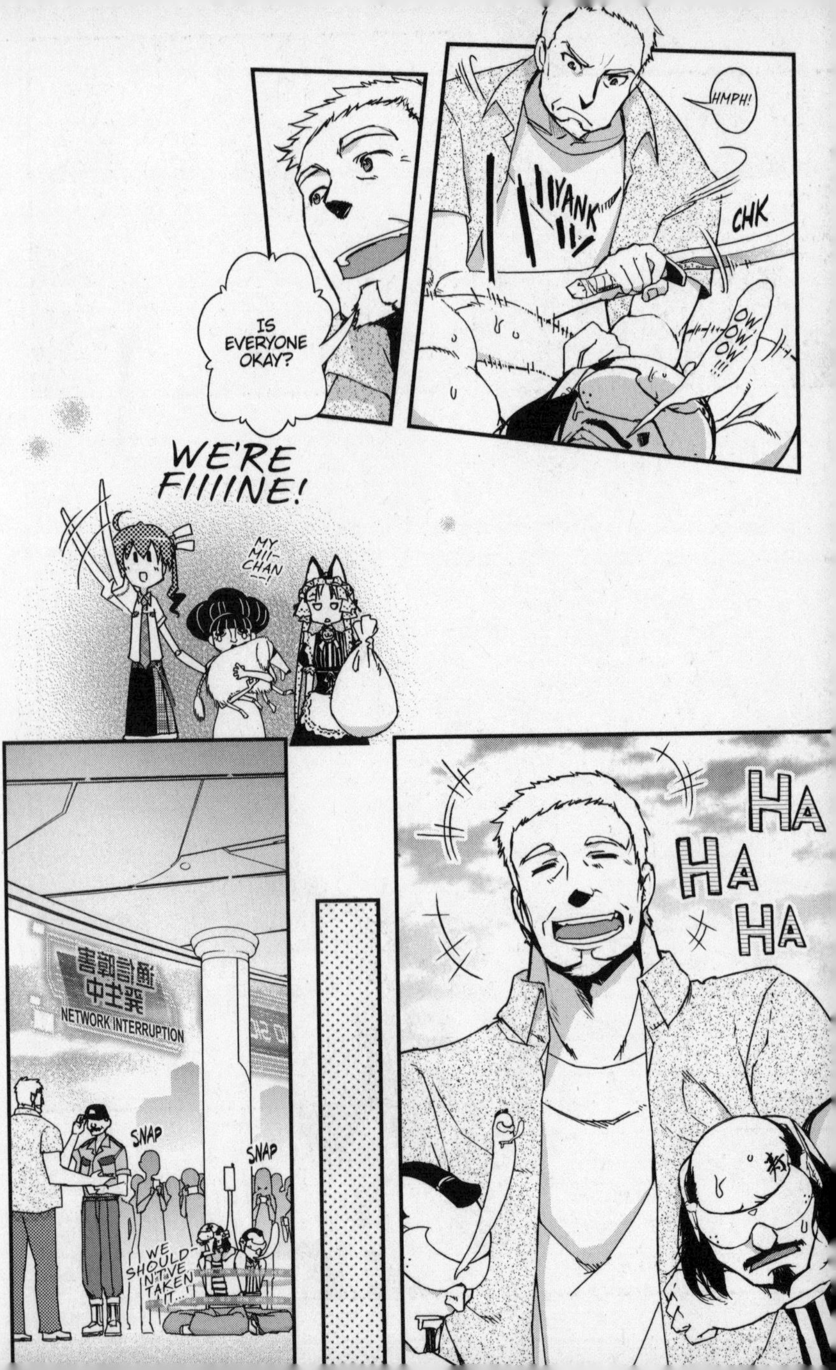
HMPH!
YANK
CHK
OW OW OW!!!
IS EVERYONE OKAY?
WE'RE FIIIINE!
MY MII-CHAN~!
HA HA HA HA
NETWORK INTERRUPTION
SNAP
SNAP
WE SHOULDN'T'VE TAKEN IT...!

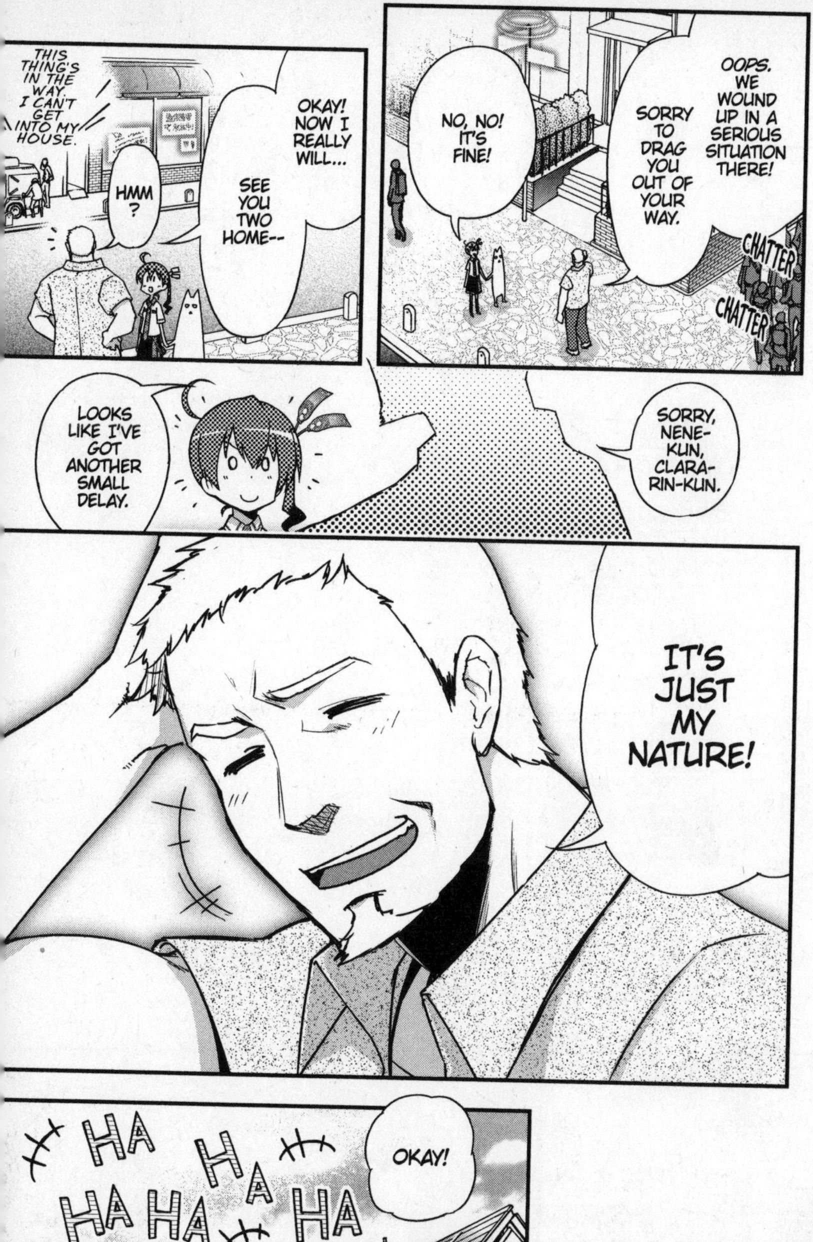
OOPS. WE WOUND UP IN A SERIOUS SITUATION THERE!
SORRY TO DRAG YOU OUT OF YOUR WAY.
NO, NO! IT'S FINE!
CHATTER
CHATTER
OKAY! NOW I REALLY WILL...
SEE YOU TWO HOME--
HMM?
THIS THING'S IN THE WAY. I CAN'T GET INTO MY HOUSE.
SORRY, NENE-KUN, CLARA-RIN-KUN.
LOOKS LIKE I'VE GOT ANOTHER SMALL DELAY.
IT'S JUST MY NATURE!
OKAY!
HA HA HA HA HA HA

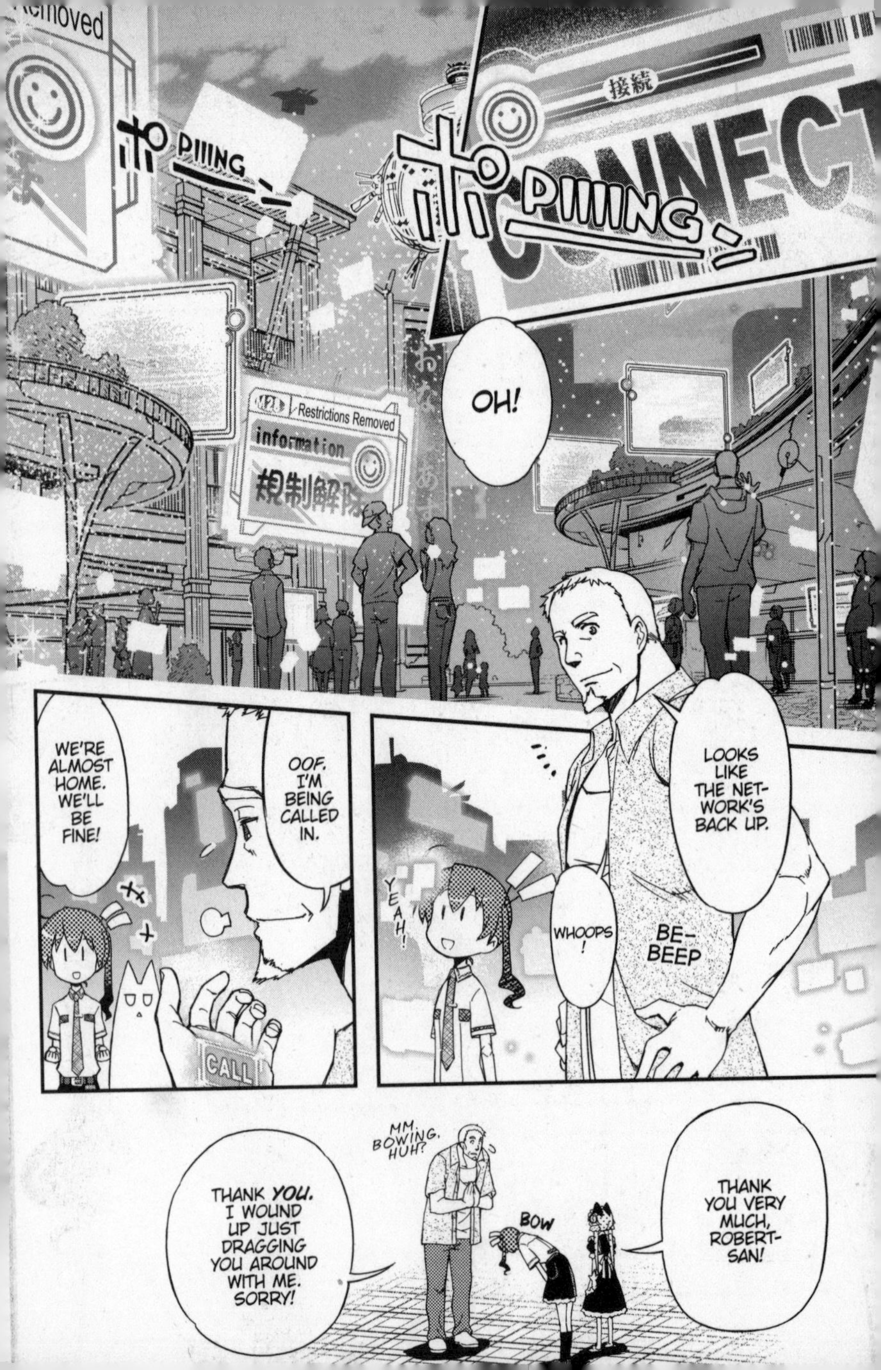
接続
CONNECT
PIIIING
Removed
PIIING
OH!
Restrictions Removed
information
規制解除
LOOKS LIKE THE NET-WORK'S BACK UP.
...
BE-BEEP
WHOOPS!
YEAH!
OOF. I'M BEING CALLED IN.
WE'RE ALMOST HOME. WE'LL BE FINE!
CALL
THANK YOU VERY MUCH, ROBERT-SAN!
MM, BOWING, HUH?
BOW
THANK YOU. I WOUND UP JUST DRAGGING YOU AROUND WITH ME. SORRY!

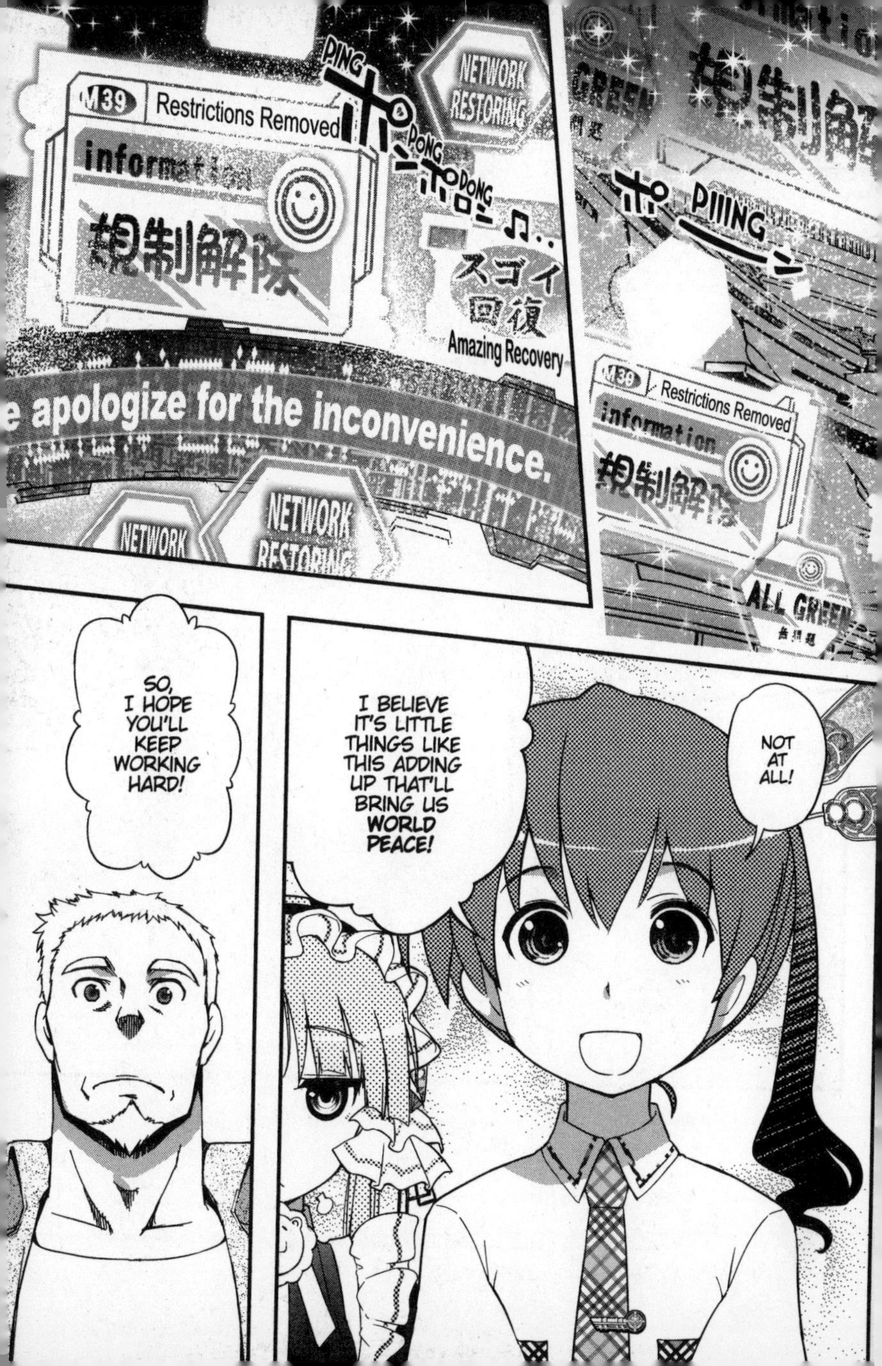
ポーーン
PIIING
M39 Restrictions Removed
information
規制解除
ALL GREEN
M39 Restrictions Removed
規制解除
ポーンポロン♪..
PING PONG PONG DONG
NETWORK RESTORING
スゴイ回復
Amazing Recovery
e apologize for the inconvenience.
NETWORK RESTORING
NOT AT ALL!
I BELIEVE IT'S LITTLE THINGS LIKE THIS ADDING UP THAT'LL BRING US WORLD PEACE!
SO, I HOPE YOU'LL KEEP WORKING HARD!

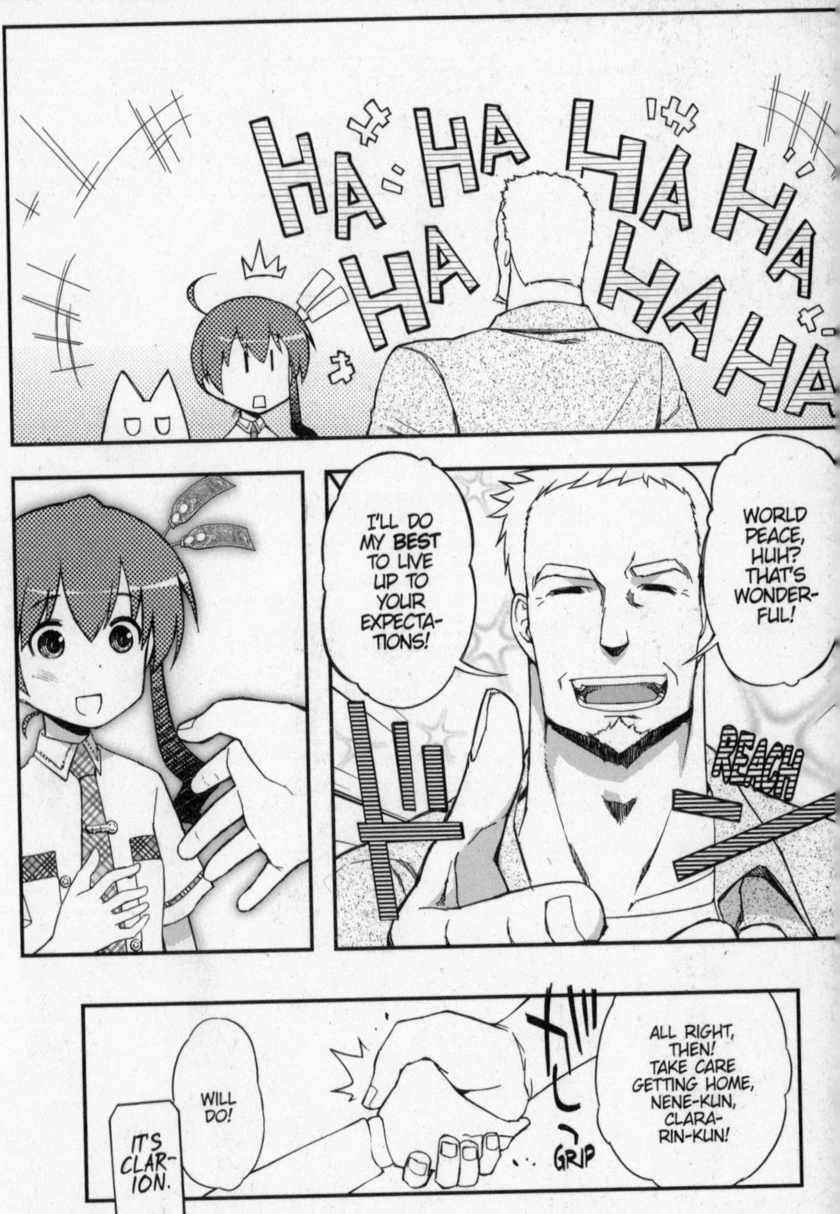
HA HA HA HA HA HA HA HA HA
WORLD PEACE, HUH? THAT'S WONDERFUL!
I'LL DO MY BEST TO LIVE UP TO YOUR EXPECTATIONS!
REACH
ALL RIGHT, THEN! TAKE CARE GETTING HOME, NENE-KUN, CLARA-RIN-KUN!
GRIP
WILL DO!
IT'S CLARION.

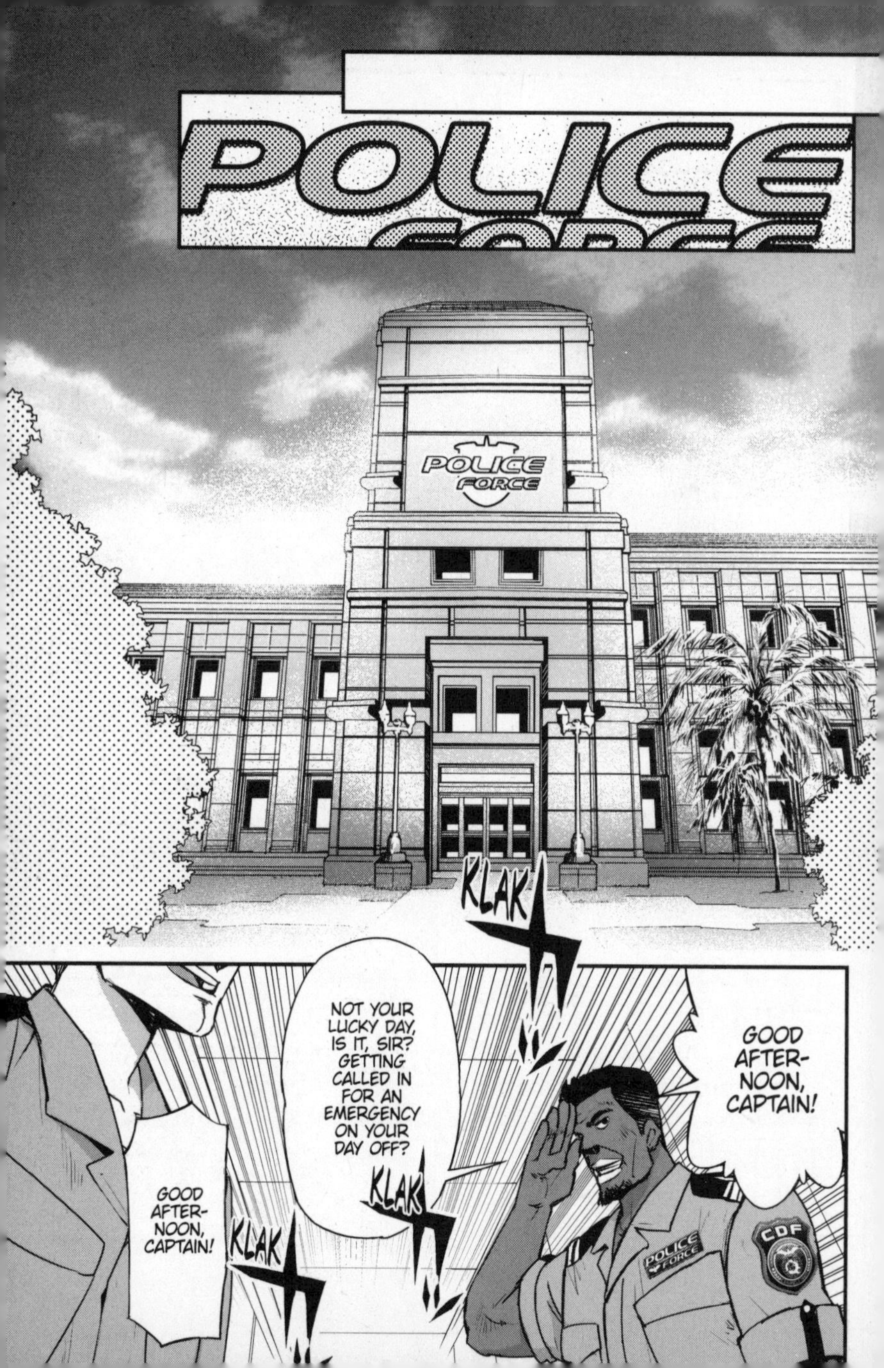
POLICE
POLICE FORCE
KLAK
GOOD AFTER-NOON, CAPTAIN!
NOT YOUR LUCKY DAY, IS IT, SIR? GETTING CALLED IN FOR AN EMERGENCY ON YOUR DAY OFF?
KLAK
GOOD AFTER-NOON, CAPTAIN!
KLAK
CDF
POLICE FORCE

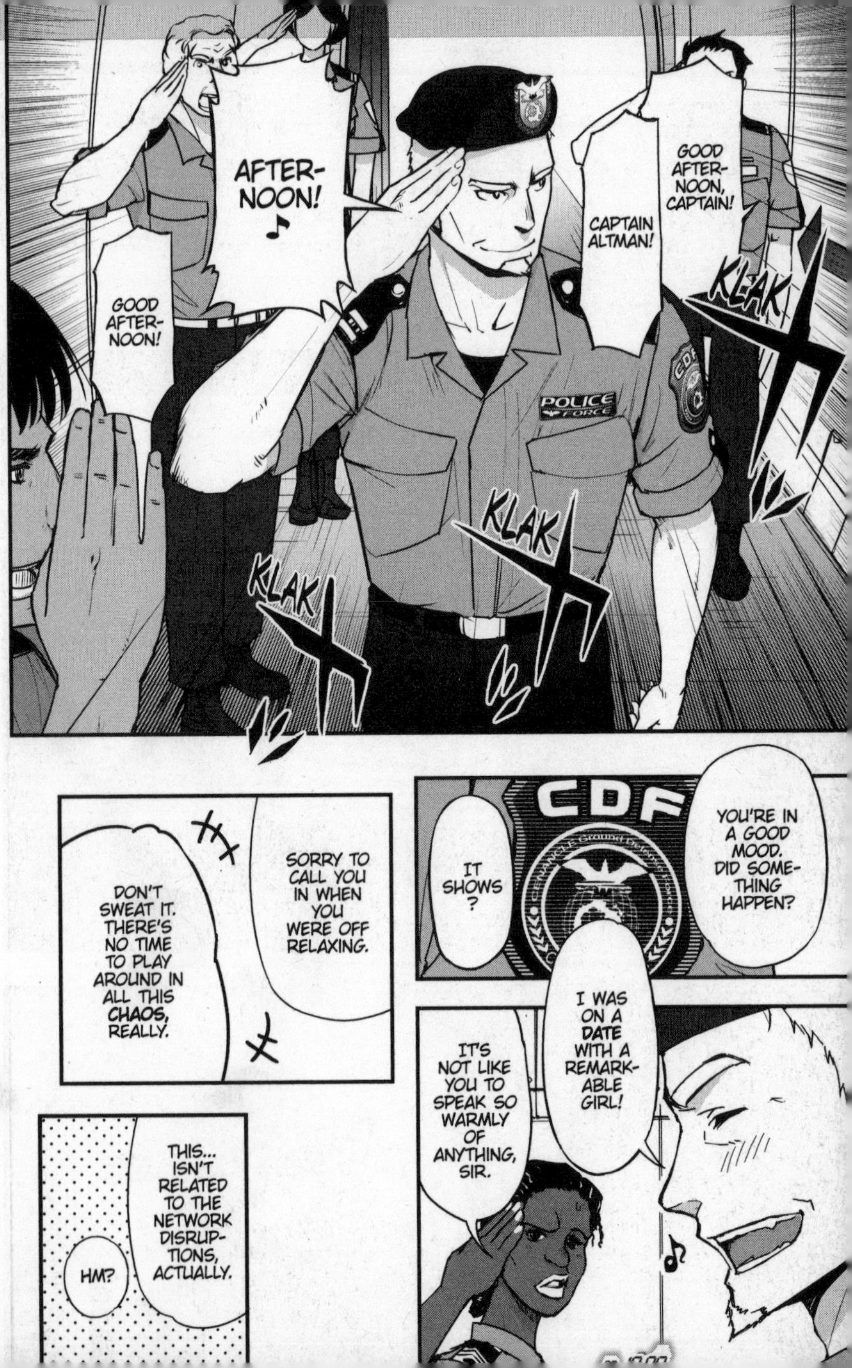
GOOD AFTERNOON, CAPTAIN!
CAPTAIN ALTMAN!
AFTERNOON! ♪
GOOD AFTERNOON!
POLICE FORCE
CDF
KLAK
KLAK
KLAK
CDF
YOU'RE IN A GOOD MOOD. DID SOMETHING HAPPEN?
IT SHOWS?
SORRY TO CALL YOU IN WHEN YOU WERE OFF RELAXING.
DON'T SWEAT IT. THERE'S NO TIME TO PLAY AROUND IN ALL THIS **CHAOS**, REALLY.
I WAS ON A **DATE** WITH A REMARKABLE GIRL!
IT'S NOT LIKE YOU TO SPEAK SO WARMLY OF ANYTHING, SIR.
THIS... ISN'T RELATED TO THE NETWORK DISRUPTIONS, ACTUALLY.
HM?

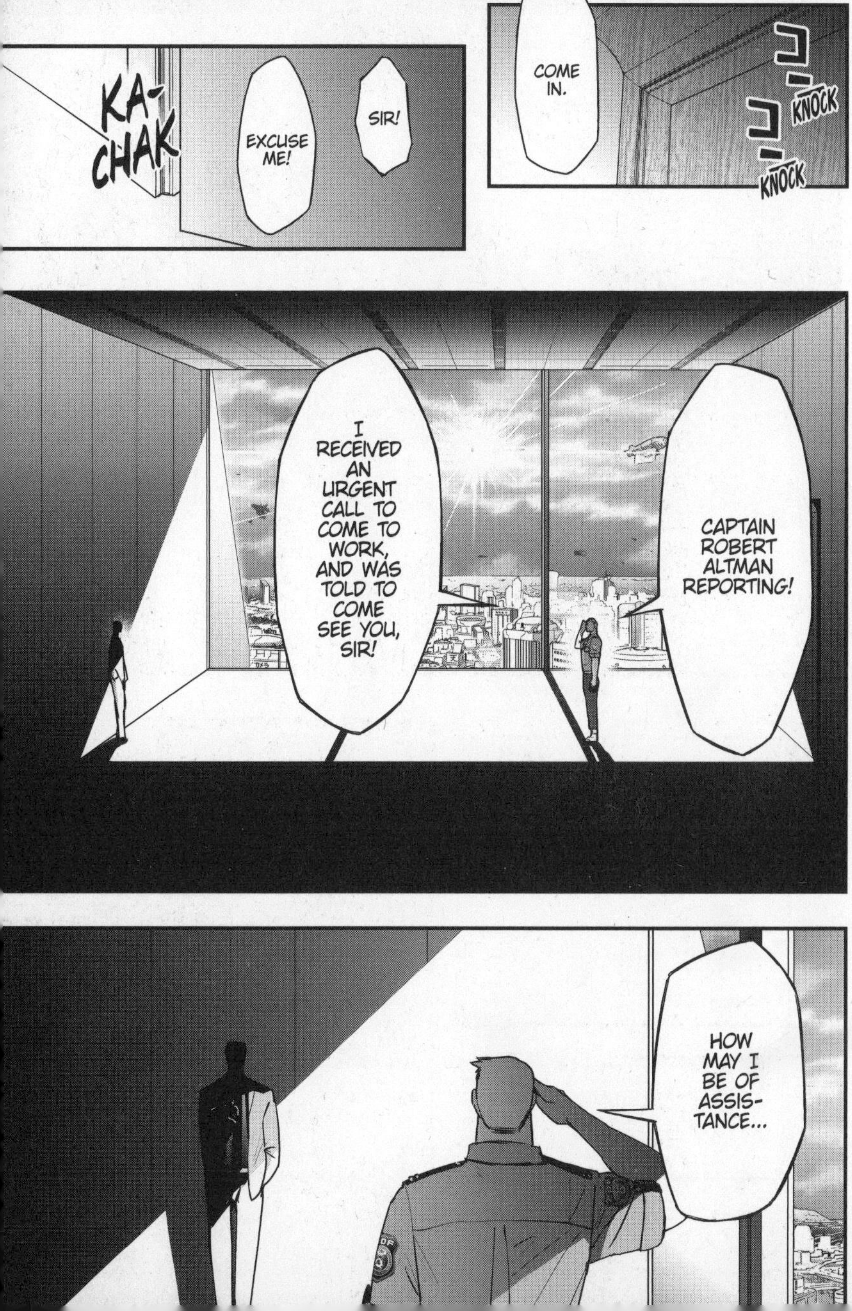
KNOCK
KNOCK
COME IN.
SIR!
EXCUSE ME!
KA-CHAK
CAPTAIN ROBERT ALTMAN REPORTING!
I RECEIVED AN URGENT CALL TO COME TO WORK, AND WAS TOLD TO COME SEE YOU, SIR!
HOW MAY I BE OF ASSIS-TANCE...

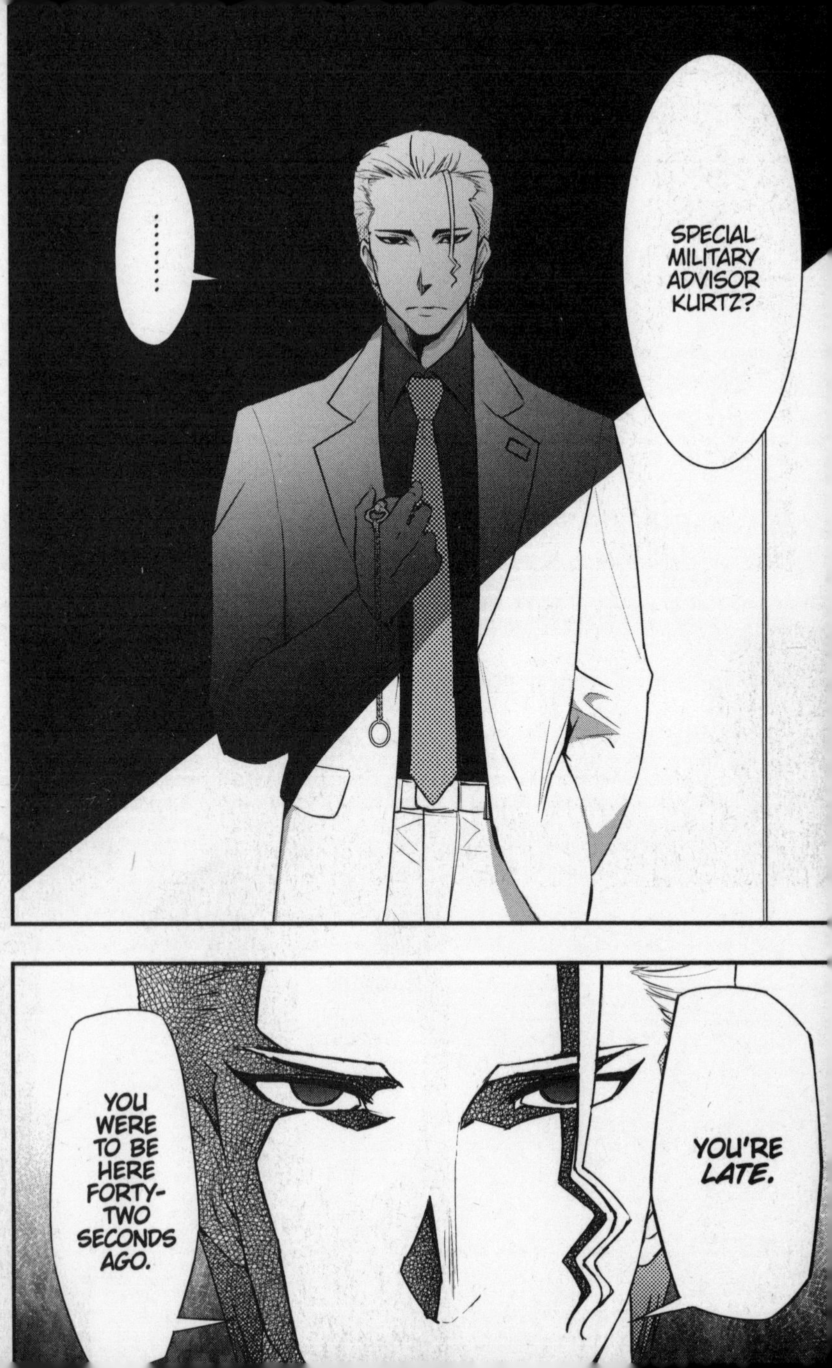
SPECIAL MILITARY ADVISOR KURTZ?
......
YOU'RE LATE.
YOU WERE TO BE HERE FORTY-TWO SECONDS AGO.

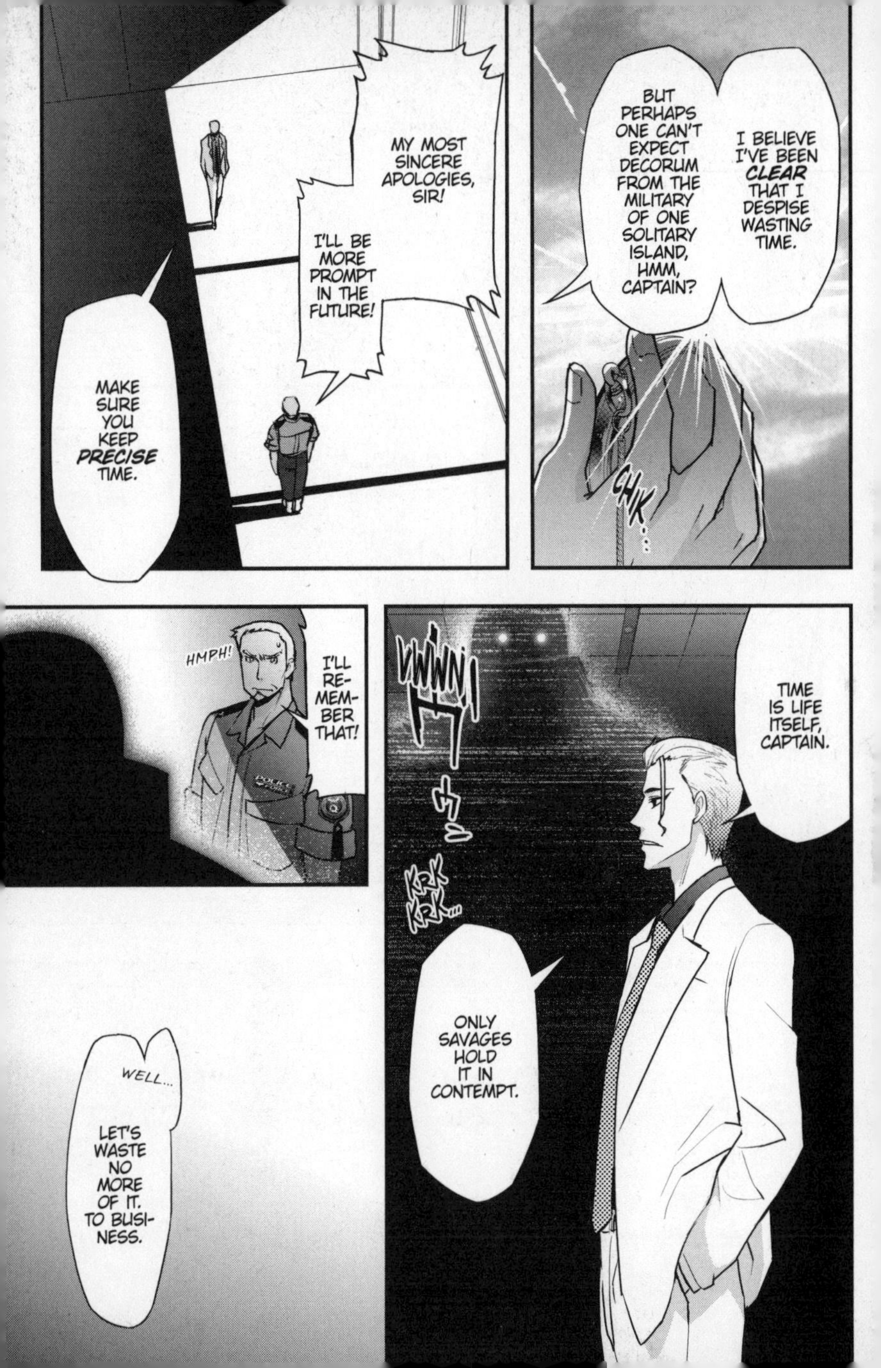
I BELIEVE I'VE BEEN CLEAR THAT I DESPISE WASTING TIME.
BUT PERHAPS ONE CAN'T EXPECT DECORUM FROM THE MILITARY OF ONE SOLITARY ISLAND, HMM, CAPTAIN?
CHIK...
MY MOST SINCERE APOLOGIES, SIR!
I'LL BE MORE PROMPT IN THE FUTURE!
MAKE SURE YOU KEEP PRECISE TIME.
TIME IS LIFE ITSELF, CAPTAIN.
KRK KRK...
ONLY SAVAGES HOLD IT IN CONTEMPT.
HMPH!
I'LL REMEMBER THAT!
WELL...
LET'S WASTE NO MORE OF IT. TO BUSINESS.

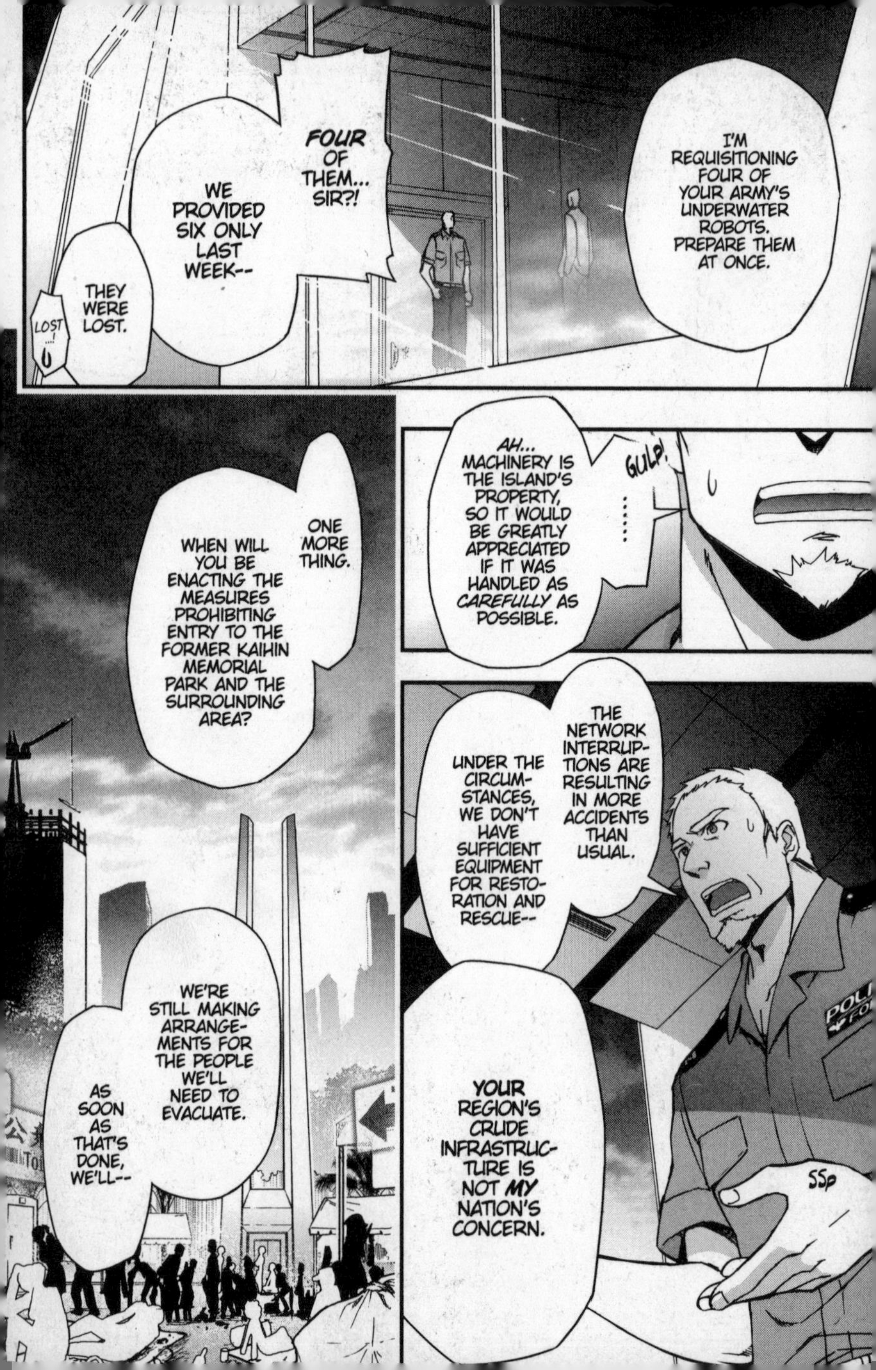

I'M REQUISITIONING FOUR OF YOUR ARMY'S UNDERWATER ROBOTS. PREPARE THEM AT ONCE.
FOUR OF THEM... SIR?!
WE PROVIDED SIX ONLY LAST WEEK--
THEY WERE LOST.
LOST...!
GULP!
......
AH... MACHINERY IS THE ISLAND'S PROPERTY, SO IT WOULD BE GREATLY APPRECIATED IF IT WAS HANDLED AS CAREFULLY AS POSSIBLE.
THE NETWORK INTERRUPTIONS ARE RESULTING IN MORE ACCIDENTS THAN USUAL.
UNDER THE CIRCUMSTANCES, WE DON'T HAVE SUFFICIENT EQUIPMENT FOR RESTORATION AND RESCUE--
YOUR REGION'S CRUDE INFRASTRUCTURE IS NOT MY NATION'S CONCERN.
SSP
ONE MORE THING.
WHEN WILL YOU BE ENACTING THE MEASURES PROHIBITING ENTRY TO THE FORMER KAIHIN MEMORIAL PARK AND THE SURROUNDING AREA?
WE'RE STILL MAKING ARRANGEMENTS FOR THE PEOPLE WE'LL NEED TO EVACUATE.
AS SOON AS THAT'S DONE, WE'LL--

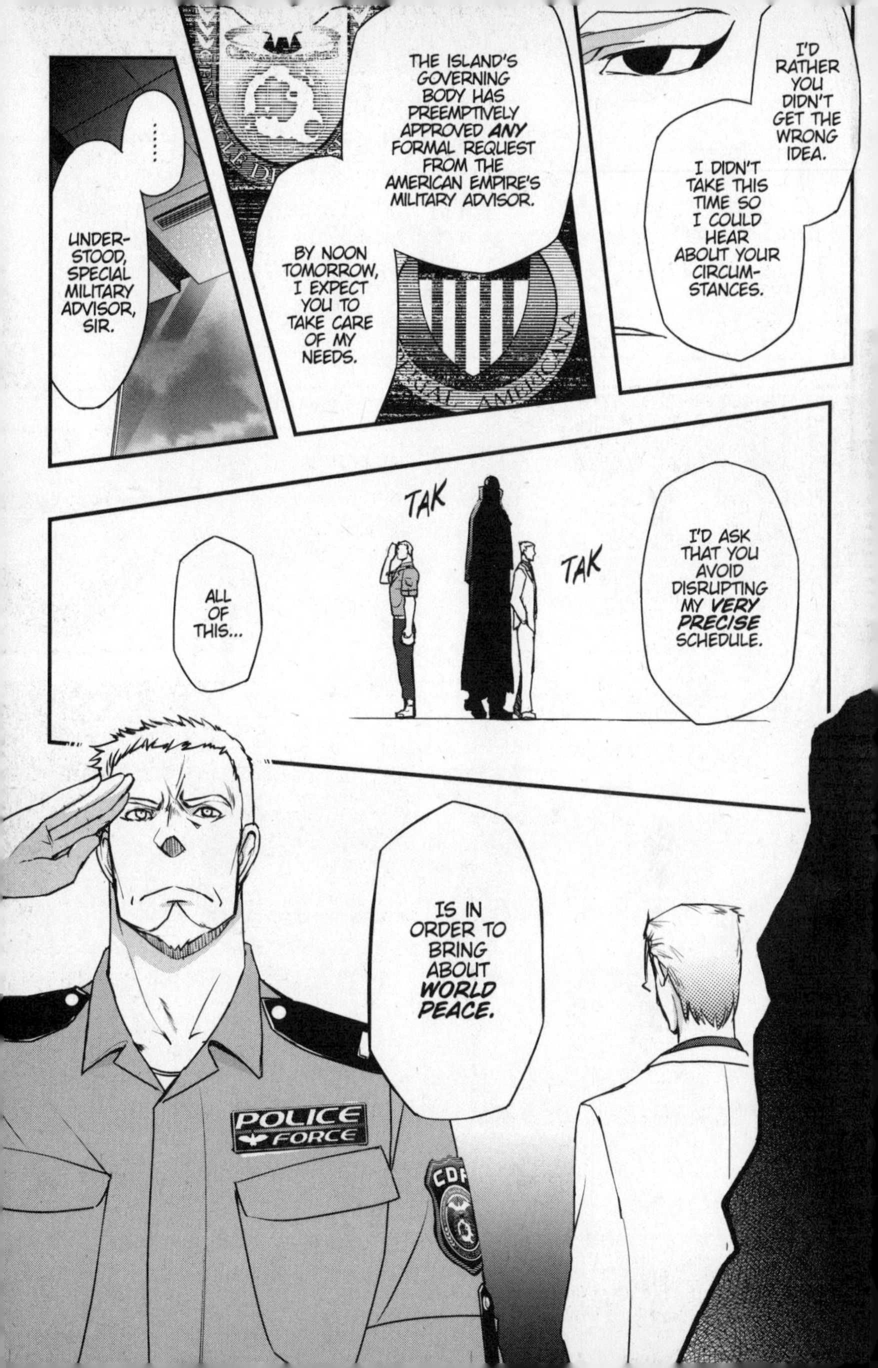
I'D RATHER YOU DIDN'T GET THE WRONG IDEA.
I DIDN'T TAKE THIS TIME SO I COULD HEAR ABOUT YOUR CIRCUMSTANCES.
THE ISLAND'S GOVERNING BODY HAS PREEMPTIVELY APPROVED ANY FORMAL REQUEST FROM THE AMERICAN EMPIRE'S MILITARY ADVISOR.
BY NOON TOMORROW, I EXPECT YOU TO TAKE CARE OF MY NEEDS.
......
UNDER-STOOD, SPECIAL MILITARY ADVISOR, SIR.
I'D ASK THAT YOU AVOID DISRUPTING MY VERY PRECISE SCHEDULE.
TAK
TAK
ALL OF THIS...
IS IN ORDER TO BRING ABOUT WORLD PEACE.
POLICE FORCE
CDF

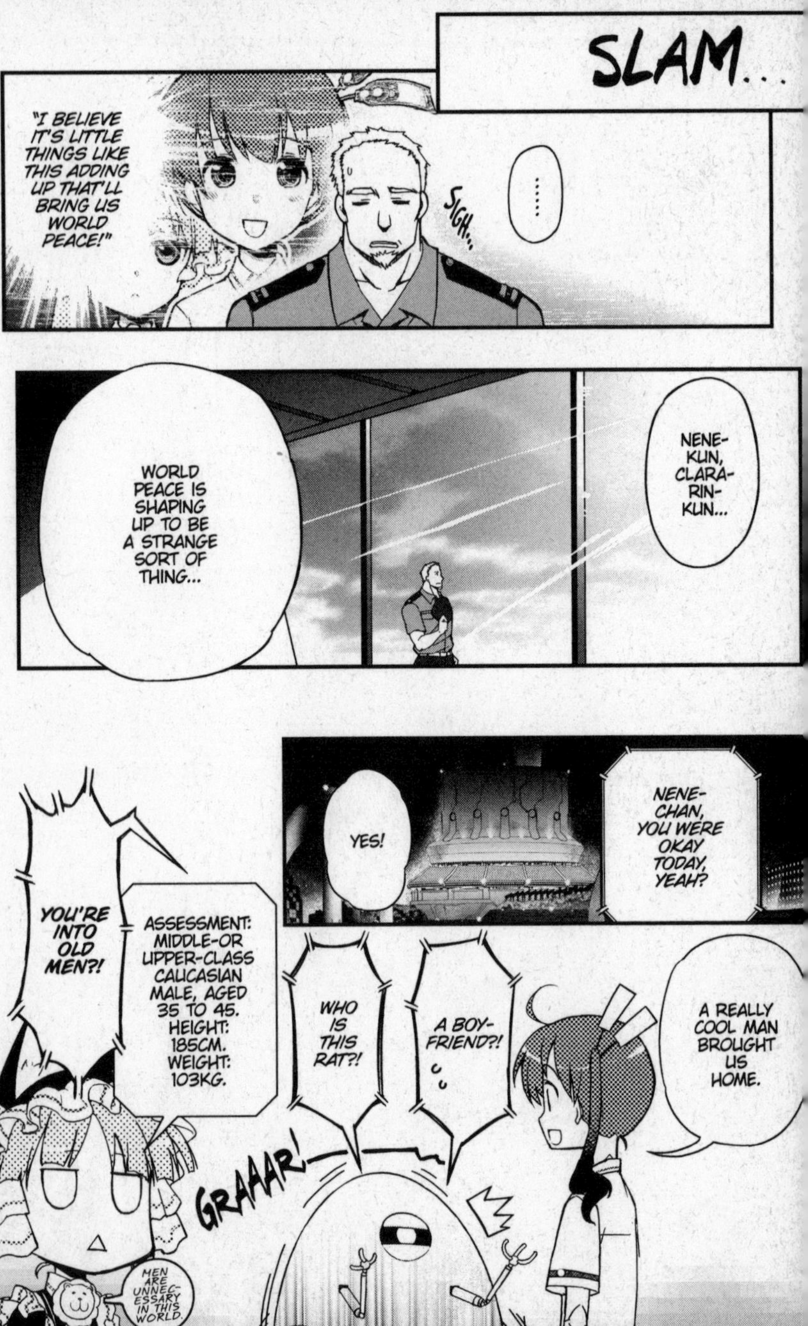
SLAM...
......
SIGH...
"I BELIEVE IT'S LITTLE THINGS LIKE THIS ADDING UP THAT'LL BRING US WORLD PEACE!"
NENE-KUN, CLARA-RIN-KUN...
WORLD PEACE IS SHAPING UP TO BE A STRANGE SORT OF THING...
NENE-CHAN, YOU WERE OKAY TODAY, YEAH?
YES!
A REALLY COOL MAN BROUGHT US HOME.
A BOY-FRIEND?!
WHO IS THIS RAT?!
ASSESSMENT: MIDDLE-OR UPPER-CLASS CAUCASIAN MALE, AGED 35 TO 45. HEIGHT: 185CM. WEIGHT: 103KG.
YOU'RE INTO OLD MEN?!
GRAAAR!
MEN ARE UNNEC-ESSARY IN THIS WORLD.

GHOST URN

GHOST URN

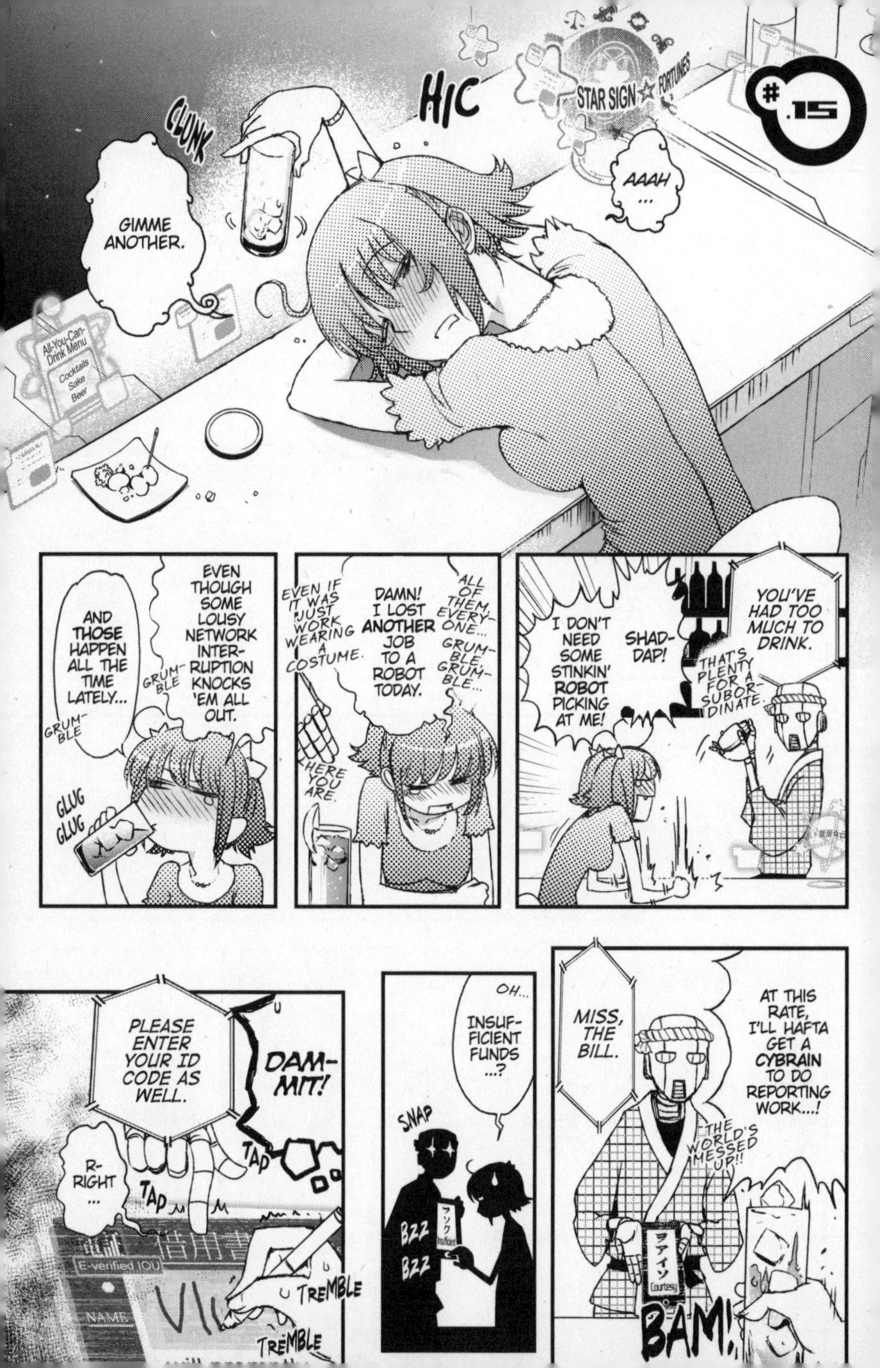
#.15
STAR SIGN ☆ FORTUNES
AAAH ...
HIC
CLUNK
GIMME ANOTHER.
All-You-Can-Drink Menu
Cocktails
Sake
Beer
YOU'VE HAD TOO MUCH TO DRINK.
THAT'S PLENTY FOR A SUBORDINATE.
SHAD-DAP!
I DON'T NEED SOME STINKIN' ROBOT PICKING AT ME!
ALL OF THEM, EVERYONE... GRUMBLE GRUMBLE...
DAMN! I LOST ANOTHER JOB TO A ROBOT TODAY.
EVEN IF IT WAS JUST WORK WEARING A COSTUME.
HERE YOU ARE.
EVEN THOUGH SOME LOUSY NETWORK INTERRUPTION KNOCKS 'EM ALL OUT.
GRUMBLE
AND THOSE HAPPEN ALL THE TIME LATELY...
GRUMBLE
GLUG GLUG
AT THIS RATE, I'LL HAFTA GET A CYBRAIN TO DO REPORTING WORK...!
MISS, THE BILL.
THE WORLD'S MESSED UP!!
Courtesy
BAM!
OH...
INSUFFICIENT FUNDS ...?
SNAP
BZZ BZZ
Insufficient
DAMMIT!
PLEASE ENTER YOUR ID CODE AS WELL.
TAP
TAP
R-RIGHT ...
借用書
E-verified IOU
NAME
TREMBLE
TREMBLE

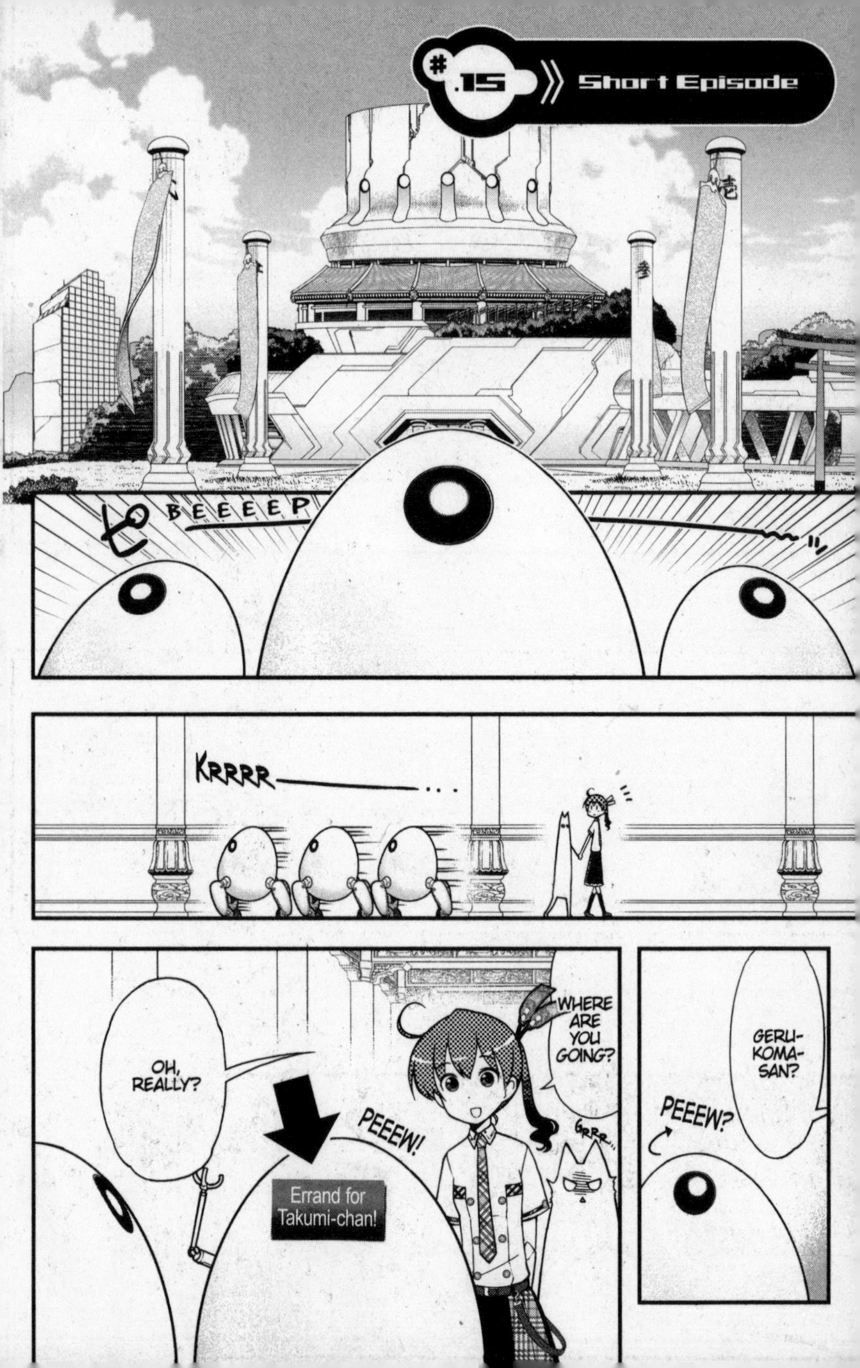
#.15
Short Episode
ピ
BEEEEP
KRRRR...
GERU-KOMA-SAN?
PEEEW?
WHERE ARE YOU GOING?
PEEEW!
GRRR...
OH, REALLY?
Errand for Takumi-chan!

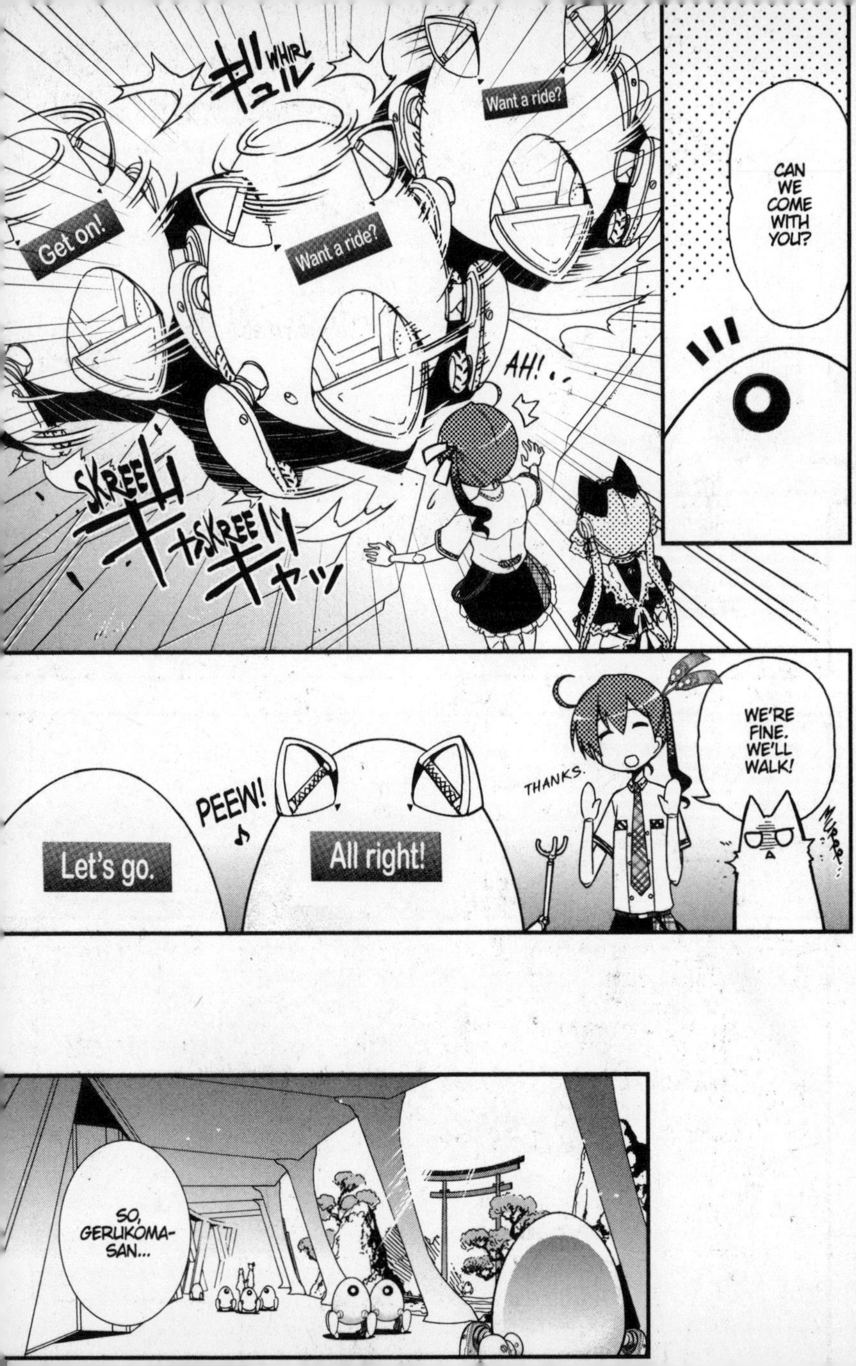
CAN WE COME WITH YOU?
Want a ride?
WHIRL
ギュル
Want a ride?
Get on!
AH!
SKREE
SKREE
キャッ
WE'RE FINE. WE'LL WALK!
MURRR...
THANKS.
All right!
PEEW!
Let's go.
SO, GERUKOMA-SAN...

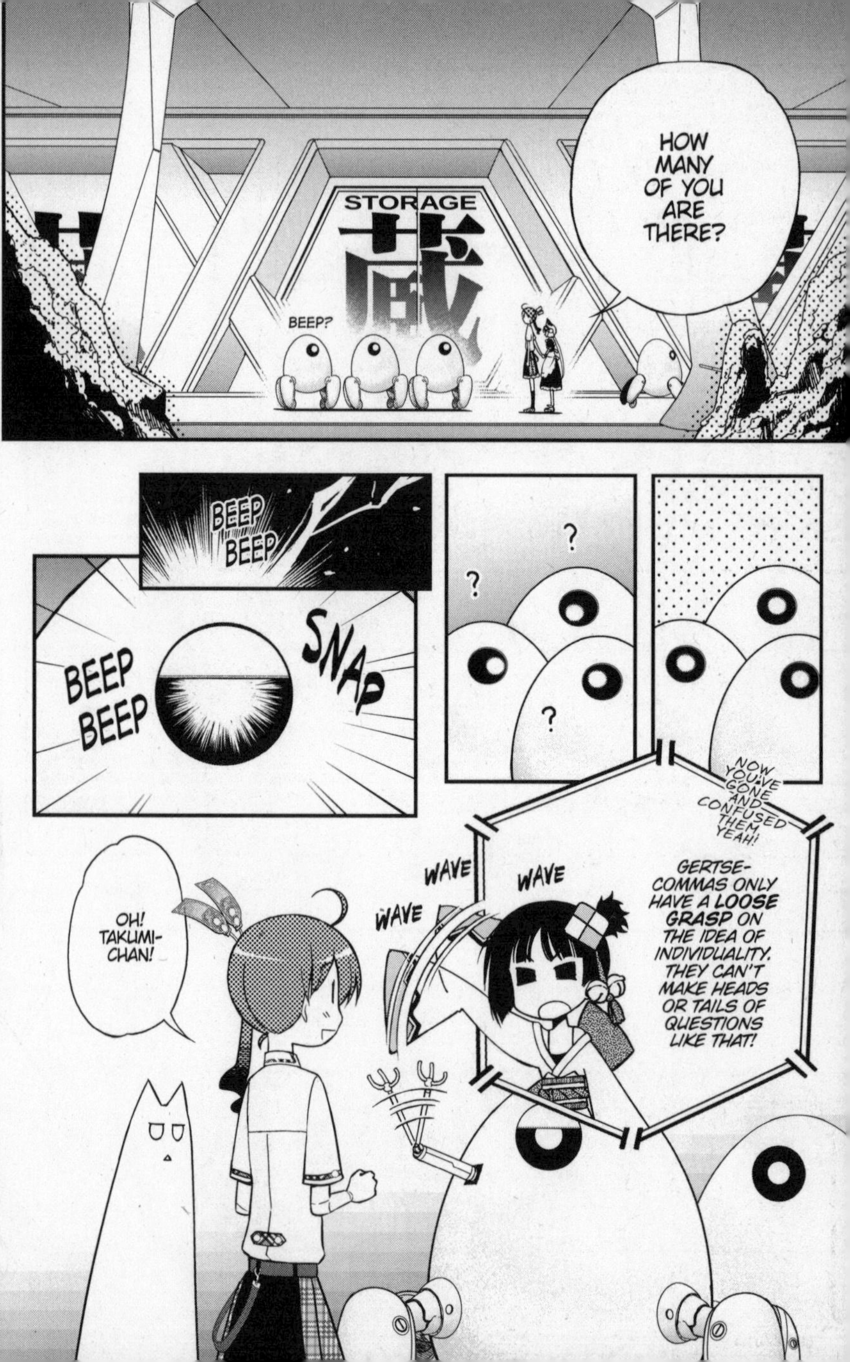
HOW MANY OF YOU ARE THERE?
STORAGE
蔵
BEEP?
?
?
?
BEEP BEEP
SNAP
BEEP BEEP
NOW YOU'VE GONE AND CONFUSED THEM, YEAH!
GERTSE-COMMAS ONLY HAVE A **LOOSE GRASP** ON THE IDEA OF INDIVIDUALITY. THEY CAN'T MAKE HEADS OR TAILS OF QUESTIONS LIKE THAT!
WAVE
WAVE
WAVE
OH! TAKUMI-CHAN!

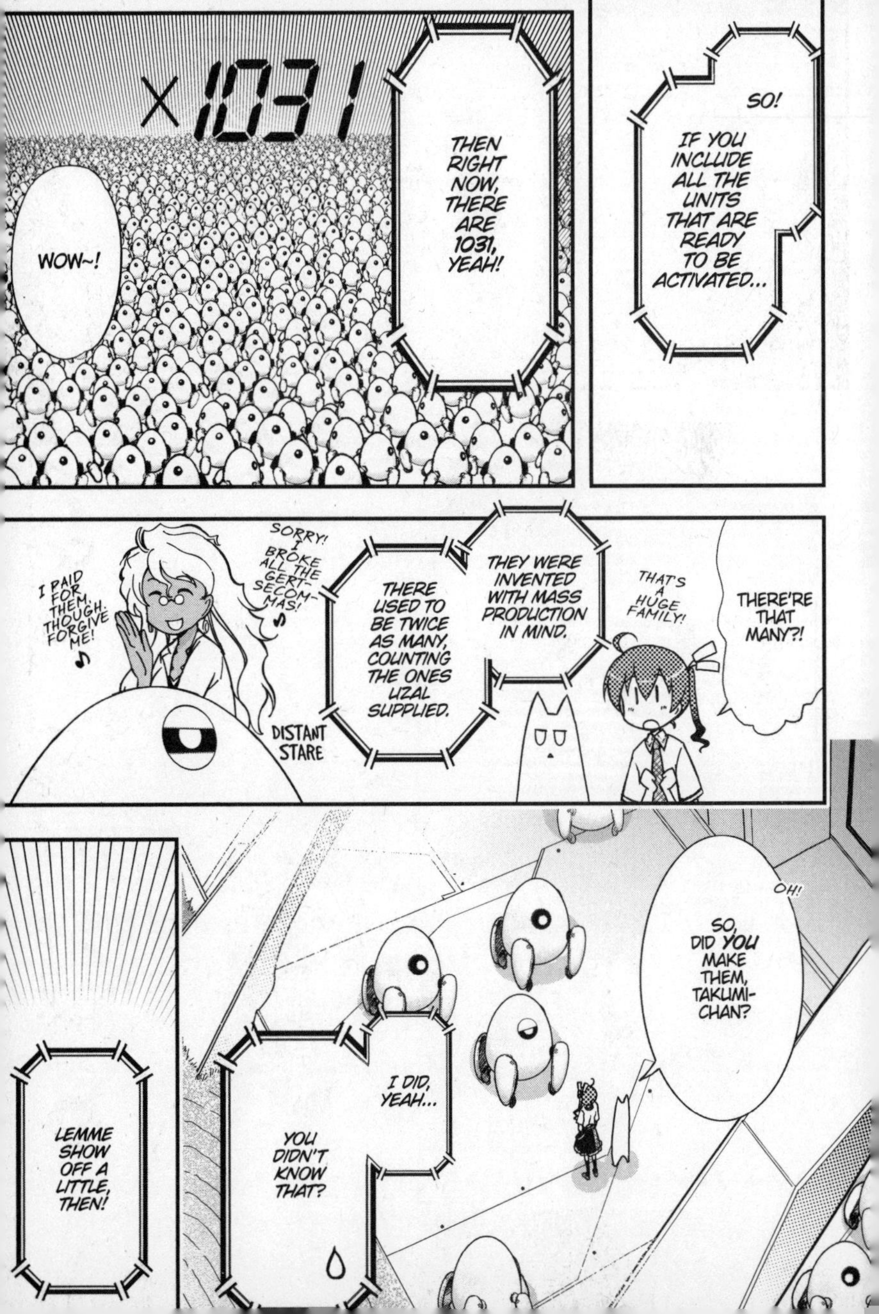
SO!
IF YOU INCLUDE ALL THE UNITS THAT ARE READY TO BE ACTIVATED...
THEN RIGHT NOW, THERE ARE 1031, YEAH!
×1031
WOW~!
THERE'RE THAT MANY?!
THAT'S A HUGE FAMILY!
THEY WERE INVENTED WITH MASS PRODUCTION IN MIND.
THERE USED TO BE TWICE AS MANY, COUNTING THE ONES UZAL SUPPLIED.
DISTANT STARE
SORRY! I BROKE ALL THE GERT-SECOM-MAS! ♪
I PAID FOR THEM, THOUGH. FORGIVE ME! ♪
OH!
SO, DID YOU MAKE THEM, TAKUMI-CHAN?
I DID, YEAH...
YOU DIDN'T KNOW THAT?
LEMME SHOW OFF A LITTLE, THEN!

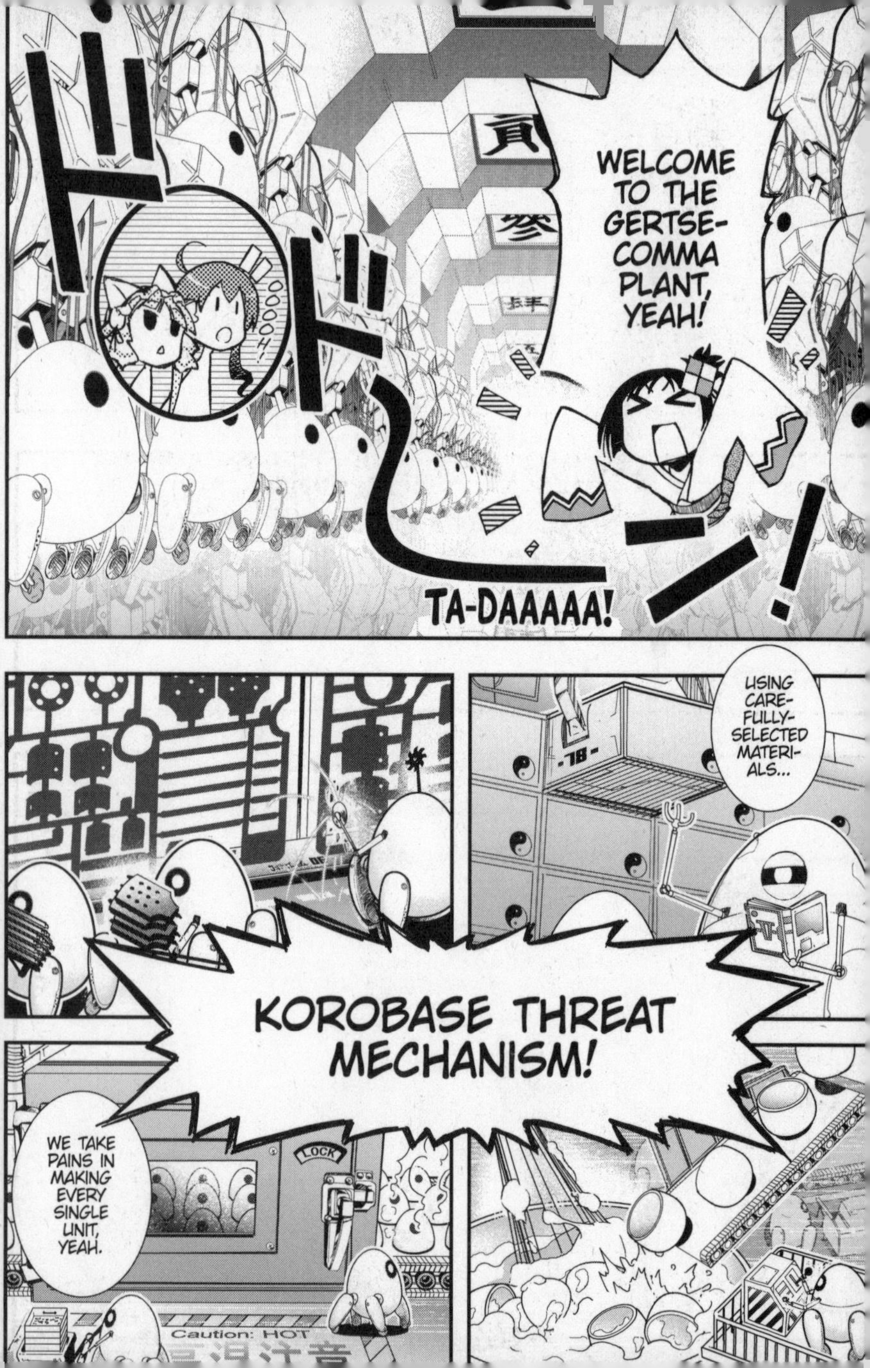

WELCOME TO THE GERTSE-COMMA PLANT, YEAH!
TA-DAAAAA!
OOOOOH!
USING CAREFULLY-SELECTED MATERIALS...
KOROBASE THREAT MECHANISM!
WE TAKE PAINS IN MAKING EVERY SINGLE UNIT, YEAH.
LOCK
Caution: HOT

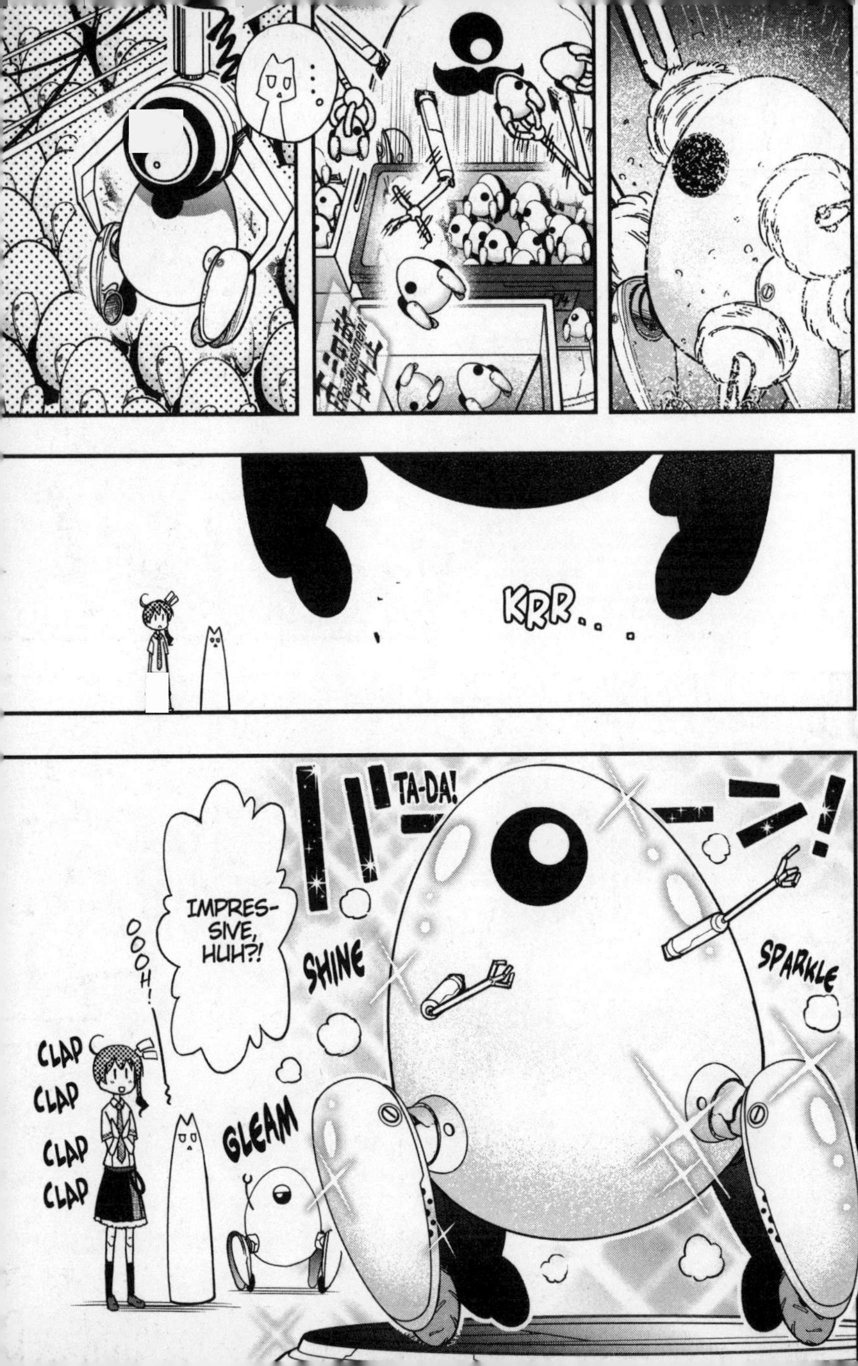

Readjustment
...
KRR...
TA-DA!
SPARKLE
SHINE
IMPRES-SIVE, HUH?!
OOOH!
GLEAM
CLAP
CLAP
CLAP
CLAP

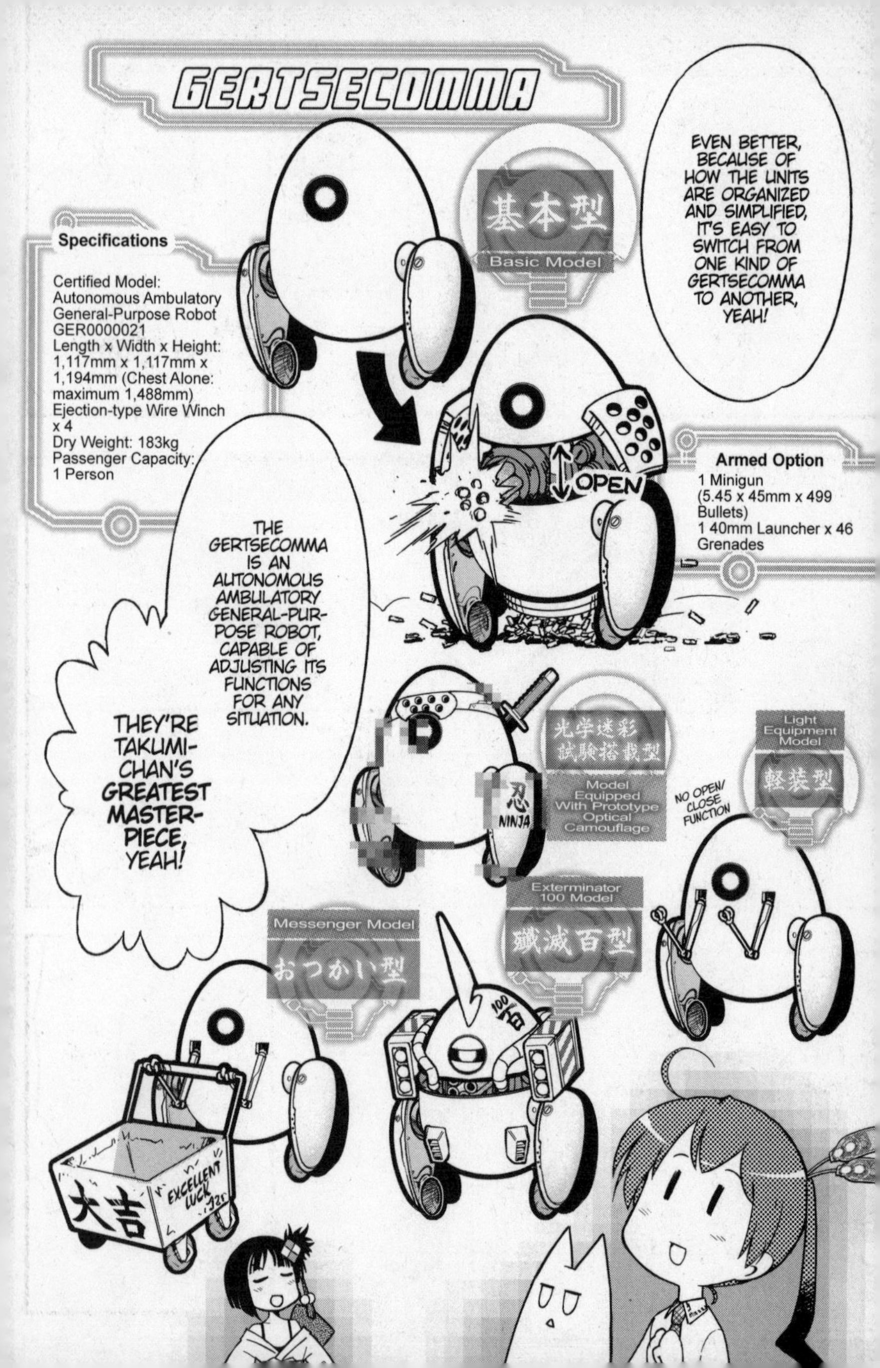
GERTSECOMMA
EVEN BETTER, BECAUSE OF HOW THE UNITS ARE ORGANIZED AND SIMPLIFIED, IT'S EASY TO SWITCH FROM ONE KIND OF GERTSECOMMA TO ANOTHER, YEAH!
基本型
Basic Model
Specifications
Certified Model: Autonomous Ambulatory General-Purpose Robot GER0000021
Length x Width x Height: 1,117mm x 1,117mm x 1,194mm (Chest Alone: maximum 1,488mm)
Ejection-type Wire Winch x 4
Dry Weight: 183kg
Passenger Capacity: 1 Person
OPEN
Armed Option
1 Minigun (5.45 x 45mm x 499 Bullets)
1 40mm Launcher x 46 Grenades
THE GERTSECOMMA IS AN AUTONOMOUS AMBULATORY GENERAL-PURPOSE ROBOT, CAPABLE OF ADJUSTING ITS FUNCTIONS FOR ANY SITUATION.
THEY'RE TAKUMI-CHAN'S GREATEST MASTER-PIECE, YEAH!
Light Equipment Model
軽装型
NO OPEN/CLOSE FUNCTION
光学迷彩試験搭載型
Model Equipped With Prototype Optical Camouflage
忍
NINJA
Exterminator 100 Model
殲滅百型
100
Messenger Model
おつかい型
大吉
EXCELLENT LUCK

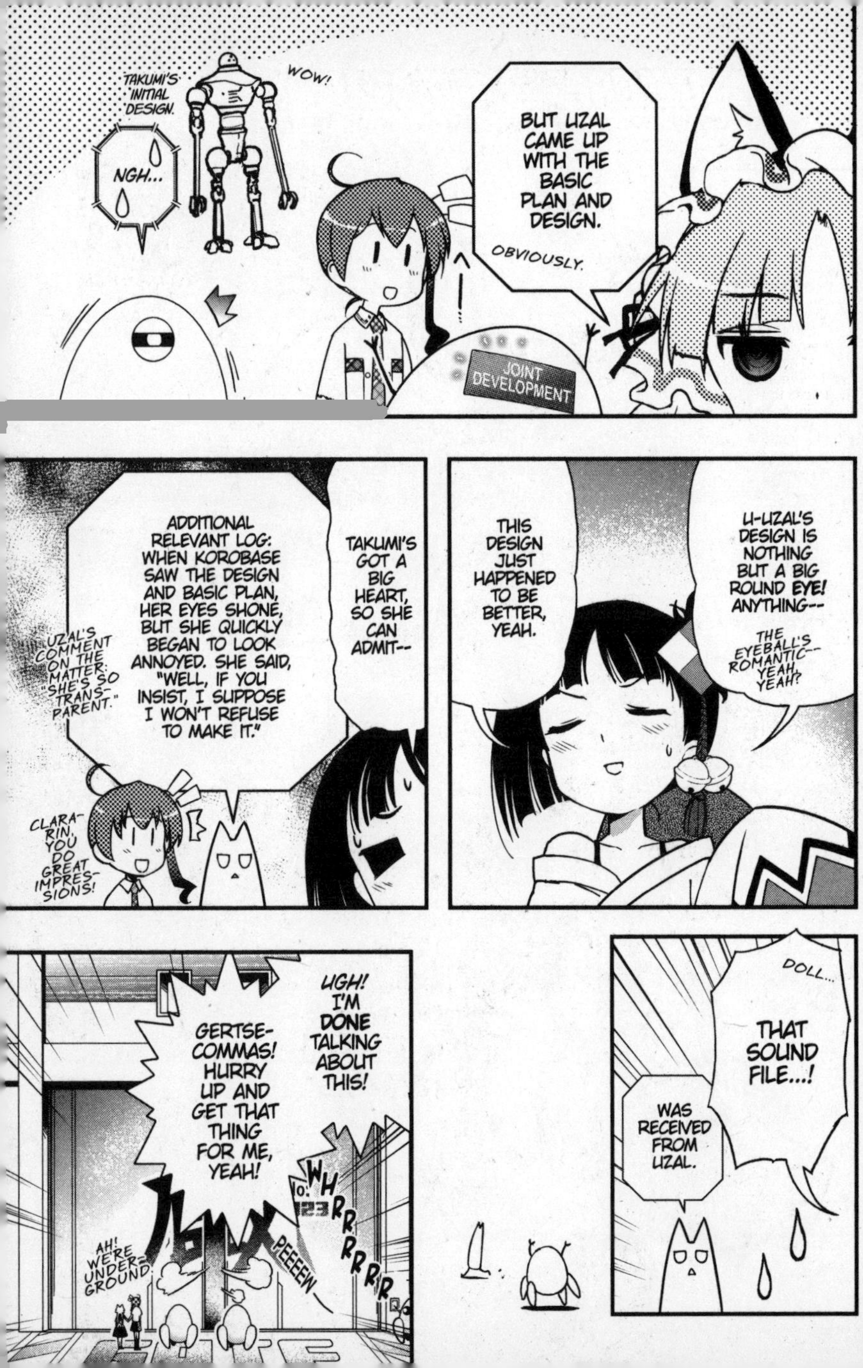
BUT UZAL CAME UP WITH THE BASIC PLAN AND DESIGN.
OBVIOUSLY.
JOINT DEVELOPMENT
WOW!
TAKUMI'S INITIAL DESIGN.
NGH...
U-UZAL'S DESIGN IS NOTHING BUT A BIG ROUND EYE! ANYTHING--
THE EYEBALL'S ROMANTIC--YEAH, YEAH?
THIS DESIGN JUST HAPPENED TO BE BETTER, YEAH.
TAKUMI'S GOT A BIG HEART, SO SHE CAN ADMIT--
ADDITIONAL RELEVANT LOG: WHEN KOROBASE SAW THE DESIGN AND BASIC PLAN, HER EYES SHONE, BUT SHE QUICKLY BEGAN TO LOOK ANNOYED. SHE SAID, "WELL, IF YOU INSIST, I SUPPOSE I WON'T REFUSE TO MAKE IT."
UZAL'S COMMENT ON THE MATTER: "SHE'S SO TRANS-PARENT."
CLARA-RIN, YOU DO GREAT IMPRES-SIONS!
DOLL...
THAT SOUND FILE...!
WAS RECEIVED FROM UZAL.
UGH! I'M DONE TALKING ABOUT THIS!
GERTSE-COMMAS! HURRY UP AND GET THAT THING FOR ME, YEAH!
WHRRRRRRR
PEEEEW
AH! WE'RE UNDER-GROUND!

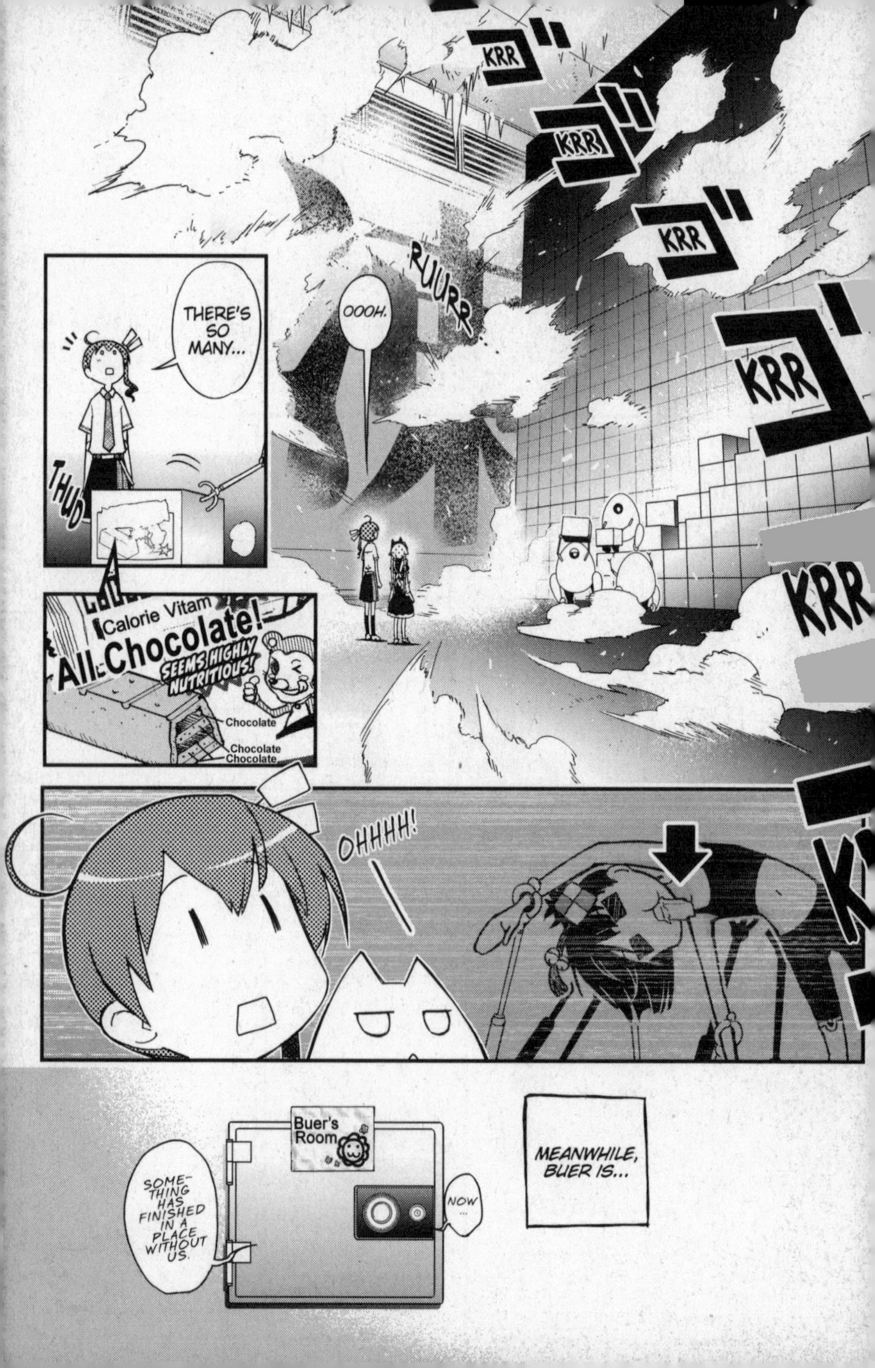

KRR
KRR
KRR
KRR
KRR
RUURR
OOOH.
THERE'S SO MANY...
THUD
Calorie Vitam
All Chocolate!
SEEMS HIGHLY NUTRITIOUS!
Chocolate
Chocolate
Chocolate
OHHHH!
MEANWHILE, BUER IS...
Buer's Room
NOW...
SOMETHING HAS FINISHED IN A PLACE WITHOUT US.

GHOST URN

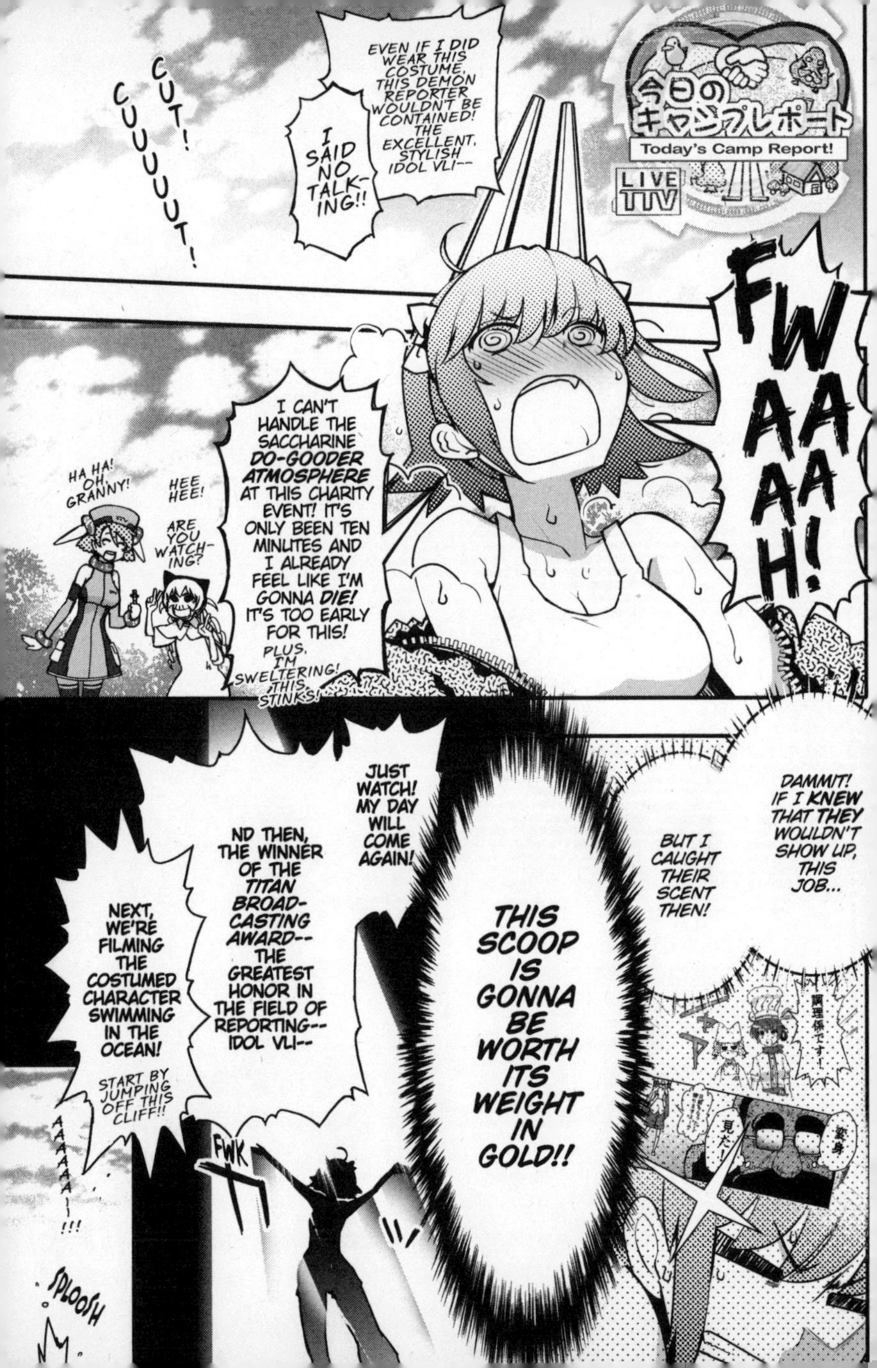

今日のキャンプレポート
Today's Camp Report!
LIVE TTV
EVEN IF I DID WEAR THIS COSTUME, THIS DEMON REPORTER WOULDN'T BE CONTAINED! THE EXCELLENT, STYLISH IDOL VLI--
I SAID NO TALKING!!
CUT! CUUUUUUUT!
FWAAAAH!
I CAN'T HANDLE THE SACCHARINE DO-GOODER ATMOSPHERE AT THIS CHARITY EVENT! IT'S ONLY BEEN TEN MINUTES AND I ALREADY FEEL LIKE I'M GONNA DIE! IT'S TOO EARLY FOR THIS!
PLUS, I'M SWELTERING! THIS STINKS!
HEE HEE!
ARE YOU WATCHING?
HA HA! OH, GRANNY!
DAMMIT! IF I KNEW THAT THEY WOULDN'T SHOW UP, THIS JOB...
BUT I CAUGHT THEIR SCENT THEN!
調理係です!
変身
見た!
THIS SCOOP IS GONNA BE WORTH ITS WEIGHT IN GOLD!!
JUST WATCH! MY DAY WILL COME AGAIN!
ND THEN, THE WINNER OF THE TITAN BROADCASTING AWARD-- THE GREATEST HONOR IN THE FIELD OF REPORTING-- IDOL VLI--
NEXT, WE'RE FILMING THE COSTUMED CHARACTER SWIMMING IN THE OCEAN!
START BY JUMPING OFF THIS CLIFF!!
FWK
AAAAAAA!!!
SPLOOSH

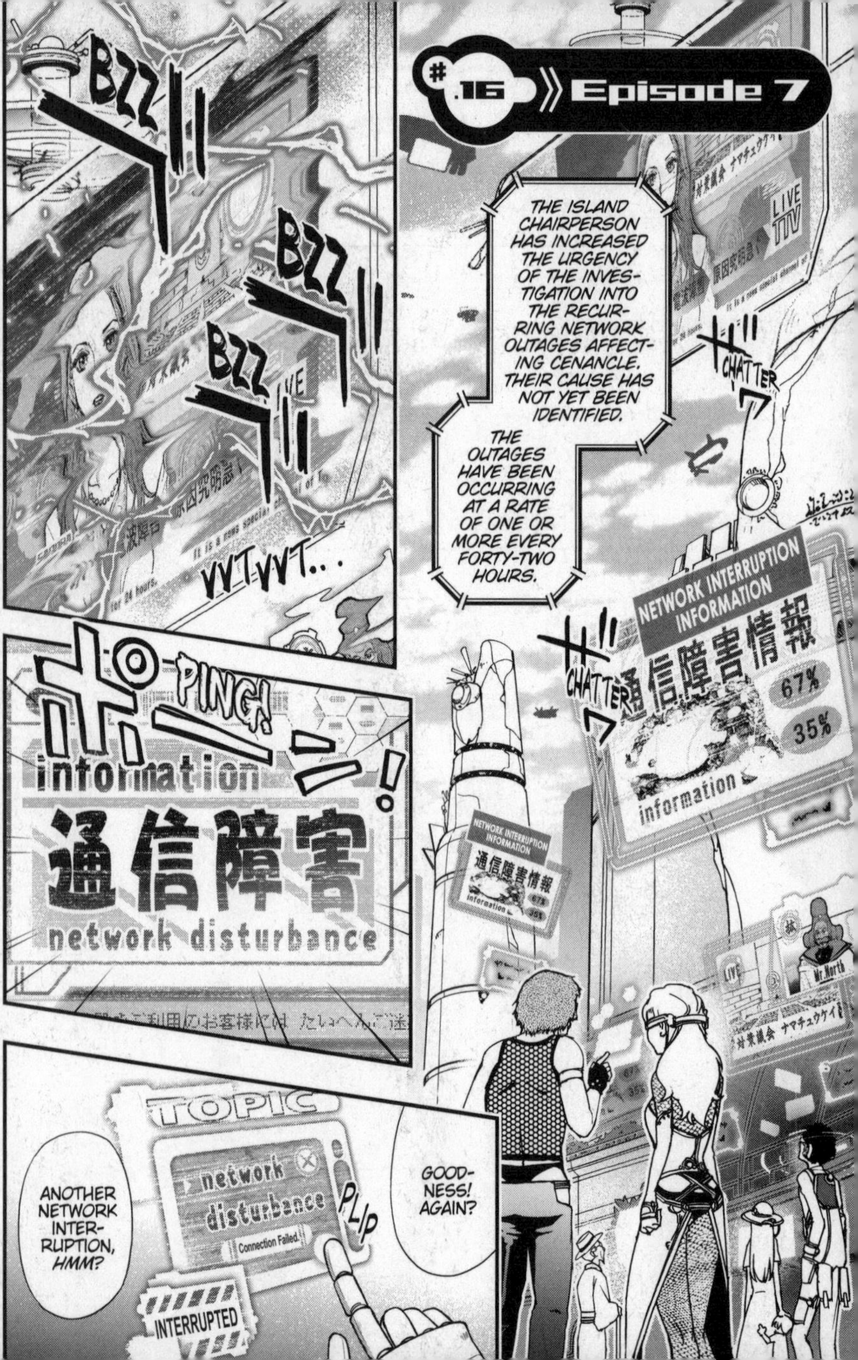
#.16 Episode 7
THE ISLAND CHAIRPERSON HAS INCREASED THE URGENCY OF THE INVESTIGATION INTO THE RECURRING NETWORK OUTAGES AFFECTING CENANCLE. THEIR CAUSE HAS NOT YET BEEN IDENTIFIED.
THE OUTAGES HAVE BEEN OCCURRING AT A RATE OF ONE OR MORE EVERY FORTY-TWO HOURS.
LIVE TV
CHATTER
CHATTER
NETWORK INTERRUPTION INFORMATION
通信障害情報
67%
35%
information
NETWORK INTERRUPTION INFORMATION
通信障害情報
Mr.North
対策議会 ナマチュウケイ
GOOD-NESS! AGAIN?
BZZ
BZZ
BZZ
LIVE
It is a news special
for 24 hours.
VVTVVT...
ポーン
PING!
information
通信障害
network disturbance
TOPIC
ANOTHER NETWORK INTER-RUPTION, HMM?
network disturbance
Connection Failed.
PLIP
INTERRUPTED

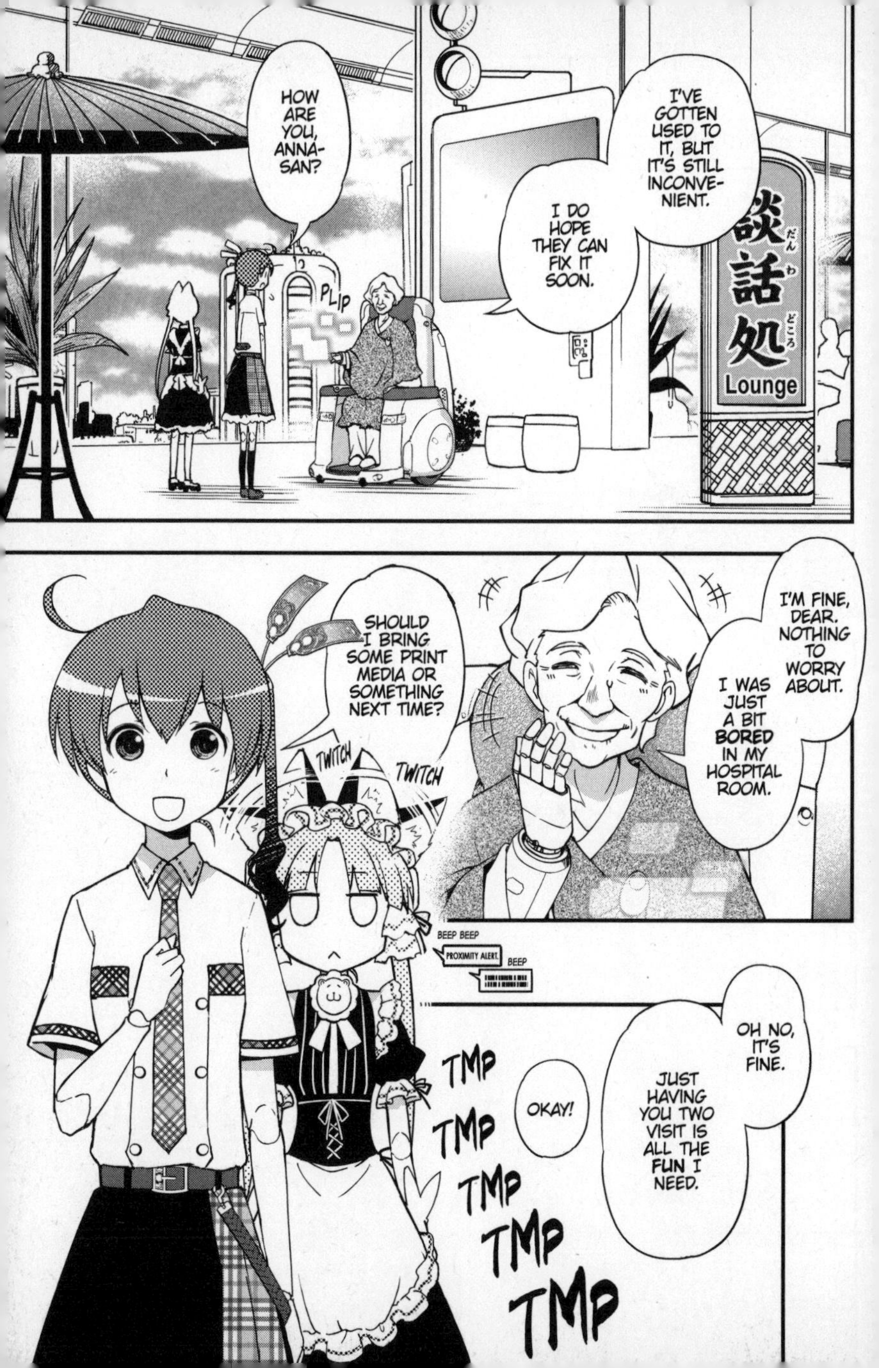
I'VE GOTTEN USED TO IT, BUT IT'S STILL INCONVENIENT.
HOW ARE YOU, ANNA-SAN?
談話処
だんわどころ
Lounge
I DO HOPE THEY CAN FIX IT SOON.
PLIP
I'M FINE, DEAR. NOTHING TO WORRY ABOUT.
I WAS JUST A BIT BORED IN MY HOSPITAL ROOM.
SHOULD I BRING SOME PRINT MEDIA OR SOMETHING NEXT TIME?
TWITCH
TWITCH
BEEP BEEP
PROXIMITY ALERT.
BEEP
OH NO, IT'S FINE.
JUST HAVING YOU TWO VISIT IS ALL THE FUN I NEED.
OKAY!
TMP
TMP
TMP
TMP
TMP

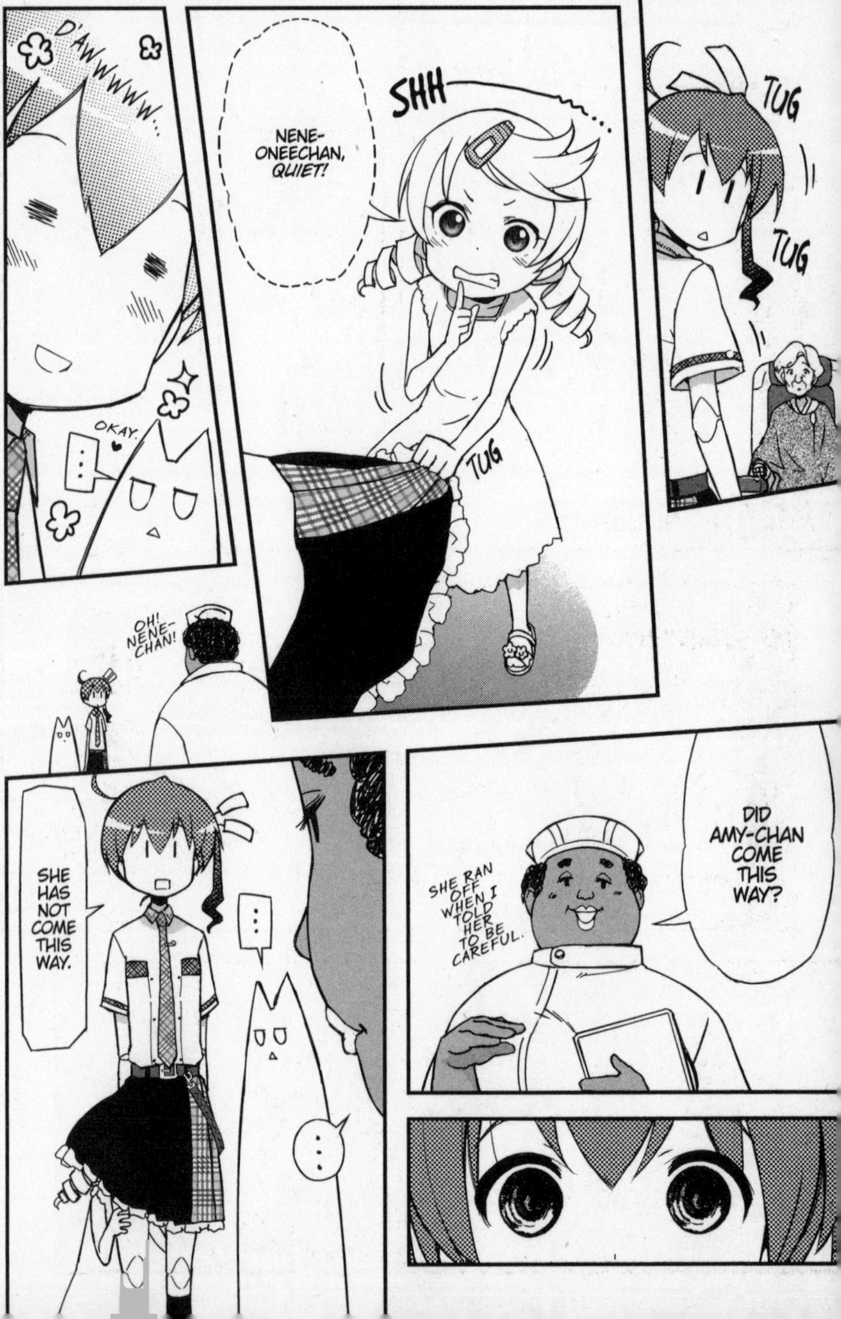
TUG
TUG
SHH
NENE-ONEECHAN, QUIET!
TUG
D'AWWWWWW...
OKAY. ♥
...
OH! NENE-CHAN!
DID AMY-CHAN COME THIS WAY?
SHE RAN OFF WHEN I TOLD HER TO BE CAREFUL.
SHE HAS NOT COME THIS WAY.
...
...

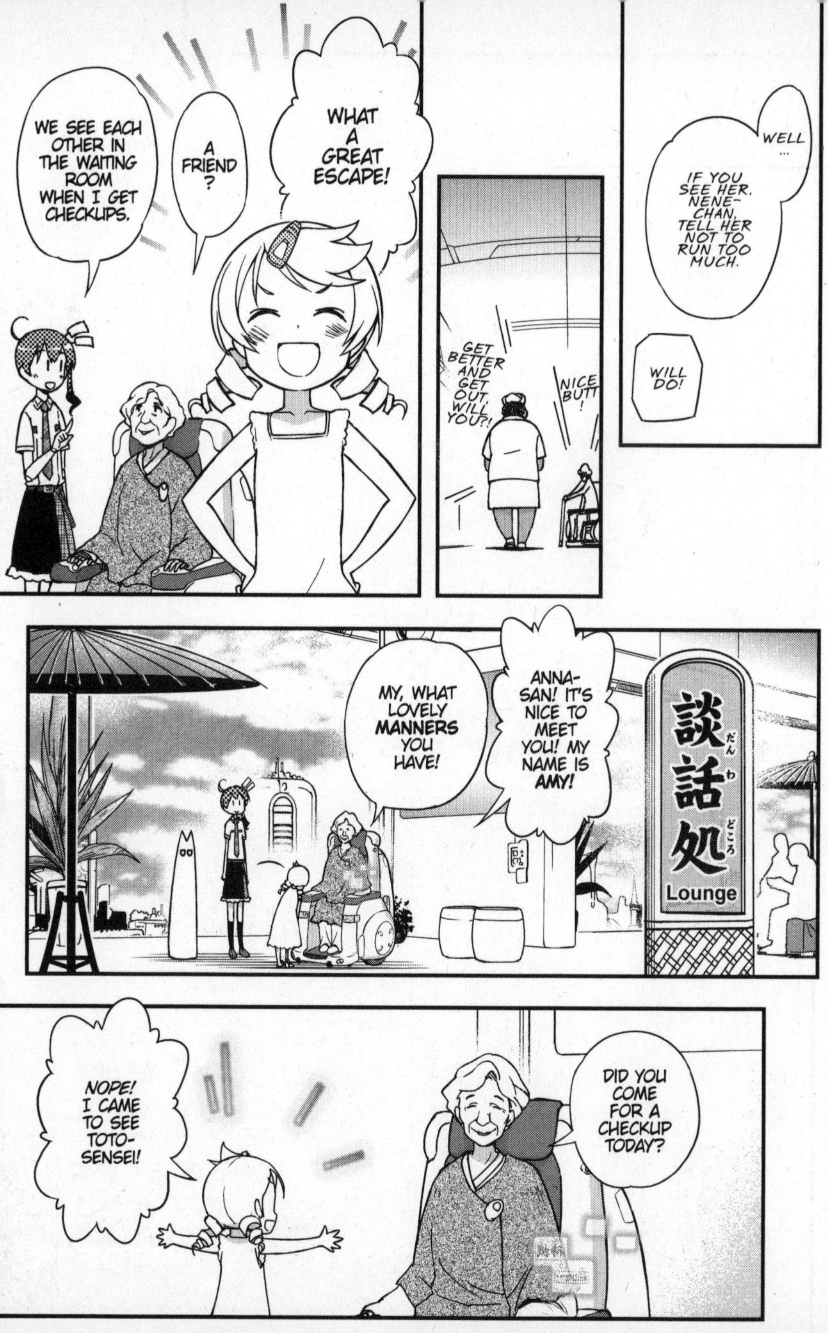
WELL ...
IF YOU SEE HER, NENE-CHAN, TELL HER NOT TO RUN TOO MUCH.
WILL DO!
NICE BUTT!
GET BETTER AND GET OUT, WILL YOU?!
WHAT A GREAT ESCAPE!
A FRIEND?
WE SEE EACH OTHER IN THE WAITING ROOM WHEN I GET CHECKUPS.
談話処 だんわどころ
Lounge
ANNA-SAN! IT'S NICE TO MEET YOU! MY NAME IS AMY!
MY, WHAT LOVELY MANNERS YOU HAVE!
DID YOU COME FOR A CHECKUP TODAY?
NOPE! I CAME TO SEE TOTO-SENSEI!

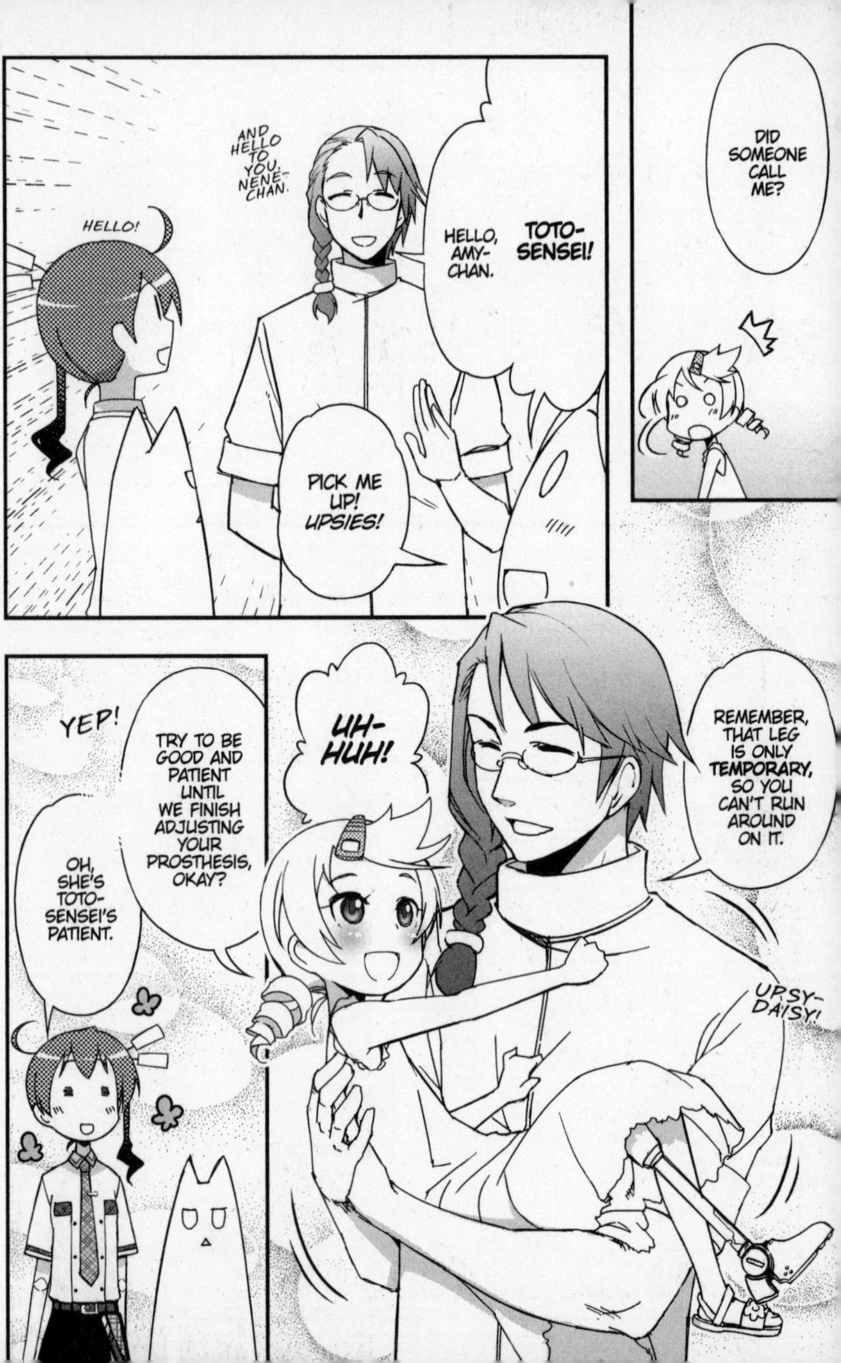
DID SOMEONE CALL ME?
TOTO-SENSEI!
HELLO, AMY-CHAN.
AND HELLO TO YOU, NENE-CHAN.
HELLO!
PICK ME UP! UPSIES!
REMEMBER, THAT LEG IS ONLY TEMPORARY, SO YOU CAN'T RUN AROUND ON IT.
UH-HUH!
UPSY-DAISY!
TRY TO BE GOOD AND PATIENT UNTIL WE FINISH ADJUSTING YOUR PROSTHESIS, OKAY?
YEP!
OH, SHE'S TOTO-SENSEI'S PATIENT.

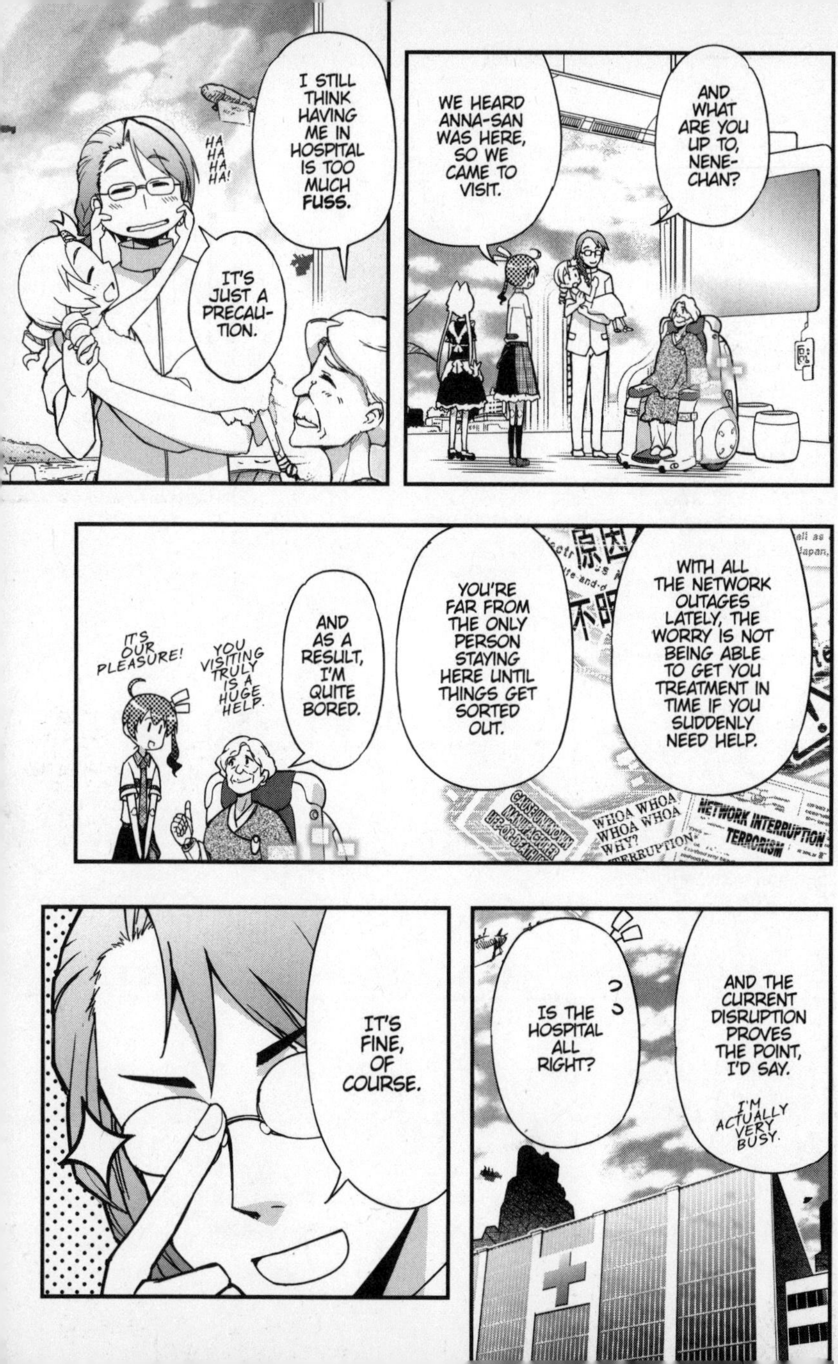
AND WHAT ARE YOU UP TO, NENE-CHAN?
WE HEARD ANNA-SAN WAS HERE, SO WE CAME TO VISIT.
I STILL THINK HAVING ME IN HOSPITAL IS TOO MUCH FUSS.
HA HA HA HA!
IT'S JUST A PRECAUTION.
WITH ALL THE NETWORK OUTAGES LATELY, THE WORRY IS NOT BEING ABLE TO GET YOU TREATMENT IN TIME IF YOU SUDDENLY NEED HELP.
YOU'RE FAR FROM THE ONLY PERSON STAYING HERE UNTIL THINGS GET SORTED OUT.
AND AS A RESULT, I'M QUITE BORED.
YOU VISITING TRULY IS A HUGE HELP.
IT'S OUR PLEASURE!
NETWORK INTERRUPTION TERRORISM
WHOA WHOA WHOA WHOA WHY?
INTERRUPTION
AND THE CURRENT DISRUPTION PROVES THE POINT, I'D SAY.
I'M ACTUALLY VERY BUSY.
IS THE HOSPITAL ALL RIGHT?
IT'S FINE, OF COURSE.

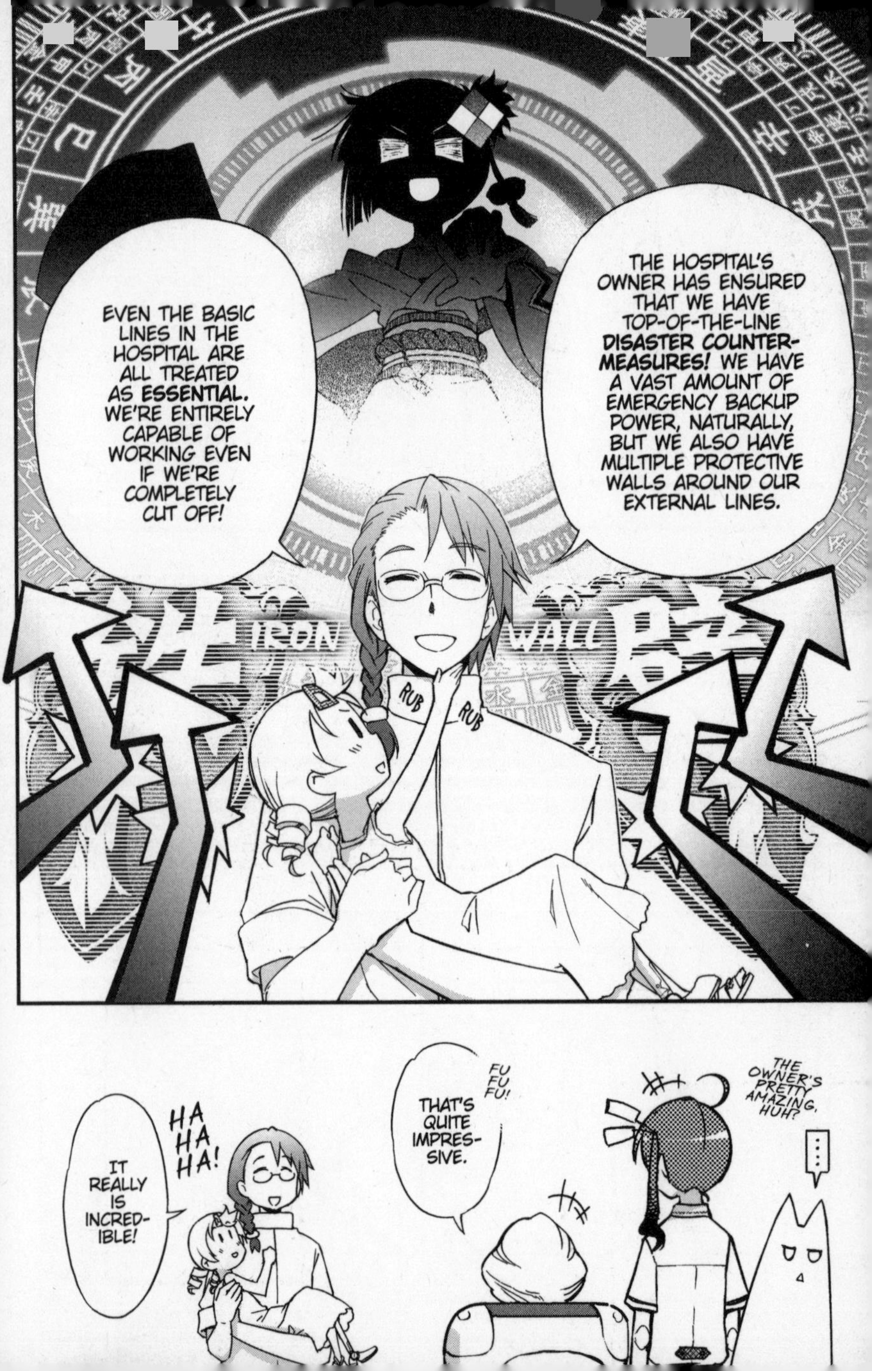
THE HOSPITAL'S OWNER HAS ENSURED THAT WE HAVE TOP-OF-THE-LINE **DISASTER COUNTER-MEASURES!** WE HAVE A VAST AMOUNT OF EMERGENCY BACKUP POWER, NATURALLY, BUT WE ALSO HAVE MULTIPLE PROTECTIVE WALLS AROUND OUR EXTERNAL LINES.
EVEN THE BASIC LINES IN THE HOSPITAL ARE ALL TREATED AS **ESSENTIAL.** WE'RE ENTIRELY CAPABLE OF WORKING EVEN IF WE'RE COMPLETELY CUT OFF!
IRON WALL
RUB
RUB
THE OWNER'S PRETTY AMAZING, HUH?
....
FU FU FU!
THAT'S QUITE IMPRESSIVE.
HA HA HA!
IT REALLY IS INCREDIBLE!

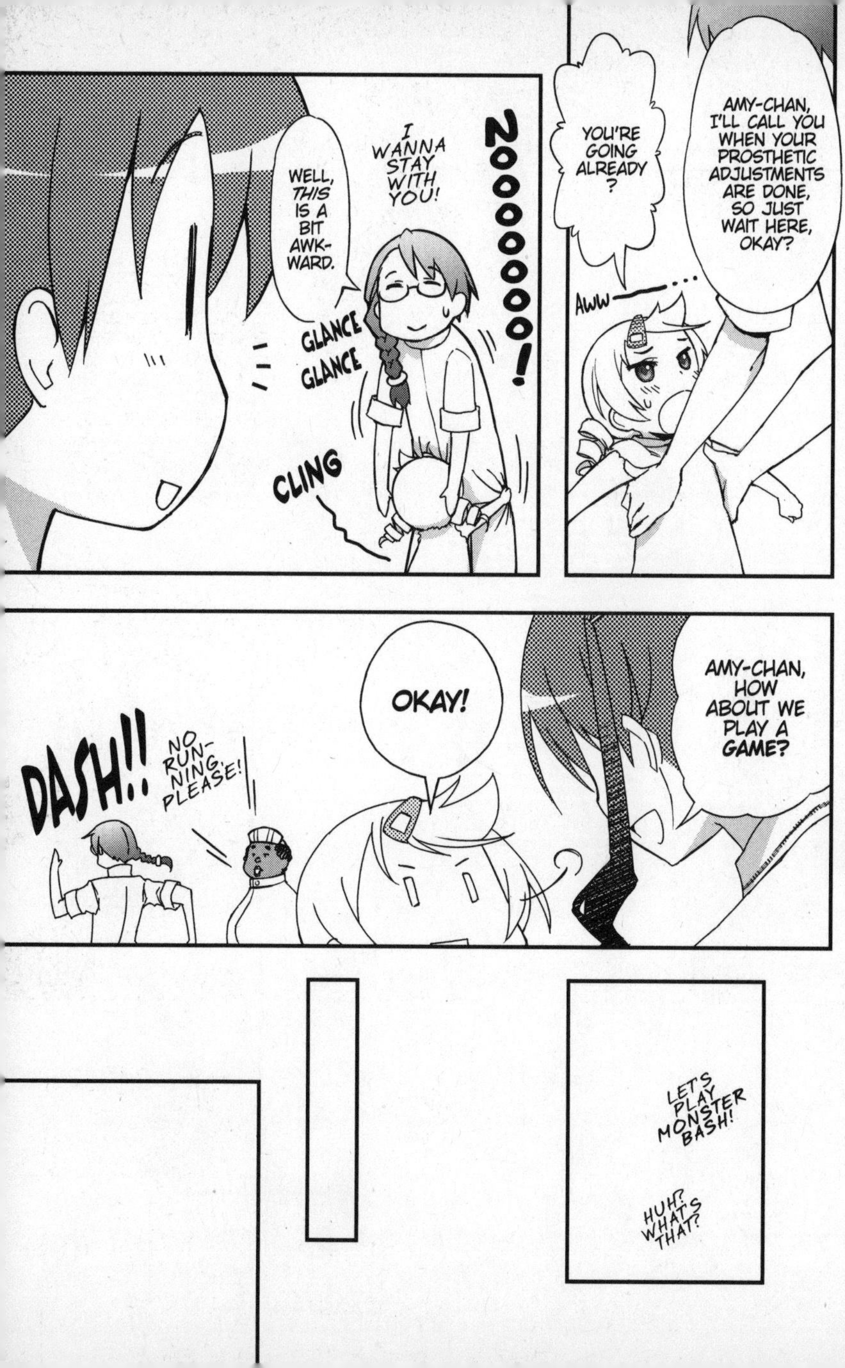
AMY-CHAN, I'LL CALL YOU WHEN YOUR PROSTHETIC ADJUSTMENTS ARE DONE, SO JUST WAIT HERE, OKAY?
YOU'RE GOING ALREADY?
AWW———...
NOOOOOOOO!
I WANNA STAY WITH YOU!
WELL, THIS IS A BIT AWK-WARD.
GLANCE GLANCE
CLING
AMY-CHAN, HOW ABOUT WE PLAY A GAME?
OKAY!
NO RUN-NING, PLEASE!
DASH!!
LET'S PLAY MONSTER BASH!
HUH? WHAT'S THAT?

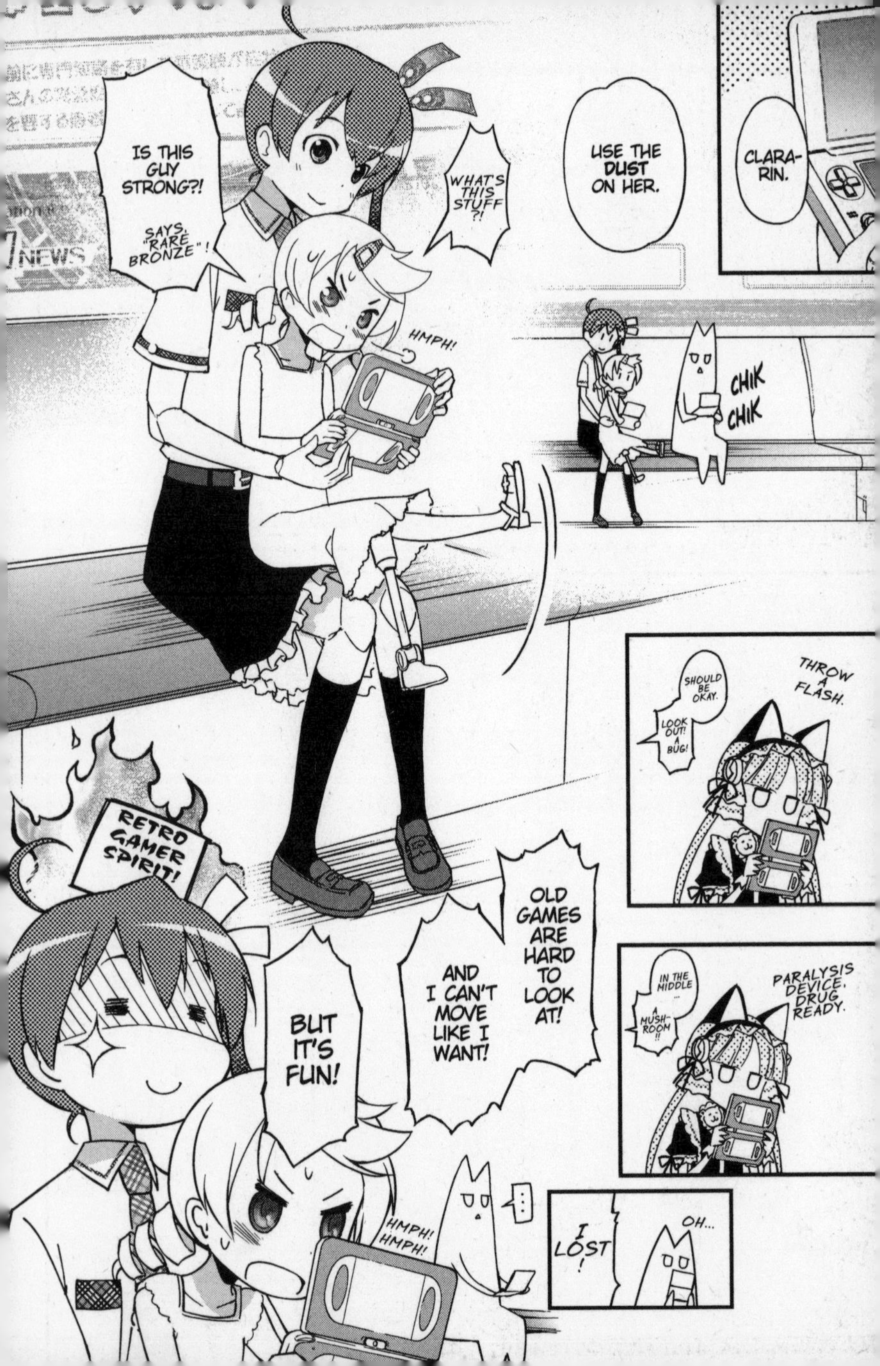

CLARA-RIN.
USE THE DUST ON HER.
WHAT'S THIS STUFF?!
IS THIS GUY STRONG?!
SAYS, "RARE BRONZE"!
HMPH!
CHIK CHIK
THROW A FLASH.
SHOULD BE OKAY.
LOOK OUT! A BUG!
PARALYSIS DEVICE, DRUG READY.
IN THE MIDDLE...
A MUSH-ROOM!!
OH...
I LOST!
OLD GAMES ARE HARD TO LOOK AT!
AND I CAN'T MOVE LIKE I WANT!
BUT IT'S FUN!
RETRO GAMER SPIRIT!
...
HMPH! HMPH!

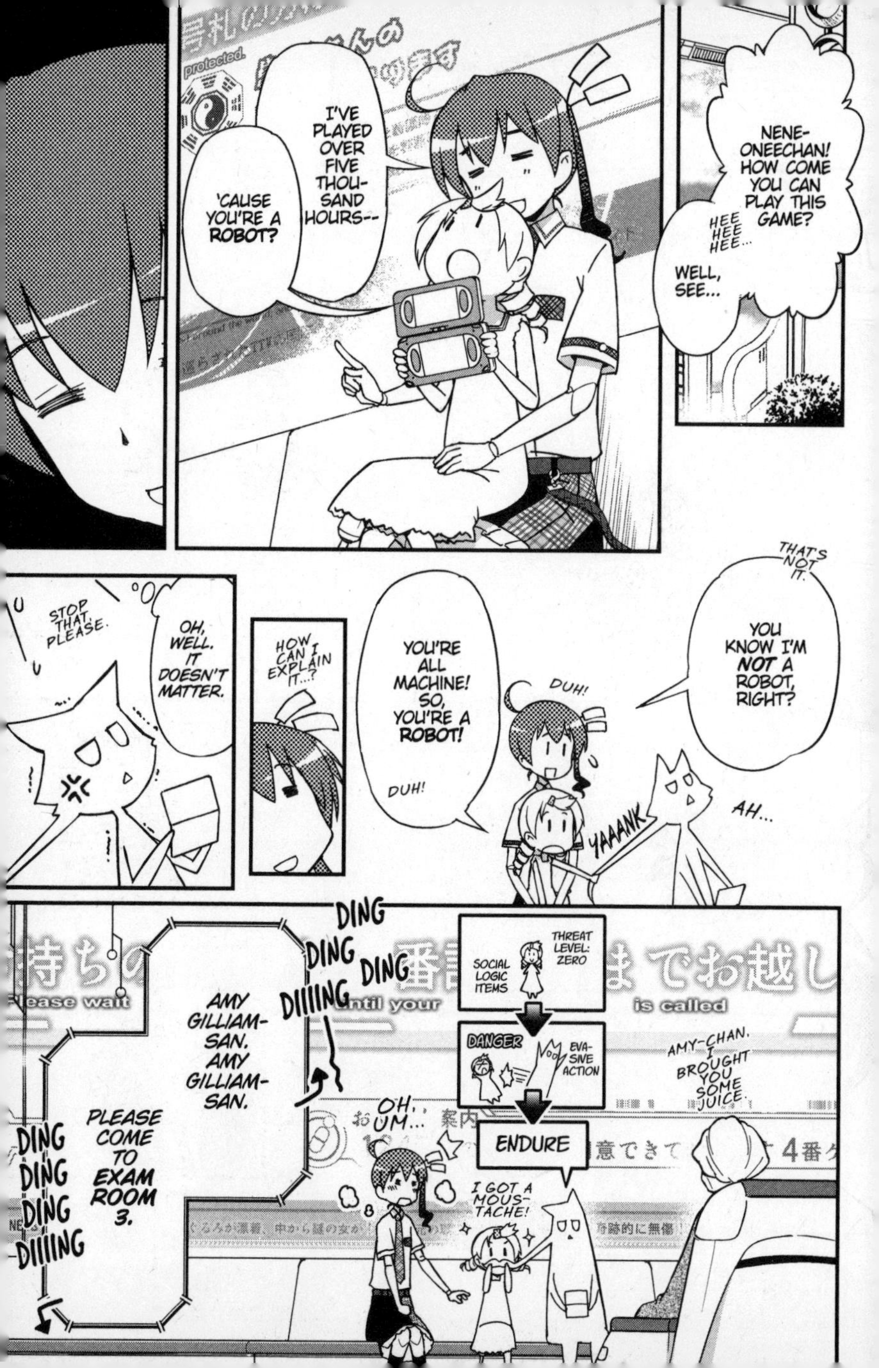
NENE-ONEECHAN! HOW COME YOU CAN PLAY THIS GAME?
HEE HEE HEE...
WELL, SEE...
I'VE PLAYED OVER FIVE THOUSAND HOURS--
'CAUSE YOU'RE A ROBOT?
THAT'S NOT IT.
YOU KNOW I'M NOT A ROBOT, RIGHT?
DUH!
YOU'RE ALL MACHINE! SO, YOU'RE A ROBOT!
DUH!
AH...
YAAANK
HOW CAN I EXPLAIN IT...?
OH, WELL. IT DOESN'T MATTER.
STOP THAT, PLEASE.
AMY-CHAN, I BROUGHT YOU SOME JUICE.
THREAT LEVEL: ZERO
SOCIAL LOGIC ITEMS
DANGER
EVASIVE ACTION
ENDURE
I GOT A MOUSTACHE!
OH, UM...
DING DING DING DIIIING
AMY GILLIAM-SAN. AMY GILLIAM-SAN.
PLEASE COME TO EXAM ROOM 3.
DING DING DING DIIIING

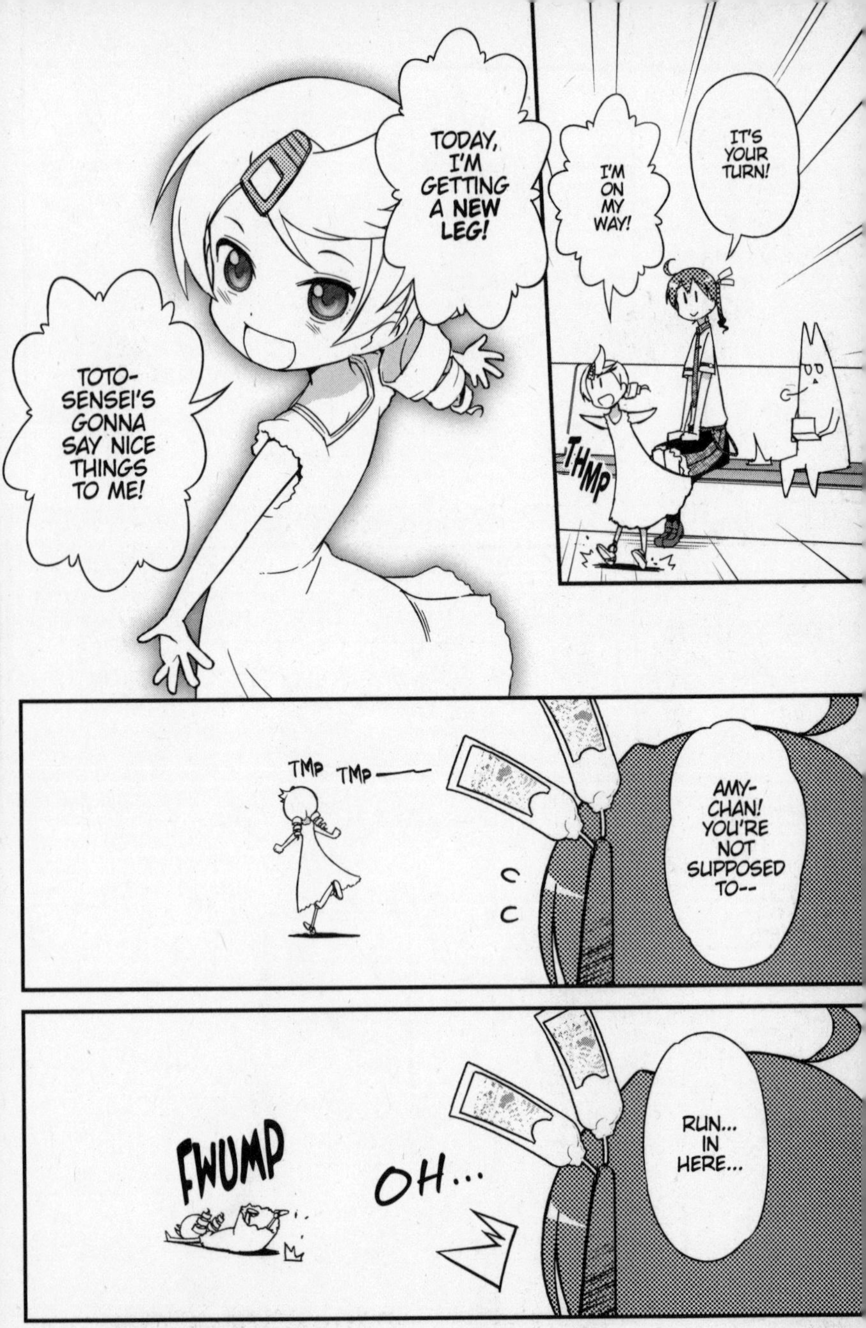
IT'S YOUR TURN!
I'M ON MY WAY!
THMP
TODAY, I'M GETTING A NEW LEG!
TOTO-SENSEI'S GONNA SAY NICE THINGS TO ME!
AMY-CHAN! YOU'RE NOT SUPPOSED TO--
TMP TMP
RUN... IN HERE...
OH...
FWUMP

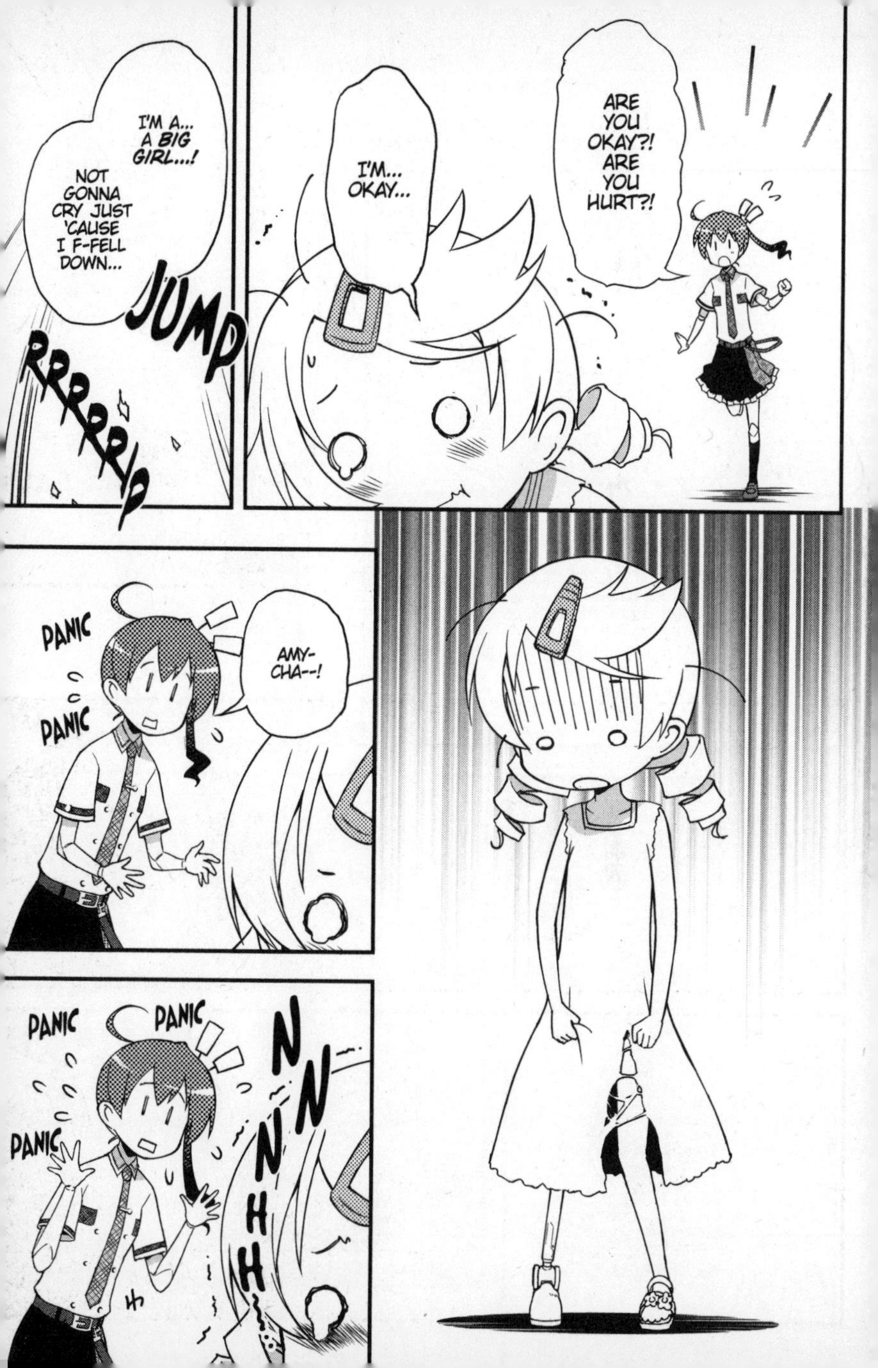
ARE YOU OKAY?! ARE YOU HURT?!
I'M... OKAY...
I'M A... A BIG GIRL...!
NOT GONNA CRY JUST 'CAUSE I F-FELL DOWN...
JUMP
RRRRRRIP
AMY-CHA--!
PANIC
PANIC
NNNHH~
PANIC
PANIC
PANIC

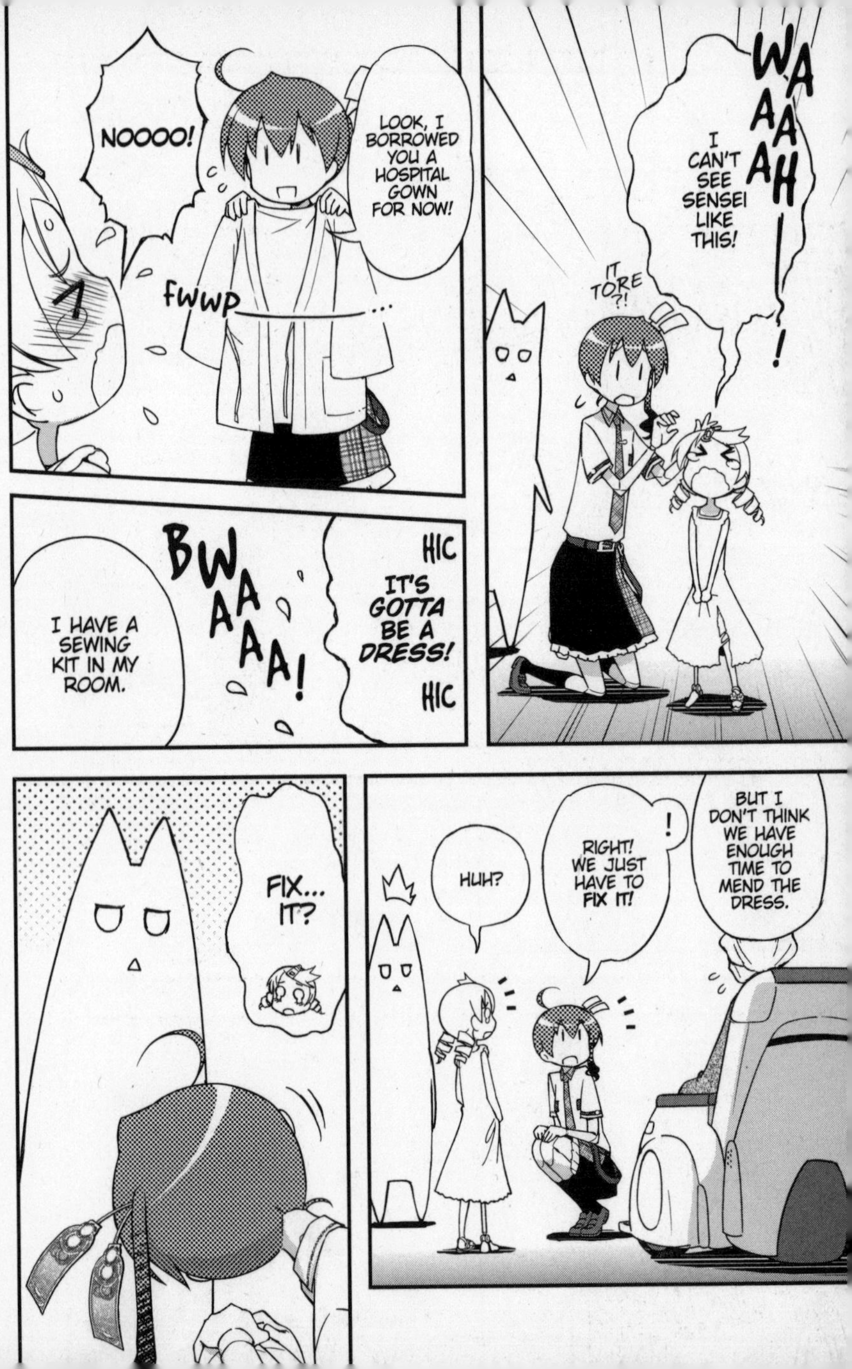
WAAAAH!
I CAN'T SEE SENSEI LIKE THIS!
IT TORE?!
LOOK, I BORROWED YOU A HOSPITAL GOWN FOR NOW!
NOOOO!
FWWP...
HIC
IT'S GOTTA BE A DRESS!
HIC
BWAAAAA!
I HAVE A SEWING KIT IN MY ROOM.
BUT I DON'T THINK WE HAVE ENOUGH TIME TO MEND THE DRESS.
RIGHT! WE JUST HAVE TO FIX IT!
!
HUH?
FIX... IT?

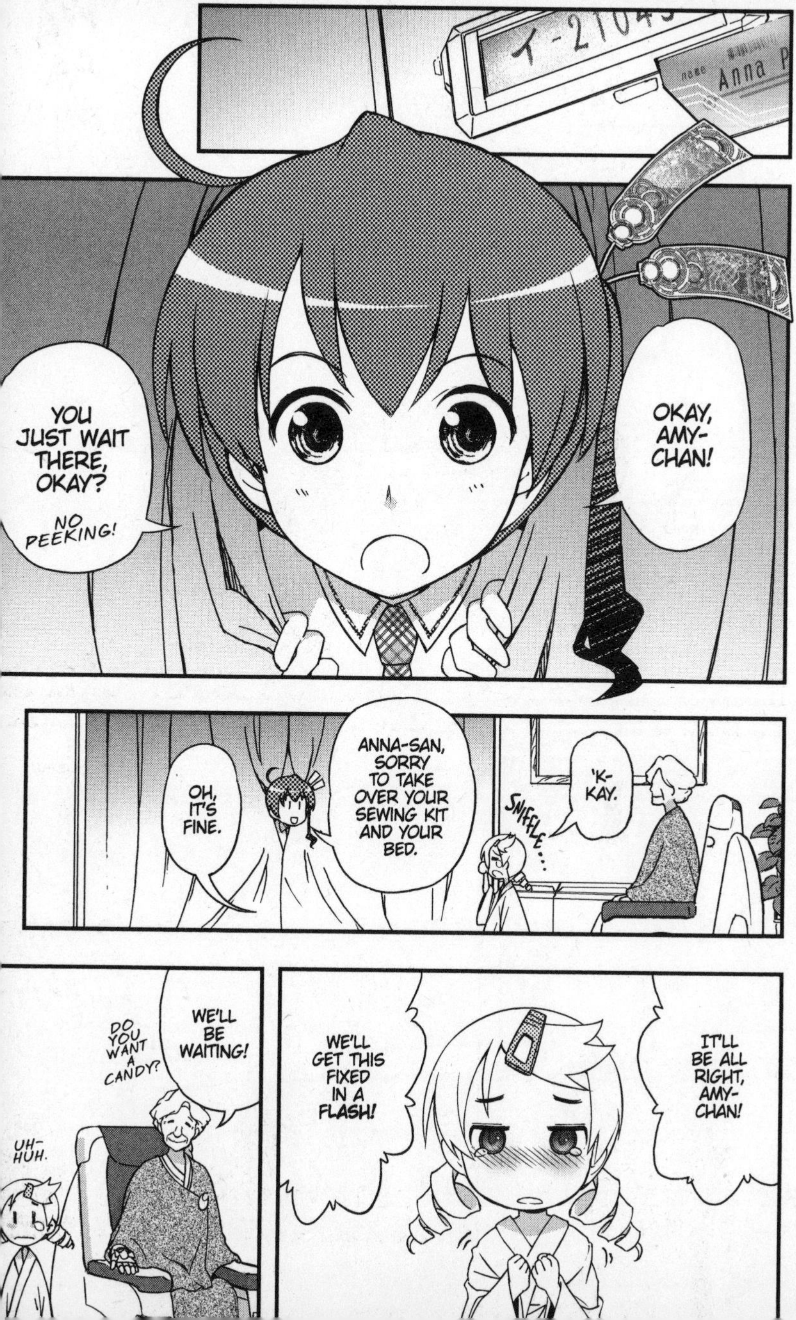
Anna
OKAY, AMY-CHAN!
YOU JUST WAIT THERE, OKAY?
NO PEEKING!
'K-KAY.
SNIFFLE...
ANNA-SAN, SORRY TO TAKE OVER YOUR SEWING KIT AND YOUR BED.
OH, IT'S FINE.
IT'LL BE ALL RIGHT, AMY-CHAN!
WE'LL GET THIS FIXED IN A FLASH!
WE'LL BE WAITING!
DO YOU WANT A CANDY?
UH-HUH.

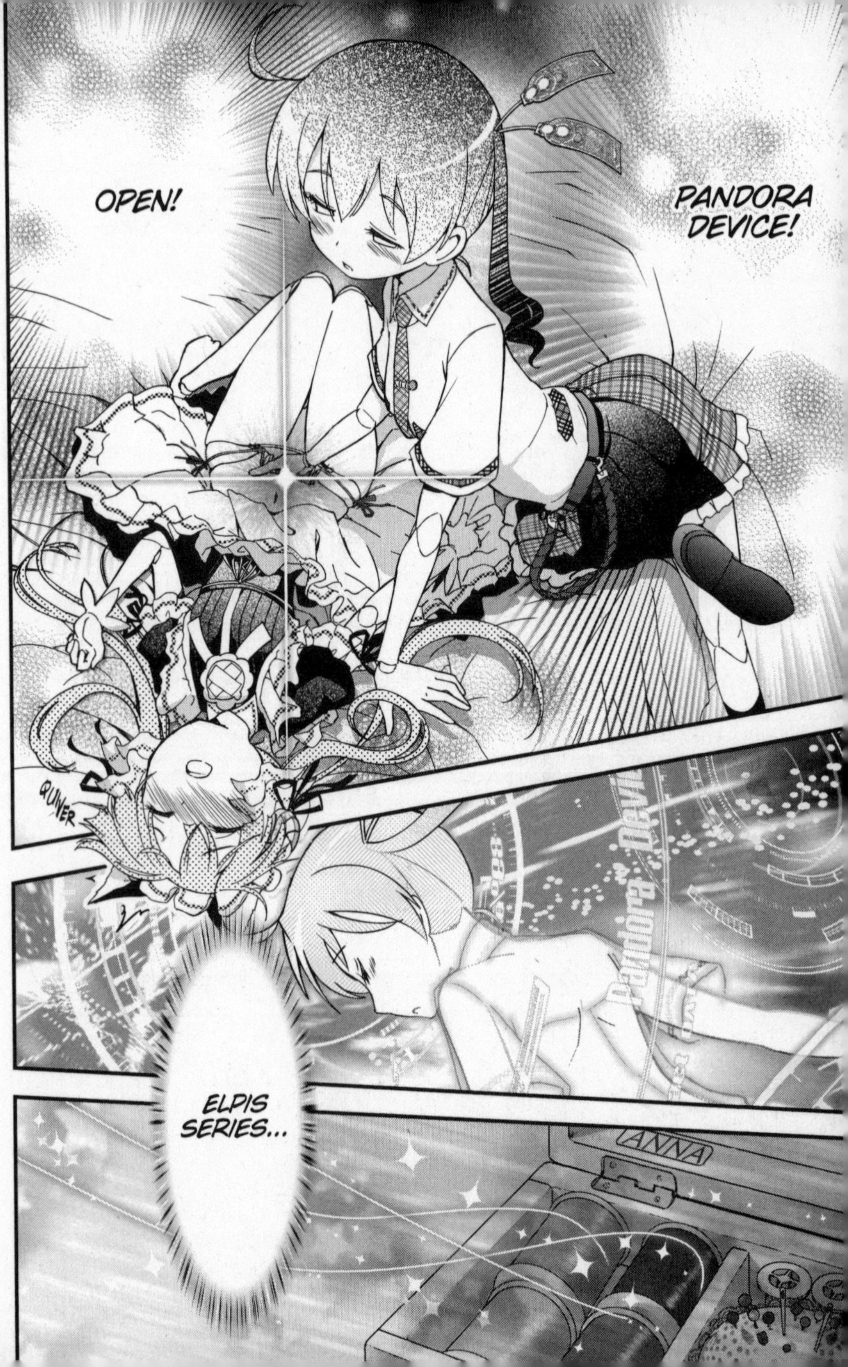
PANDORA DEVICE!
OPEN!
QUIVER
ELPIS SERIES...
ANNA

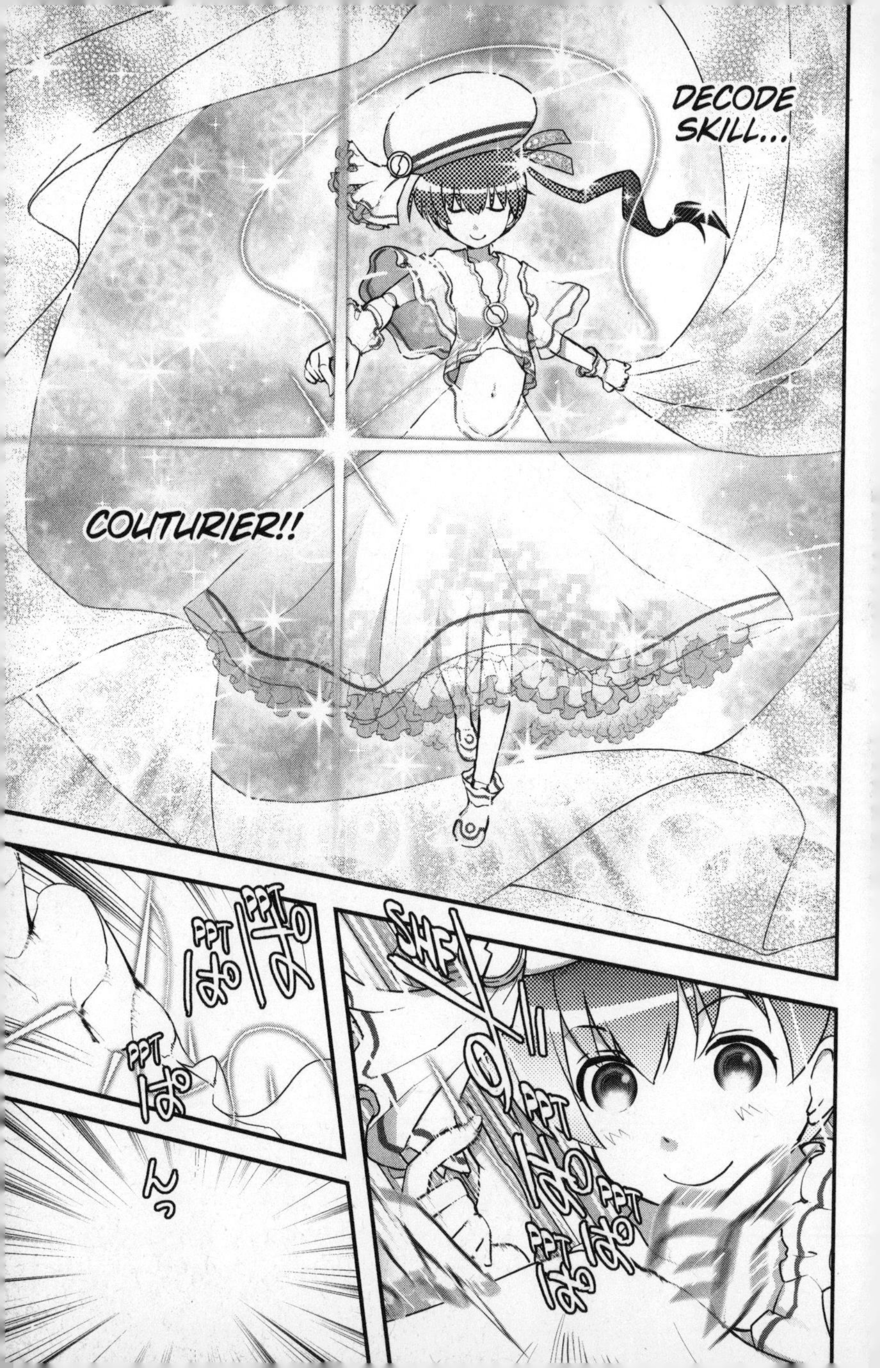
DECODE SKILL...
COUTURIER!!
SHF
PPT
PPT
PPT
PPT
PPT
PPT
PPT
ん

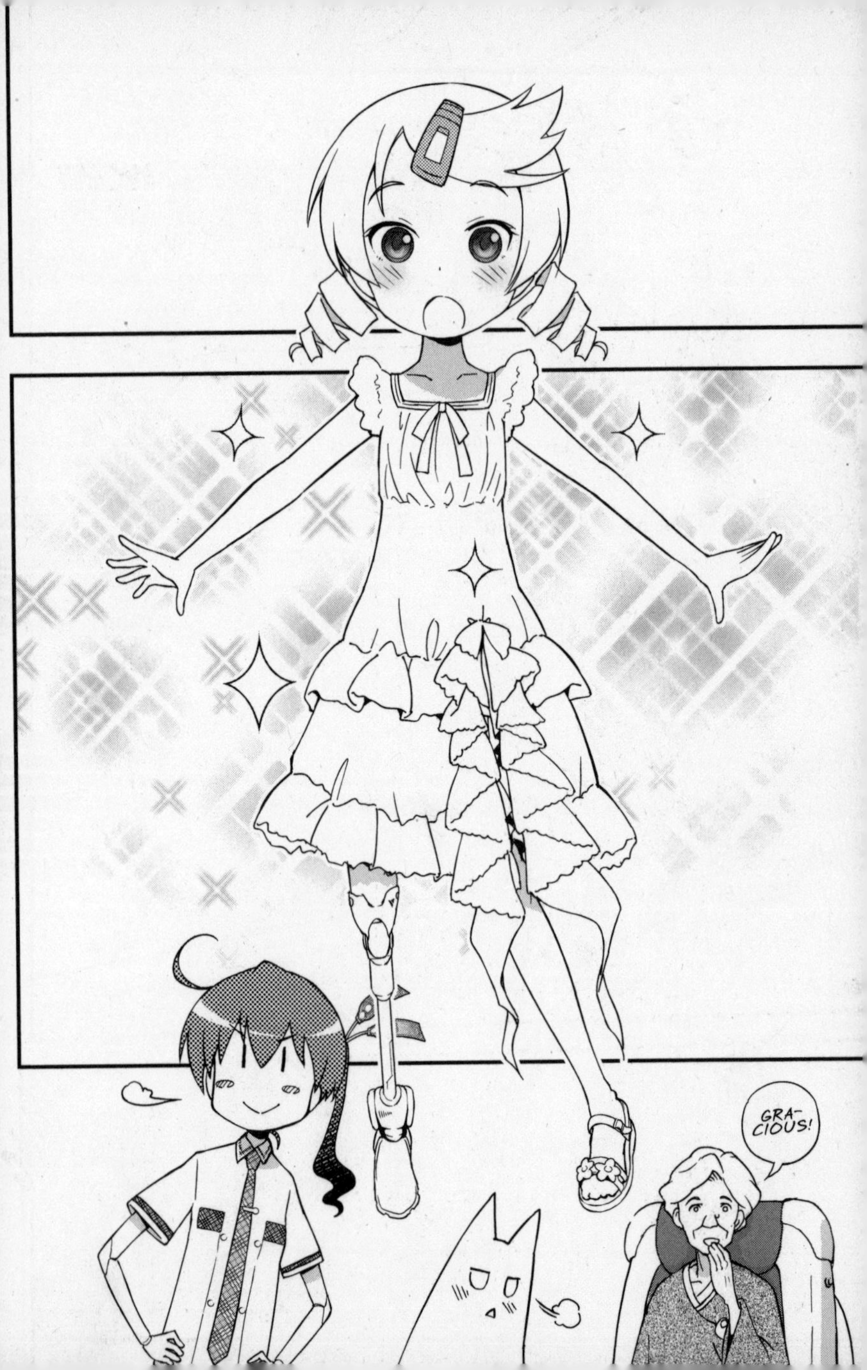
GRA-
CIOUS!

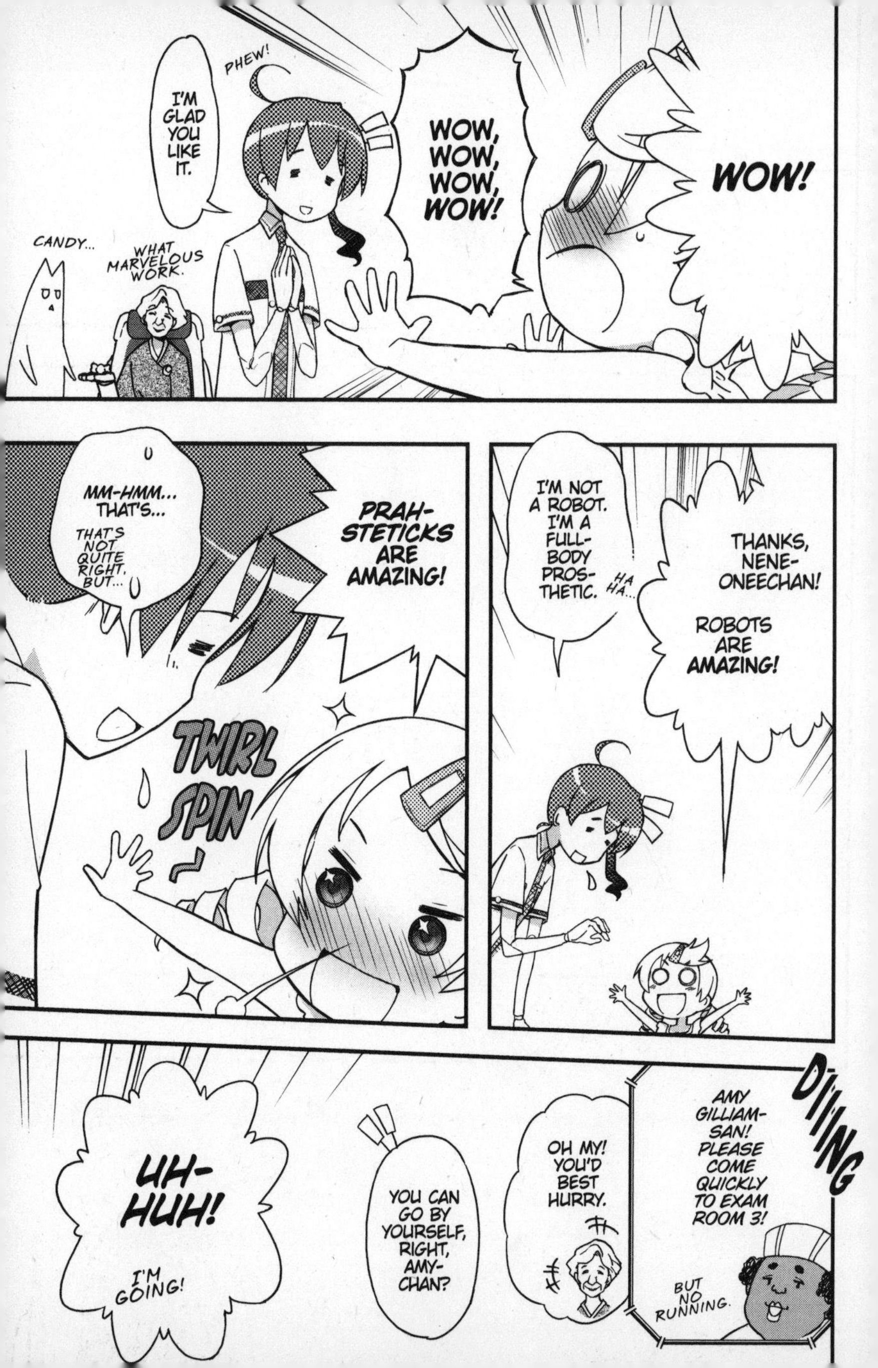
WOW!
WOW, WOW, WOW, WOW!
PHEW!
I'M GLAD YOU LIKE IT.
WHAT MARVELOUS WORK.
CANDY...
THANKS, NENE-ONEECHAN!
ROBOTS ARE AMAZING!
I'M NOT A ROBOT. I'M A FULL-BODY PROS-THETIC.
HA HA...
PRAH-STETICKS ARE AMAZING!
MM-HMM... THAT'S...
THAT'S NOT QUITE RIGHT, BUT...
TWIRL SPIN
DIIING
AMY GILLIAM-SAN! PLEASE COME QUICKLY TO EXAM ROOM 3!
BUT NO RUNNING.
OH MY! YOU'D BEST HURRY.
YOU CAN GO BY YOURSELF, RIGHT, AMY-CHAN?
UH-HUH!
I'M GOING!

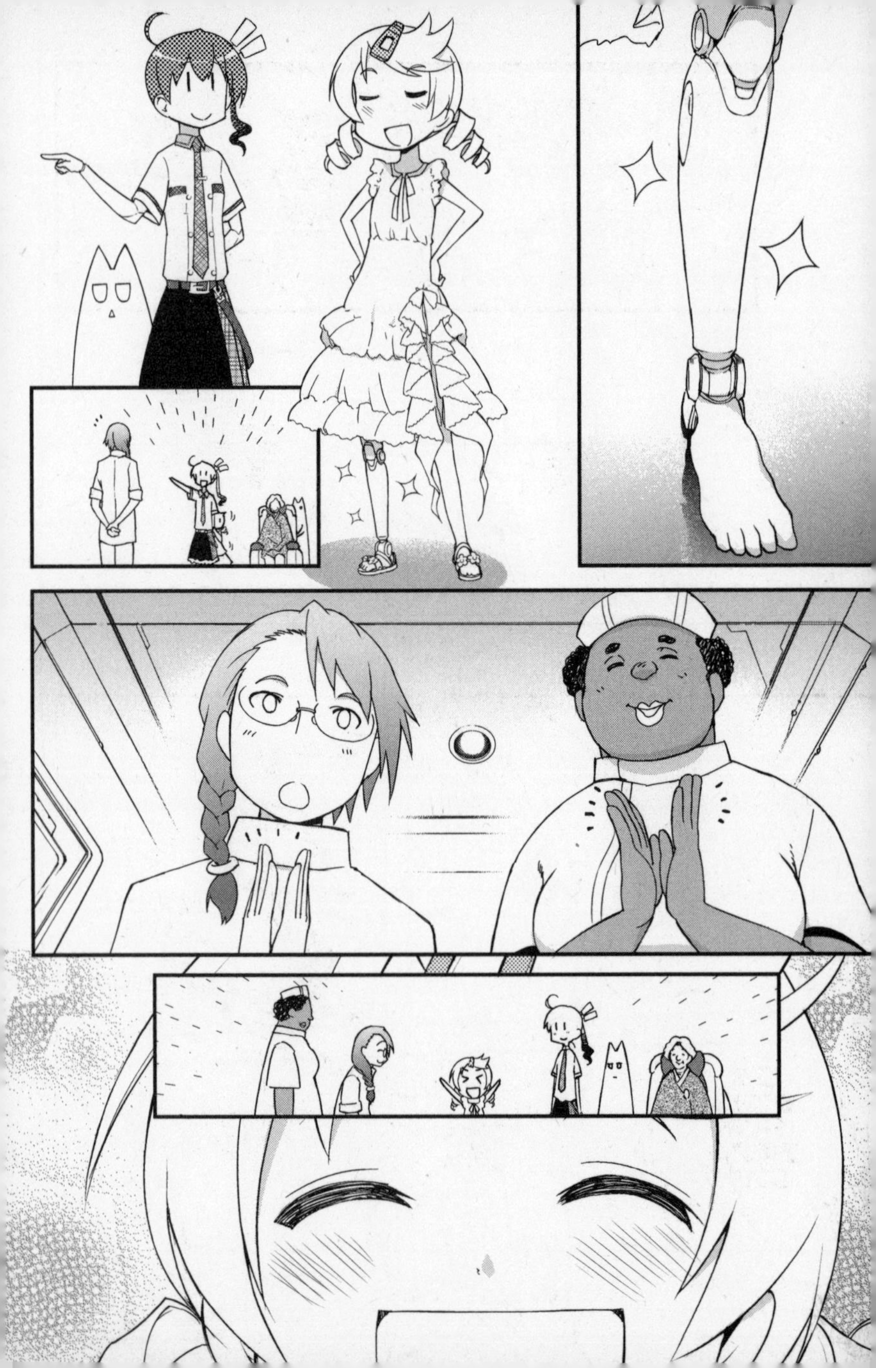

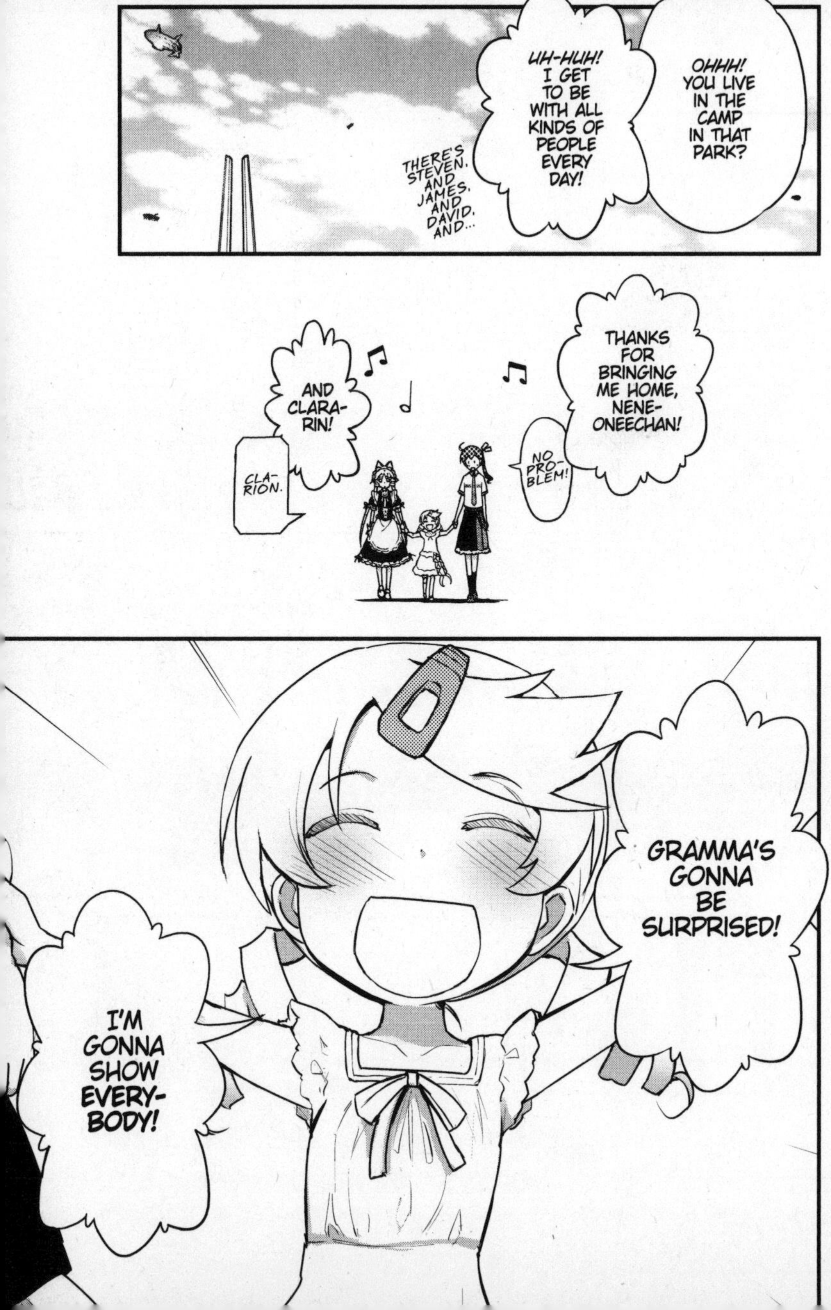
OHHH! YOU LIVE IN THE CAMP IN THAT PARK?
UH-HUH! I GET TO BE WITH ALL KINDS OF PEOPLE EVERY DAY!
THERE'S STEVEN, AND JAMES, AND DAVID, AND...
THANKS FOR BRINGING ME HOME, NENE-ONEECHAN!
NO PROBLEM!
AND CLARA-RIN!
CLARION.
GRAMMA'S GONNA BE SURPRISED!
I'M GONNA SHOW EVERYBODY!

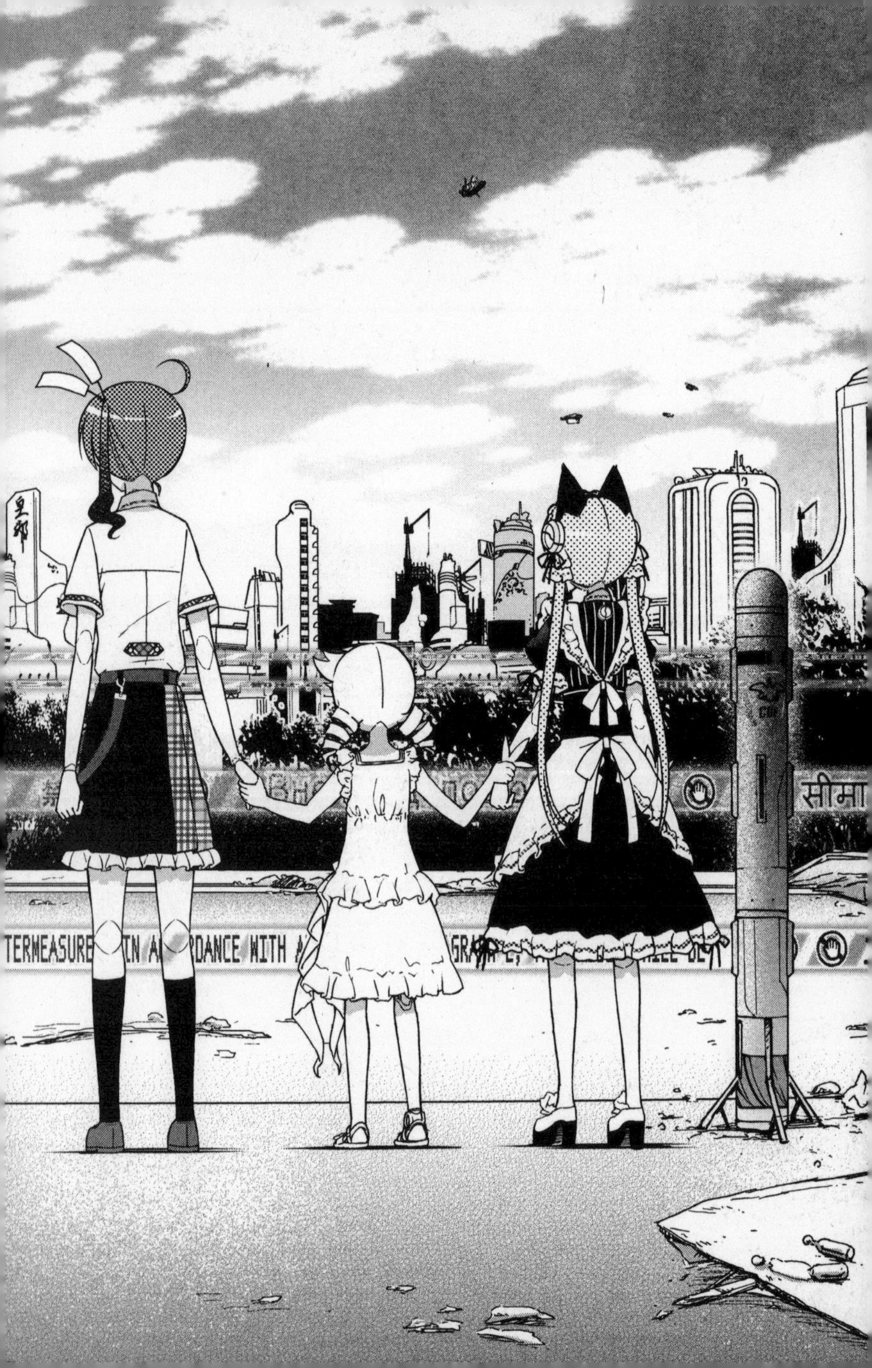

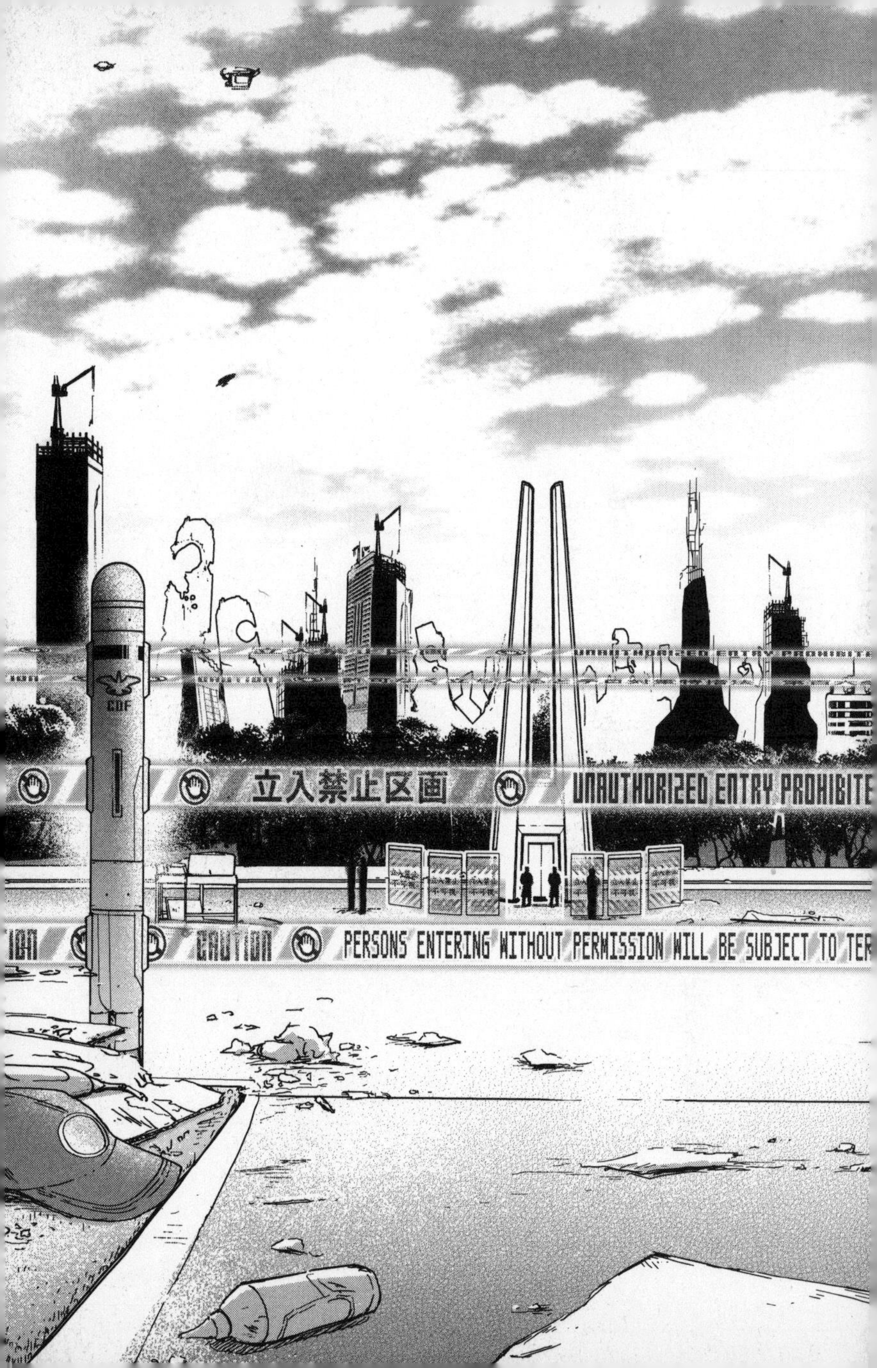
CDF
立入禁止区画
UNAUTHORIZED ENTRY PROHIBITE
CAUTION
PERSONS ENTERING WITHOUT PERMISSION WILL BE SUBJECT TO TER

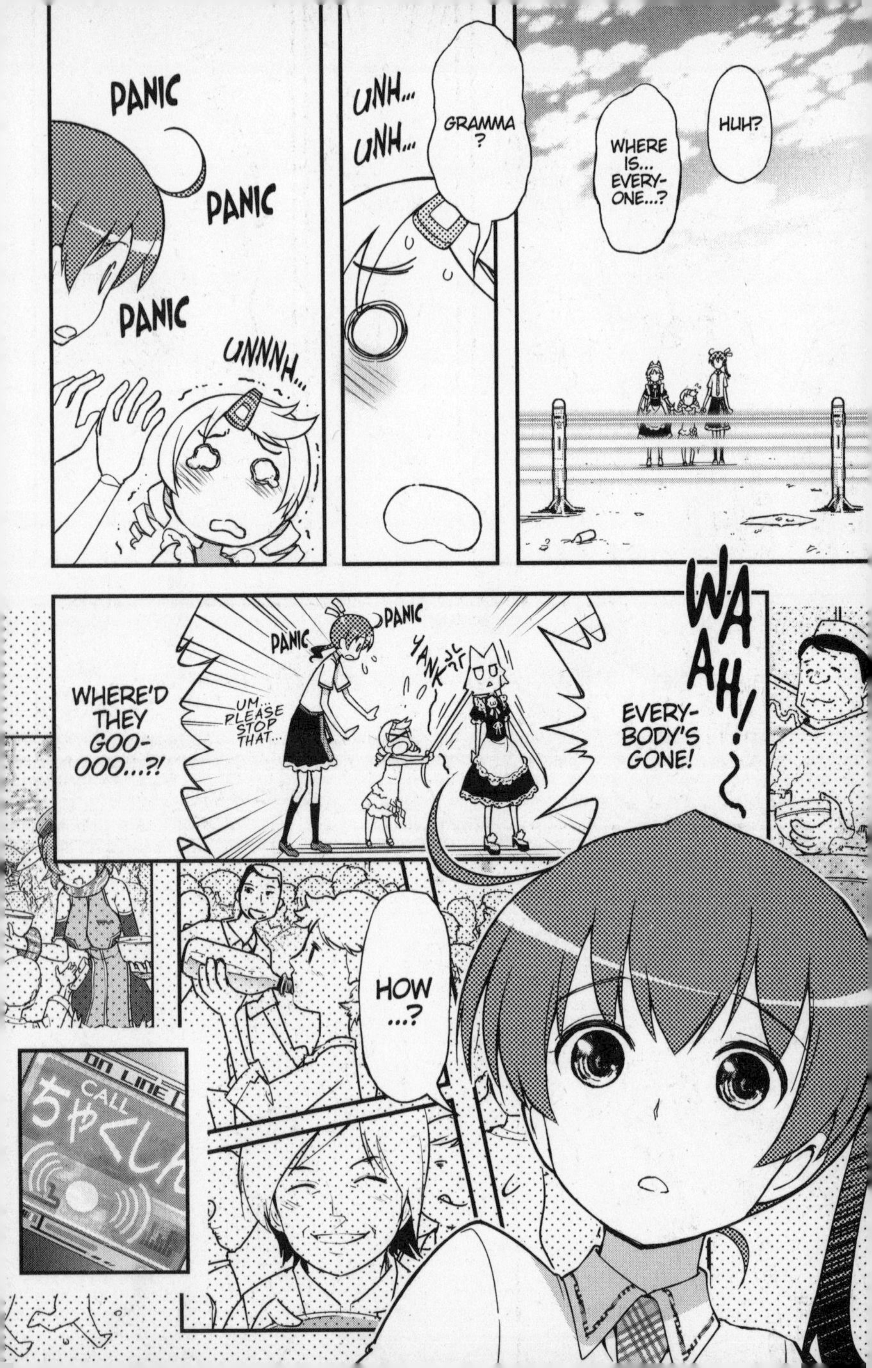
HUH?
WHERE IS... EVERY-ONE...?
GRAMMA?
UNH... UNH...
PANIC
PANIC
PANIC
UNNNH...
WAAH!~
EVERY-BODY'S GONE!
PANIC
PANIC
YANK
UM... PLEASE STOP THAT...
WHERE'D THEY GOO-OOO...?!
HOW...?
ON LINE
CALL
ちゃくしん

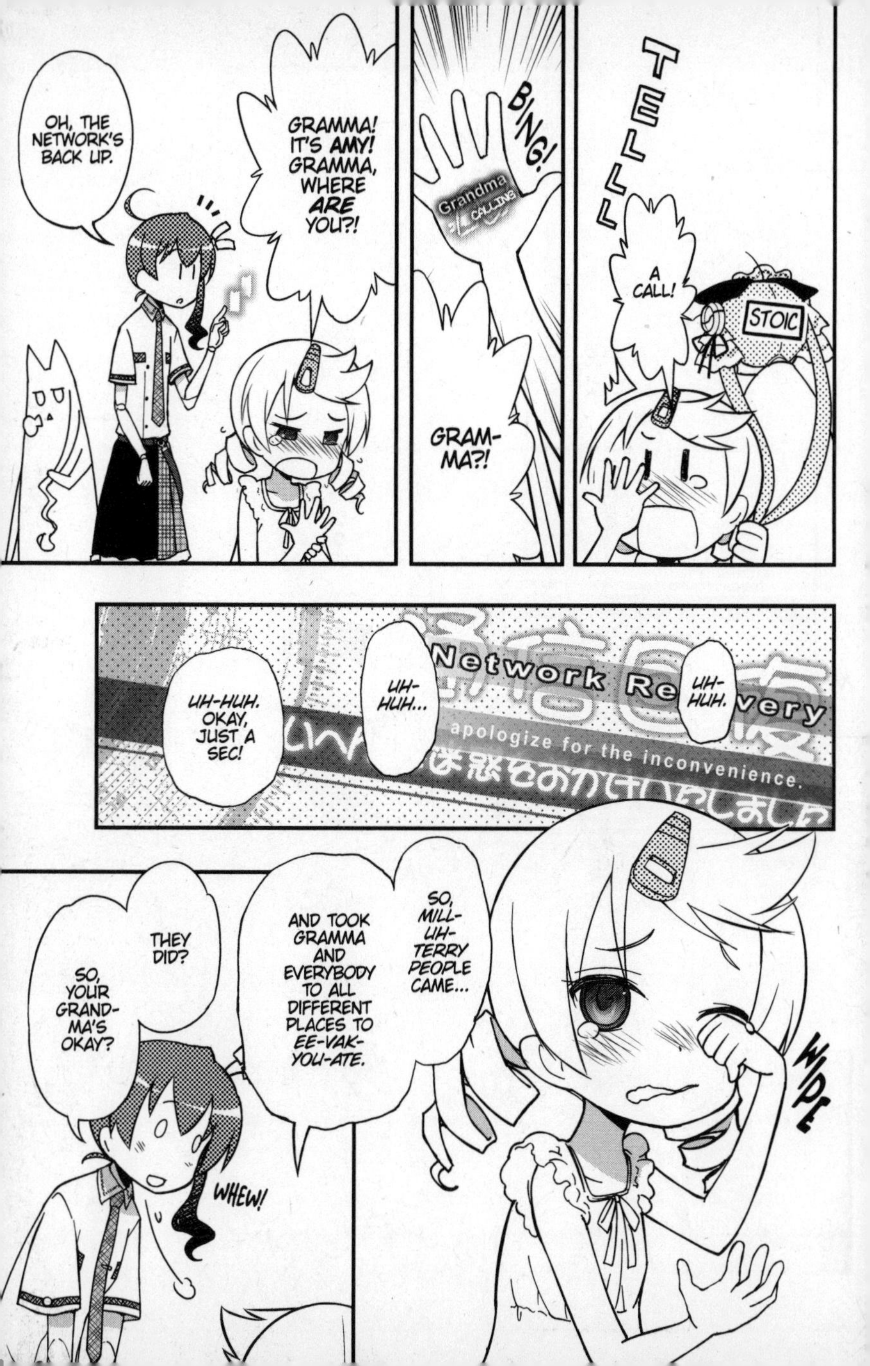
TELLL
A CALL!
STOIC
BING!
Grandma CALLING
GRAM-MA?!
GRAMMA! IT'S **AMY!** GRAMMA, WHERE **ARE** YOU?!
OH, THE NETWORK'S BACK UP.
UH-HUH.
UH-HUH...
UH-HUH. OKAY, JUST A SEC!
Network Re very
apologize for the inconvenience.
WIPE
SO, MILL-UH-TERRY PEOPLE CAME...
AND TOOK GRAMMA AND EVERYBODY TO ALL DIFFERENT PLACES TO EE-VAK-YOU-ATE.
THEY DID?
SO, YOUR GRAND-MA'S OKAY?
WHEW!

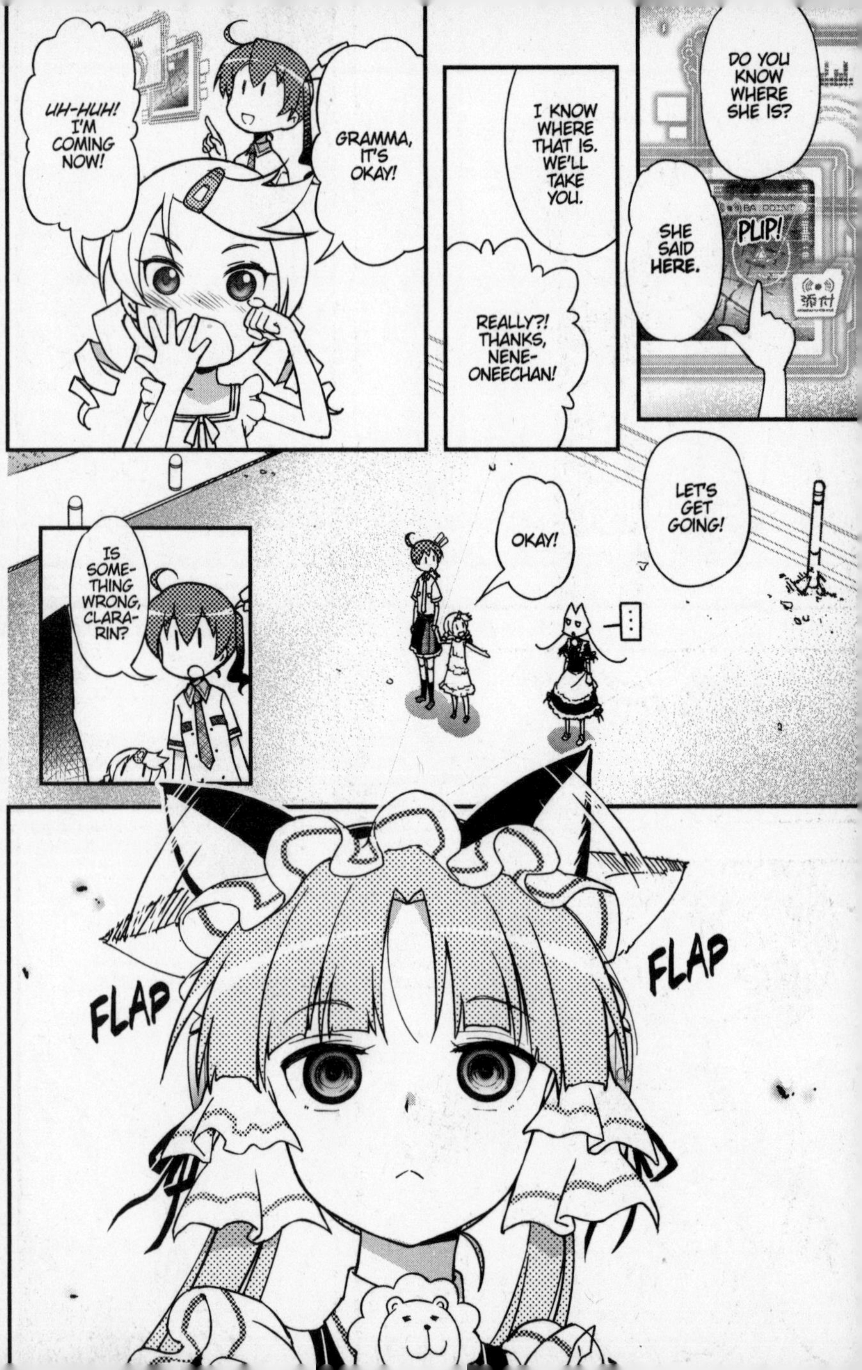
DO YOU KNOW WHERE SHE IS?
PLIP!
SHE SAID HERE.
I KNOW WHERE THAT IS. WE'LL TAKE YOU.
REALLY?! THANKS, NENE-ONEECHAN!
GRAMMA, IT'S OKAY!
UH-HUH! I'M COMING NOW!
LET'S GET GOING!
OKAY!
...
IS SOME-THING WRONG, CLARA-RIN?
FLAP
FLAP

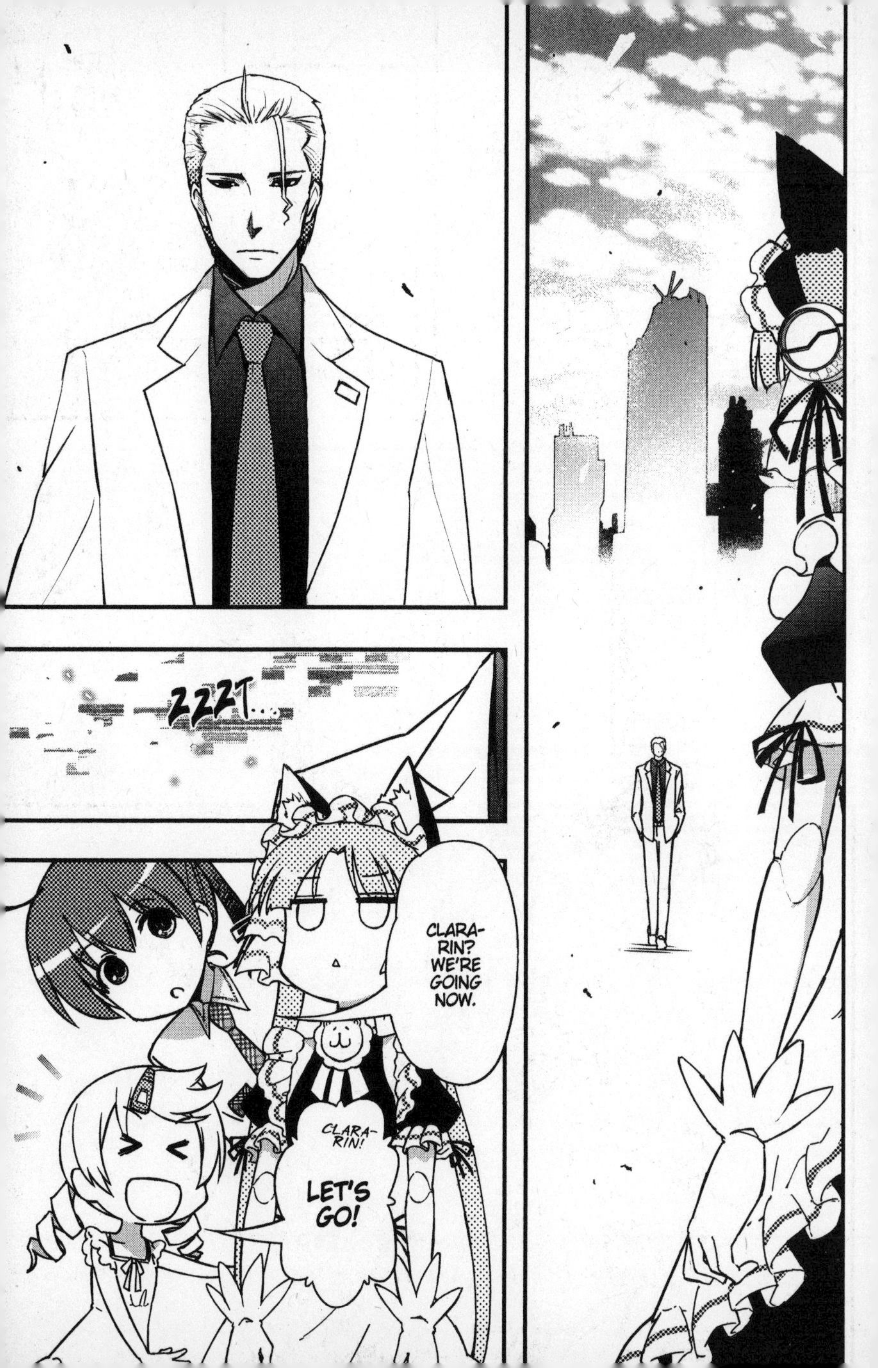
ZZZT...
CLARA-RIN? WE'RE GOING NOW.
CLARA-RIN!
LET'S GO!

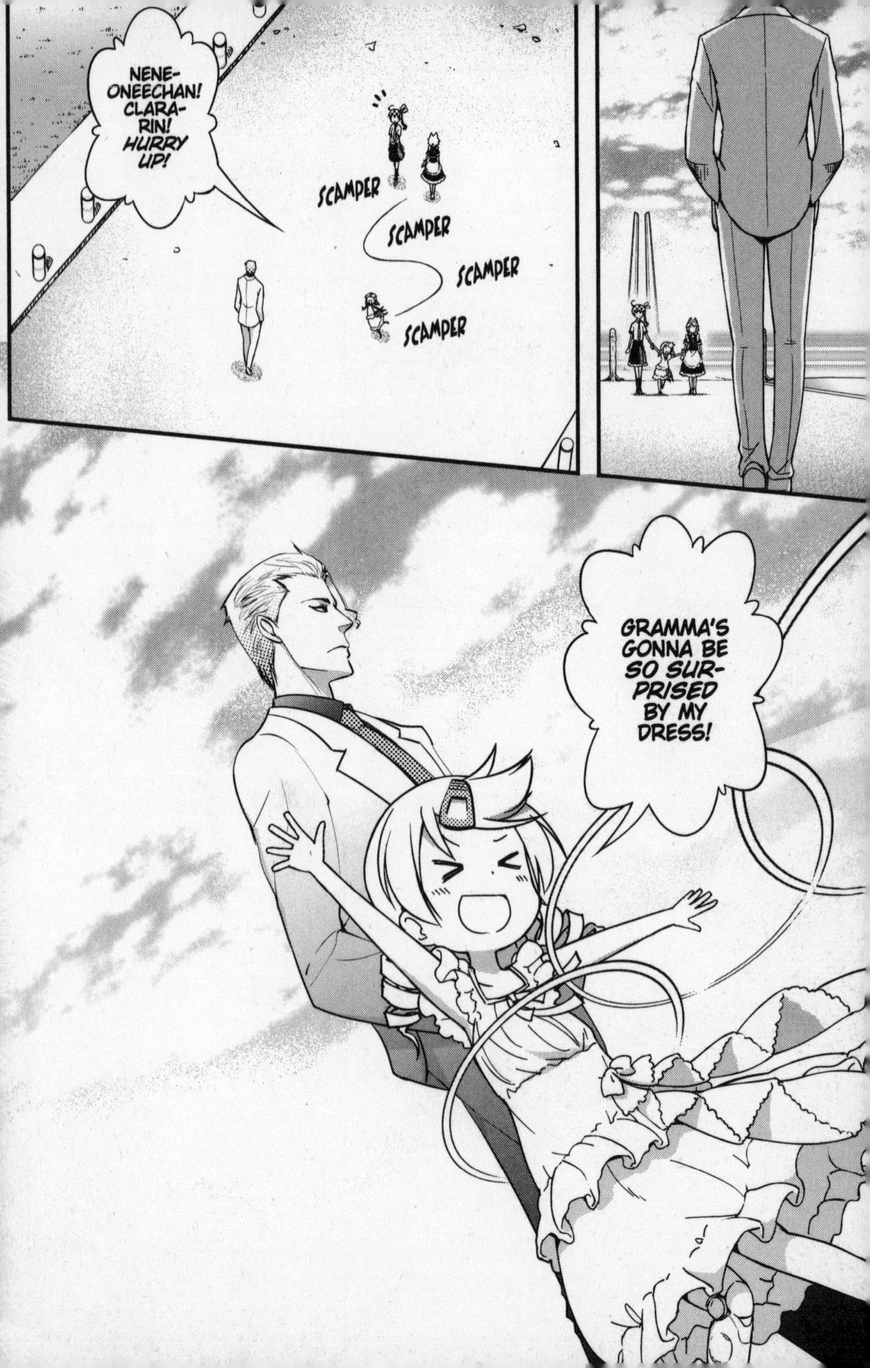
NENE-ONEECHAN! CLARA-RIN! HURRY UP!
SCAMPER
SCAMPER
SCAMPER
SCAMPER
GRAMMA'S GONNA BE SO SURPRISED BY MY DRESS!

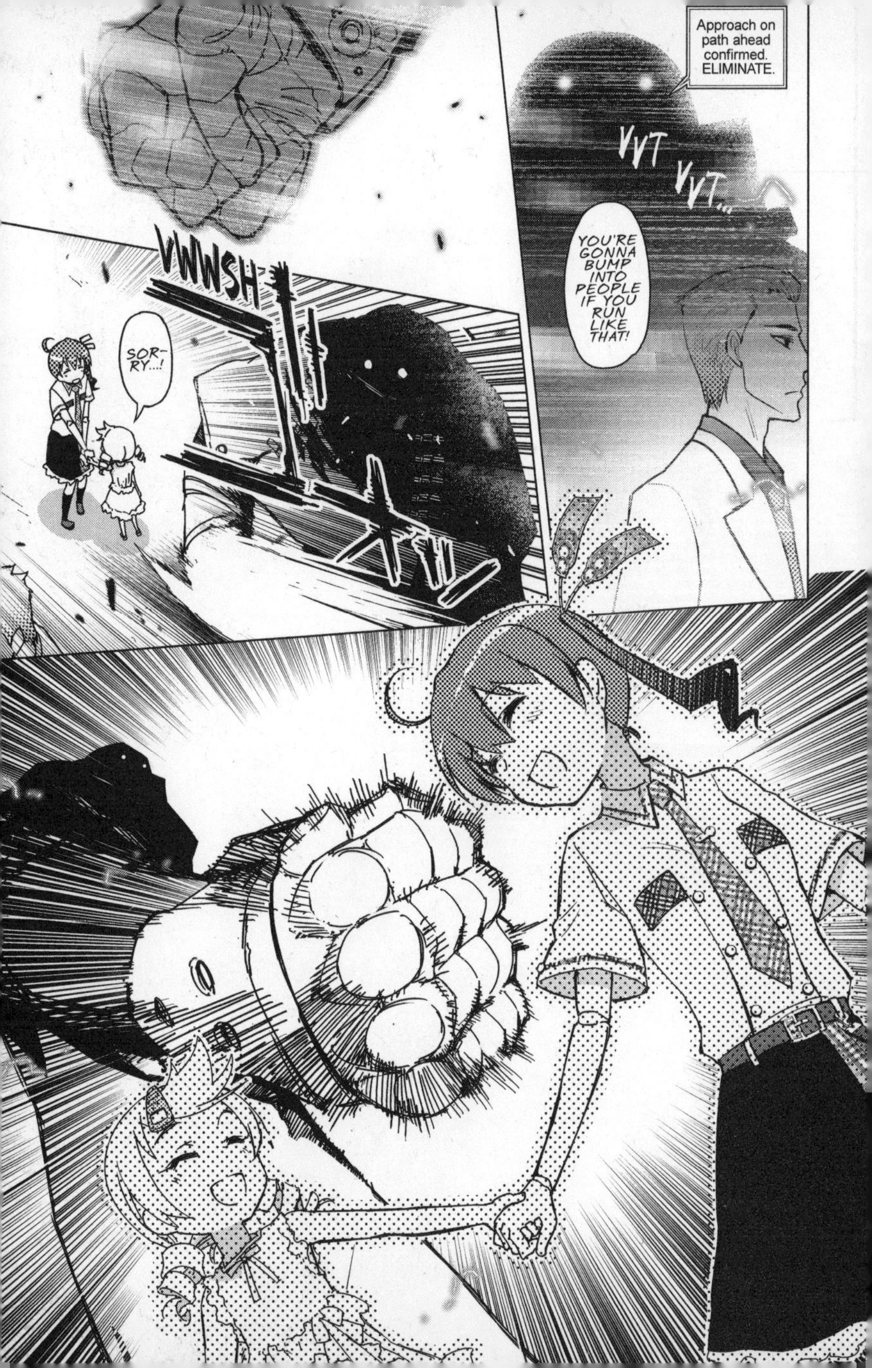

Approach on path ahead confirmed. ELIMINATE.
VVT VVT...
YOU'RE GONNA BUMP INTO PEOPLE IF YOU RUN LIKE THAT!
VWWSH
SOR-RY...!

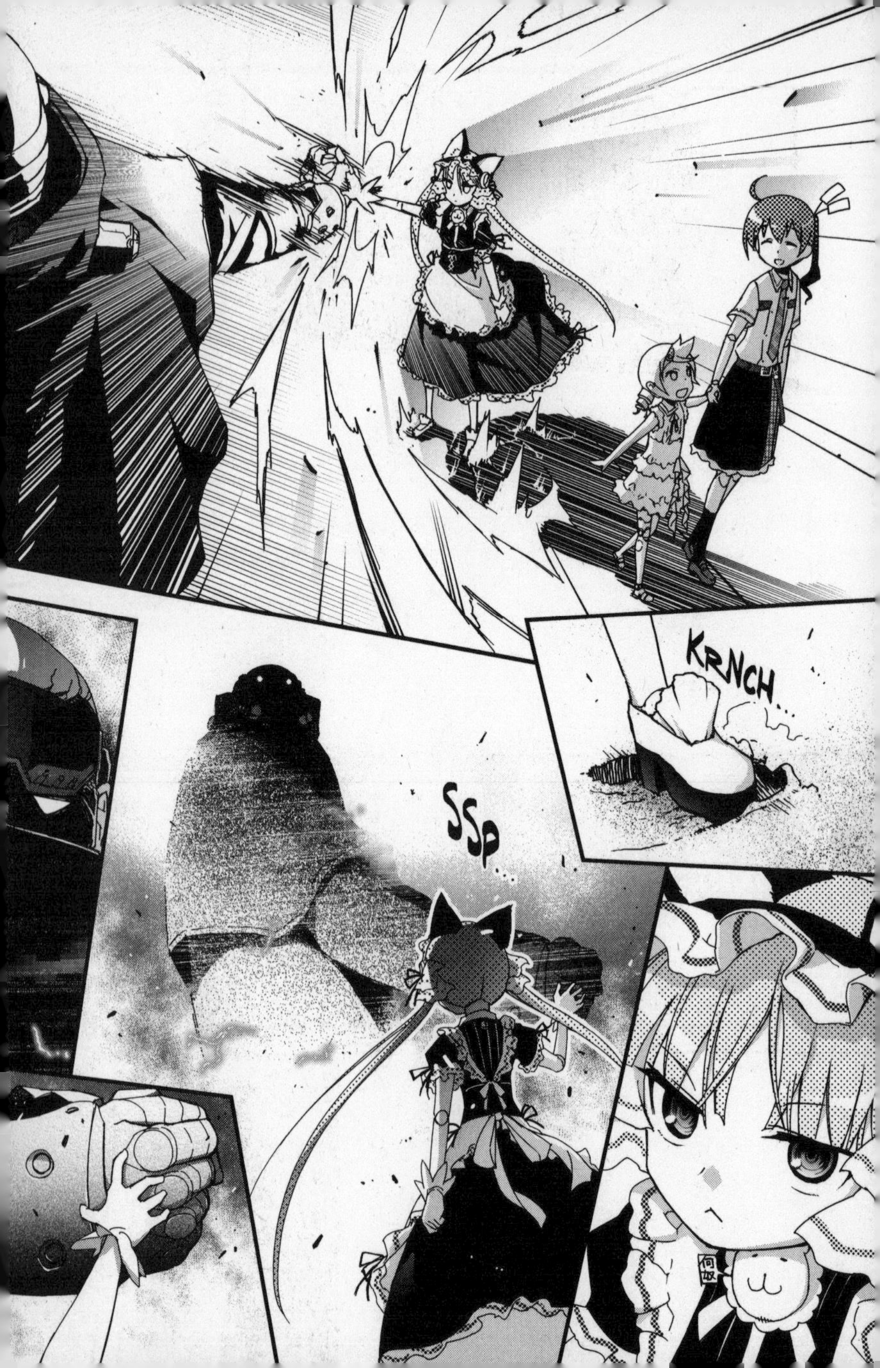
KRNCH...
SSP...
何奴

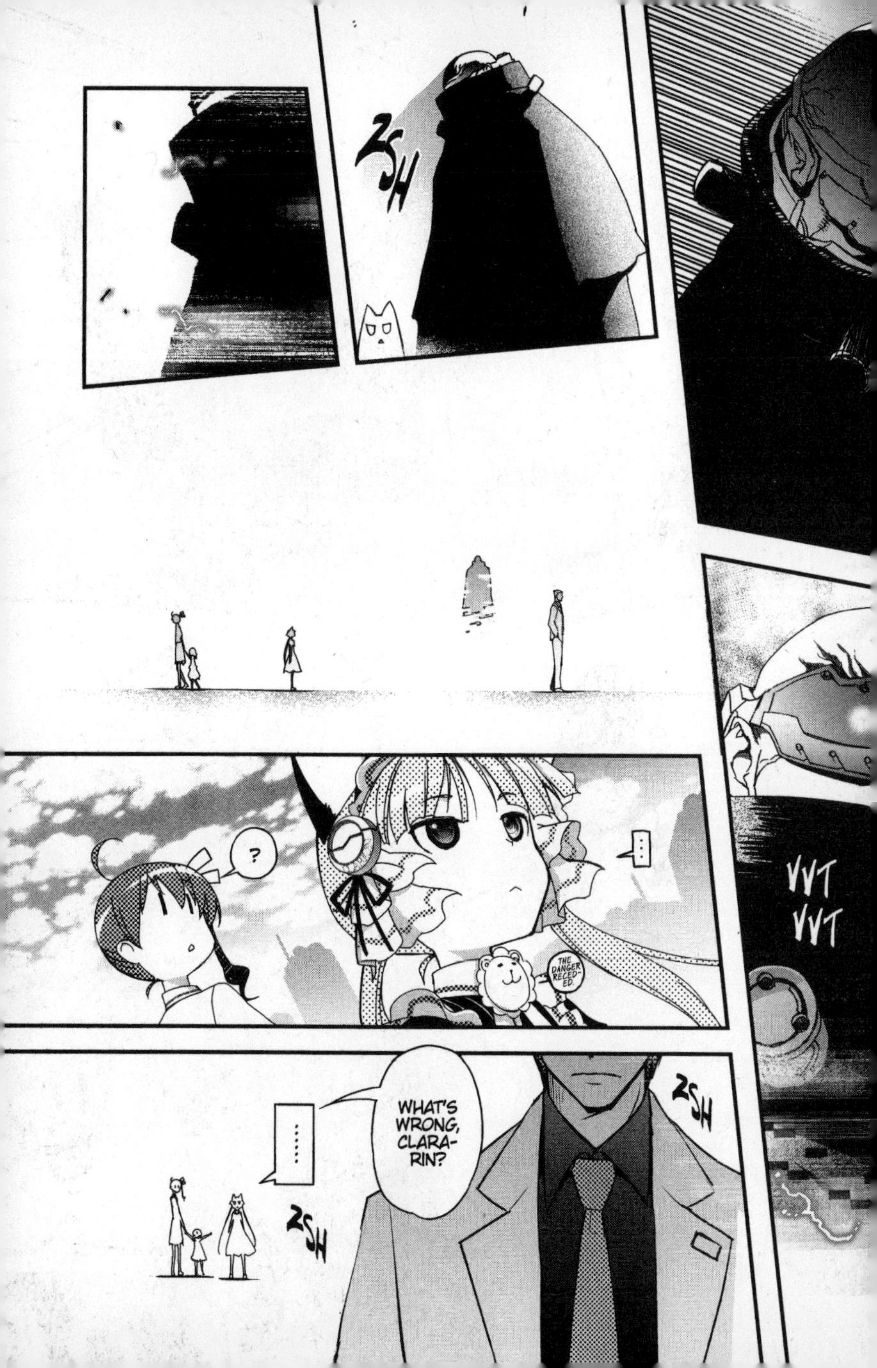
ZSH
VVT VVT
...
THE DANGER RECEDED.
?
ZSH
WHAT'S WRONG, CLARA-RIN?
......
ZSH

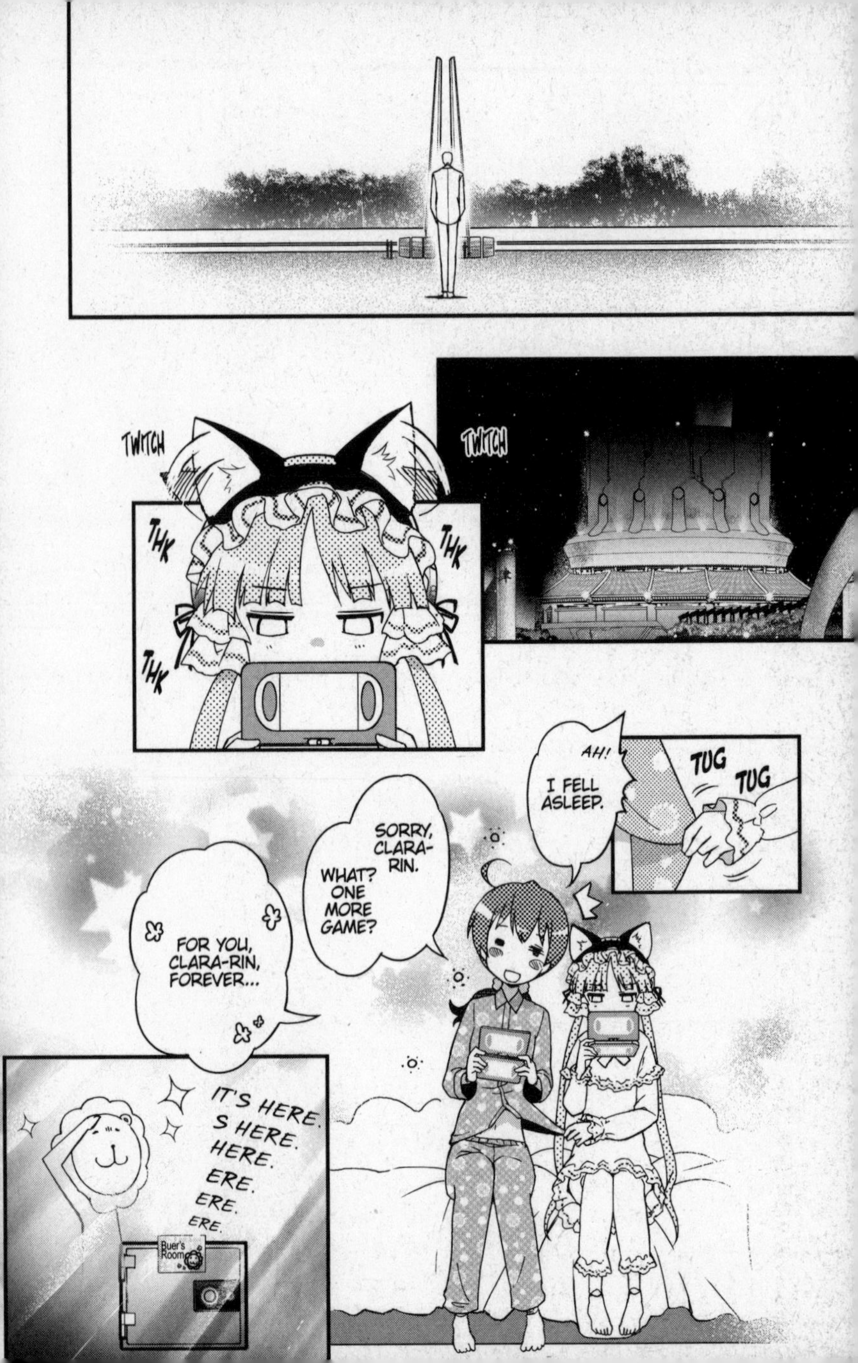
TWITCH
TWITCH
THK
THK
THK
TUG TUG
AH! I FELL ASLEEP.
SORRY, CLARA-RIN.
WHAT? ONE MORE GAME?
FOR YOU, CLARA-RIN, FOREVER...
IT'S HERE. S HERE. HERE. ERE. ERE. ERE.
Buer's Room

GHOST URN

GHOST URN

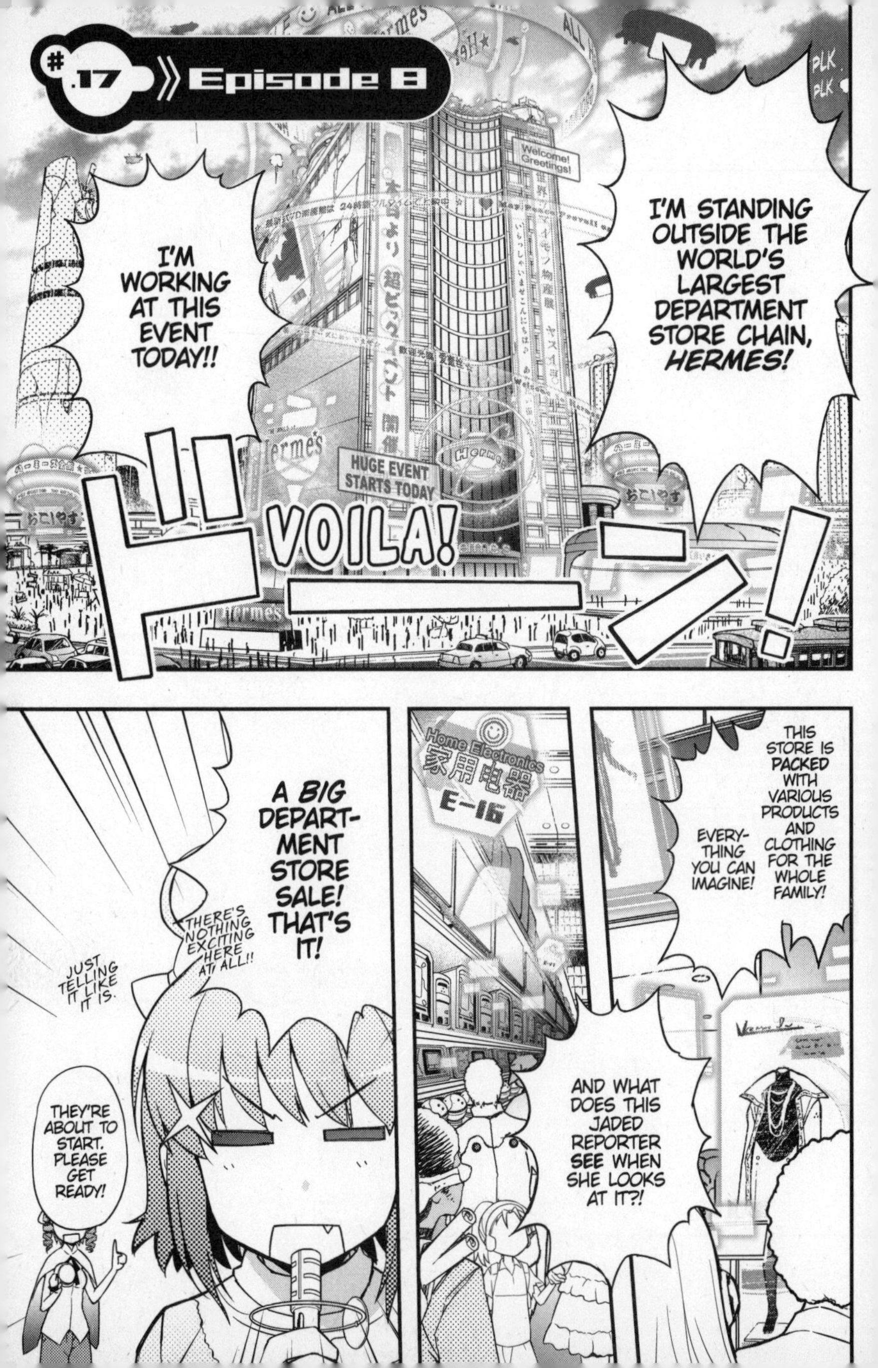
#.17 Episode 8
I'M STANDING OUTSIDE THE WORLD'S LARGEST DEPARTMENT STORE CHAIN, *HERMES!*
I'M WORKING AT THIS EVENT TODAY!!
Welcome! Greetings!
HUGE EVENT STARTS TODAY
VOILA!
Hermes
THIS STORE IS PACKED WITH VARIOUS PRODUCTS AND CLOTHING FOR THE WHOLE FAMILY!
EVERY-THING YOU CAN IMAGINE!
AND WHAT DOES THIS JADED REPORTER SEE WHEN SHE LOOKS AT IT?!
Home Electronics
家用电器
E-16
A *BIG* DEPART-MENT STORE SALE! THAT'S IT!
THERE'S NOTHING EXCITING HERE AT ALL!!
JUST TELLING IT LIKE IT IS.
THEY'RE ABOUT TO START. PLEASE GET READY!

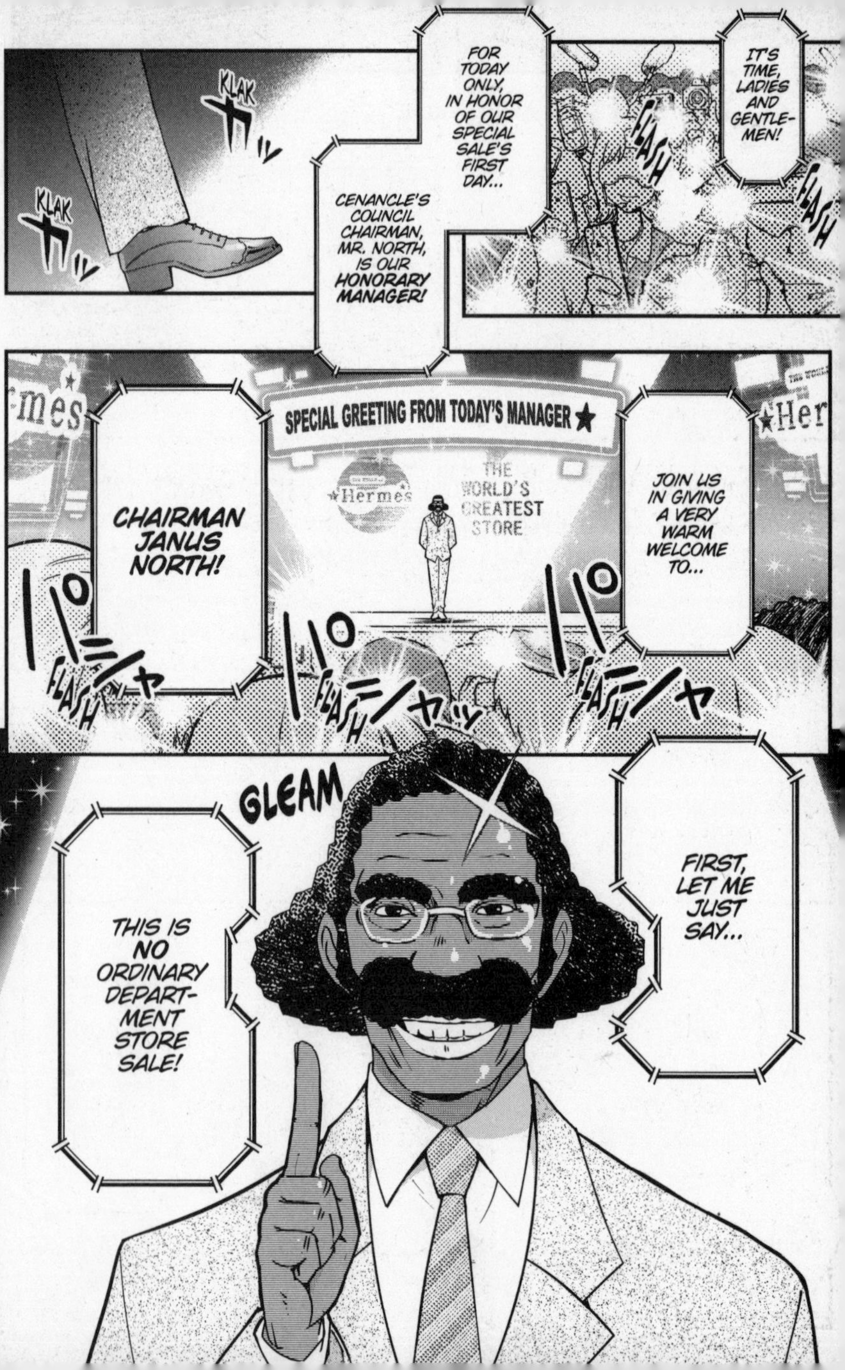
IT'S TIME, LADIES AND GENTLEMEN!
FLASH
FLASH
FOR TODAY ONLY, IN HONOR OF OUR SPECIAL SALE'S FIRST DAY...
CENANCLE'S COUNCIL CHAIRMAN, MR. NORTH, IS OUR HONORARY MANAGER!
KLAK
KLAK
JOIN US IN GIVING A VERY WARM WELCOME TO...
SPECIAL GREETING FROM TODAY'S MANAGER ★
THE WORLD'S GREATEST STORE
Hermes
CHAIRMAN JANUS NORTH!
FLASH
FLASH
FLASH
GLEAM
FIRST, LET ME JUST SAY...
THIS IS NO ORDINARY DEPART-MENT STORE SALE!

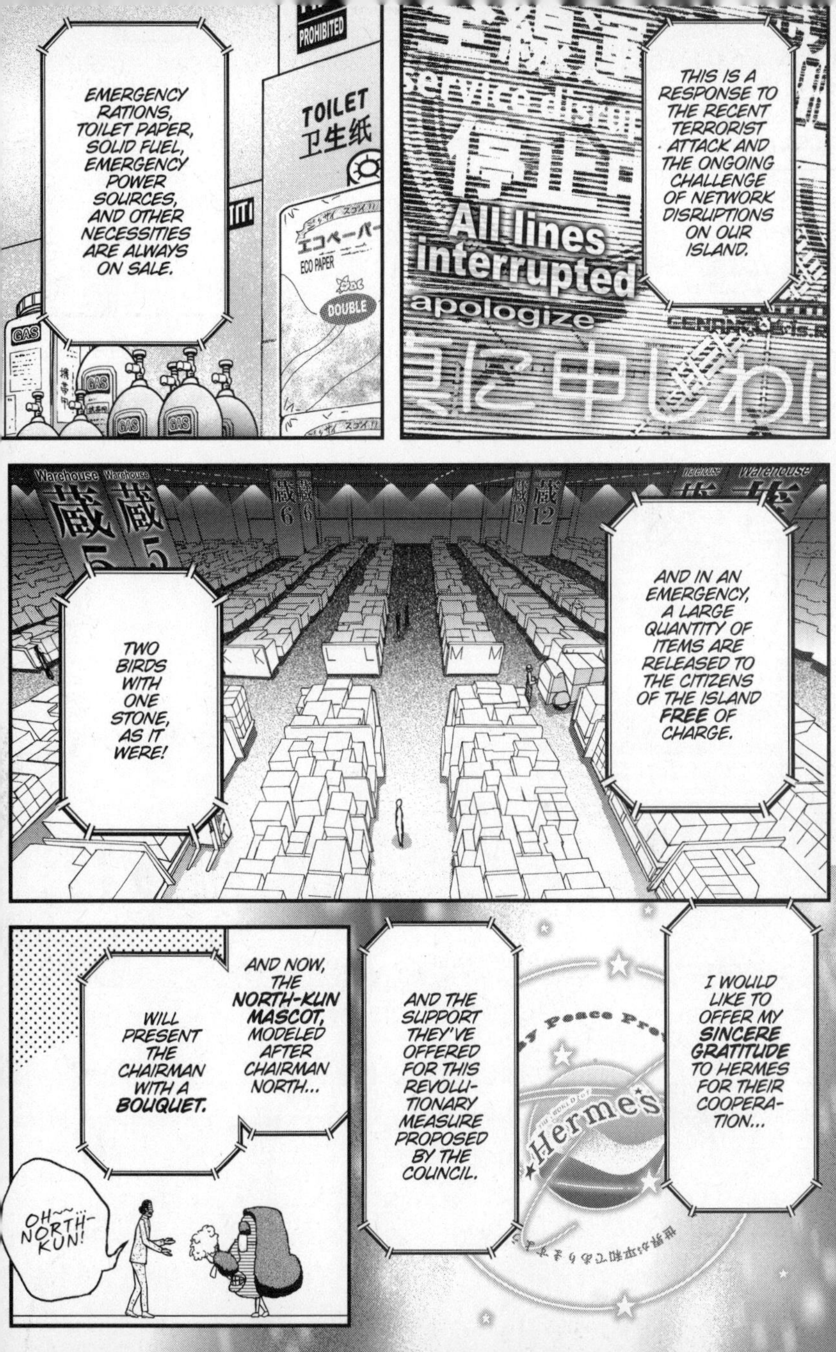
All lines interrupted
apologize
THIS IS A RESPONSE TO THE RECENT TERRORIST ATTACK AND THE ONGOING CHALLENGE OF NETWORK DISRUPTIONS ON OUR ISLAND.
PROHIBITED
TOILET
卫生纸
ECO PAPER
DOUBLE
GAS
EMERGENCY RATIONS, TOILET PAPER, SOLID FUEL, EMERGENCY POWER SOURCES, AND OTHER NECESSITIES ARE ALWAYS ON SALE.
Warehouse
AND IN AN EMERGENCY, A LARGE QUANTITY OF ITEMS ARE RELEASED TO THE CITIZENS OF THE ISLAND **FREE** OF CHARGE.
TWO BIRDS WITH ONE STONE, AS IT WERE!
I WOULD LIKE TO OFFER MY **SINCERE GRATITUDE** TO HERMES FOR THEIR COOPERATION...
AND THE SUPPORT THEY'VE OFFERED FOR THIS REVOLUTIONARY MEASURE PROPOSED BY THE COUNCIL.
Hermes
AND NOW, THE **NORTH-KUN MASCOT,** MODELED AFTER CHAIRMAN NORTH...
WILL PRESENT THE CHAIRMAN WITH A **BOUQUET.**
OH~~... NORTH-KUN!

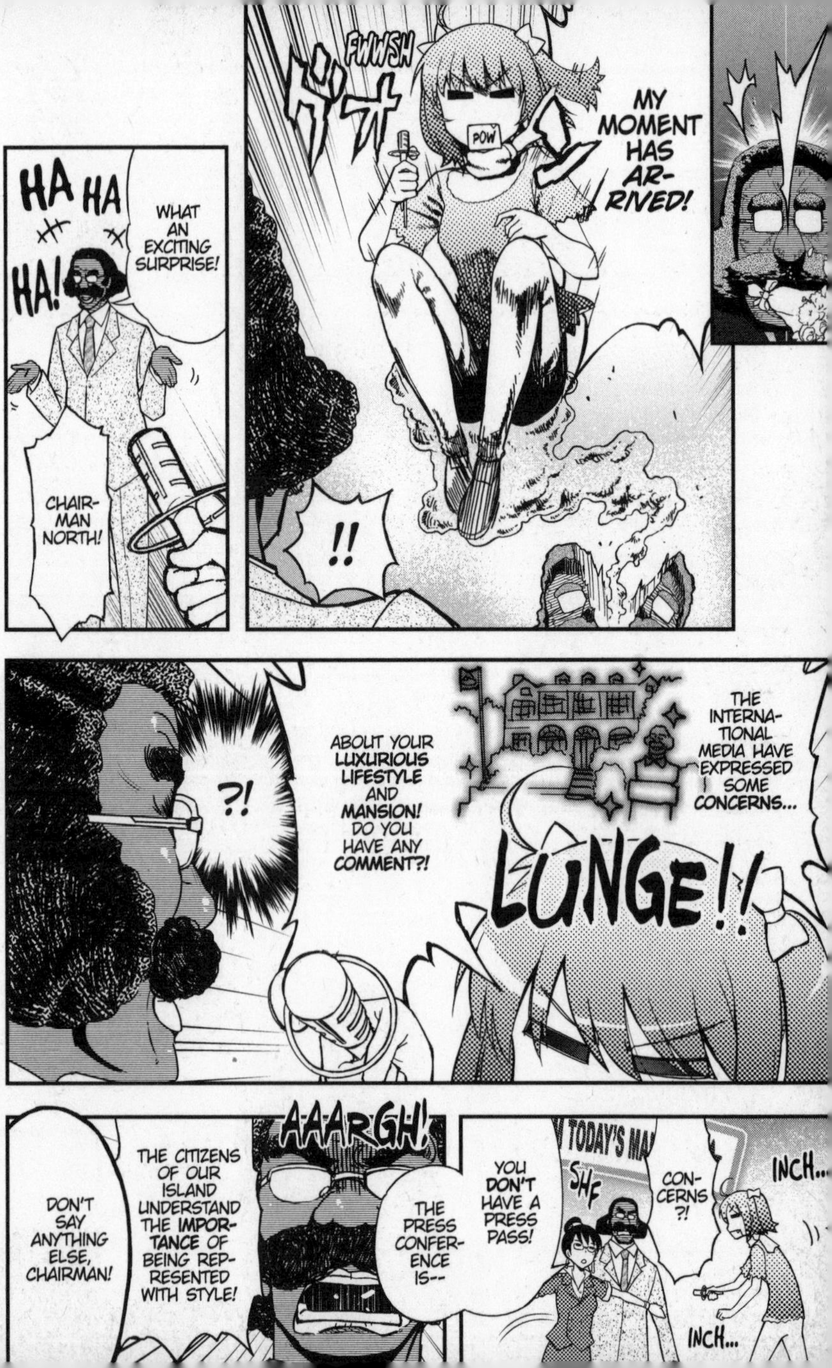

FWWSH
POW
MY MOMENT HAS AR-RIVED!
!!
HA HA HA!
WHAT AN EXCITING SURPRISE!
CHAIR-MAN NORTH!
THE INTERNATIONAL MEDIA HAVE EXPRESSED SOME CONCERNS...
LUNGE!!
ABOUT YOUR LUXURIOUS LIFESTYLE AND MANSION! DO YOU HAVE ANY COMMENT?!
?!
INCH...
CON-CERNS?!
TODAY'S MA
SHF
YOU DON'T HAVE A PRESS PASS!
INCH...
AAARGH!
THE PRESS CONFERENCE IS--
THE CITIZENS OF OUR ISLAND UNDERSTAND THE IMPORTANCE OF BEING REPRESENTED WITH STYLE!
DON'T SAY ANYTHING ELSE, CHAIRMAN!

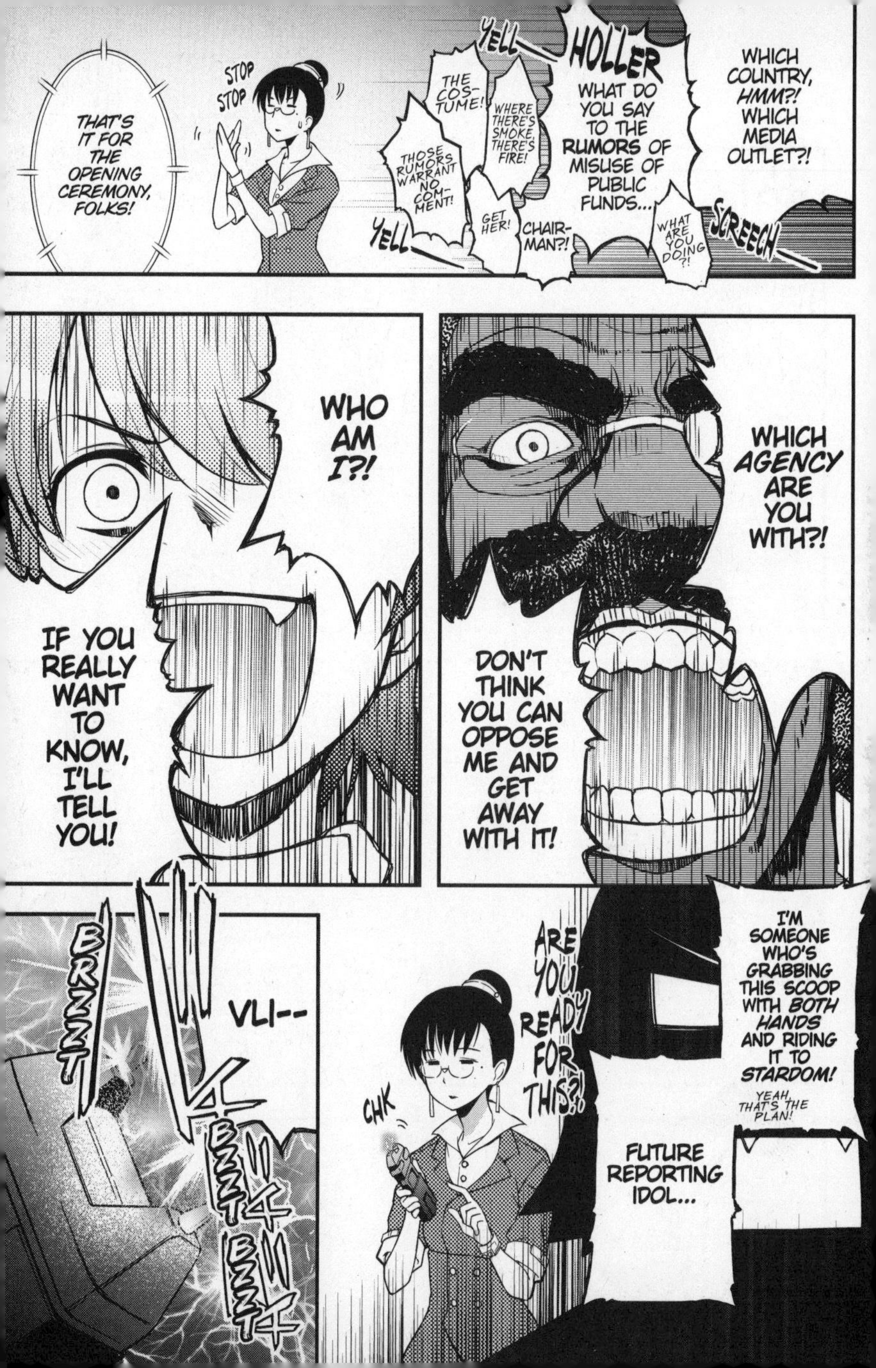
WHICH COUNTRY, HMM?! WHICH MEDIA OUTLET?!
SCREECH
WHAT ARE YOU DOING?!
HOLLER
WHAT DO YOU SAY TO THE RUMORS OF MISUSE OF PUBLIC FUNDS...
YELL
CHAIRMAN?!
WHERE THERE'S SMOKE, THERE'S FIRE!
THE COS-TUME!
GET HER!
THOSE RUMORS WARRANT NO COM-MENT!
YELL
STOP STOP
THAT'S IT FOR THE OPENING CEREMONY, FOLKS!
WHICH AGENCY ARE YOU WITH?!
DON'T THINK YOU CAN OPPOSE ME AND GET AWAY WITH IT!
WHO AM I?!
IF YOU REALLY WANT TO KNOW, I'LL TELL YOU!
I'M SOMEONE WHO'S GRABBING THIS SCOOP WITH BOTH HANDS AND RIDING IT TO STARDOM!
YEAH, THAT'S THE PLAN!
FUTURE REPORTING IDOL...
ARE YOU READY FOR THIS?!
CHK
VLI--
BRZZZT
BZZT BZZT

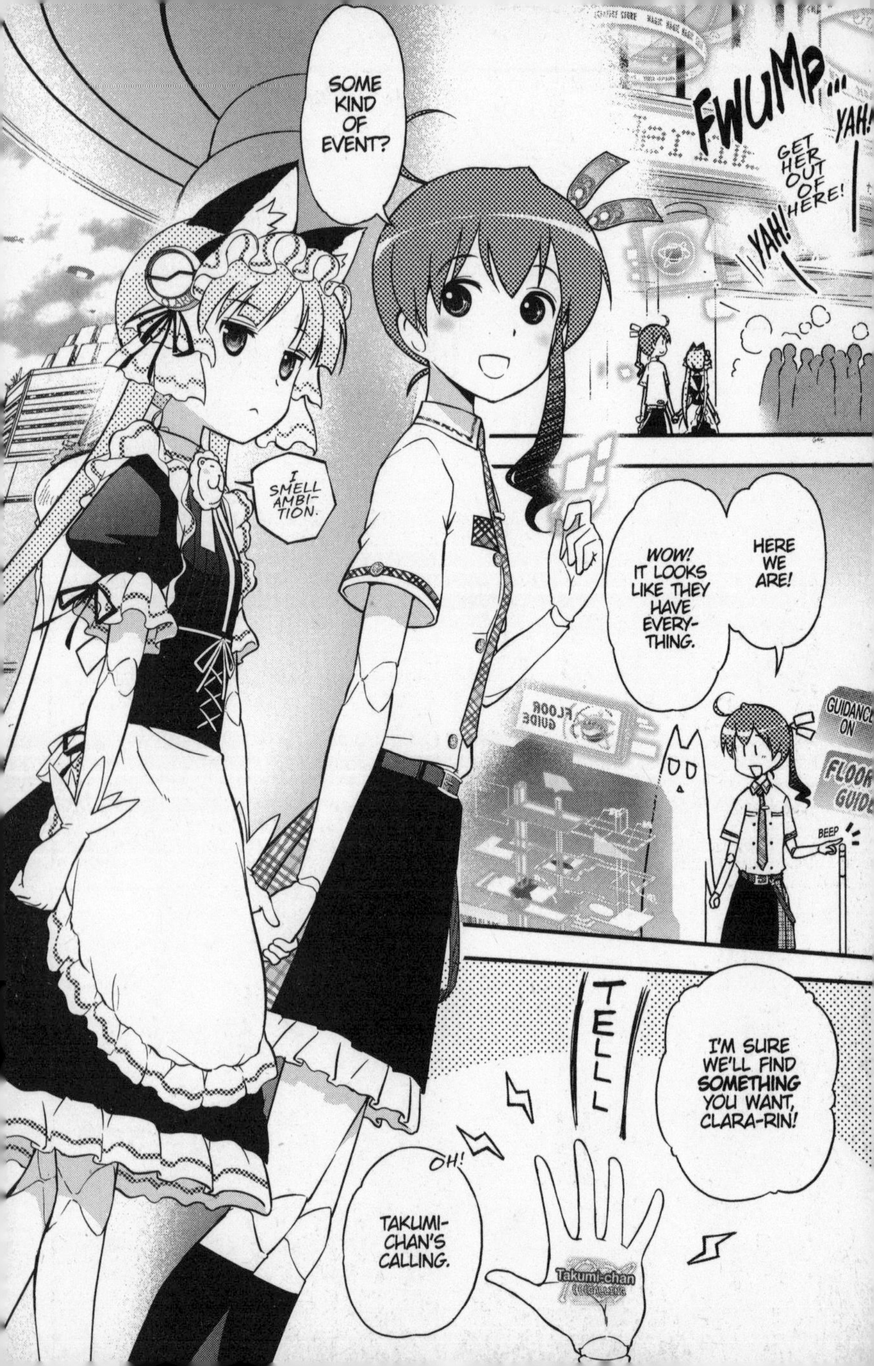
YAH!
GET HER OUT OF HERE!
YAH!
FWUMP...
SOME KIND OF EVENT?
I SMELL AMBITION.
HERE WE ARE!
WOW! IT LOOKS LIKE THEY HAVE EVERYTHING.
GUIDANCE ON
FLOOR GUIDE
BEEP
FLOOR GUIDE
I'M SURE WE'LL FIND SOMETHING YOU WANT, CLARA-RIN!
TELLL
OH!
TAKUMI-CHAN'S CALLING.
Takumi-chan CALLING

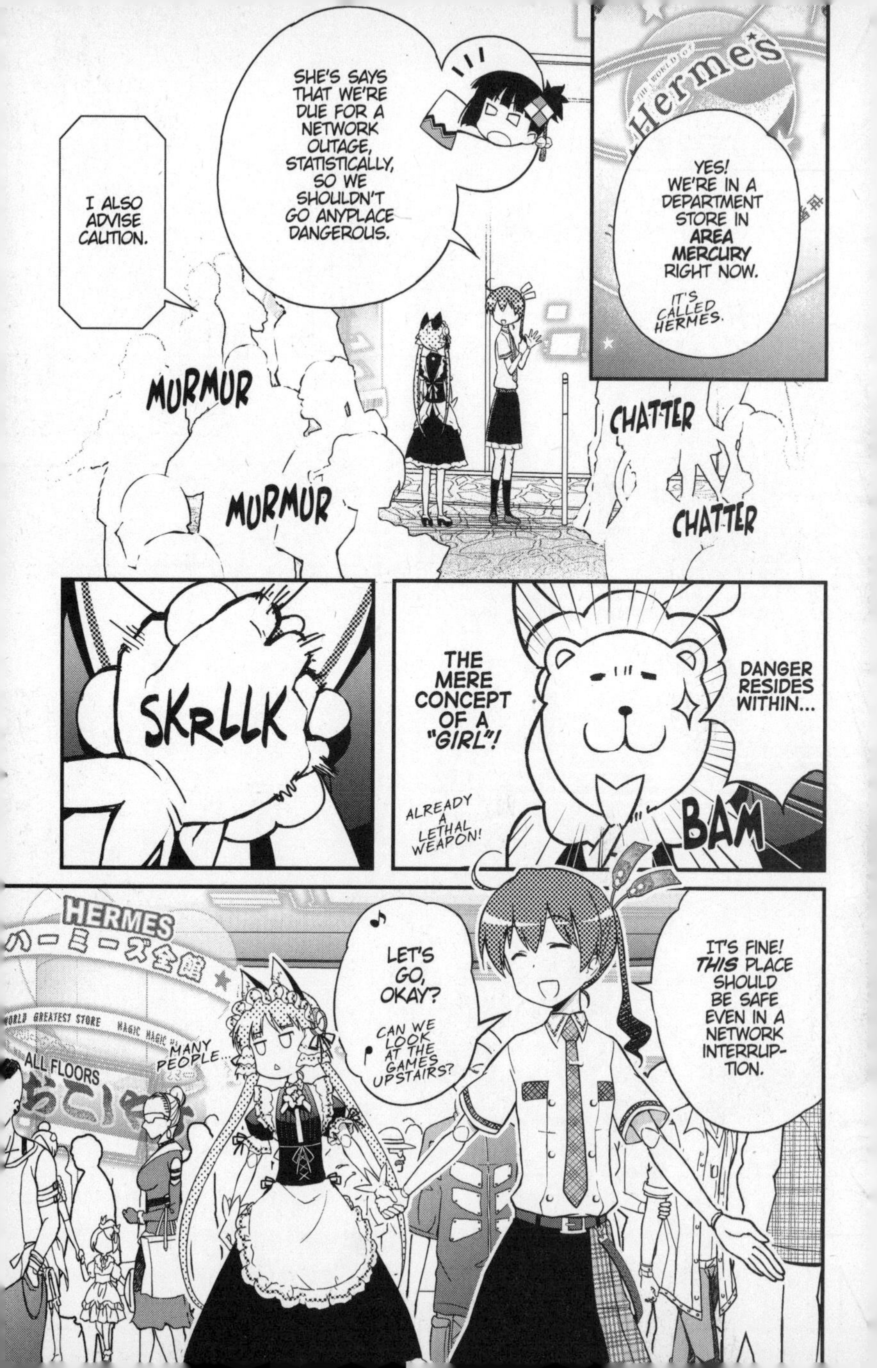
THE WORLD OF Hermes
YES! WE'RE IN A DEPARTMENT STORE IN **AREA MERCURY** RIGHT NOW.
IT'S CALLED HERMES.
SHE'S SAYS THAT WE'RE DUE FOR A NETWORK OUTAGE, STATISTICALLY, SO WE SHOULDN'T GO ANYPLACE DANGEROUS.
I ALSO ADVISE CAUTION.
CHATTER
CHATTER
MURMUR
MURMUR
DANGER RESIDES WITHIN...
THE MERE CONCEPT OF A "*GIRL*"!
ALREADY A LETHAL WEAPON!
BAM
SKRLLK
IT'S FINE! *THIS* PLACE SHOULD BE SAFE EVEN IN A NETWORK INTERRUPTION.
LET'S GO, OKAY?
CAN WE LOOK AT THE GAMES UPSTAIRS?
MANY PEOPLE...
HERMES
ハーミーズ全館
WORLD GREATEST STORE
MAGIC MAGIC
ALL FLOORS

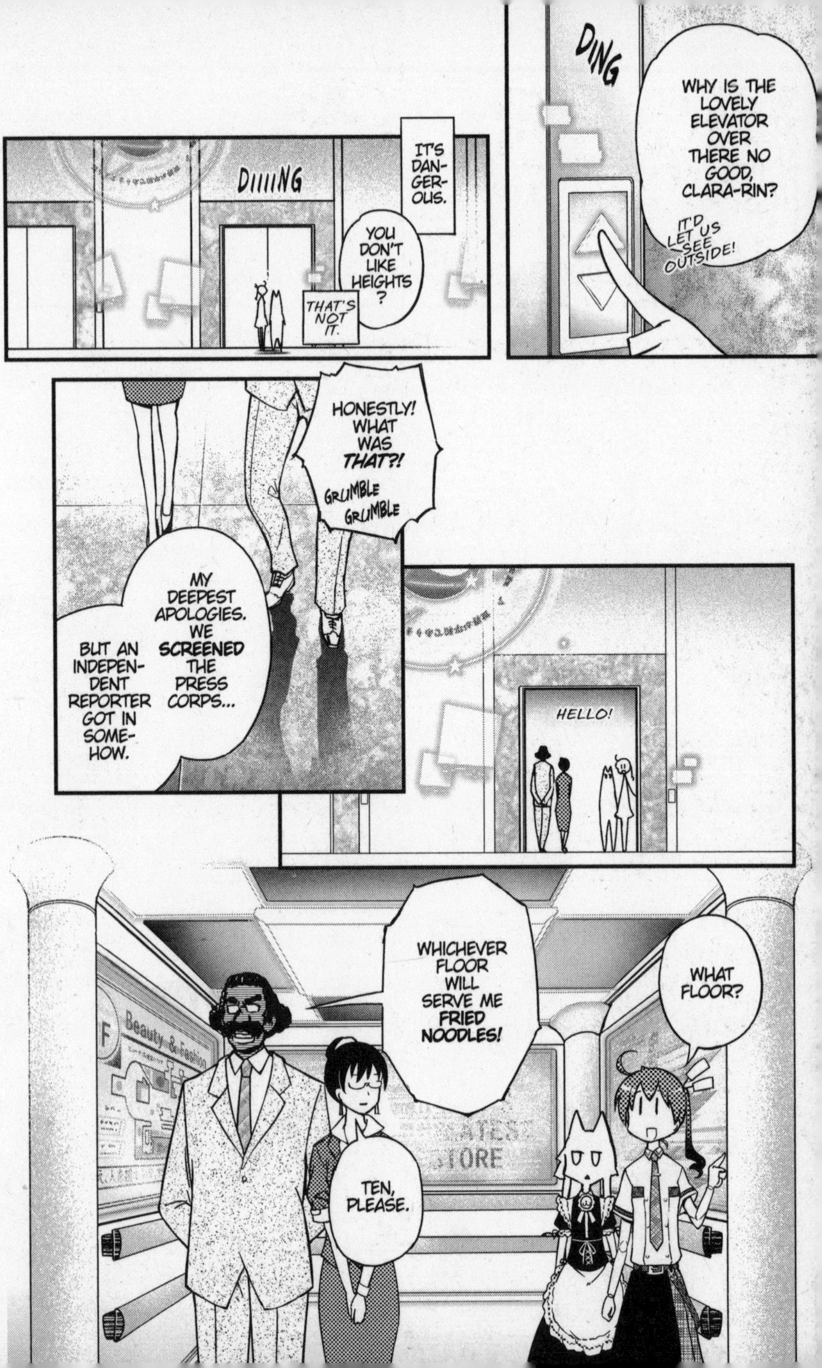
DING
WHY IS THE LOVELY ELEVATOR OVER THERE NO GOOD, CLARA-RIN?
IT'D LET US SEE OUTSIDE!
DIIIING
IT'S DANGEROUS.
YOU DON'T LIKE HEIGHTS?
THAT'S NOT IT.
HONESTLY! WHAT WAS ***THAT?!***
GRUMBLE GRUMBLE
MY DEEPEST APOLOGIES. WE **SCREENED** THE PRESS CORPS...
BUT AN INDEPENDENT REPORTER GOT IN SOMEHOW.
HELLO!
WHAT FLOOR?
WHICHEVER FLOOR WILL SERVE ME **FRIED NOODLES!**
Beauty & Fashion
TEN, PLEASE.

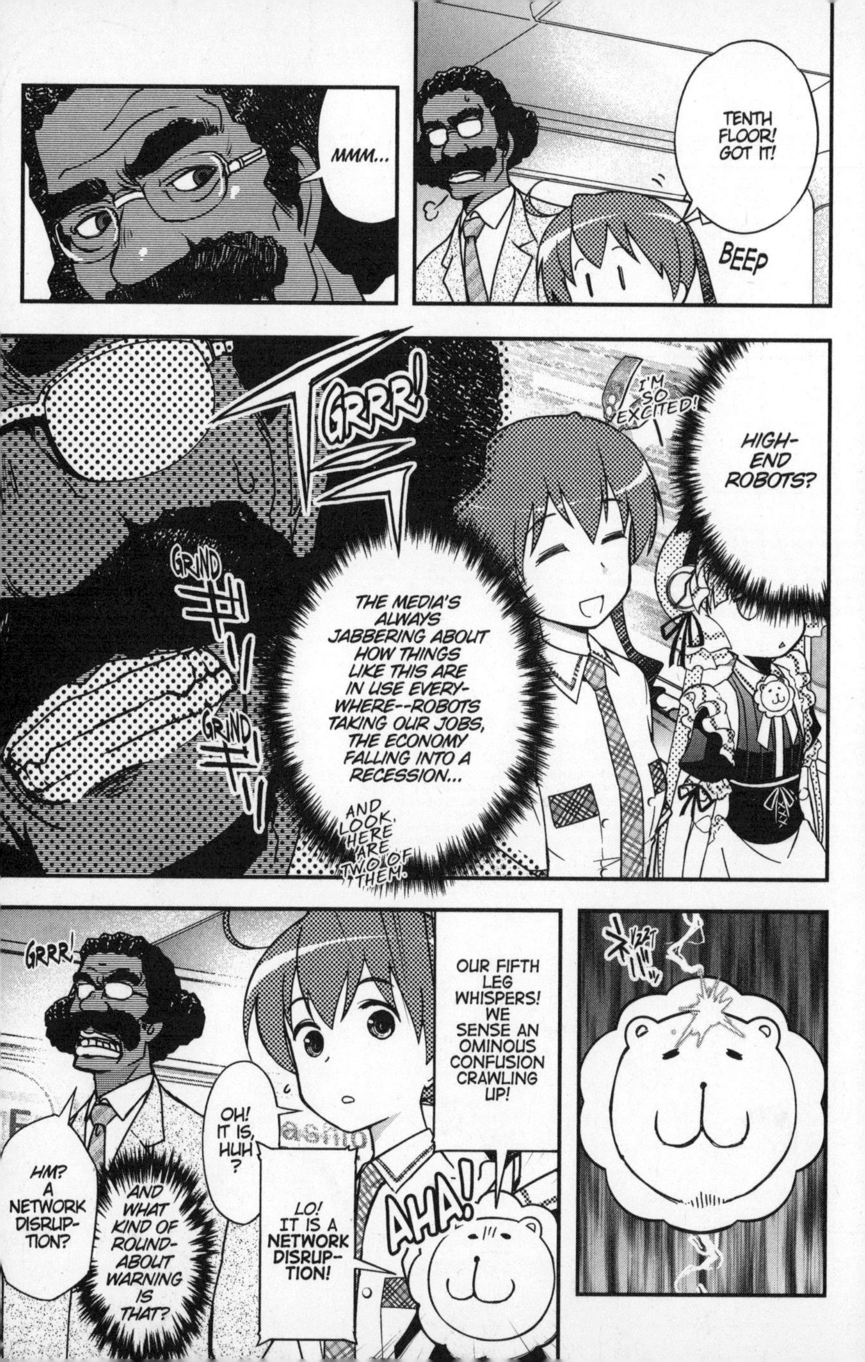
TENTH FLOOR! GOT IT!
BEEP
MMM...
HIGH-END ROBOTS?
I'M SO EXCITED!
GRRR!
THE MEDIA'S ALWAYS JABBERING ABOUT HOW THINGS LIKE THIS ARE IN USE EVERYWHERE--ROBOTS TAKING OUR JOBS, THE ECONOMY FALLING INTO A RECESSION...
AND LOOK, HERE ARE TWO OF THEM.
GRIND
GRIND
OUR FIFTH LEG WHISPERS! WE SENSE AN OMINOUS CONFUSION CRAWLING UP!
OH! IT IS, HUH?
LO! IT IS A NETWORK DISRUPTION!
AHA!
GRRR!
HM? A NETWORK DISRUPTION?
AND WHAT KIND OF ROUNDABOUT WARNING IS THAT?

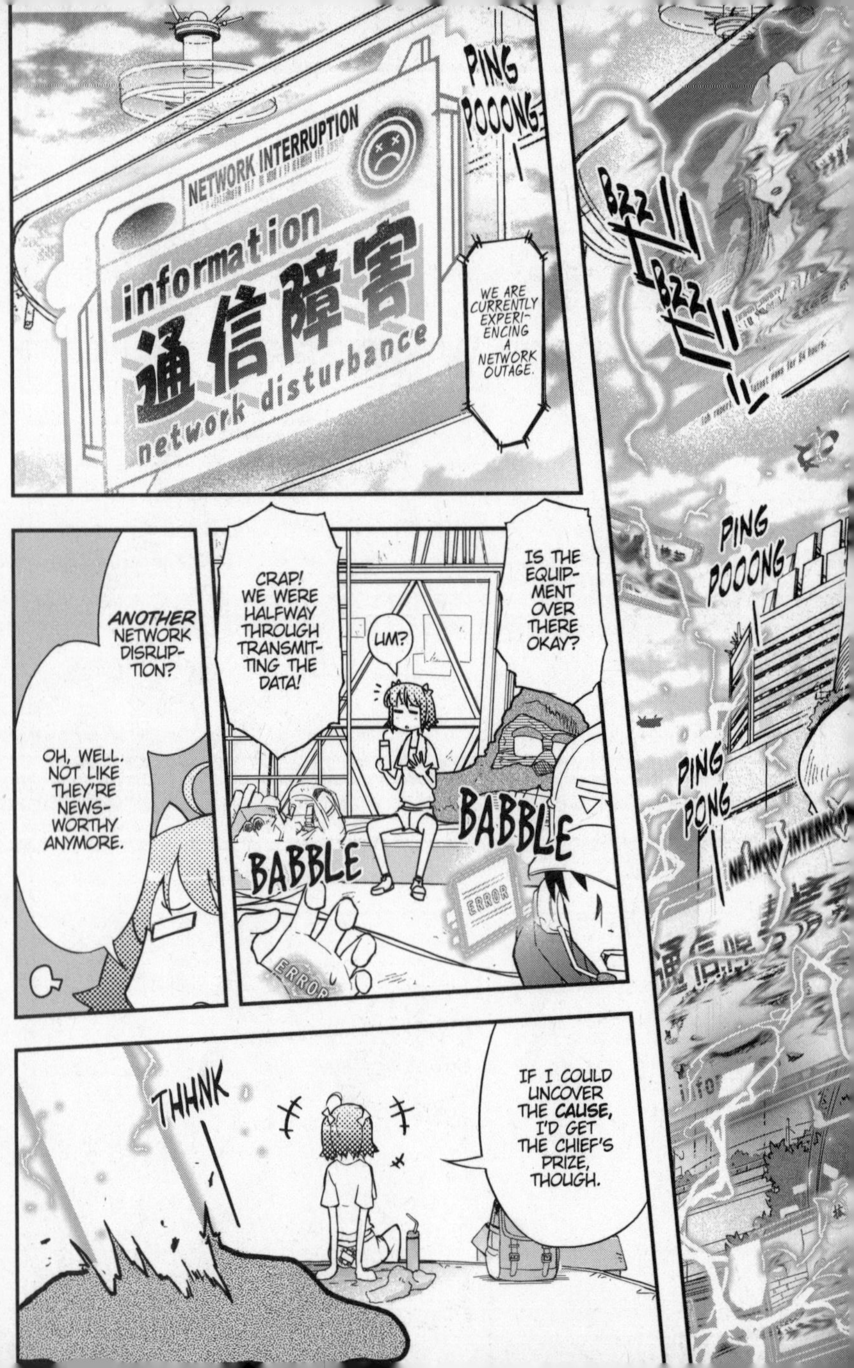
BZZ
BZZ
PING POOONG
PING PONG
PING POOONG
NETWORK INTERRUPTION
information
通信障害
network disturbance
WE ARE CURRENTLY EXPERIENCING A NETWORK OUTAGE.
IS THE EQUIPMENT OVER THERE OKAY?
CRAP! WE WERE HALFWAY THROUGH TRANSMITTING THE DATA!
UM?
BABBLE
BABBLE
ERROR
ERROR
ANOTHER NETWORK DISRUPTION?
OH, WELL. NOT LIKE THEY'RE NEWSWORTHY ANYMORE.
IF I COULD UNCOVER THE CAUSE, I'D GET THE CHIEF'S PRIZE, THOUGH.
THHNK

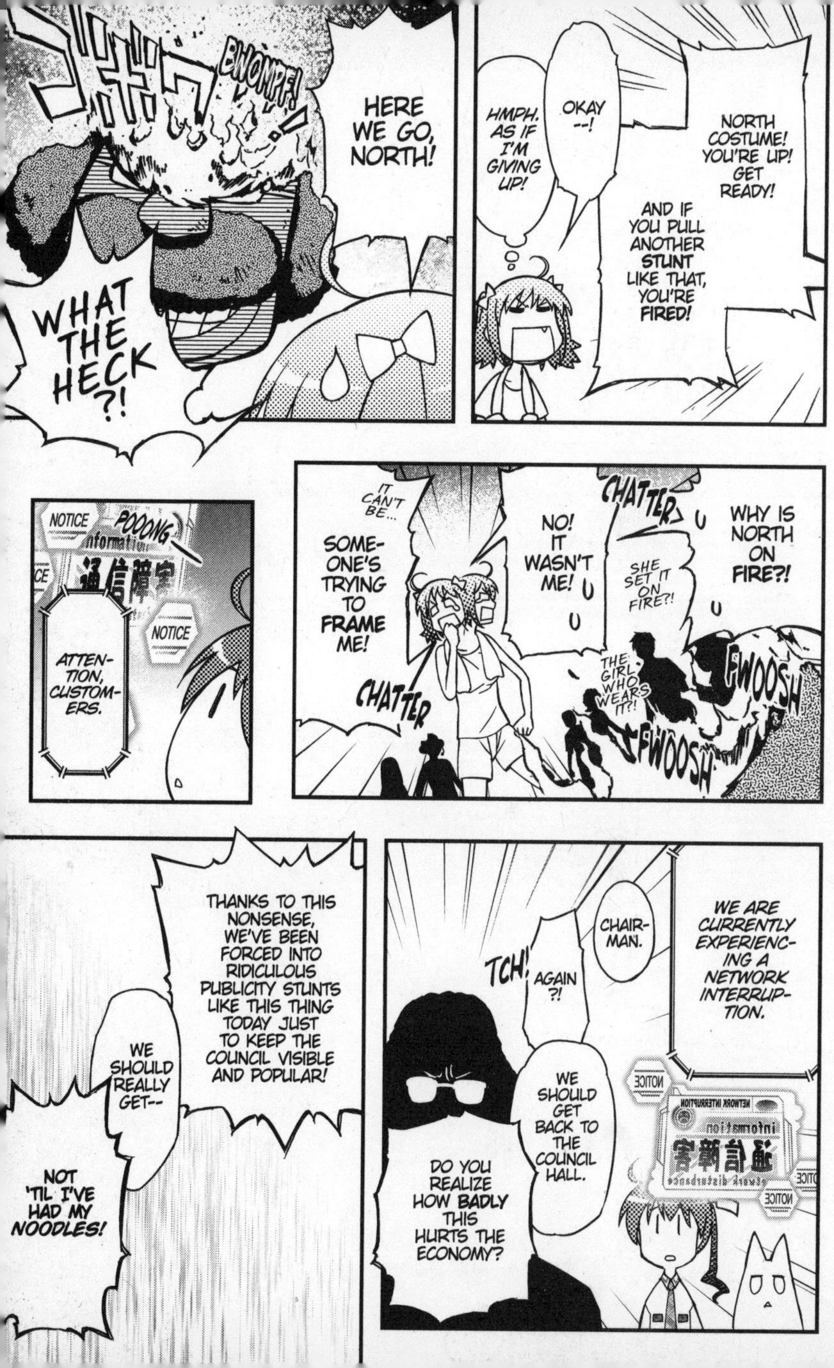
NORTH COSTUME! YOU'RE UP! GET READY!
AND IF YOU PULL ANOTHER STUNT LIKE THAT, YOU'RE FIRED!
OKAY --!
HMPH. AS IF I'M GIVING UP!
BWOMPF!
HERE WE GO, NORTH!
WHAT THE HECK ?!
WHY IS NORTH ON FIRE?!
CHATTER
SHE SET IT ON FIRE?!
FWOOSH
FWOOSH
THE GIRL WHO WEARS IT?!
NO! IT WASN'T ME!
IT CAN'T BE...
SOMEONE'S TRYING TO FRAME ME!
CHATTER
NOTICE
POOONG
通信障害
NOTICE
ATTENTION, CUSTOMERS.
WE ARE CURRENTLY EXPERIENCING A NETWORK INTERRUPTION.
CHAIRMAN.
TCH!
AGAIN ?!
WE SHOULD GET BACK TO THE COUNCIL HALL.
DO YOU REALIZE HOW BADLY THIS HURTS THE ECONOMY?
NOTICE
NETWORK INTERRUPTION
information
通信障害
NOTICE
NOTICE
THANKS TO THIS NONSENSE, WE'VE BEEN FORCED INTO RIDICULOUS PUBLICITY STUNTS LIKE THIS THING TODAY JUST TO KEEP THE COUNCIL VISIBLE AND POPULAR!
WE SHOULD REALLY GET--
NOT 'TIL I'VE HAD MY NOODLES!

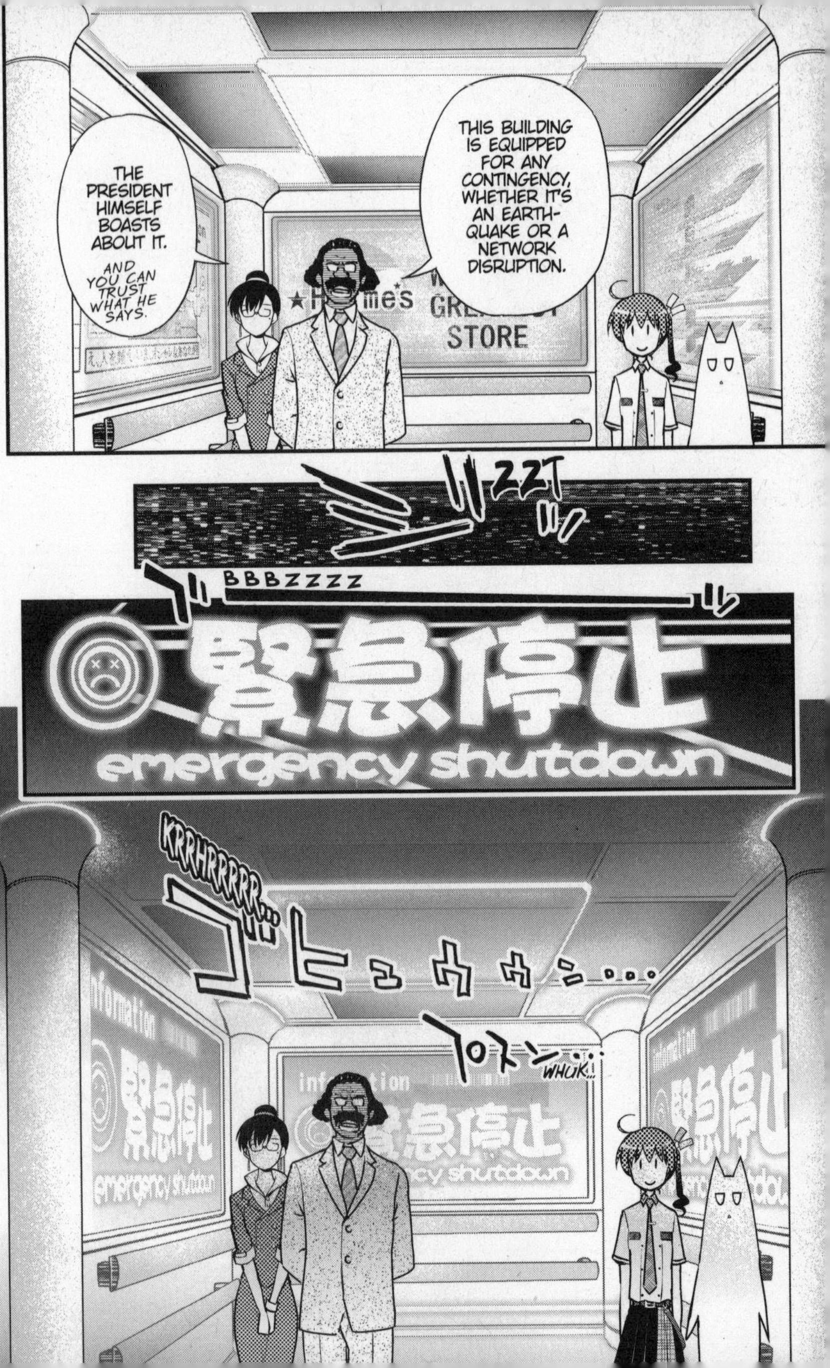
THIS BUILDING IS EQUIPPED FOR ANY CONTINGENCY, WHETHER IT'S AN EARTH-QUAKE OR A NETWORK DISRUPTION.
THE PRESIDENT HIMSELF BOASTS ABOUT IT.
AND YOU CAN TRUST WHAT HE SAYS.
STORE
ZZZT
BBBZZZZ
緊急停止
emergency shutdown
KRRHRRRRR...
ゴヒュゥゥン…
プスン…
WHUK!!
emergency shutdown

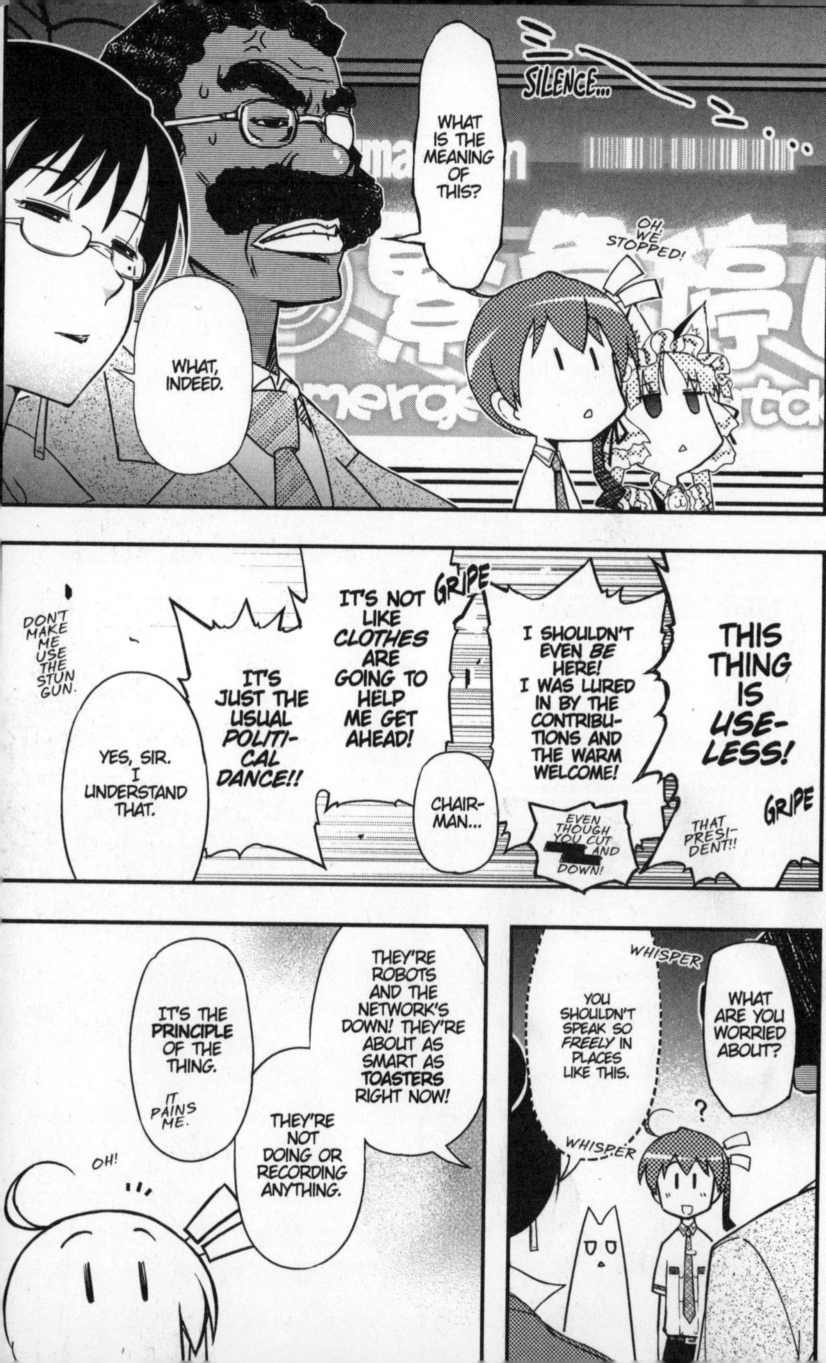
SILENCE...
OH, WE STOPPED!
WHAT IS THE MEANING OF THIS?
WHAT, INDEED.
THIS THING IS USELESS!
GRIPE
THAT PRESIDENT!!
I SHOULDN'T EVEN BE HERE! I WAS LURED IN BY THE CONTRIBUTIONS AND THE WARM WELCOME!
EVEN THOUGH YOU CUT [redacted] AND DOWN!
GRIPE
IT'S NOT LIKE CLOTHES ARE GOING TO HELP ME GET AHEAD!
CHAIRMAN...
IT'S JUST THE USUAL POLITICAL DANCE!!
DON'T MAKE ME USE THE STUN GUN.
YES, SIR. I UNDERSTAND THAT.
WHAT ARE YOU WORRIED ABOUT?
WHISPER
YOU SHOULDN'T SPEAK SO FREELY IN PLACES LIKE THIS.
WHISPER
?
THEY'RE ROBOTS AND THE NETWORK'S DOWN! THEY'RE ABOUT AS SMART AS TOASTERS RIGHT NOW!
THEY'RE NOT DOING OR RECORDING ANYTHING.
IT'S THE PRINCIPLE OF THE THING.
IT PAINS ME.
OH!

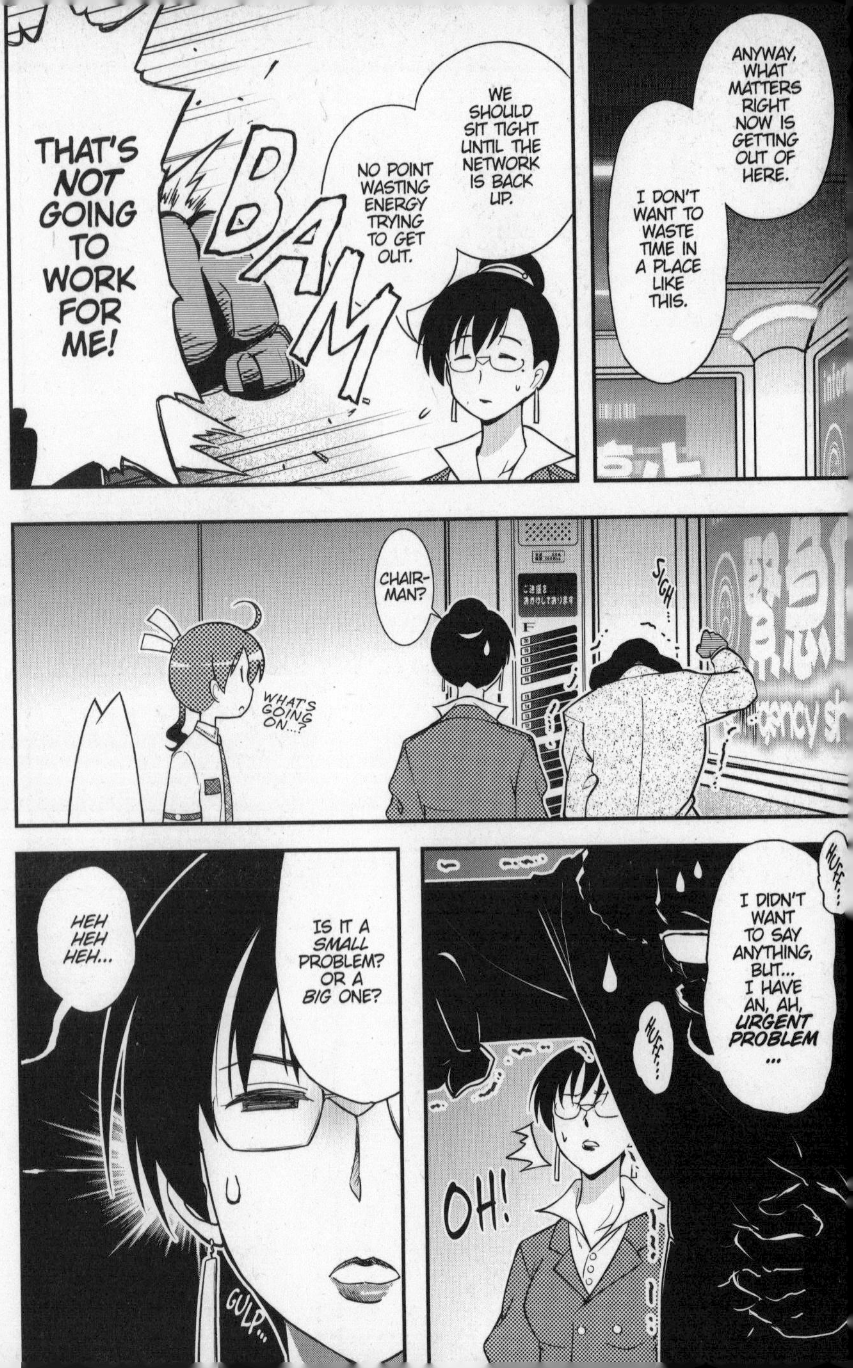
ANYWAY, WHAT MATTERS RIGHT NOW IS GETTING OUT OF HERE.
I DON'T WANT TO WASTE TIME IN A PLACE LIKE THIS.
WE SHOULD SIT TIGHT UNTIL THE NETWORK IS BACK UP.
NO POINT WASTING ENERGY TRYING TO GET OUT.
BAM
THAT'S NOT GOING TO WORK FOR ME!
SIGH...
CHAIR-MAN?
WHAT'S GOING ON...?
HUFF...
I DIDN'T WANT TO SAY ANYTHING, BUT... I HAVE AN, AH, URGENT PROBLEM...
HUFF...
OH!
IS IT A SMALL PROBLEM? OR A BIG ONE?
HEH HEH HEH...
GULP...

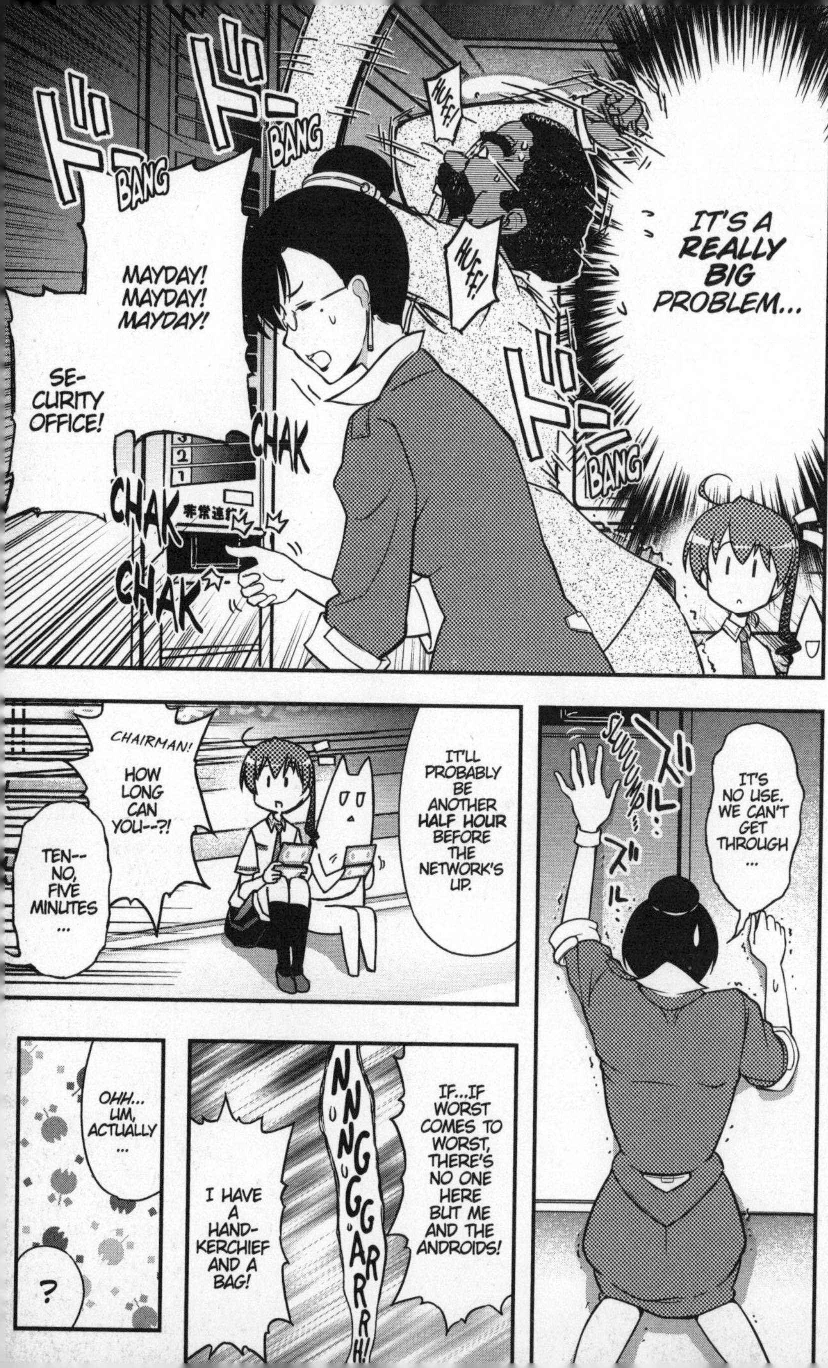
IT'S A REALLY BIG PROBLEM...
HUFF!
HUFF!
BANG
BANG
BANG
MAYDAY! MAYDAY! MAYDAY!
SE-CURITY OFFICE!
CHAK
CHAK CHAK
CHAK
IT'S NO USE. WE CAN'T GET THROUGH ...
SLUUUMP...
IT'LL PROBABLY BE ANOTHER HALF HOUR BEFORE THE NETWORK'S UP.
CHAIRMAN!
HOW LONG CAN YOU--?!
TEN-- NO, FIVE MINUTES ...
IF...IF WORST COMES TO WORST, THERE'S NO ONE HERE BUT ME AND THE ANDROIDS!
NNNGGARRRH!
I HAVE A HAND-KERCHIEF AND A BAG!
OHH... UM, ACTUALLY ...
?

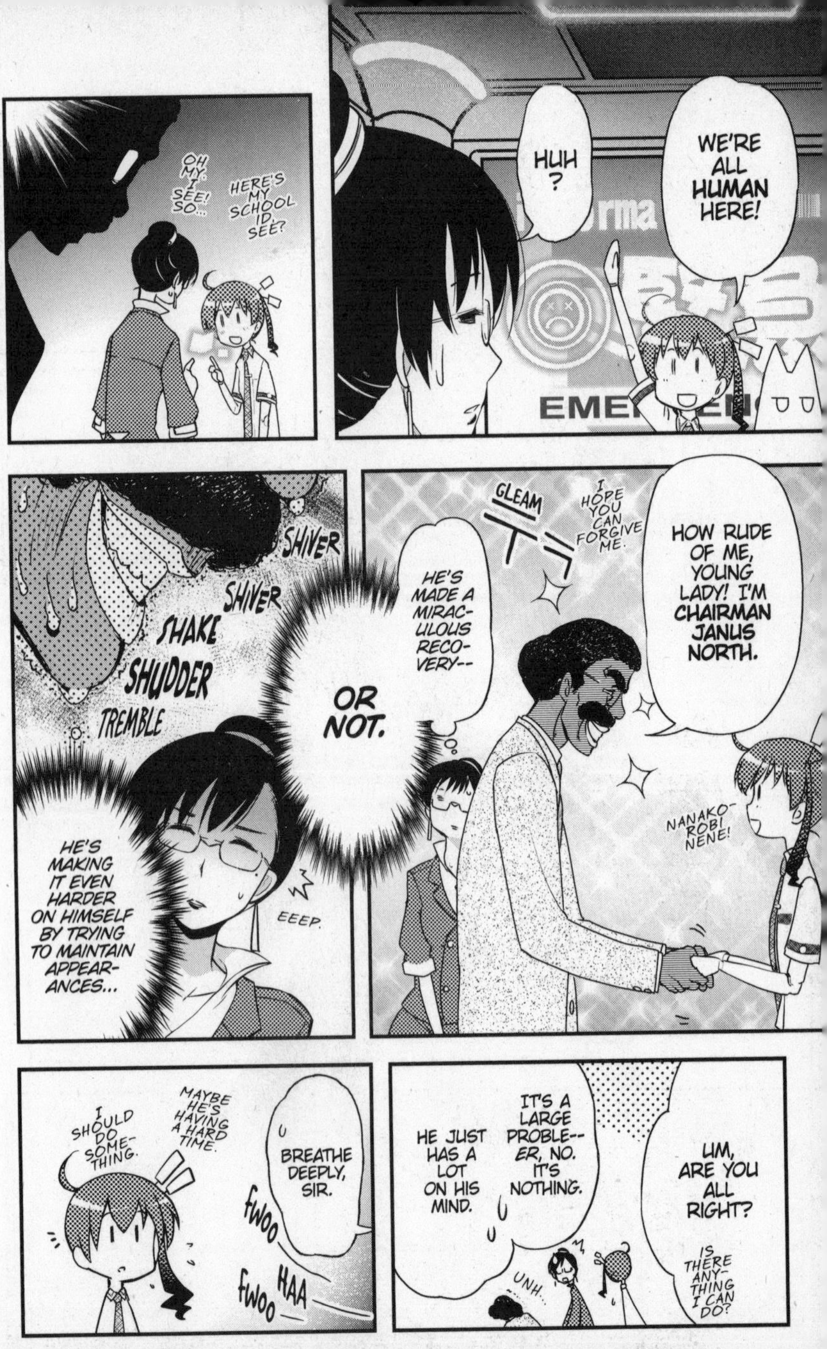
WE'RE ALL HUMAN HERE!
HUH?
HERE'S MY SCHOOL ID. SEE?
OH MY. I SEE! SO...
HOW RUDE OF ME, YOUNG LADY! I'M CHAIRMAN JANUS NORTH.
I HOPE YOU CAN FORGIVE ME.
GLEAM
NANAKOROBI NENE!
HE'S MADE A MIRACULOUS RECOVERY--
OR NOT.
SHIVER
SHIVER
SHAKE
SHUDDER
TREMBLE
HE'S MAKING IT EVEN HARDER ON HIMSELF BY TRYING TO MAINTAIN APPEARANCES...
EEEP.
UM, ARE YOU ALL RIGHT?
IS THERE ANYTHING I CAN DO?
IT'S A LARGE PROBLE-- ER, NO. IT'S NOTHING.
HE JUST HAS A LOT ON HIS MIND.
UNH...
BREATHE DEEPLY, SIR.
MAYBE HE'S HAVING A HARD TIME.
I SHOULD DO SOMETHING.
FWOO
HAA
FWOO

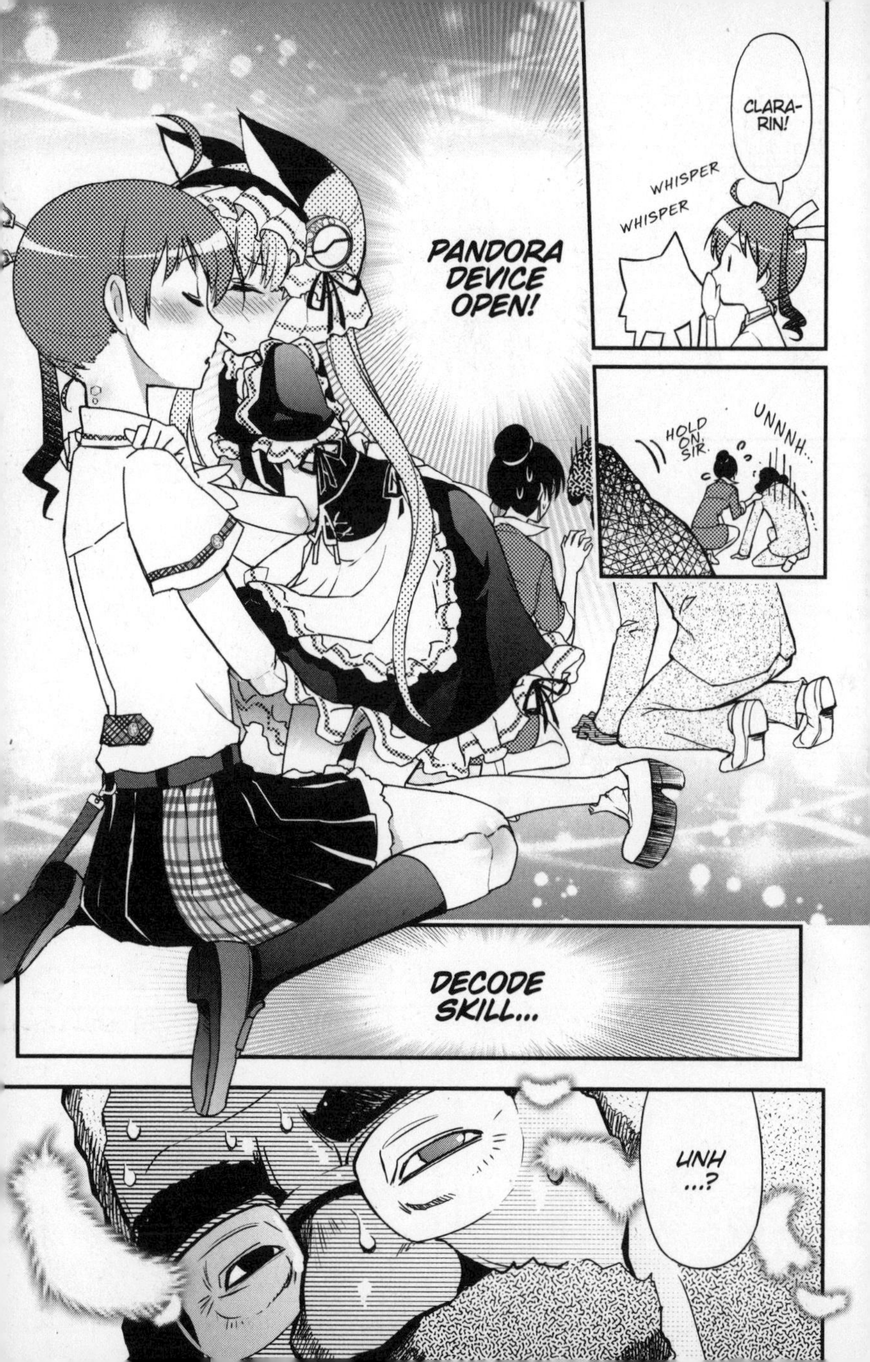
CLARA-RIN!
WHISPER
WHISPER
HOLD ON, SIR.
UNNNH...
PANDORA DEVICE OPEN!
DECODE SKILL...
UNH ...?

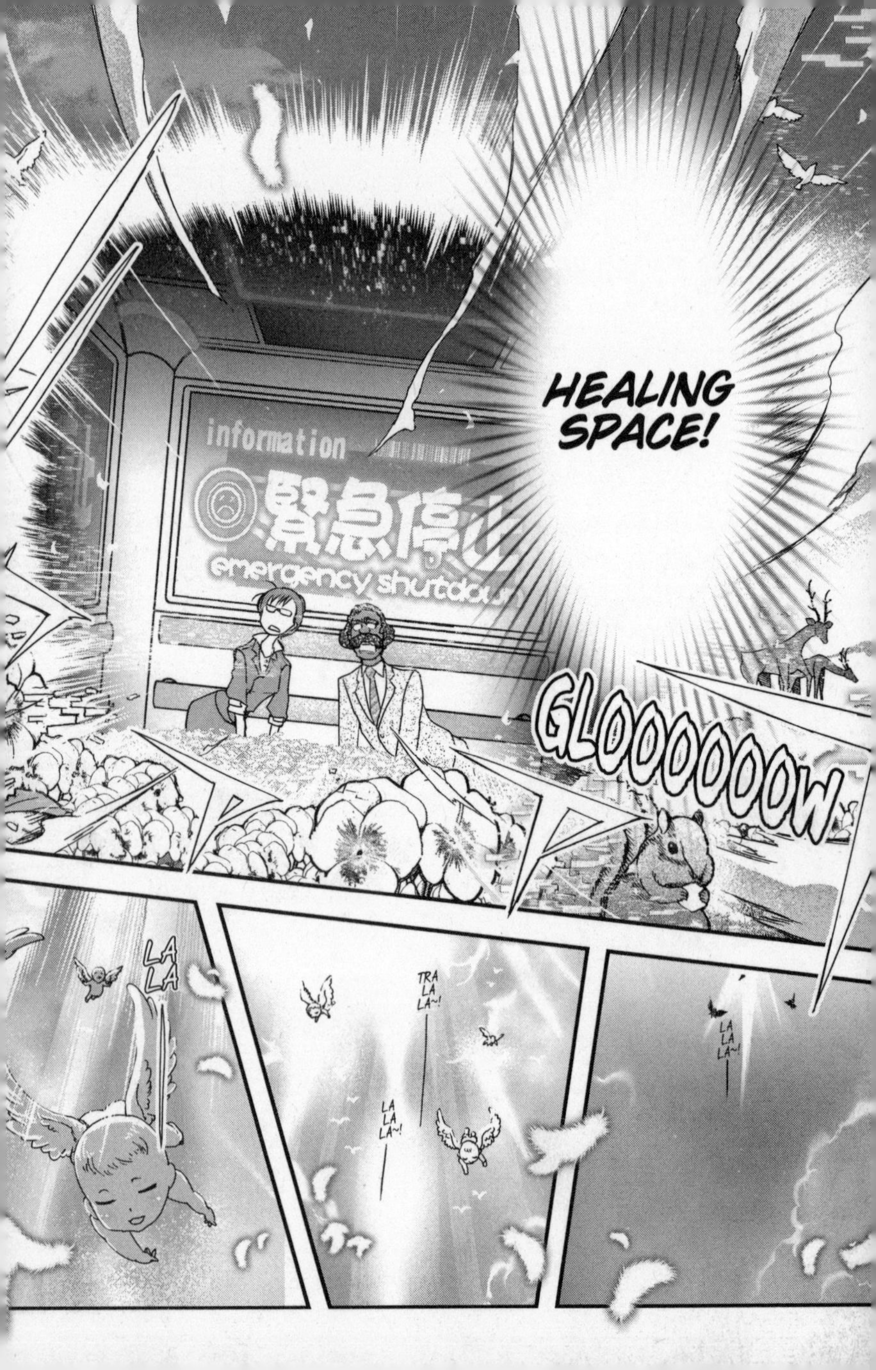

HEALING SPACE!
information
GLOOOOOOW
LA LA LA~!
TRA LA LA~!
LA LA LA~!
LA LA

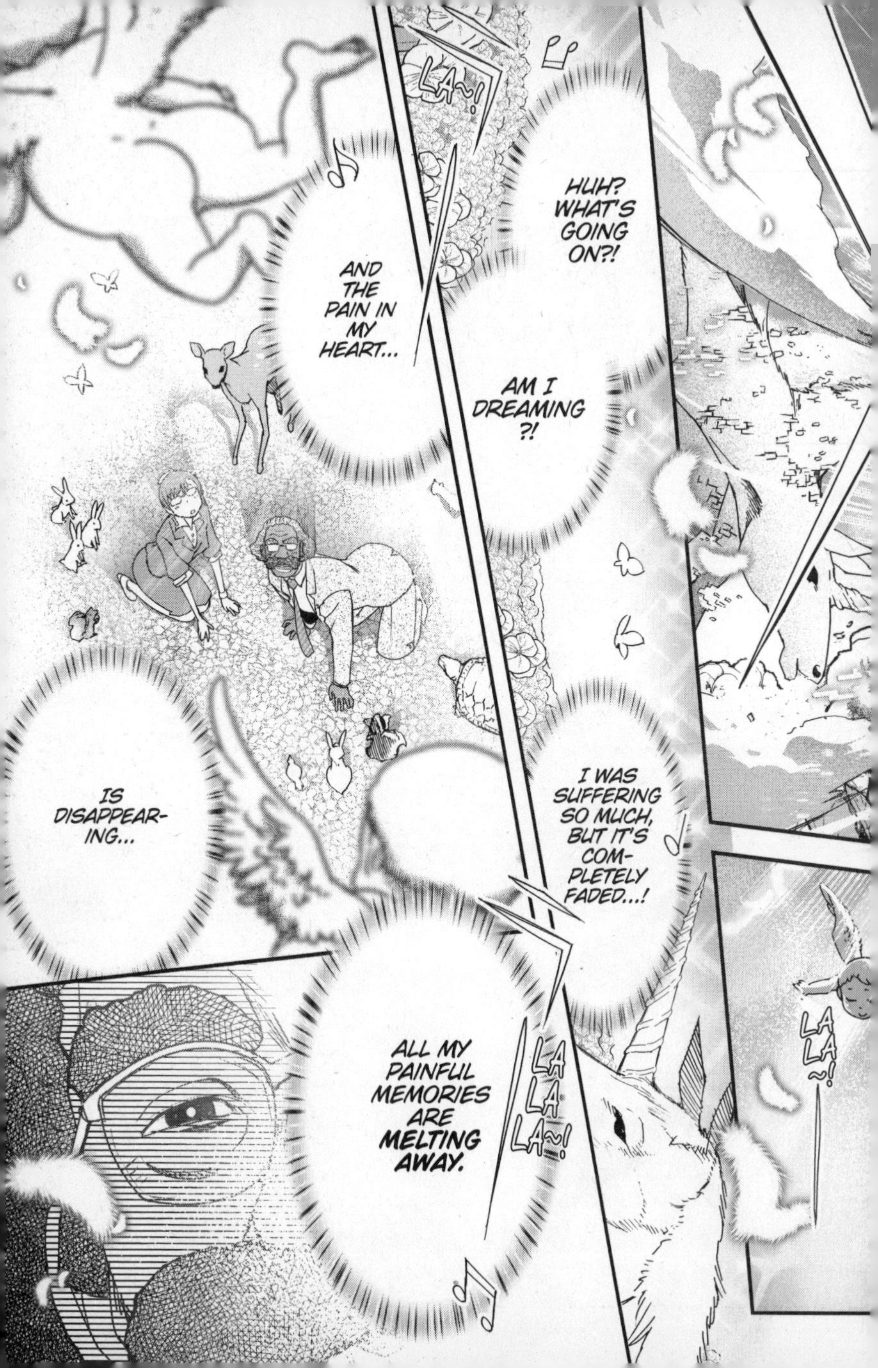
LA~!
HUH? WHAT'S GOING ON?!
AM I DREAMING?!
AND THE PAIN IN MY HEART...
IS DISAPPEAR-ING...
I WAS SUFFERING SO MUCH, BUT IT'S COM-PLETELY FADED...!
LA LA LA~!
ALL MY PAINFUL MEMORIES ARE MELTING AWAY.
LA LA~!

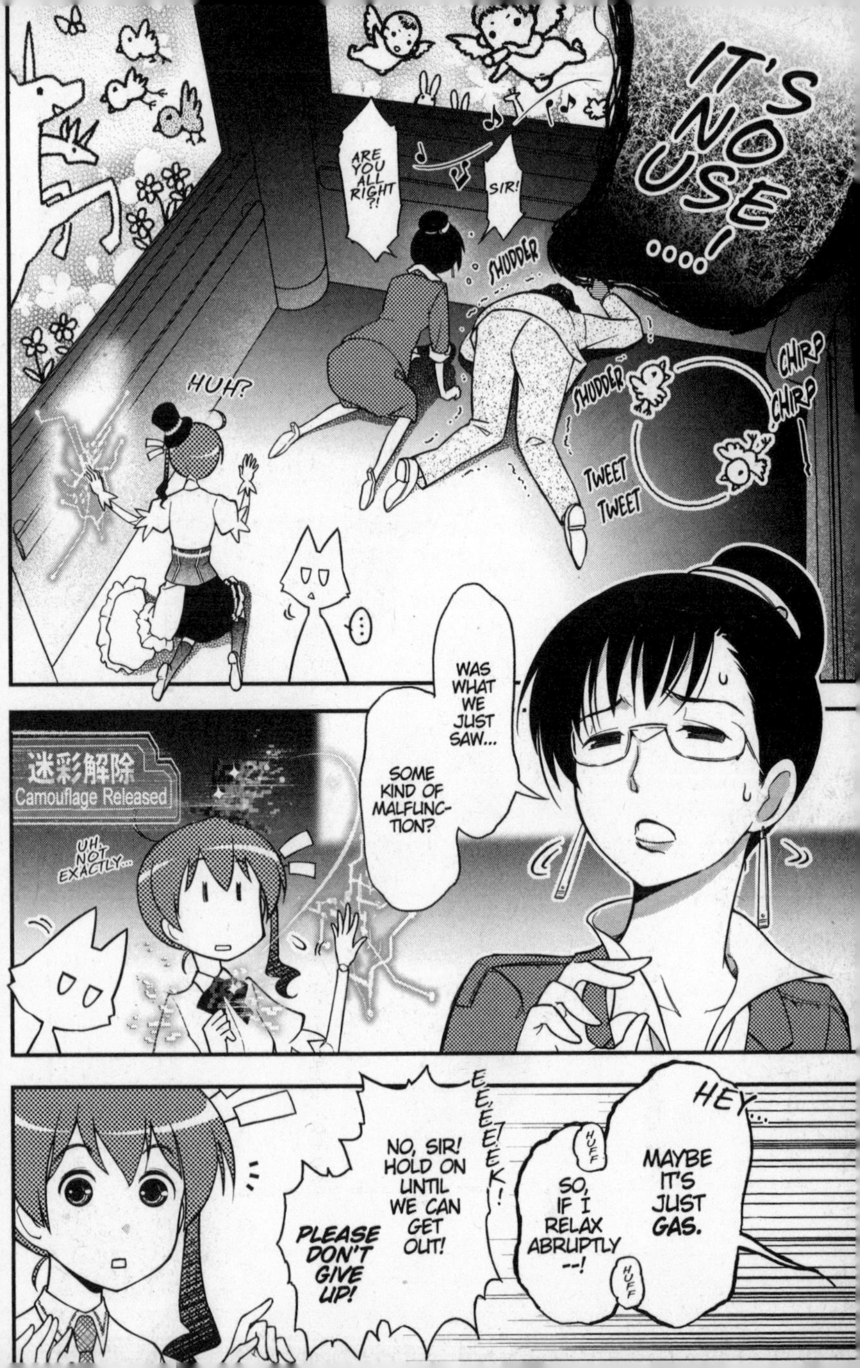
IT'S NO USE! OOOO
SHUDDER
SIR!
ARE YOU ALL RIGHT?!
CHIRP
CHIRP
SHUDDER
TWEET TWEET
HUH?
...
WAS WHAT WE JUST SAW... SOME KIND OF MALFUNCTION?
迷彩解除
Camouflage Released
UH, NOT EXACTLY...
HEY...
HUFF
MAYBE IT'S JUST GAS.
SO, IF I RELAX ABRUPTLY --!
HUFF
EEEEEEK!
NO, SIR! HOLD ON UNTIL WE CAN GET OUT!
PLEASE DON'T GIVE UP!

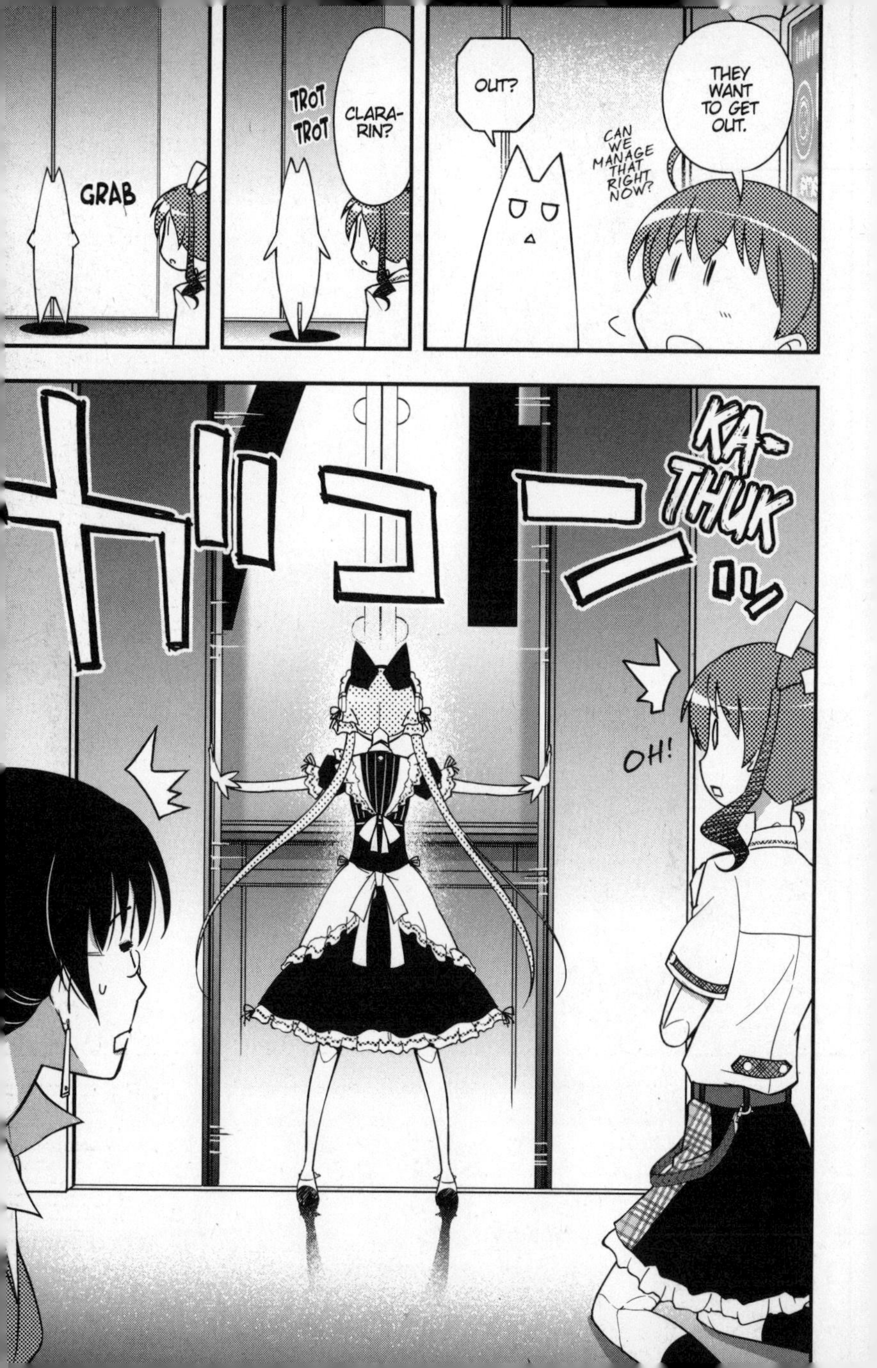
THEY WANT TO GET OUT.
OUT?
CAN WE MANAGE THAT RIGHT NOW?
CLARA-RIN?
TROT TROT
GRAB
KA-THUK
ガッコーン
OH!

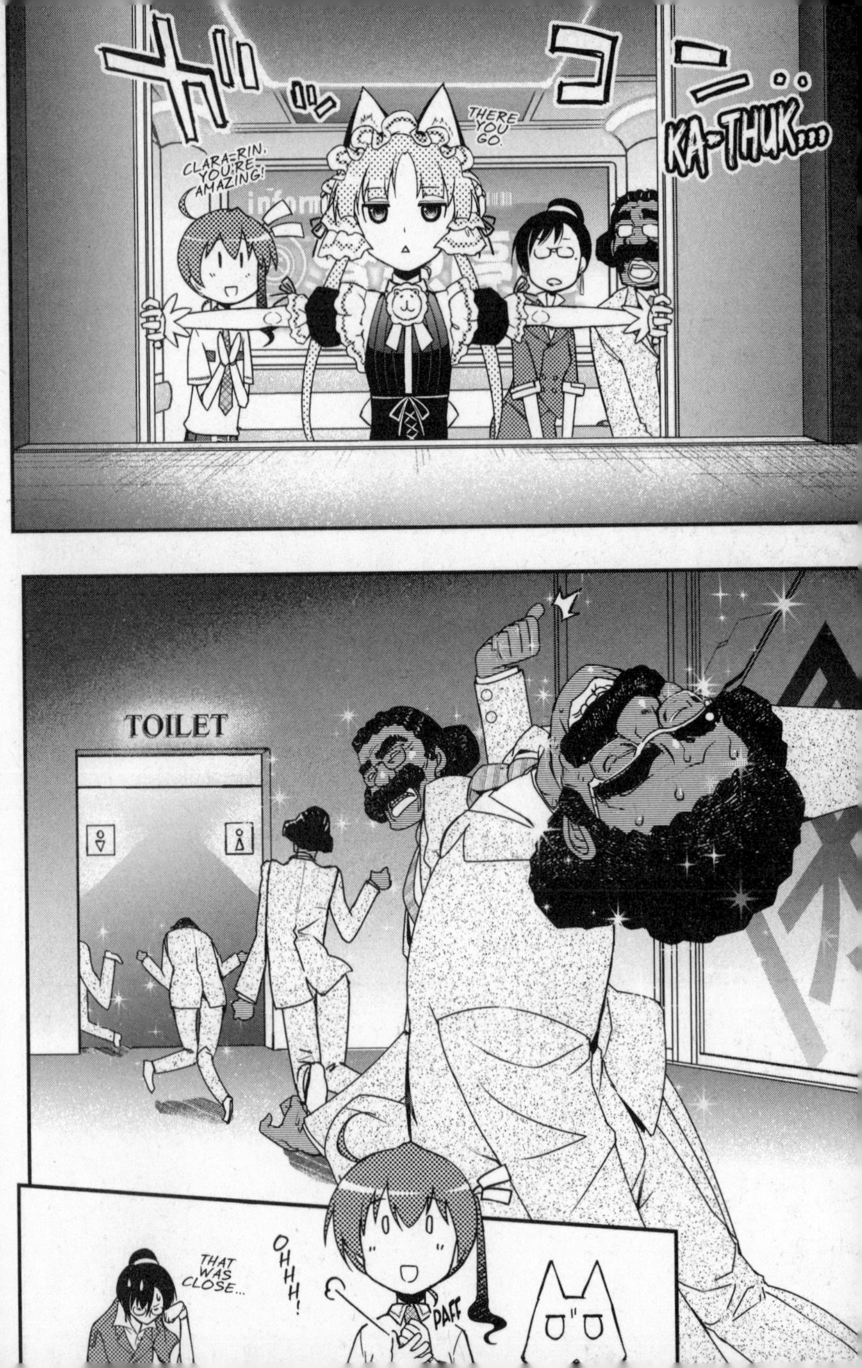
KA-THUK...
THERE YOU GO.
CLARA-RIN, YOU'RE AMAZING!
TOILET
OHHHH!
PAFF
THAT WAS CLOSE...

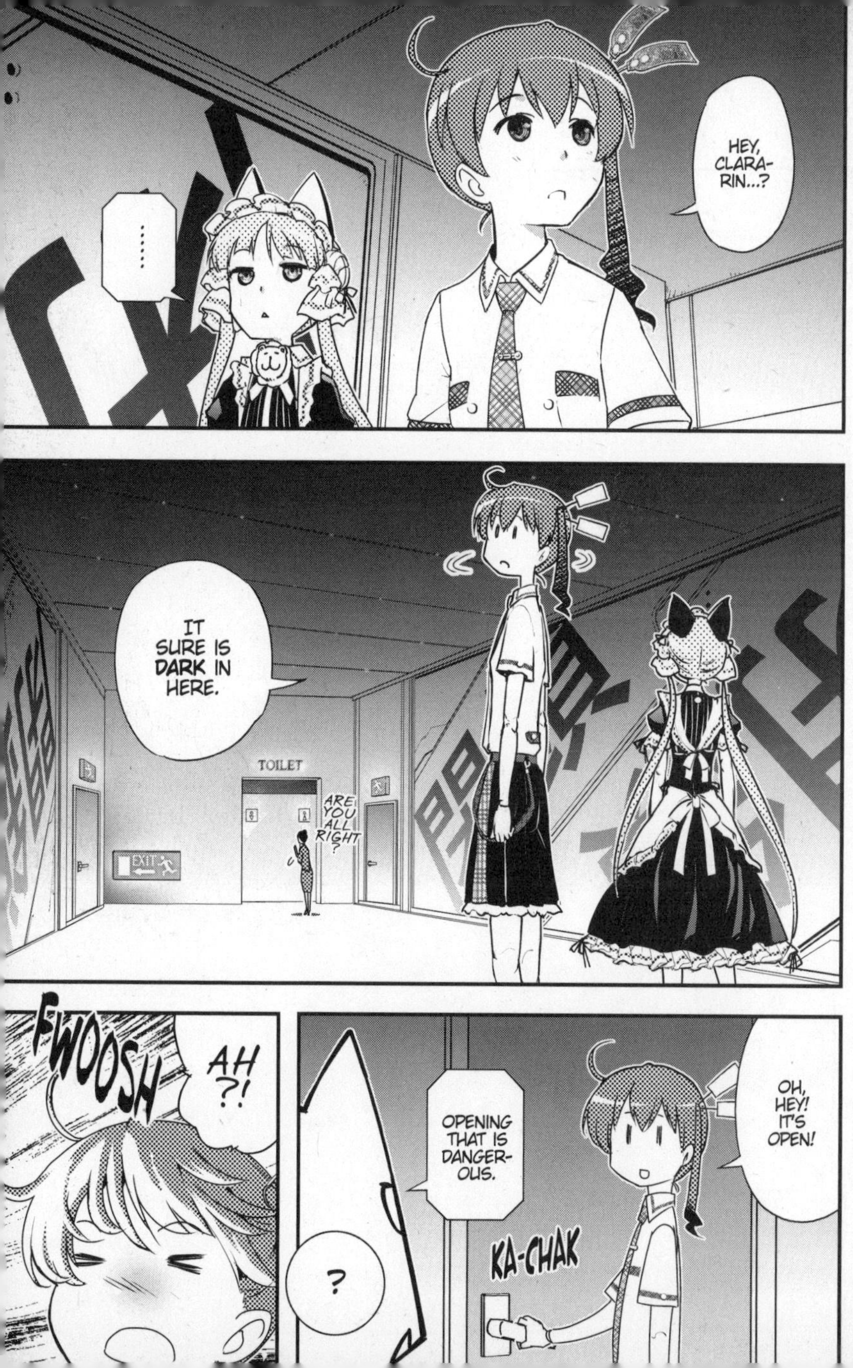
HEY, CLARA-RIN...?
......
IT SURE IS DARK IN HERE.
TOILET
ARE YOU ALL RIGHT?
EXIT
OH, HEY! IT'S OPEN!
OPENING THAT IS DANGER-OUS.
KA-CHAK
?
FWOOSH
AH ?!

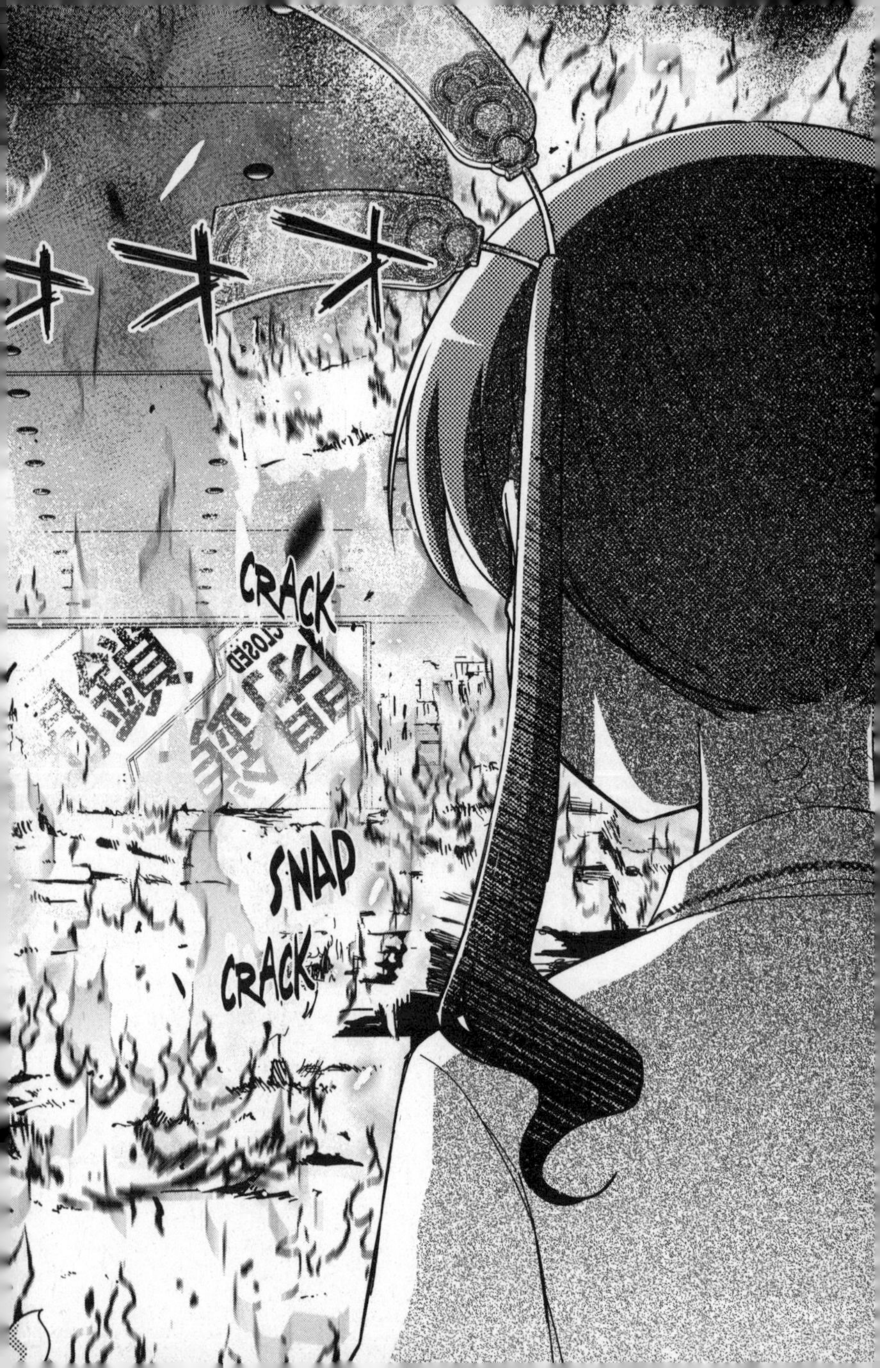
CRACK
CLOSED
SNAP
CRACK

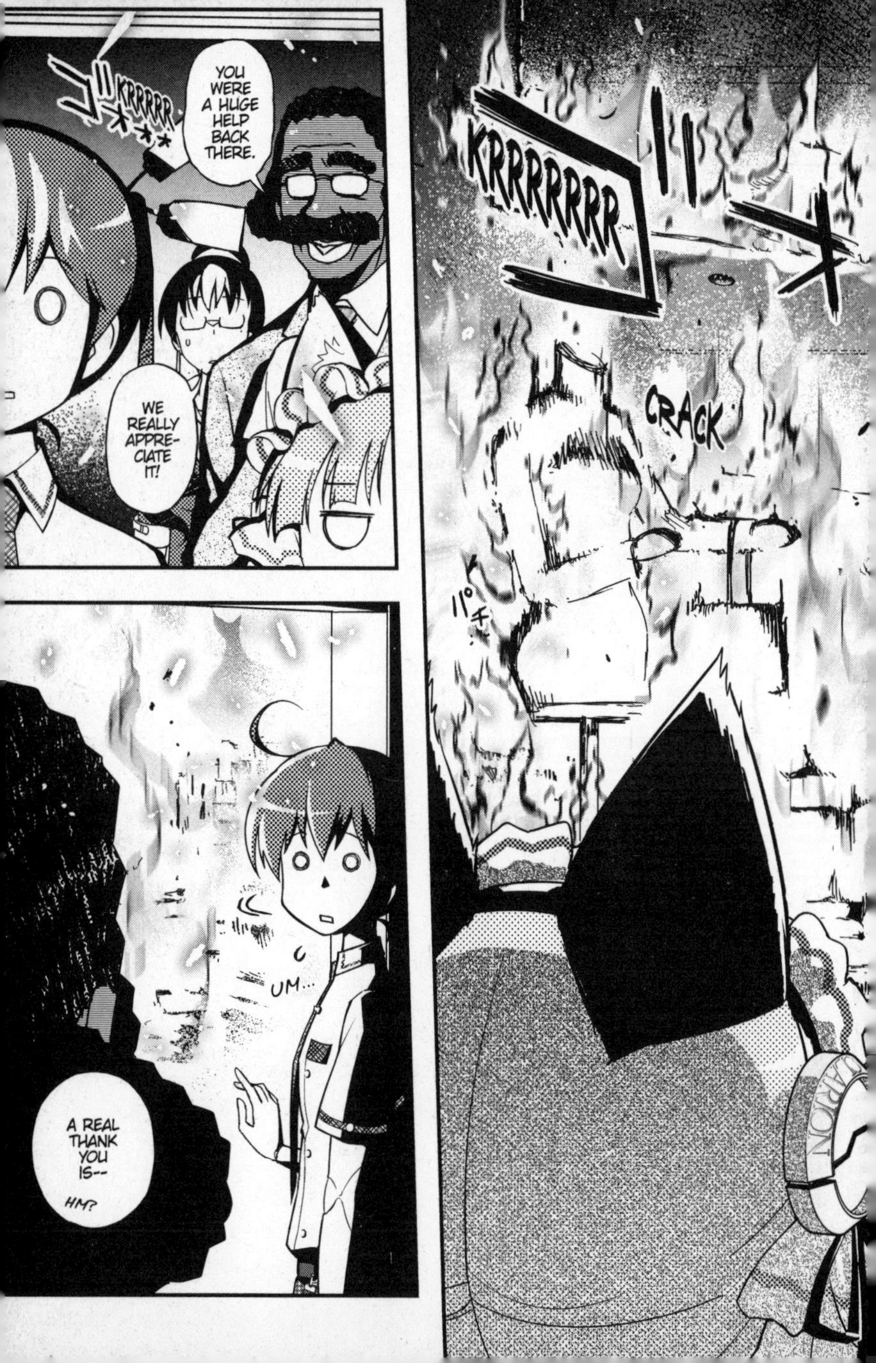
KRRRRRRRR
CRACK
パチ
KRRRRRR
YOU WERE A HUGE HELP BACK THERE.
WE REALLY APPRECIATE IT!
UM...
A REAL THANK YOU IS--
HM?

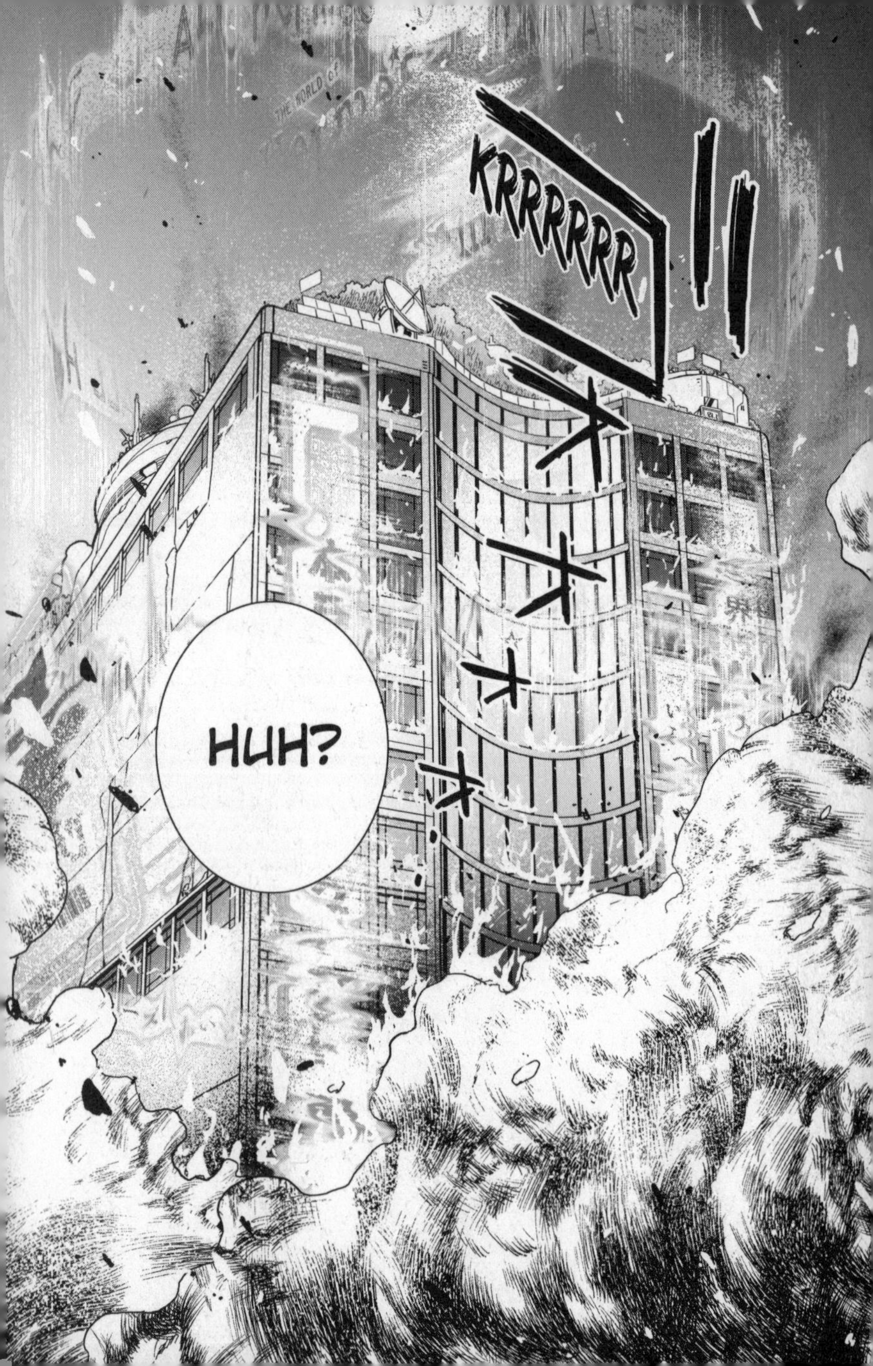
KRRRRRRR
HUH?

GHOST URN

GHOST URN

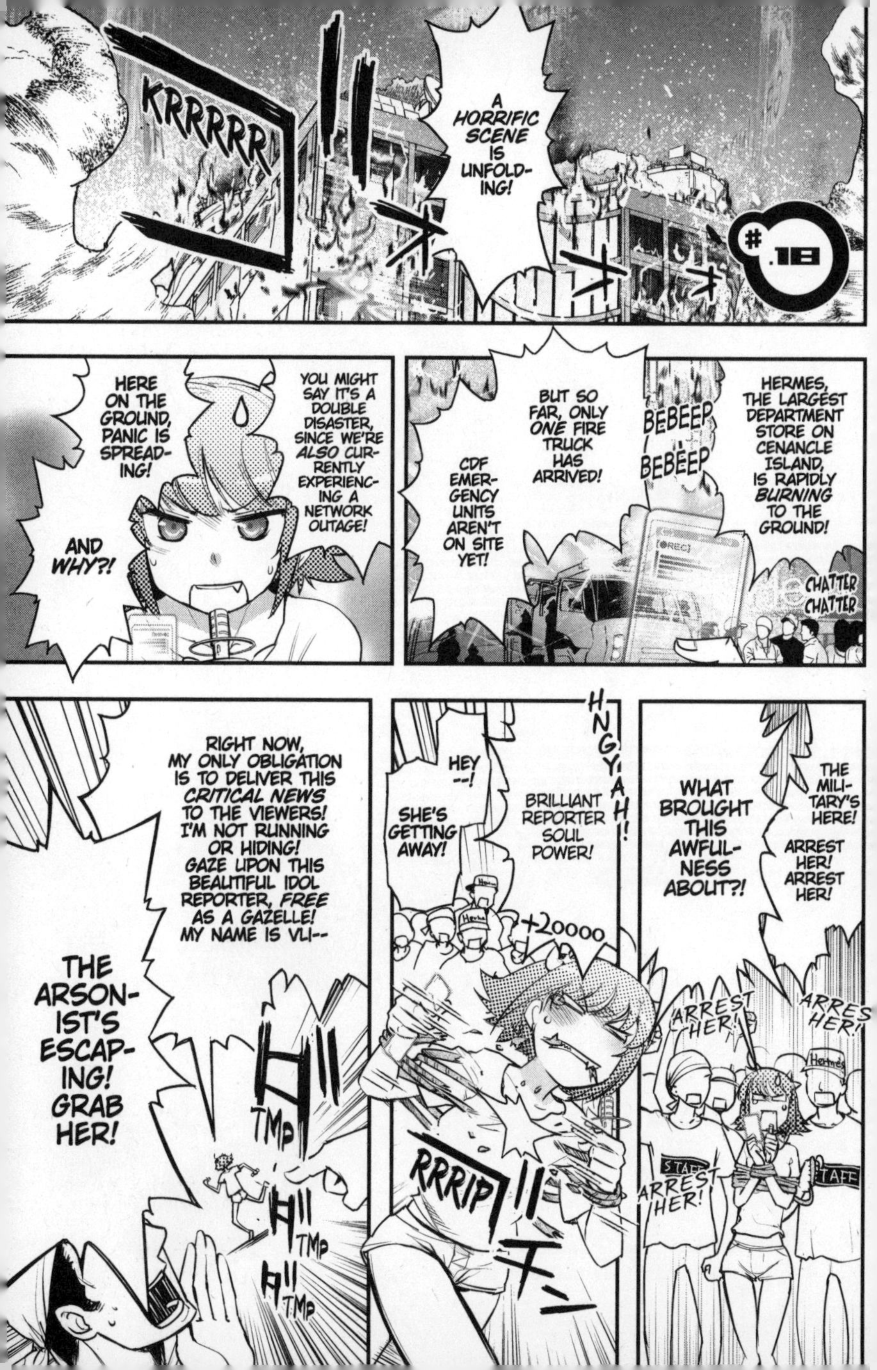
A HORRIFIC SCENE IS UNFOLDING!
KRRRRRR
#.18
HERMES, THE LARGEST DEPARTMENT STORE ON CENANCLE ISLAND, IS RAPIDLY *BURNING* TO THE GROUND!
CHATTER CHATTER
BEBEEP BEBEEP
BUT SO FAR, ONLY *ONE* FIRE TRUCK HAS ARRIVED!
CDF EMERGENCY UNITS AREN'T ON SITE YET!
YOU MIGHT SAY IT'S A DOUBLE DISASTER, SINCE WE'RE *ALSO* CURRENTLY EXPERIENCING A NETWORK OUTAGE!
HERE ON THE GROUND, PANIC IS SPREADING!
AND *WHY?!*
THE MILITARY'S HERE!
ARREST HER! ARREST HER!
WHAT BROUGHT THIS AWFULNESS ABOUT?!
ARRESS HER!
ARREST HER!
ARREST HER!
HNGYAH!
HEY--!
SHE'S GETTING AWAY!
BRILLIANT REPORTER SOUL POWER!
+20000
RRRIP
RIGHT NOW, MY ONLY OBLIGATION IS TO DELIVER THIS *CRITICAL NEWS* TO THE VIEWERS! I'M NOT RUNNING OR HIDING! GAZE UPON THIS BEAUTIFUL IDOL REPORTER, *FREE* AS A GAZELLE! MY NAME IS VLI--
THE ARSONIST'S ESCAPING! GRAB HER!
TMP
TMP
TMP

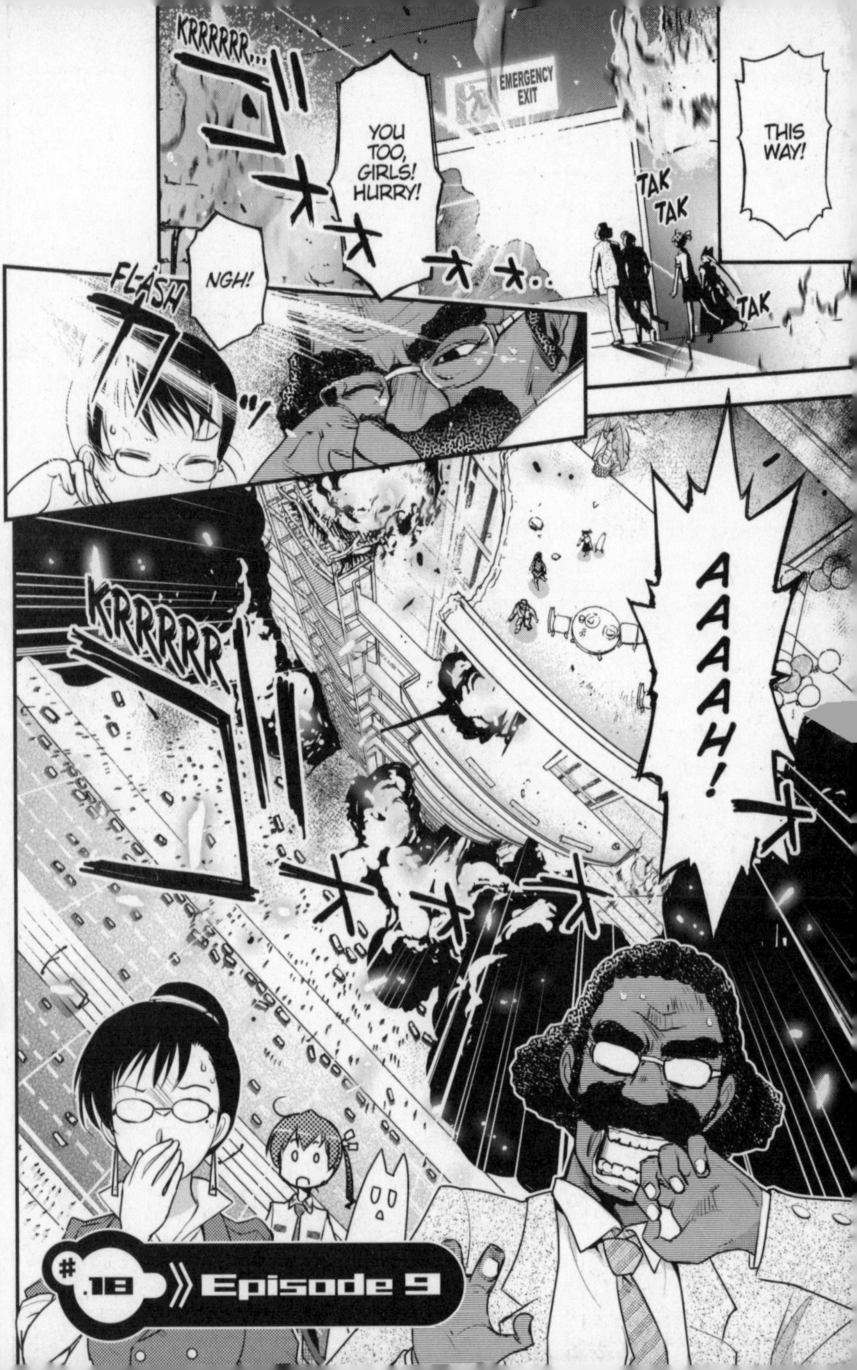
THIS WAY!
TAK TAK
TAK
EMERGENCY EXIT
YOU TOO, GIRLS! HURRY!
KRRRRRR...
NGH!
FLASH
AAAAAH!
KRRRRRR
#.18
Episode 9

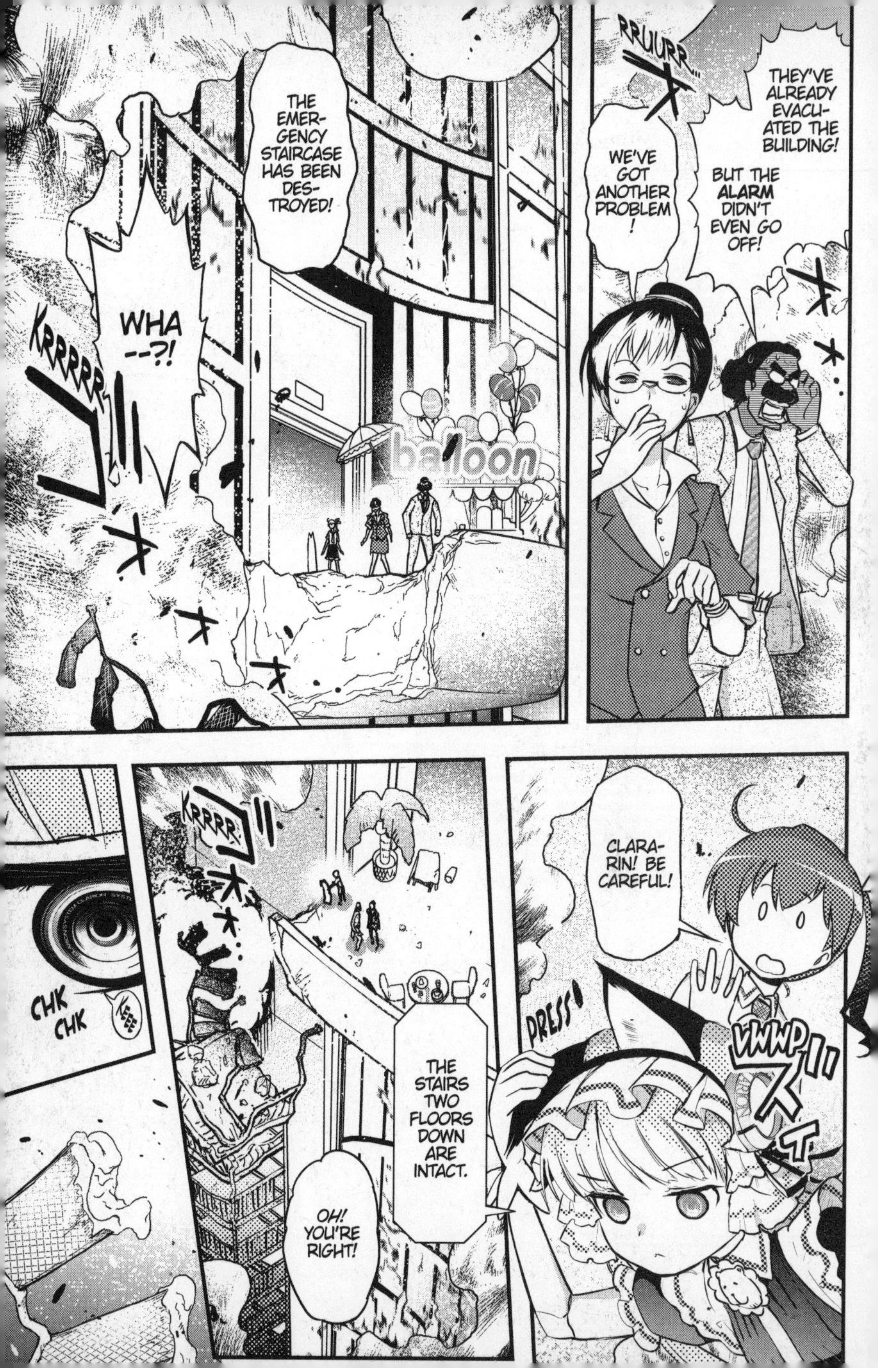
RRUIURR...
THEY'VE ALREADY EVACUATED THE BUILDING!
BUT THE ALARM DIDN'T EVEN GO OFF!
WE'VE GOT ANOTHER PROBLEM!
THE EMERGENCY STAIRCASE HAS BEEN DESTROYED!
balloon
WHA--?!
KRRRRR
CLARARIN! BE CAREFUL!
VWWPII
PRESS
KRRRR
THE STAIRS TWO FLOORS DOWN ARE INTACT.
OH! YOU'RE RIGHT!
CHK CHK

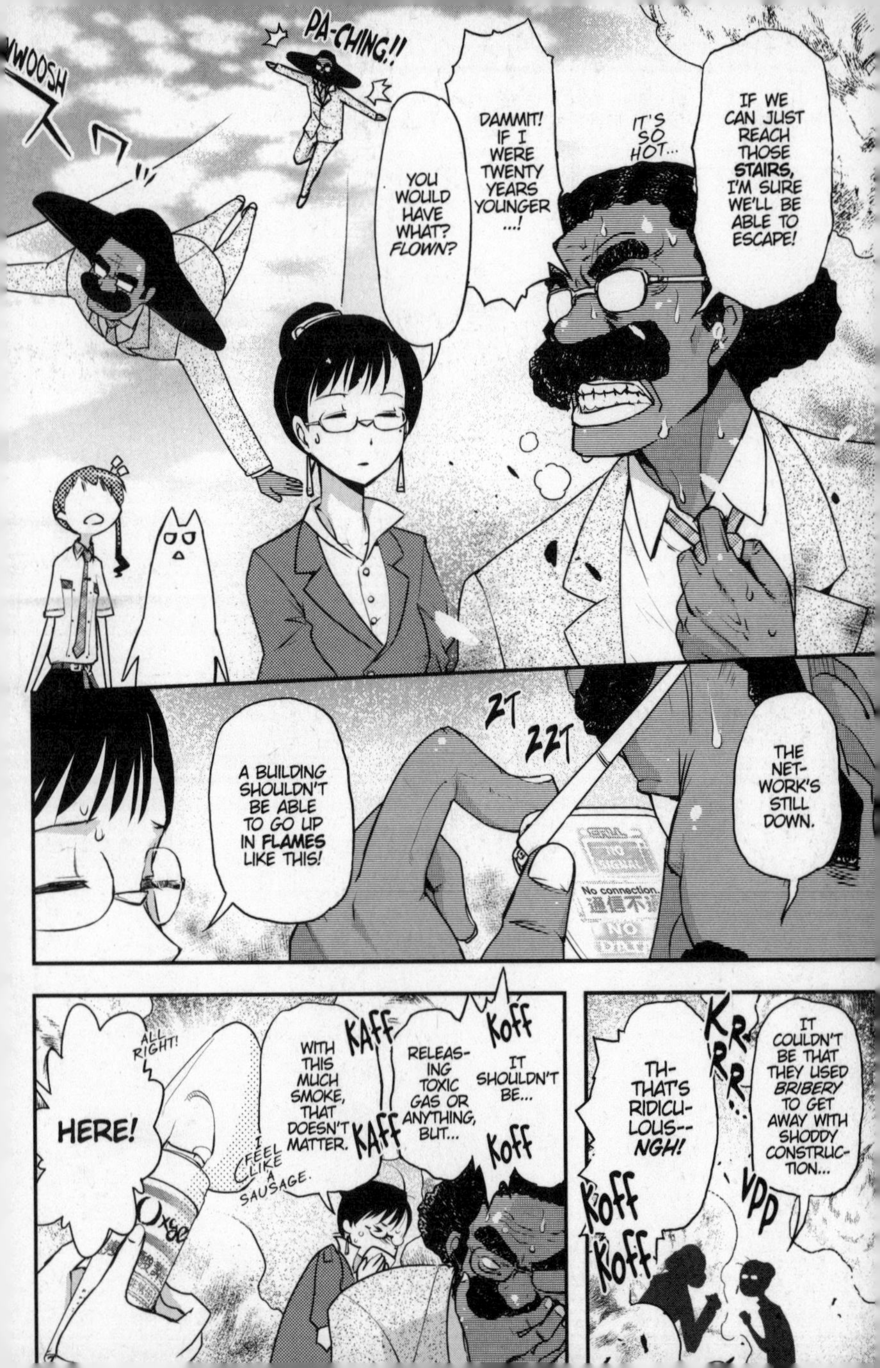
IF WE CAN JUST REACH THOSE STAIRS, I'M SURE WE'LL BE ABLE TO ESCAPE!
IT'S SO HOT...
DAMMIT! IF I WERE TWENTY YEARS YOUNGER ...!
YOU WOULD HAVE WHAT? FLOWN?
PA-CHING!!
WOOSH
THE NET-WORK'S STILL DOWN.
ZZT
ZZZT
No connection.
NO
A BUILDING SHOULDN'T BE ABLE TO GO UP IN FLAMES LIKE THIS!
IT COULDN'T BE THAT THEY USED BRIBERY TO GET AWAY WITH SHODDY CONSTRUC-TION...
KRRR...
VPP
TH-THAT'S RIDICU-LOUS--NGH!
KOFF
KOFF
IT SHOULDN'T BE...
KOFF
RELEAS-ING TOXIC GAS OR ANYTHING, BUT...
KOFF
WITH THIS MUCH SMOKE, THAT DOESN'T MATTER.
KAFF
KAFF
I FEEL LIKE A SAUSAGE.
ALL RIGHT!
HERE!

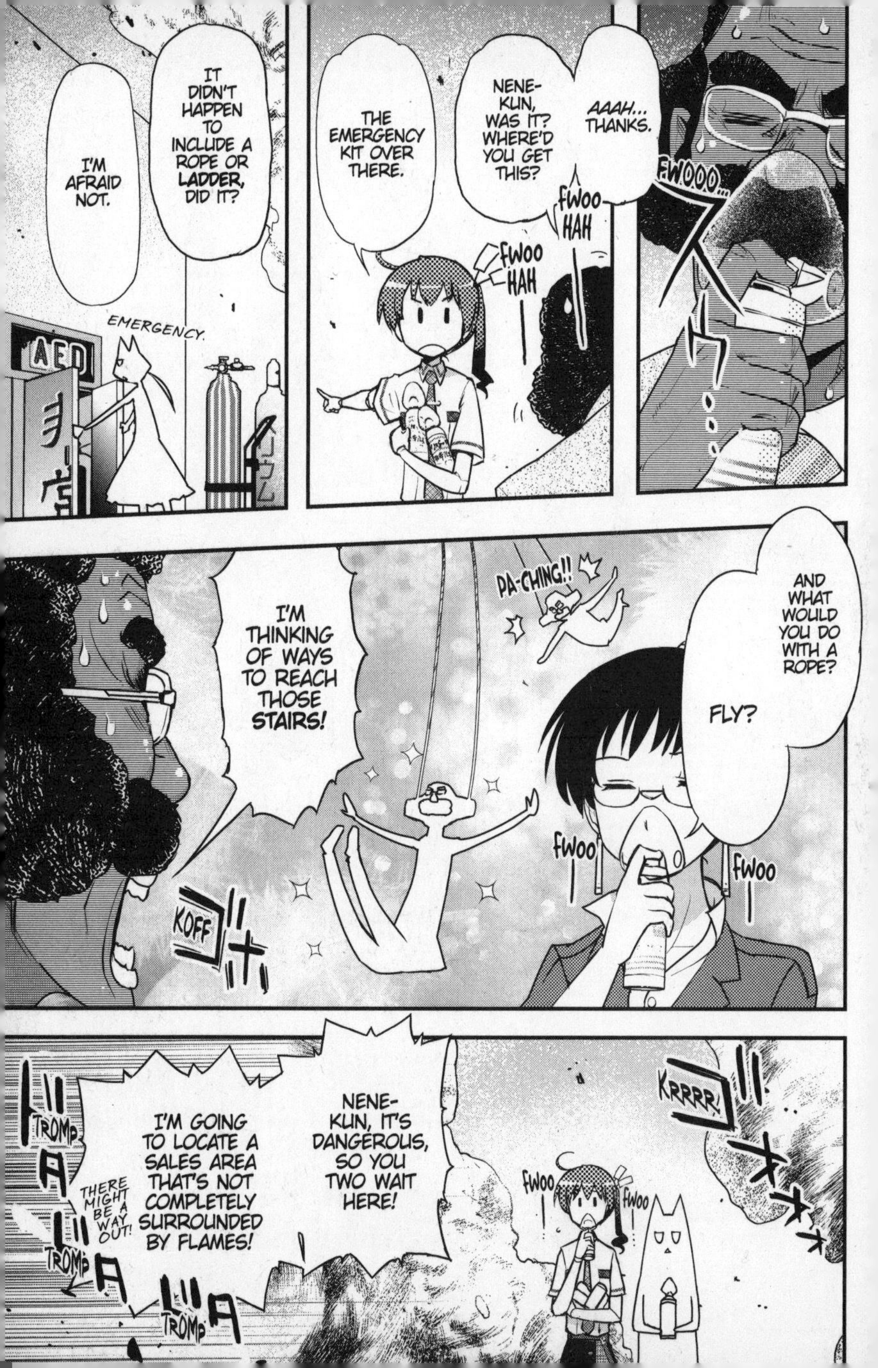
FWOOO...
AAAH... THANKS.
NENE-KUN, WAS IT? WHERE'D YOU GET THIS?
FWOO HAH
FWOO HAH
THE EMERGENCY KIT OVER THERE.
IT DIDN'T HAPPEN TO INCLUDE A ROPE OR LADDER, DID IT?
I'M AFRAID NOT.
EMERGENCY.
AED
AND WHAT WOULD YOU DO WITH A ROPE?
FLY?
PA-CHING!!
FWOO
FWOO
I'M THINKING OF WAYS TO REACH THOSE STAIRS!
KOFF
KRRRR
FWOO
FWOO
NENE-KUN, IT'S DANGEROUS, SO YOU TWO WAIT HERE!
I'M GOING TO LOCATE A SALES AREA THAT'S NOT COMPLETELY SURROUNDED BY FLAMES!
THERE MIGHT BE A WAY OUT!
TROMP
TROMP
TROMP

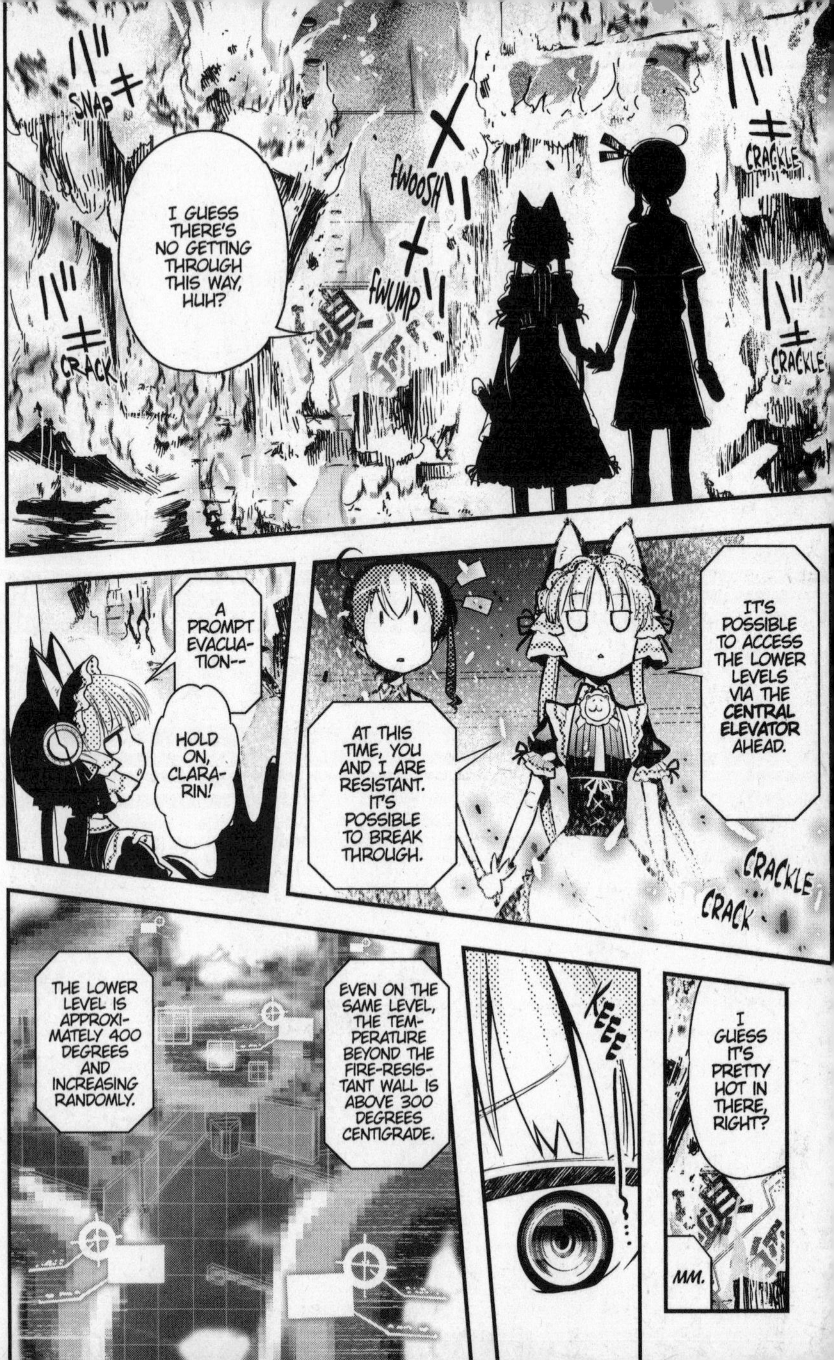
CRACKLE
FWOOSH
CRACKLE
SNAP
I GUESS THERE'S NO GETTING THROUGH THIS WAY, HUH?
FWUMP
CRACK
IT'S POSSIBLE TO ACCESS THE LOWER LEVELS VIA THE **CENTRAL ELEVATOR** AHEAD.
AT THIS TIME, YOU AND I ARE RESISTANT. IT'S POSSIBLE TO BREAK THROUGH.
CRACKLE
CRACK
A PROMPT EVACUATION--
HOLD ON, CLARARIN!
I GUESS IT'S PRETTY HOT IN THERE, RIGHT?
MM.
KEEE
EVEN ON THE SAME LEVEL, THE TEMPERATURE BEYOND THE FIRE-RESISTANT WALL IS ABOVE 300 DEGREES CENTIGRADE.
THE LOWER LEVEL IS APPROXIMATELY 400 DEGREES AND INCREASING RANDOMLY.

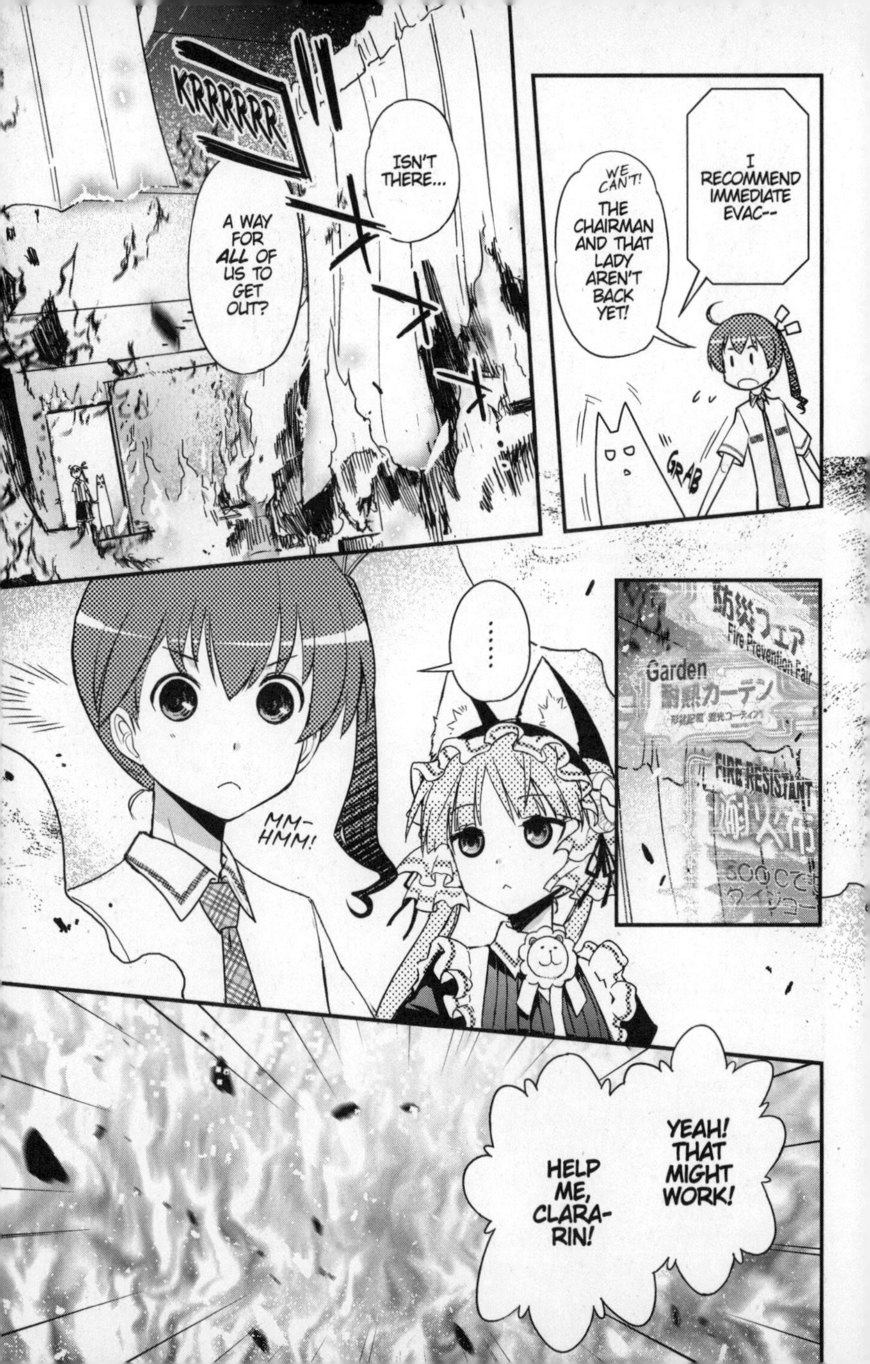
I RECOMMEND IMMEDIATE EVAC--
WE CAN'T! THE CHAIRMAN AND THAT LADY AREN'T BACK YET!
GRAB
KRRRRRRR
ISN'T THERE...
A WAY FOR ALL OF US TO GET OUT?
防災フェア
Fire Prevention Fair
Garden
FIRE RESISTANT
......
MM-HMM!
YEAH! THAT MIGHT WORK!
HELP ME, CLARA-RIN!

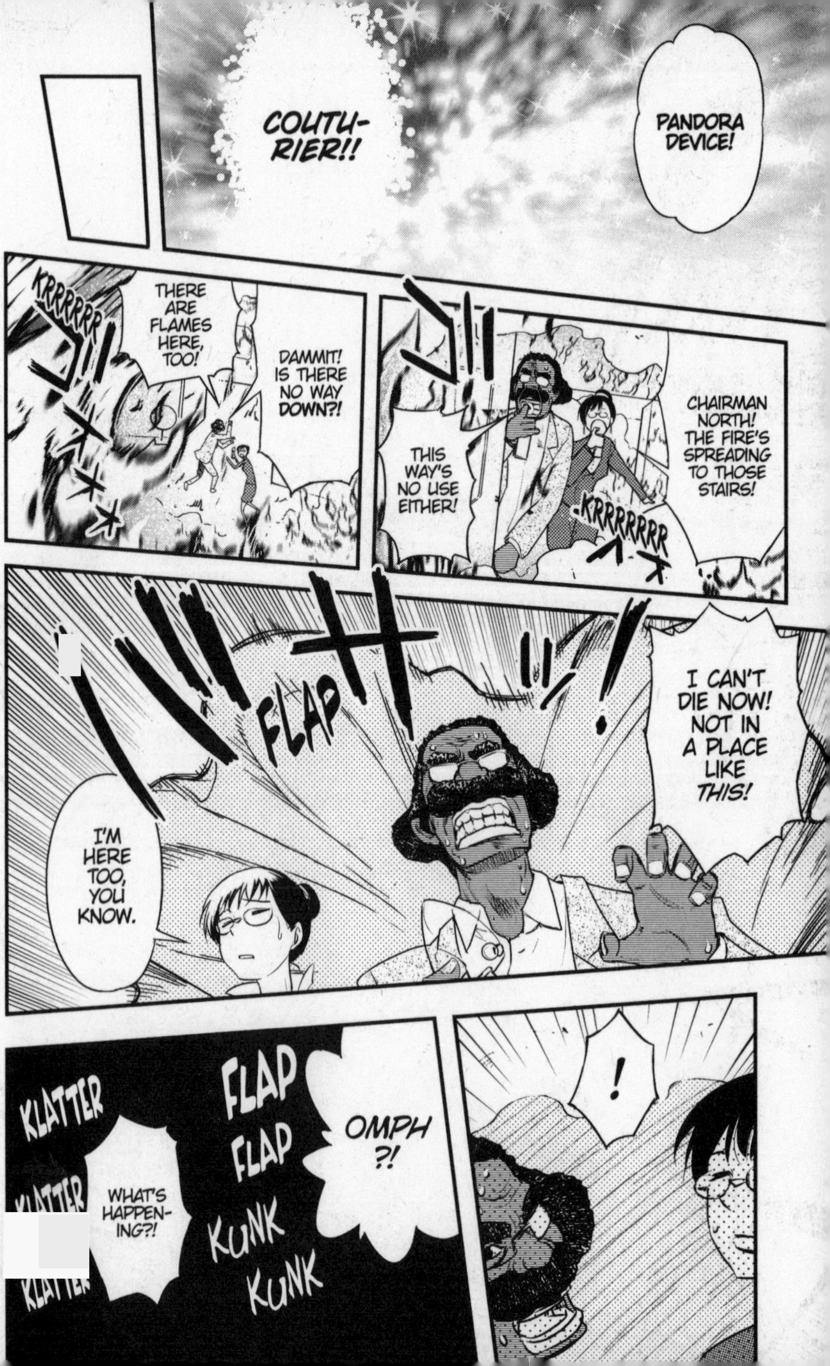
PANDORA DEVICE!
COUTURIER!!
CHAIRMAN NORTH! THE FIRE'S SPREADING TO THOSE STAIRS!
THIS WAY'S NO USE EITHER!
KRRRRRRR
DAMMIT! IS THERE NO WAY DOWN?!
THERE ARE FLAMES HERE, TOO!
KRRRRRR
I CAN'T DIE NOW! NOT IN A PLACE LIKE THIS!
FLAP
I'M HERE TOO, YOU KNOW.
!
OMPH ?!
FLAP FLAP
KUNK KUNK
WHAT'S HAPPENING?!
KLATTER
KLATTER
KLATTER

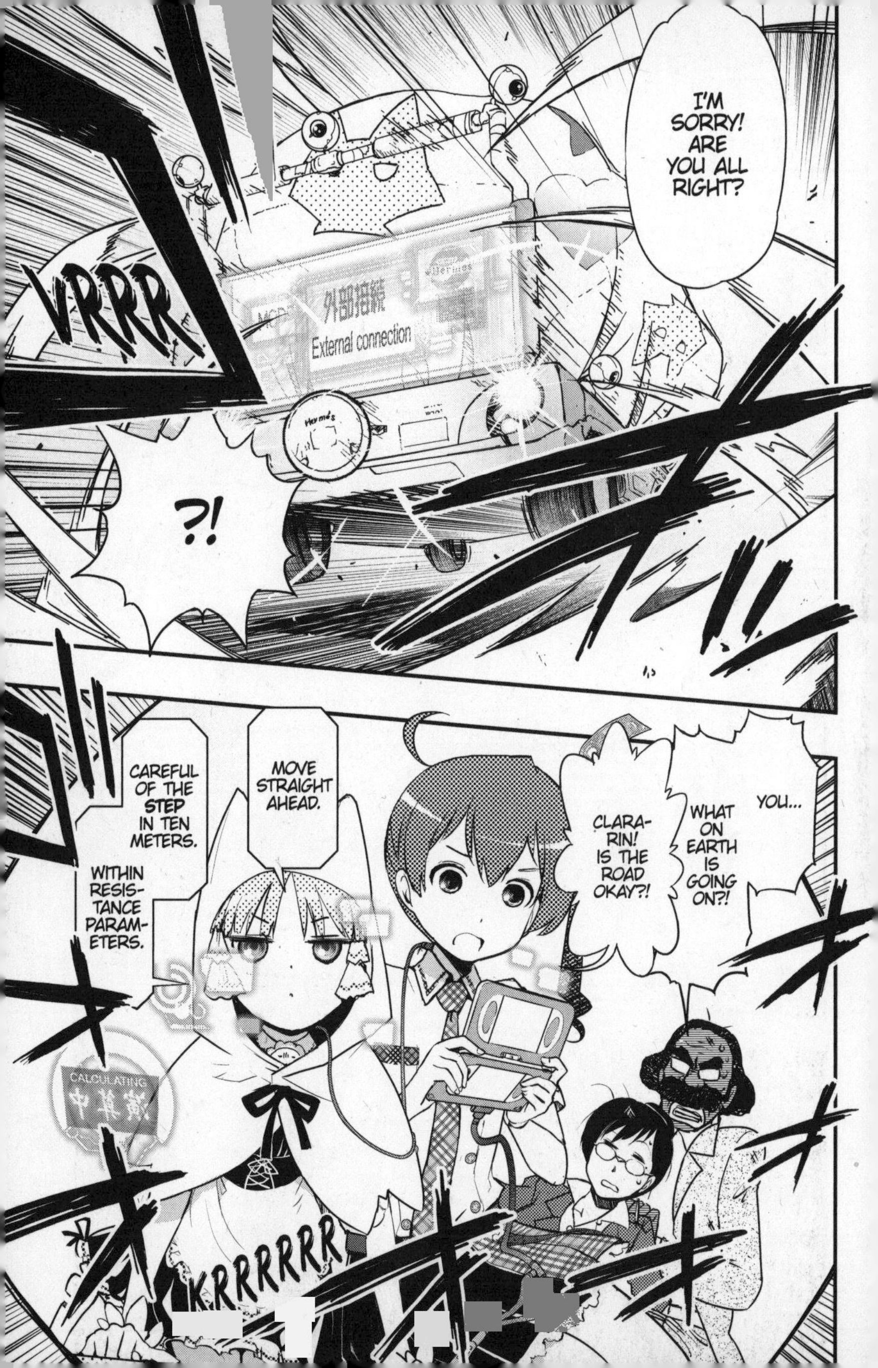
I'M SORRY! ARE YOU ALL RIGHT?
外部接続
External connection
VRRR
?!
YOU...
WHAT ON EARTH IS GOING ON?!
CLARA-RIN! IS THE ROAD OKAY?!
MOVE STRAIGHT AHEAD.
CAREFUL OF THE STEP IN TEN METERS.
WITHIN RESISTANCE PARAMETERS.
CALCULATING
KRRRRRR

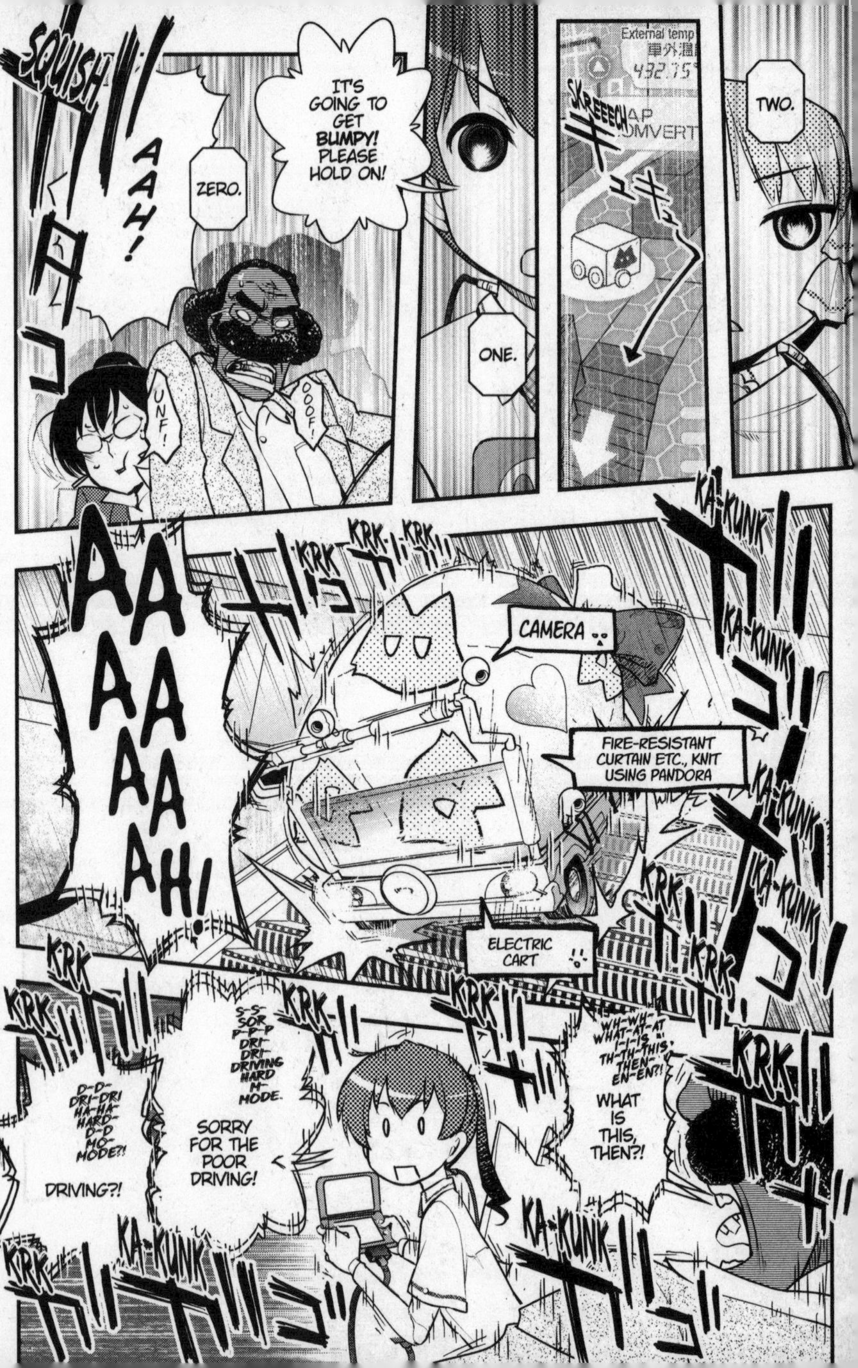
TWO.
External temp
432.75°
SKREEECH
ONE.
IT'S GOING TO GET BUMPY! PLEASE HOLD ON!
ZERO.
AAH!
SQUISH
OOOF!
UNF!
KA-KUNK
KA-KUNK
KA-KUNK
KA-KUNK
KA-KUNK
KRK-KRK
KRK
CAMERA
FIRE-RESISTANT CURTAIN ETC., KNIT USING PANDORA
ELECTRIC CART
KRK
KRK
AAAAAAAAH!
KRK
KRK
WH-WH-WHAT-AT-AT I-I-IS TH-TH-THIS THEN-EN-EN?!
WHAT IS THIS, THEN?!
KRK
KRK
S-S-SOR P-P-P DRI-DRI-DRIVING HARD M-MODE.
SORRY FOR THE POOR DRIVING!
D-D-DRI-DRI HA-HA-HARD D-D MO-MODE?!
DRIVING?!
KRK
KA-KUNK
KA-KUNK
KRK

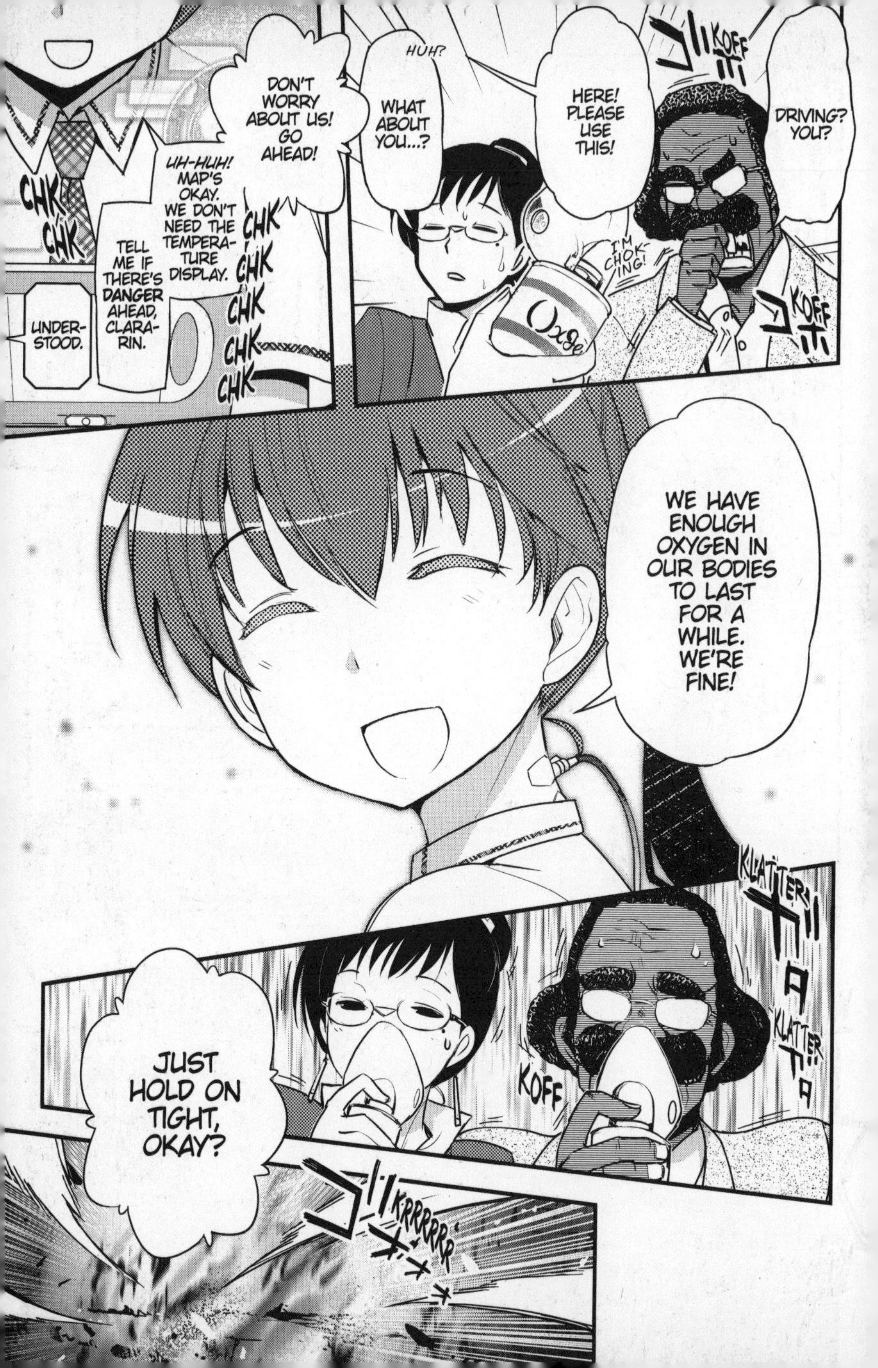
DRIVING? YOU?
KOFF
HERE! PLEASE USE THIS!
I'M CHOKING!
KOFF
HUH?
WHAT ABOUT YOU...?
DON'T WORRY ABOUT US! GO AHEAD!
UH-HUH! MAP'S OKAY. WE DON'T NEED THE TEMPERATURE DISPLAY.
CHK CHK CHK CHK CHK
TELL ME IF THERE'S DANGER AHEAD, CLARARIN.
CHK CHK
UNDERSTOOD.
WE HAVE ENOUGH OXYGEN IN OUR BODIES TO LAST FOR A WHILE. WE'RE FINE!
KLATTER
KLATTER
KOFF
JUST HOLD ON TIGHT, OKAY?
KRRRRRR

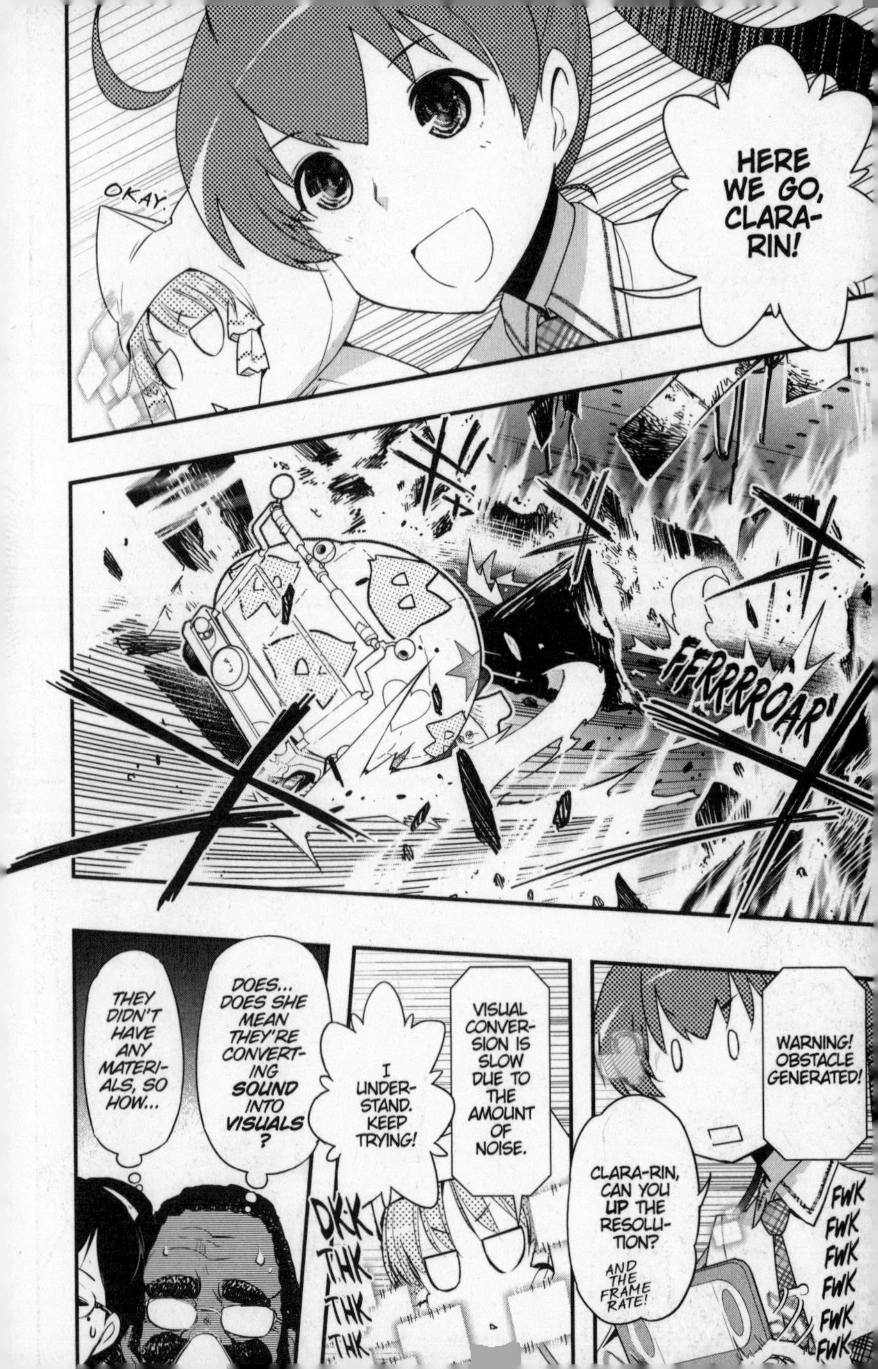
HERE WE GO, CLARA-RIN!
OKAY.
FFRRRROAR
WARNING! OBSTACLE GENERATED!
CLARA-RIN, CAN YOU **UP** THE RESOLUTION?
AND THE FRAME RATE!
FWK FWK FWK FWK FWK FWK
VISUAL CONVERSION IS SLOW DUE TO THE AMOUNT OF NOISE.
I UNDERSTAND. KEEP TRYING!
DK-K THK THK THK
DOES... DOES SHE MEAN THEY'RE CONVERTING **SOUND** INTO **VISUALS**?
THEY DIDN'T HAVE ANY MATERIALS, SO HOW...

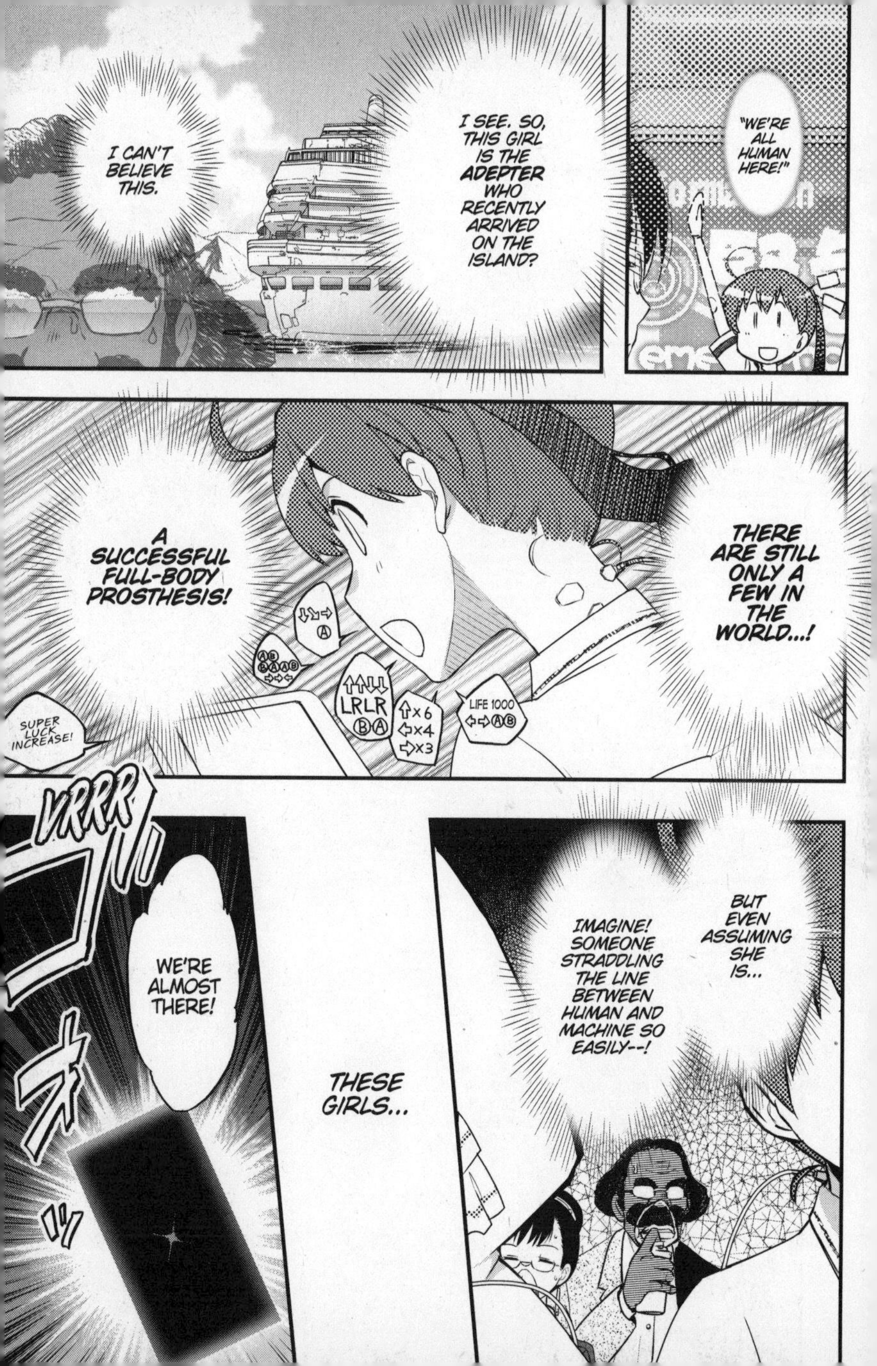
"WE'RE ALL HUMAN HERE!"
I SEE. SO, THIS GIRL IS THE ADEPTER WHO RECENTLY ARRIVED ON THE ISLAND?
I CAN'T BELIEVE THIS.
THERE ARE STILL ONLY A FEW IN THE WORLD...!
LIFE 1000
LRLR
A SUCCESSFUL FULL-BODY PROSTHESIS!
SUPER LUCK INCREASE!
BUT EVEN ASSUMING SHE IS...
IMAGINE! SOMEONE STRADDLING THE LINE BETWEEN HUMAN AND MACHINE SO EASILY--!
THESE GIRLS...
VRRR
WE'RE ALMOST THERE!

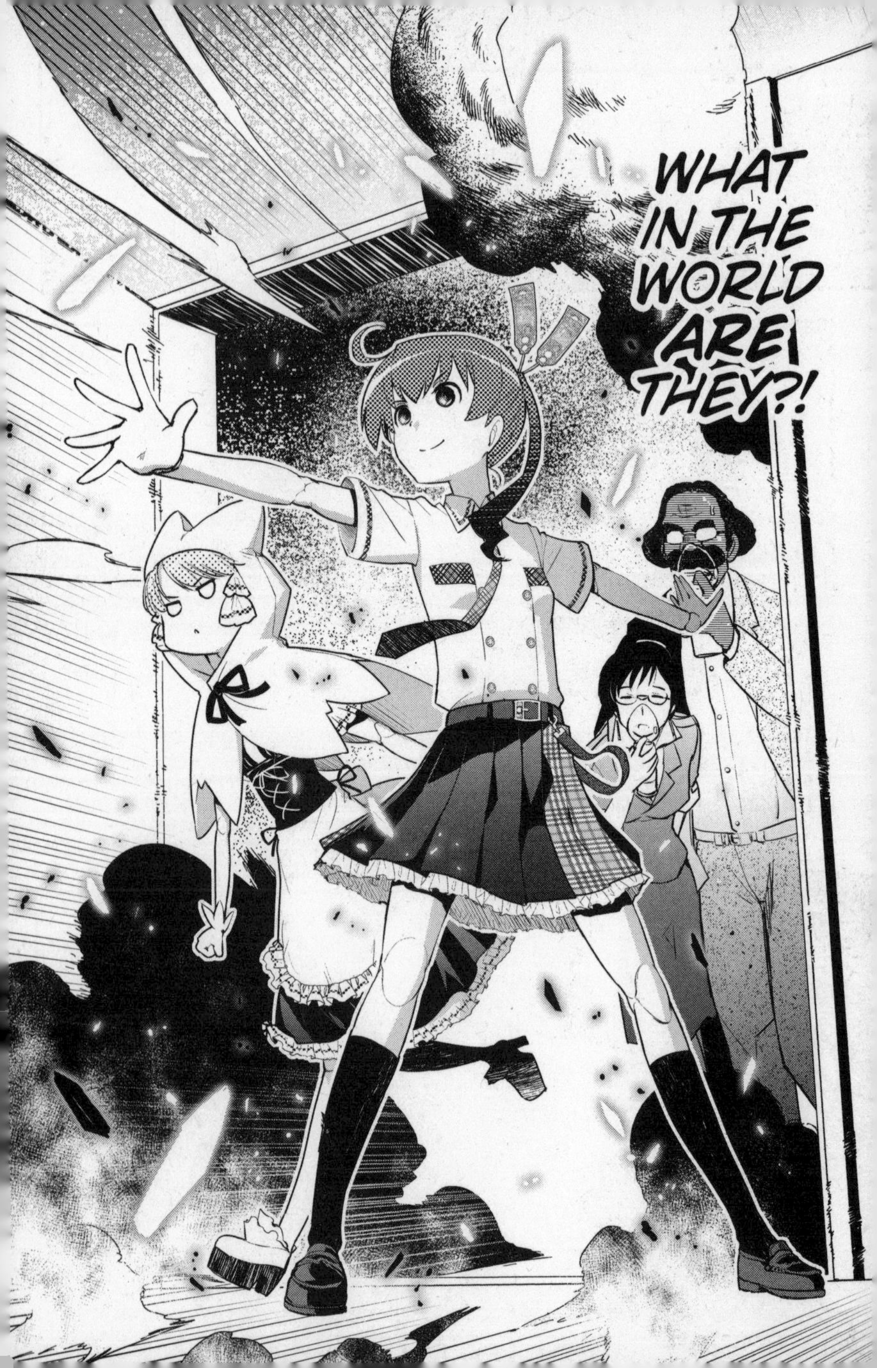
WHAT IN THE WORLD ARE THEY?!

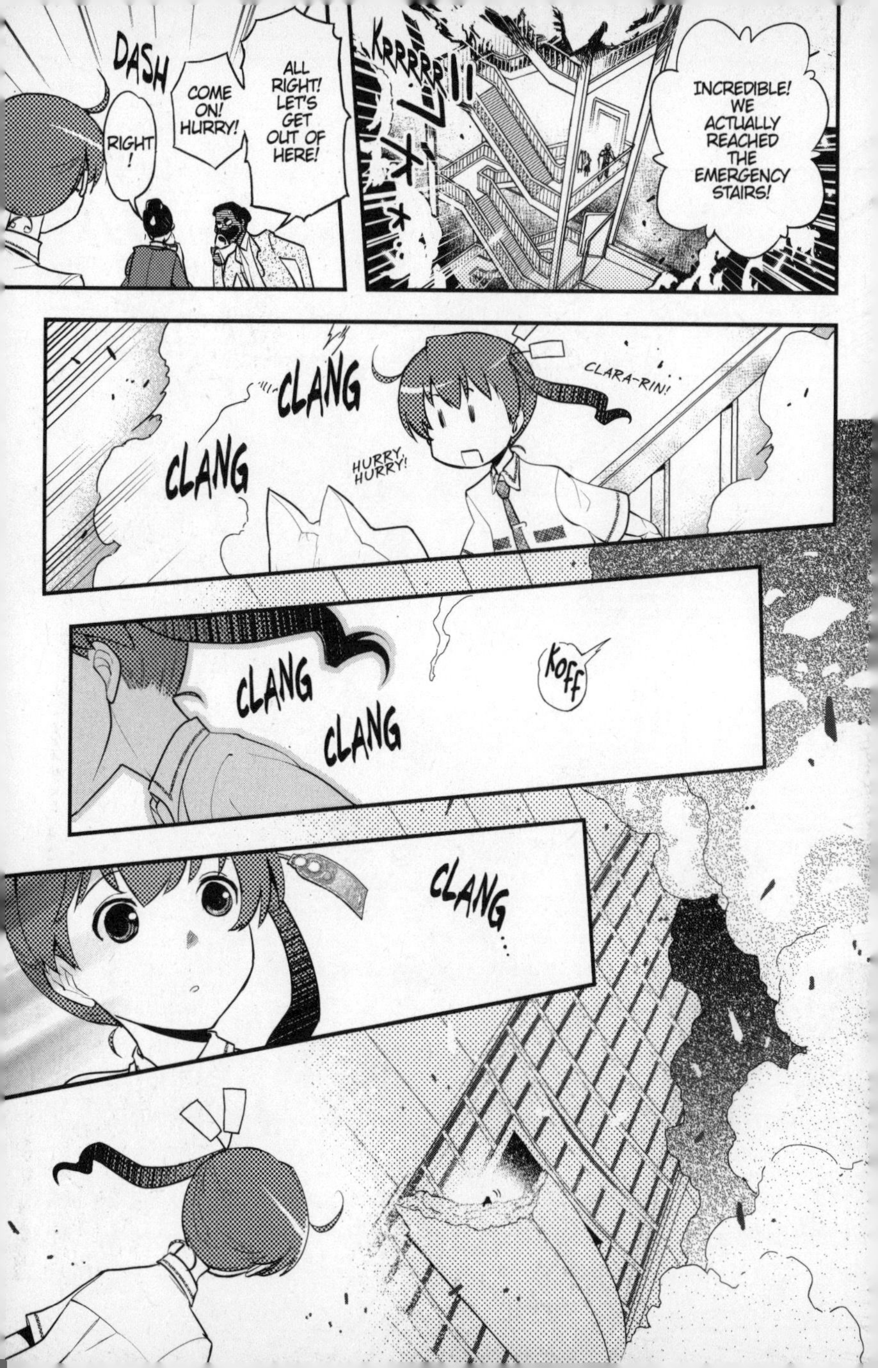
KRRRRR
INCREDIBLE! WE ACTUALLY REACHED THE EMERGENCY STAIRS!
ALL RIGHT! LET'S GET OUT OF HERE!
COME ON! HURRY!
DASH
RIGHT!
CLARA-RIN!
HURRY, HURRY!
CLANG
CLANG
KOFF
CLANG
CLANG
CLANG...

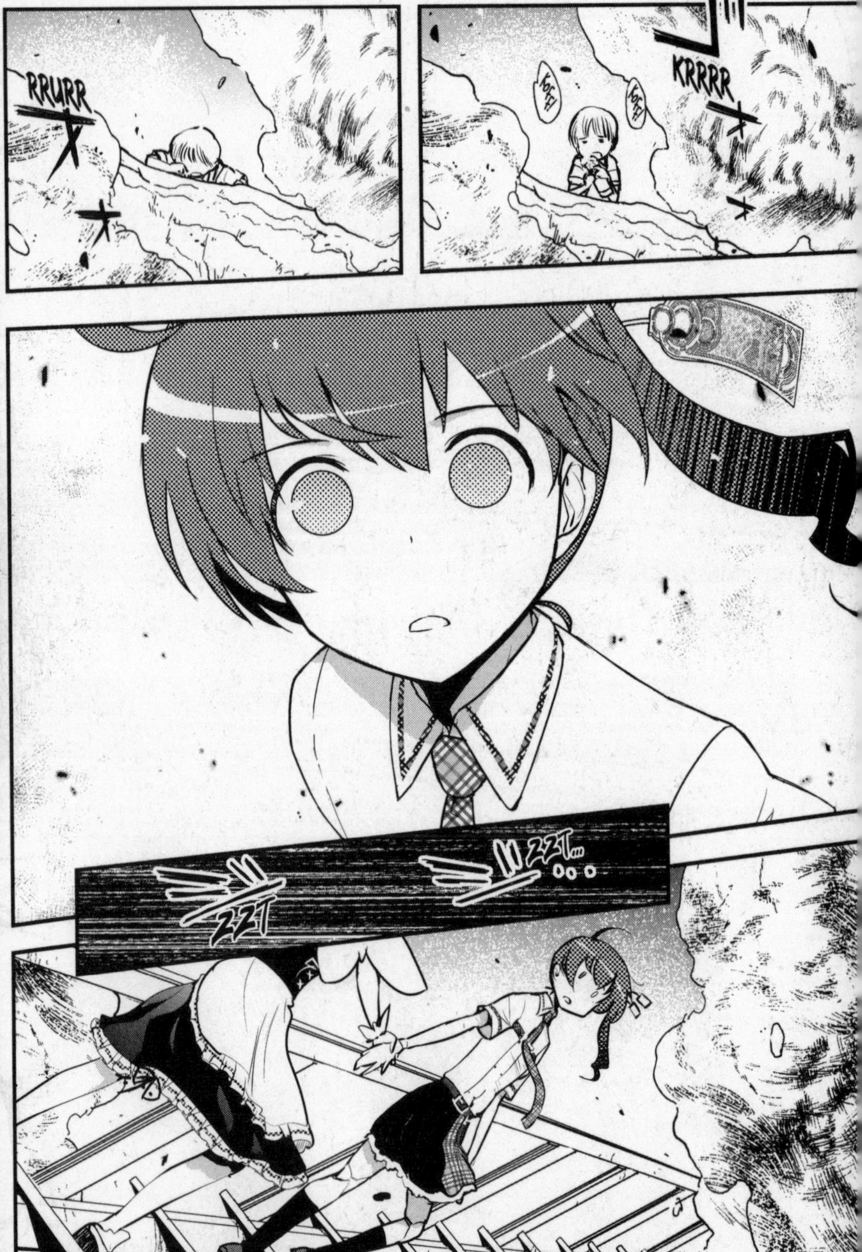
KRRRR
KOFF!
KOFF!
RRURR
ZZT...
ZZT

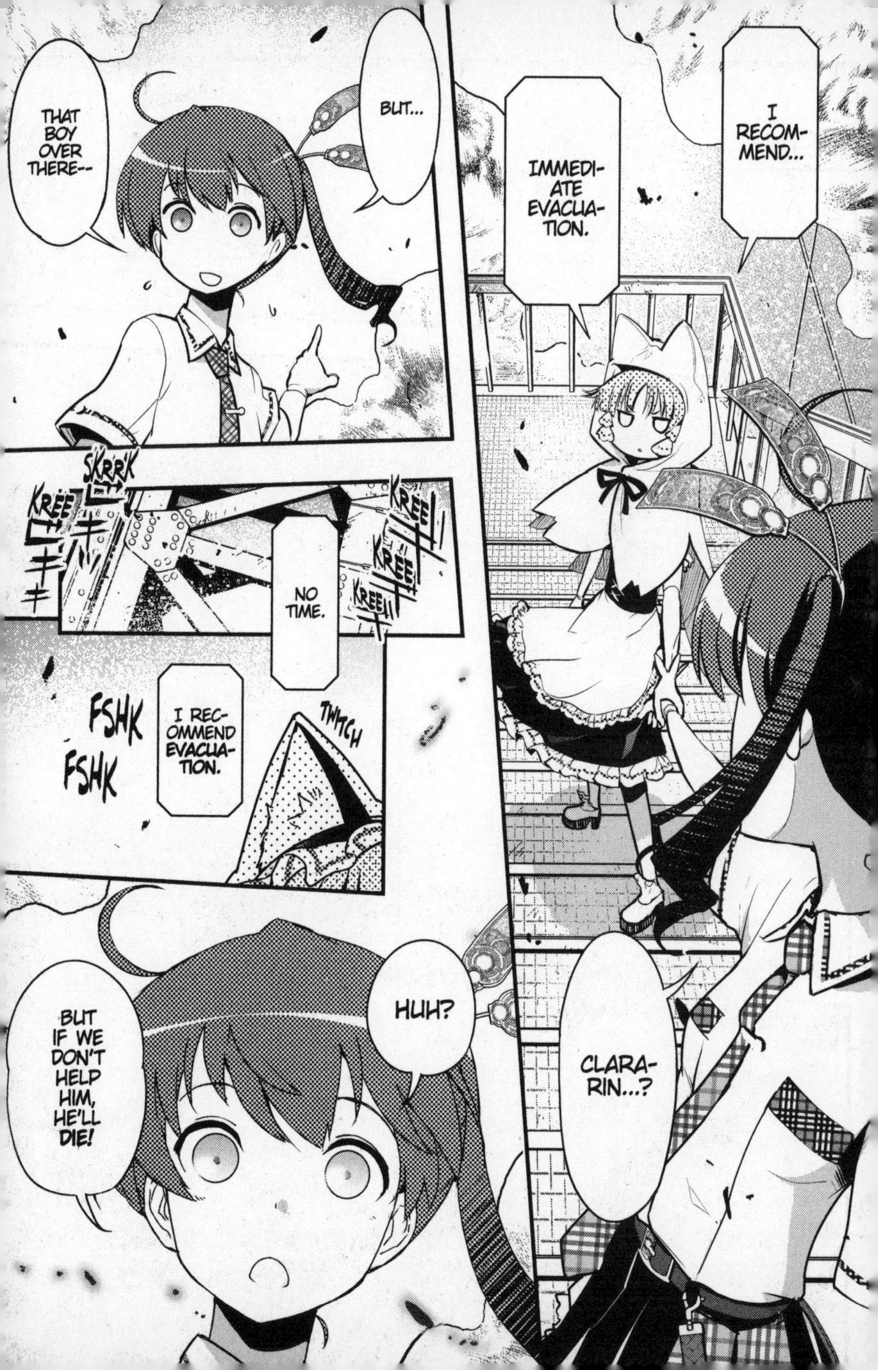
I RECOMMEND...
IMMEDIATE EVACUATION.
BUT...
THAT BOY OVER THERE--
SKRRK
KREE
KREE
KREE
KREE
NO TIME.
TWITCH
I RECOMMEND EVACUATION.
FSHK
FSHK
CLARA-RIN...?
HUH?
BUT IF WE DON'T HELP HIM, HE'LL DIE!

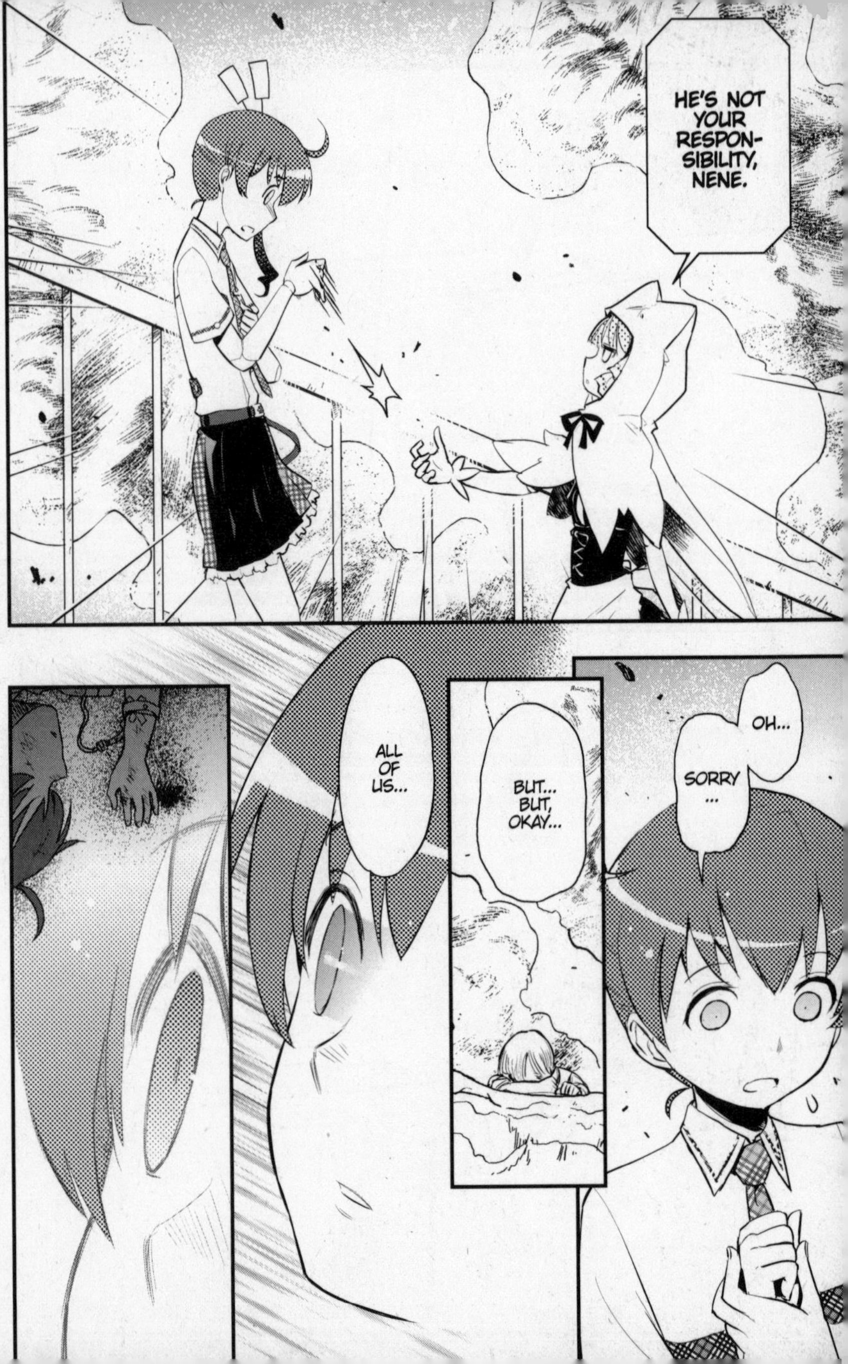
HE'S NOT YOUR RESPON-SIBILITY, NENE.
OH...
SORRY ...
BUT... BUT, OKAY...
ALL OF US...

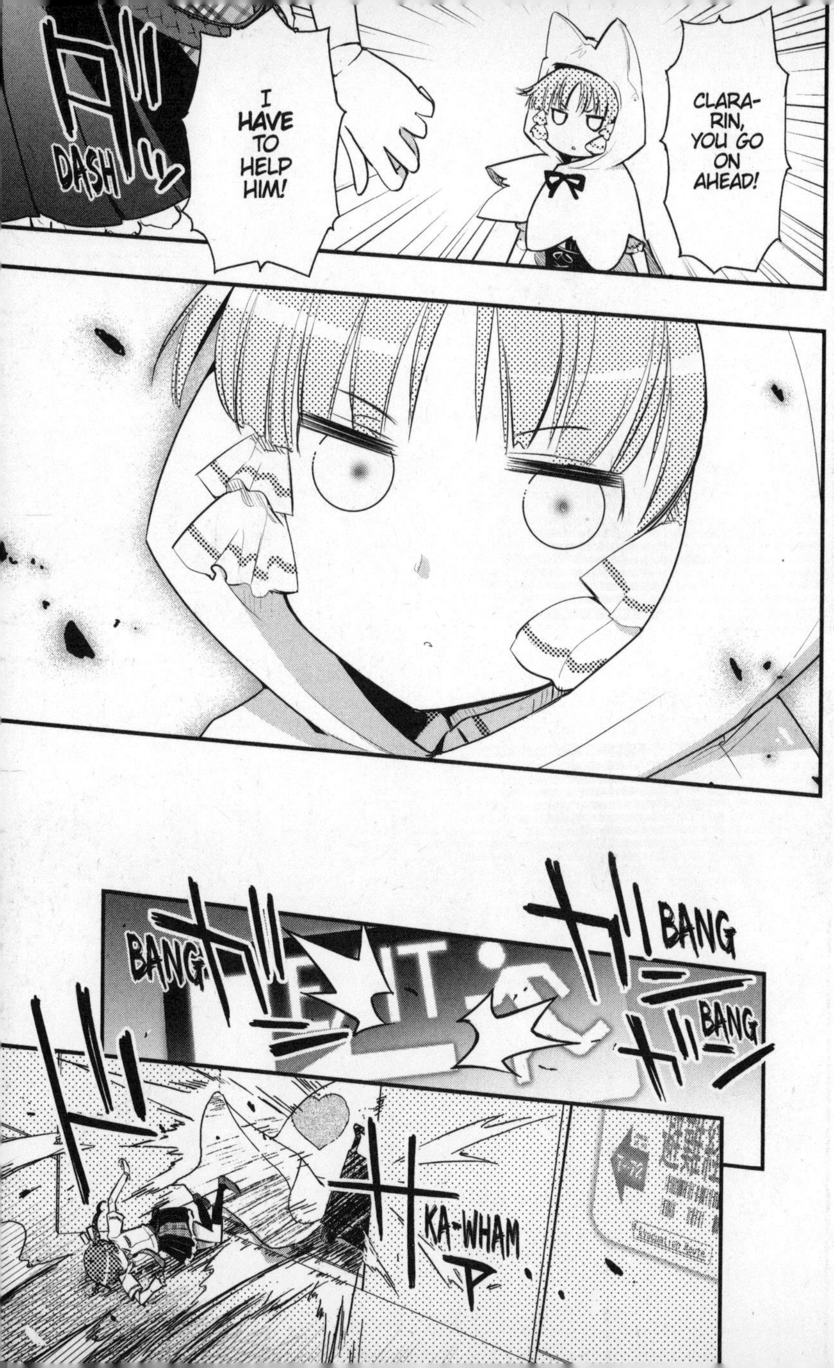
CLARA-RIN, YOU GO ON AHEAD!
I HAVE TO HELP HIM!
DASH
BANG
BANG
BANG
KA-WHAM

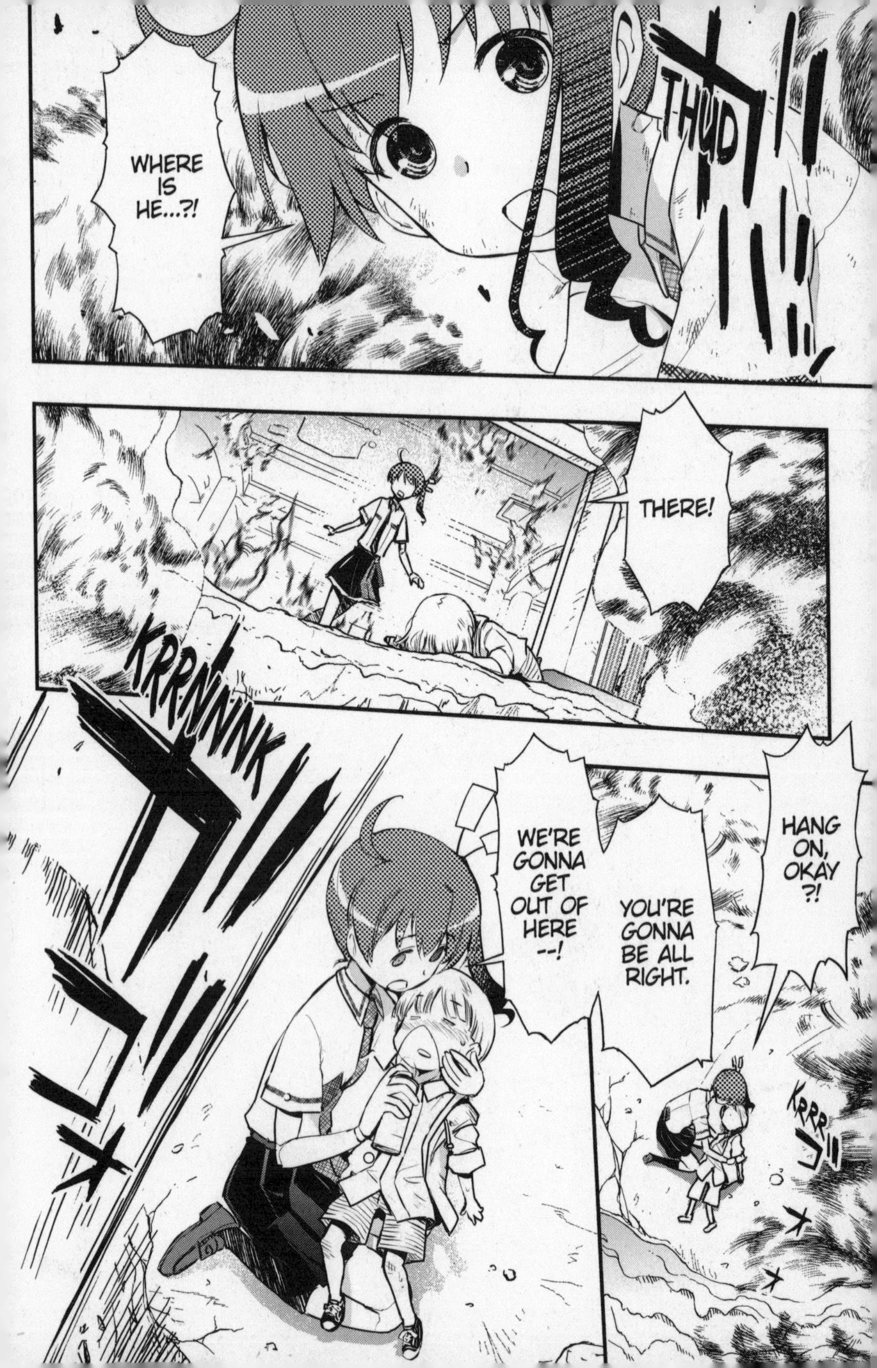
THUD
WHERE IS HE...?!
THERE!
HANG ON, OKAY?!
KRRR
YOU'RE GONNA BE ALL RIGHT.
WE'RE GONNA GET OUT OF HERE --!
KRRNNNNK

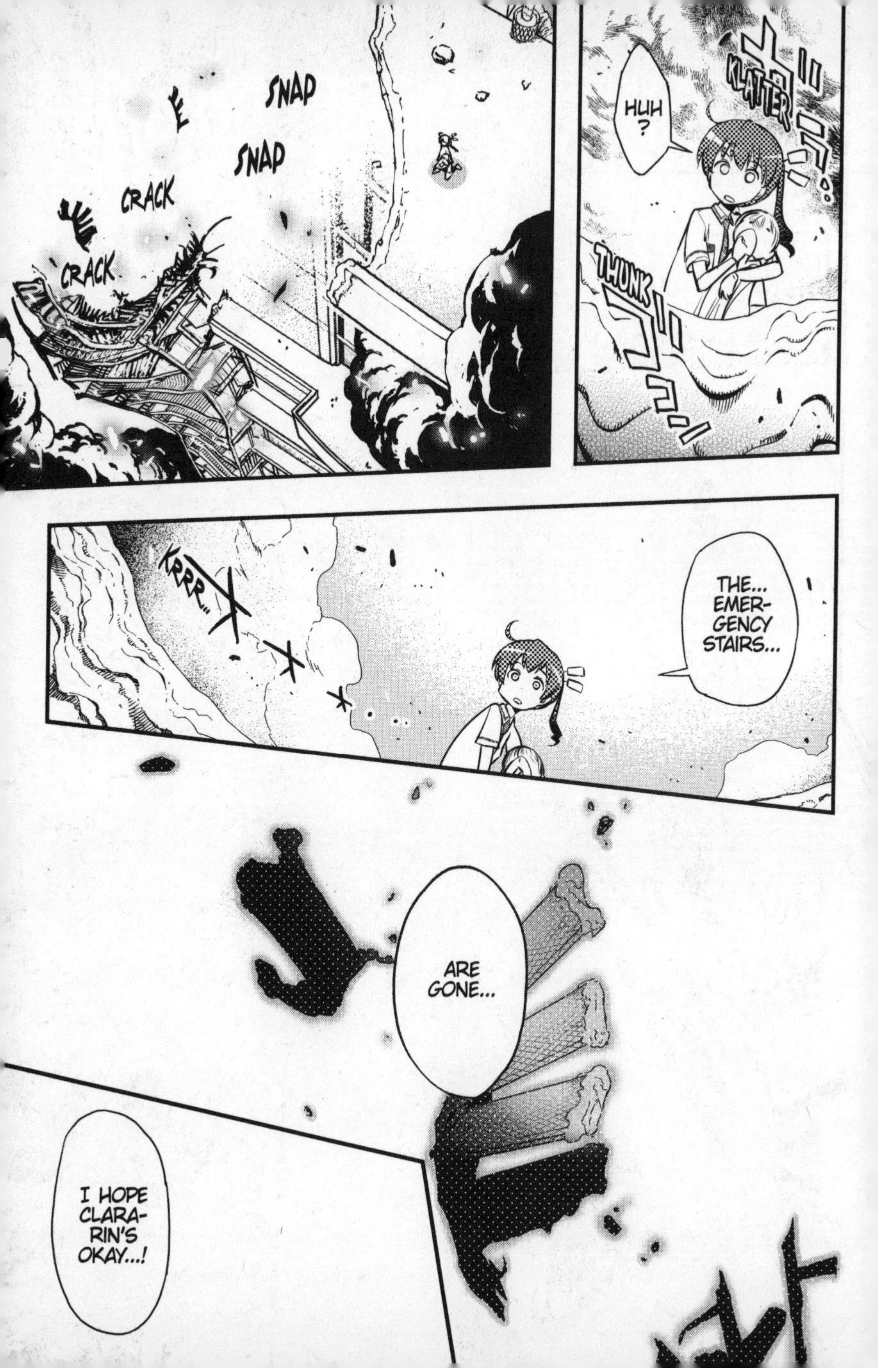
KLATTER
HUH?
THUNK
SNAP
SNAP
CRACK
CRACK
KRRR...
THE... EMER-GENCY STAIRS...
ARE GONE...
I HOPE CLARA-RIN'S OKAY...!

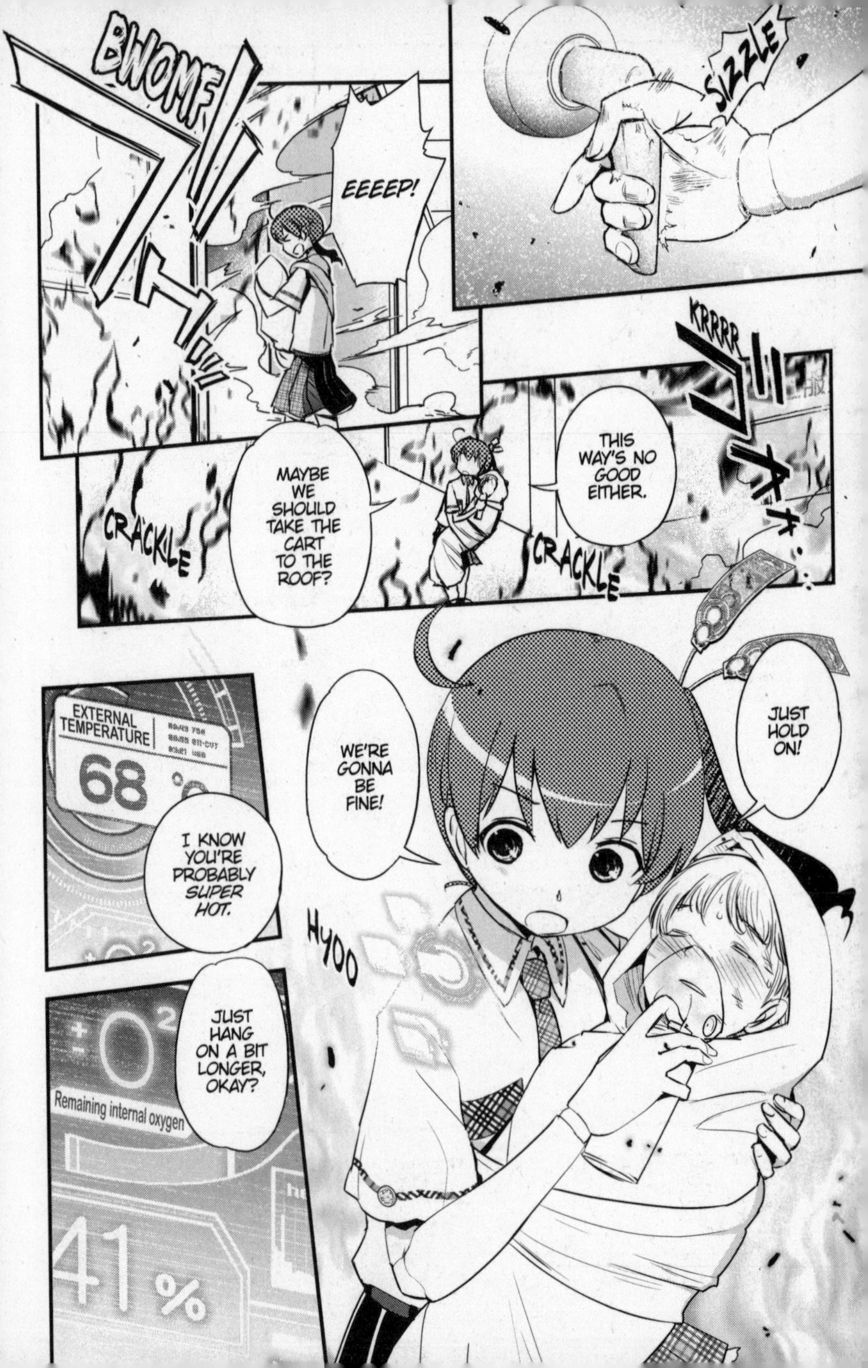
SIZZLE
BWOMF
EEEEP!
KRRRR
THIS WAY'S NO GOOD EITHER.
CRACKLE
MAYBE WE SHOULD TAKE THE CART TO THE ROOF?
CRACKLE
JUST HOLD ON!
WE'RE GONNA BE FINE!
HYOO
I KNOW YOU'RE PROBABLY SUPER HOT.
JUST HANG ON A BIT LONGER, OKAY?
EXTERNAL TEMPERATURE
68 °
Remaining internal oxygen
41 %

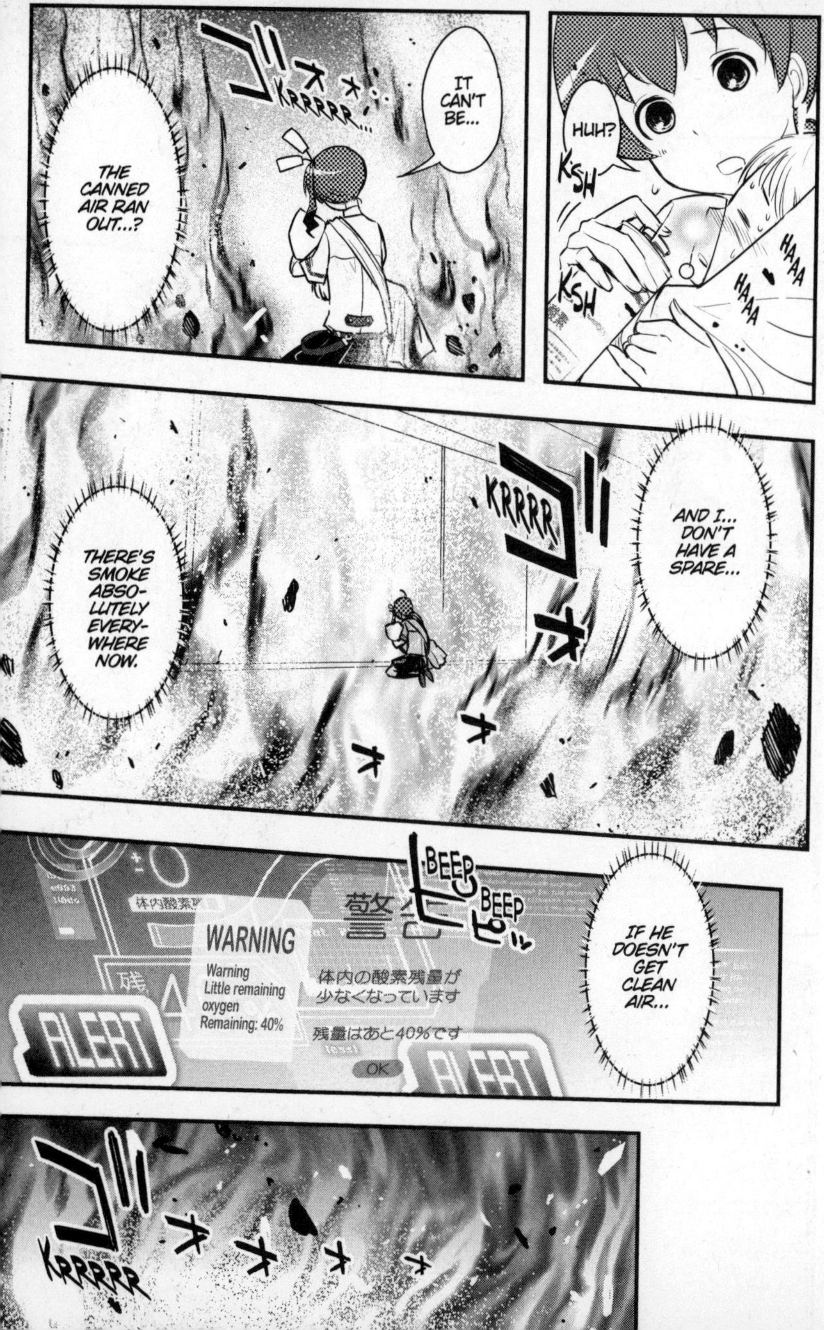
HUH?
K-SH
K-SH
HAAA
HAAA
IT CAN'T BE...
KRRRRR...
THE CANNED AIR RAN OUT...?
AND I... DON'T HAVE A SPARE...
KRRRR
THERE'S SMOKE ABSO-LUTELY EVERY-WHERE NOW.
IF HE DOESN'T GET CLEAN AIR...
BEEP
BEEP
警告
WARNING
Warning
Little remaining
oxygen
Remaining: 40%
体内の酸素残量が
少なくなっています
残量はあと40%です
OK
ALERT
ALERT
KRRRRR

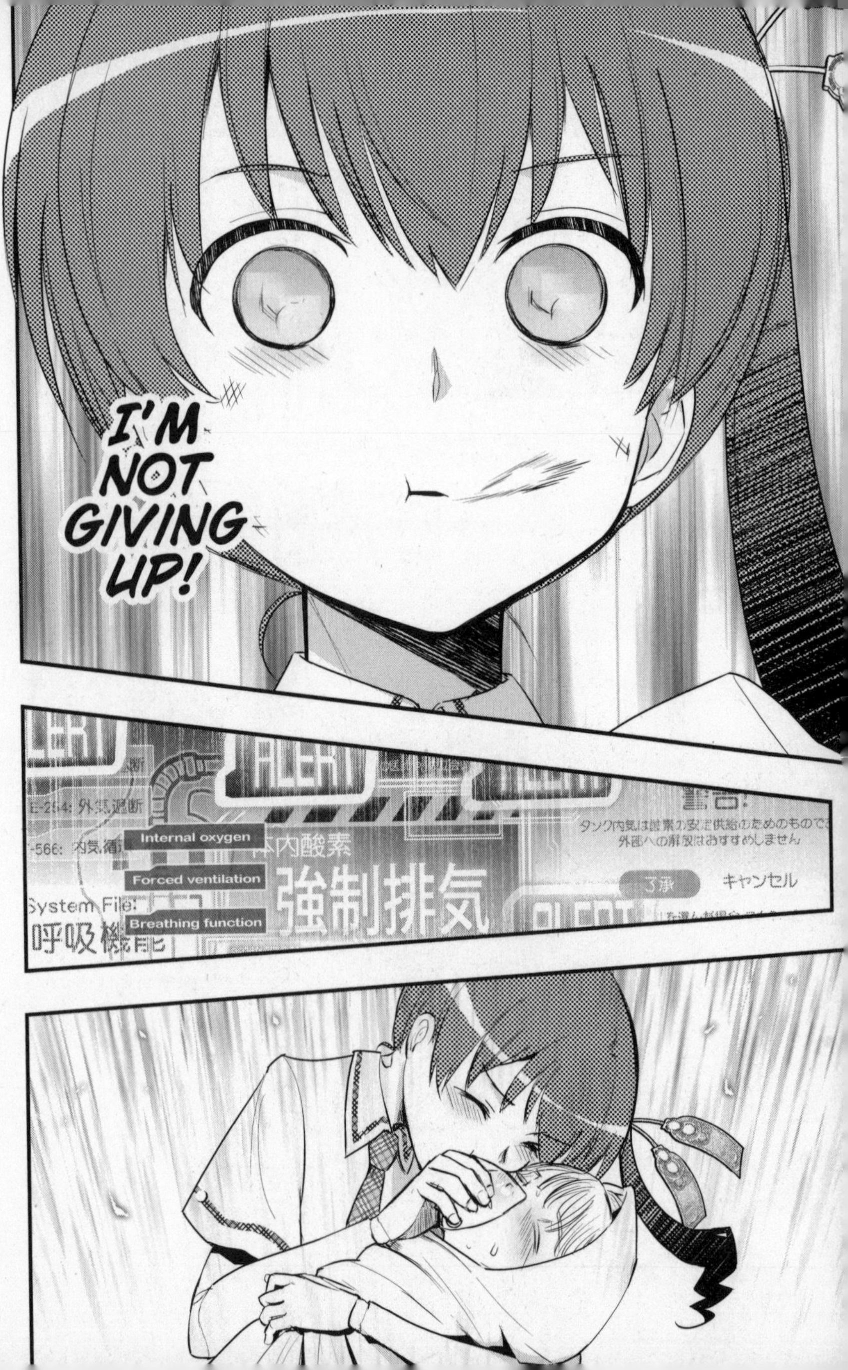
I'M NOT GIVING UP!
ALERT
Internal oxygen
Forced ventilation
強制排気
了承
キャンセル
System File:
呼吸機能
Breathing function

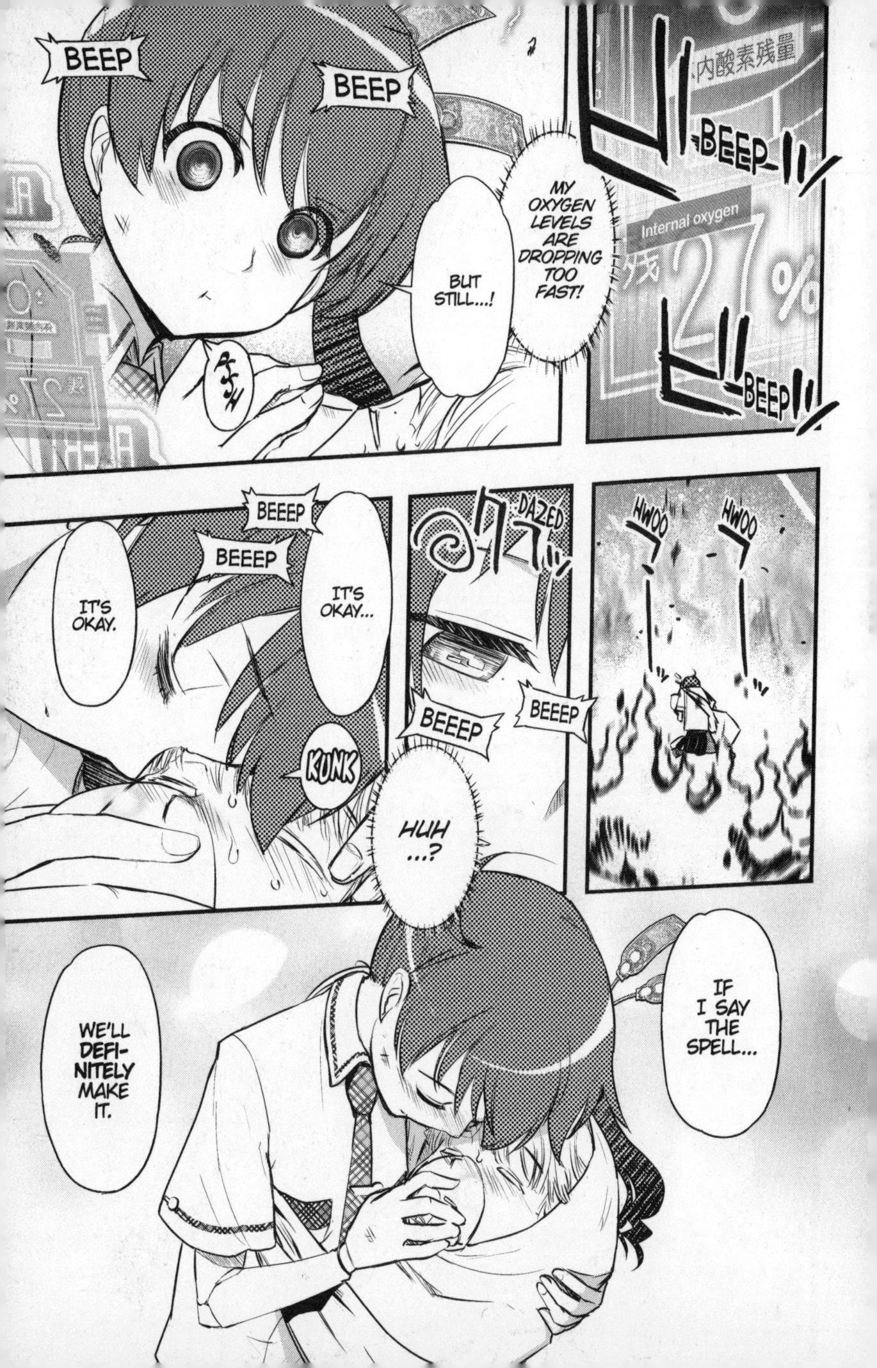
内酸素残量
BEEP
Internal oxygen
残27%
BEEP
MY OXYGEN LEVELS ARE DROPPING TOO FAST!
BUT STILL...!
BEEP
BEEP
HWOO
HWOO
DAZED
BEEEP
BEEEP
HUH ...?
BEEEP
BEEEP
IT'S OKAY...
IT'S OKAY.
KUNK
IF I SAY THE SPELL...
WE'LL DEFI-NITELY MAKE IT.

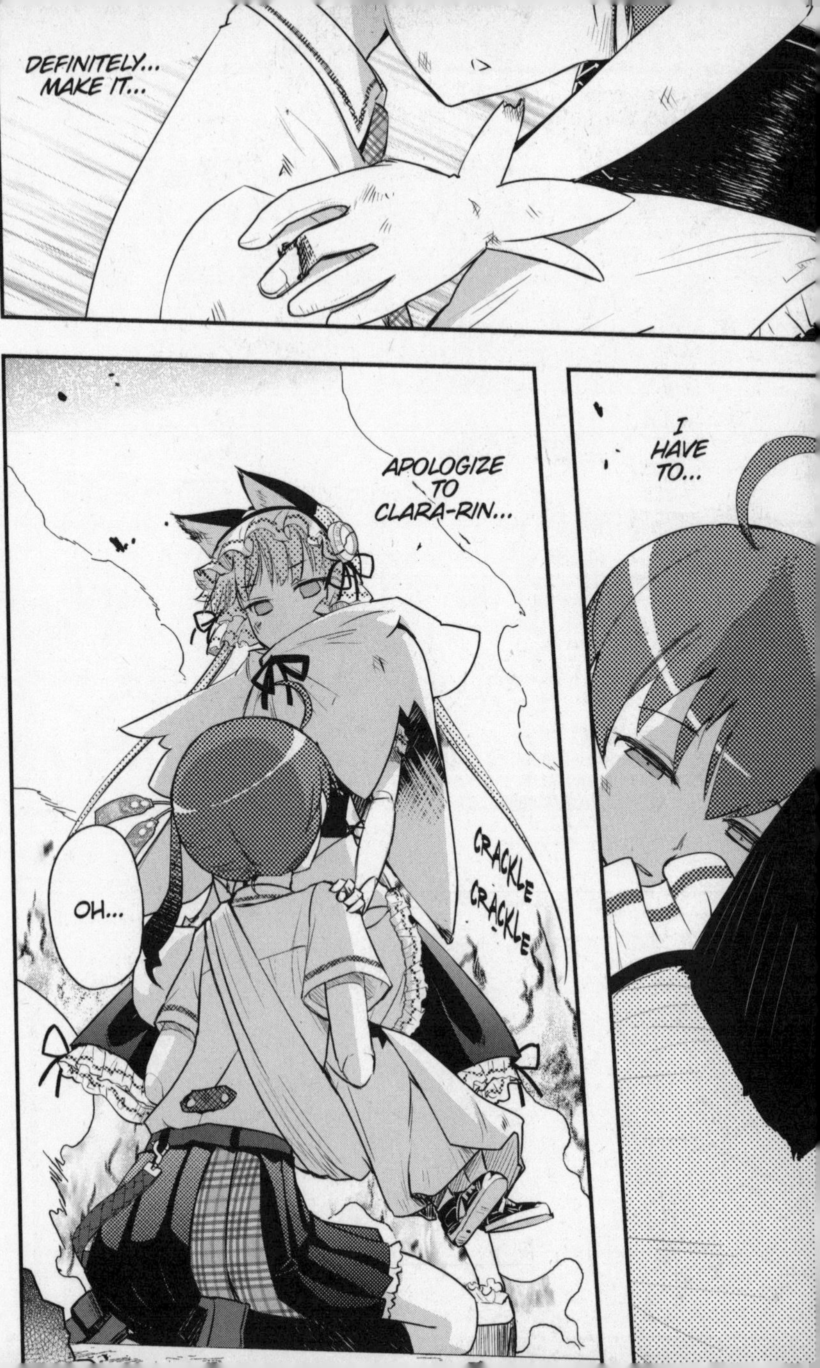
DEFINITELY... MAKE IT...
I HAVE TO...
APOLOGIZE TO CLARA-RIN...
CRACKLE CRACKLE
OH...

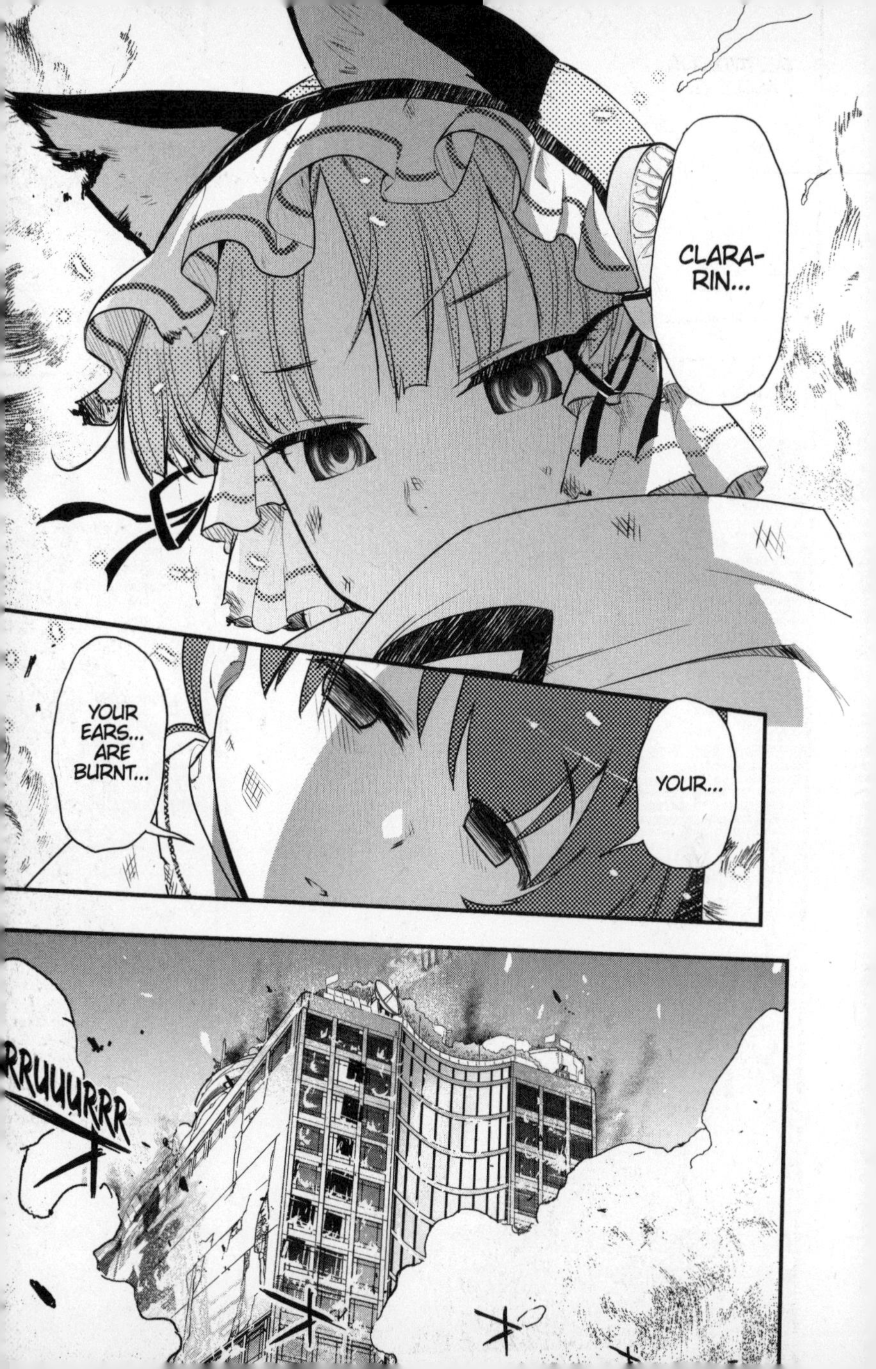
CLARA-RIN...
YOUR...
YOUR EARS... ARE BURNT...
RRUUURRR

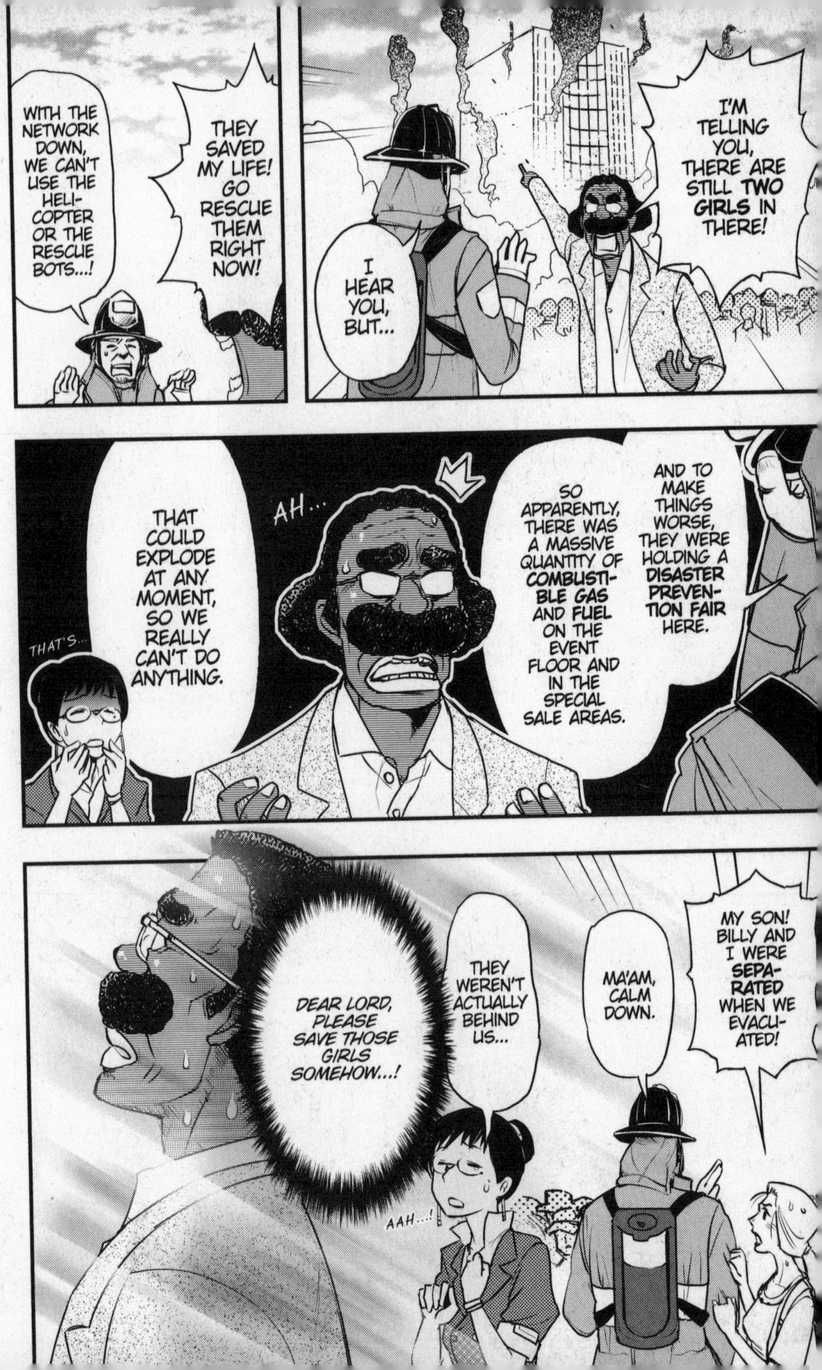
I'M TELLING YOU, THERE ARE STILL TWO GIRLS IN THERE!
I HEAR YOU, BUT...
THEY SAVED MY LIFE! GO RESCUE THEM RIGHT NOW!
WITH THE NETWORK DOWN, WE CAN'T USE THE HELI-COPTER OR THE RESCUE BOTS...!
SO APPARENTLY, THERE WAS A MASSIVE QUANTITY OF COMBUSTI-BLE GAS AND FUEL ON THE EVENT FLOOR AND IN THE SPECIAL SALE AREAS.
AND TO MAKE THINGS WORSE, THEY WERE HOLDING A DISASTER PREVEN-TION FAIR HERE.
AH...
THAT COULD EXPLODE AT ANY MOMENT, SO WE REALLY CAN'T DO ANYTHING.
THAT'S...
MY SON! BILLY AND I WERE SEPA-RATED WHEN WE EVACU-ATED!
MA'AM, CALM DOWN.
THEY WEREN'T ACTUALLY BEHIND US...
DEAR LORD, PLEASE SAVE THOSE GIRLS SOMEHOW...!
AAH...!

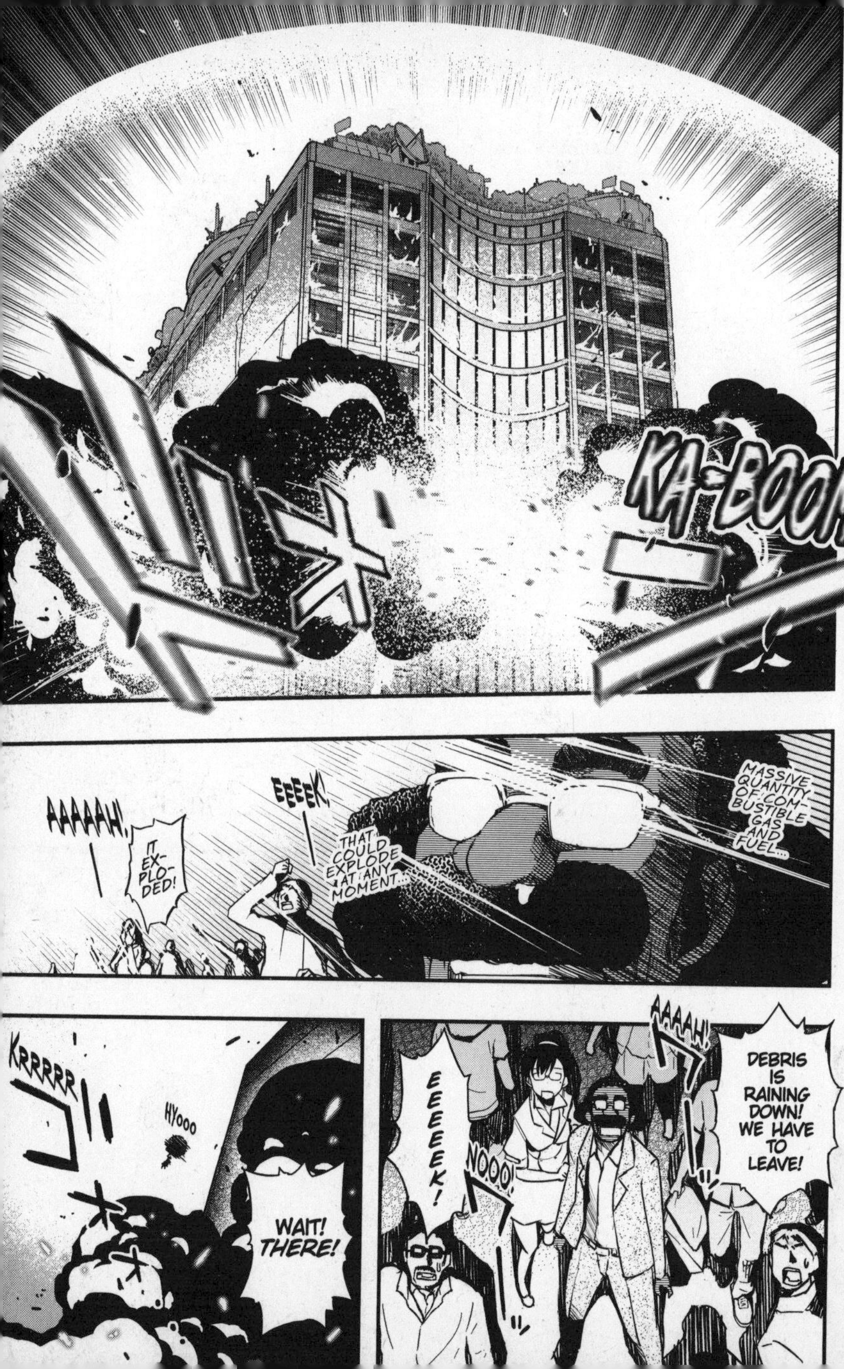
KA-BOOM
MASSIVE QUANTITY OF COM-BUSTIBLE GAS AND FUEL...
THAT COULD EXPLODE AT ANY MOMENT...
EEEEK!
IT EX-PLO-DED!
AAAAAH!
AAAAH!
DEBRIS IS RAINING DOWN! WE HAVE TO LEAVE!
EEEEEK!
NOOO!
KRRRRR
HYOOO
WAIT! THERE!

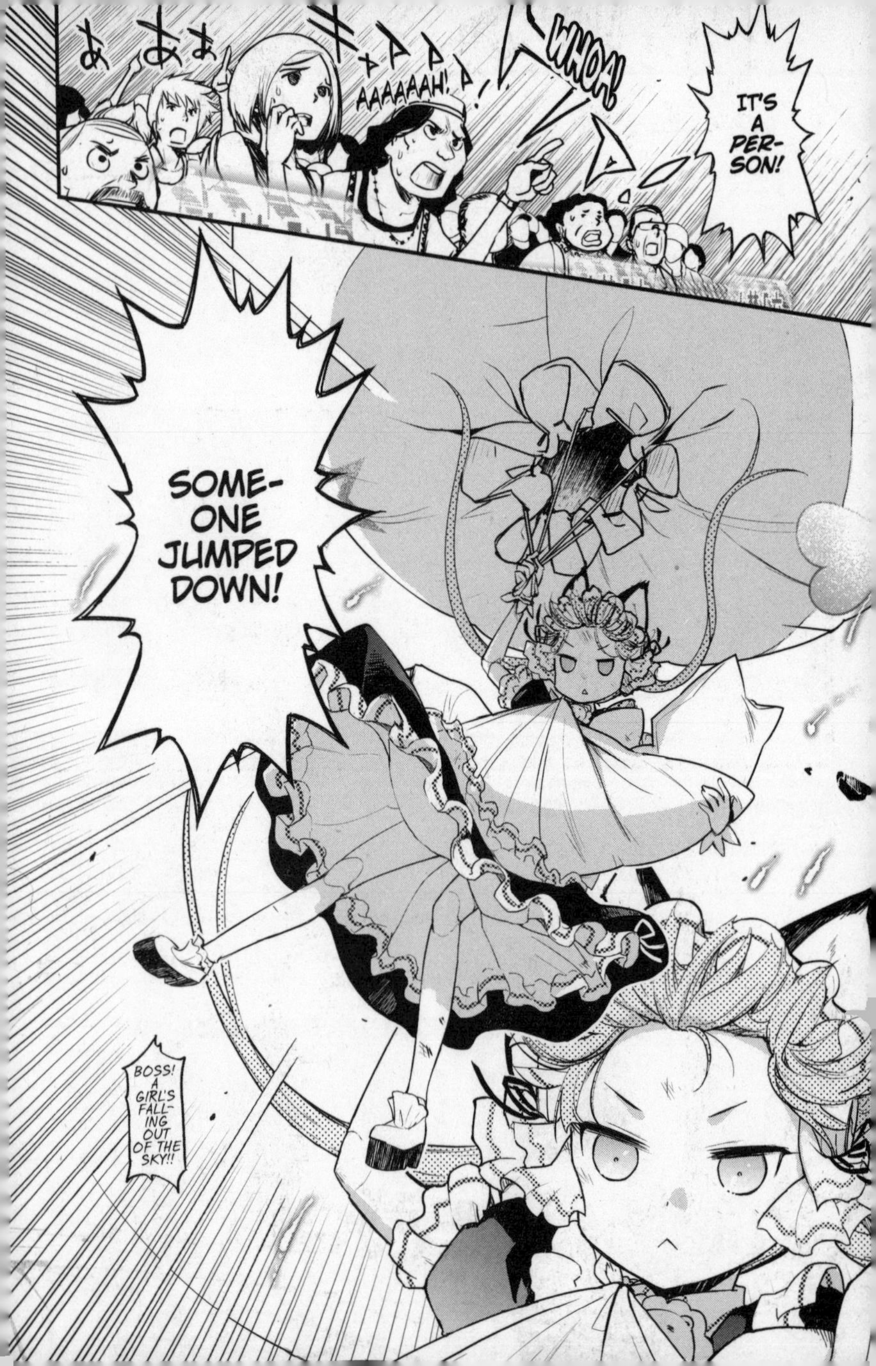
IT'S A PER-SON!
WHOA!
AAAAAAH!
SOME-ONE JUMPED DOWN!
BOSS! A GIRL'S FALL-ING OUT OF THE SKY!!

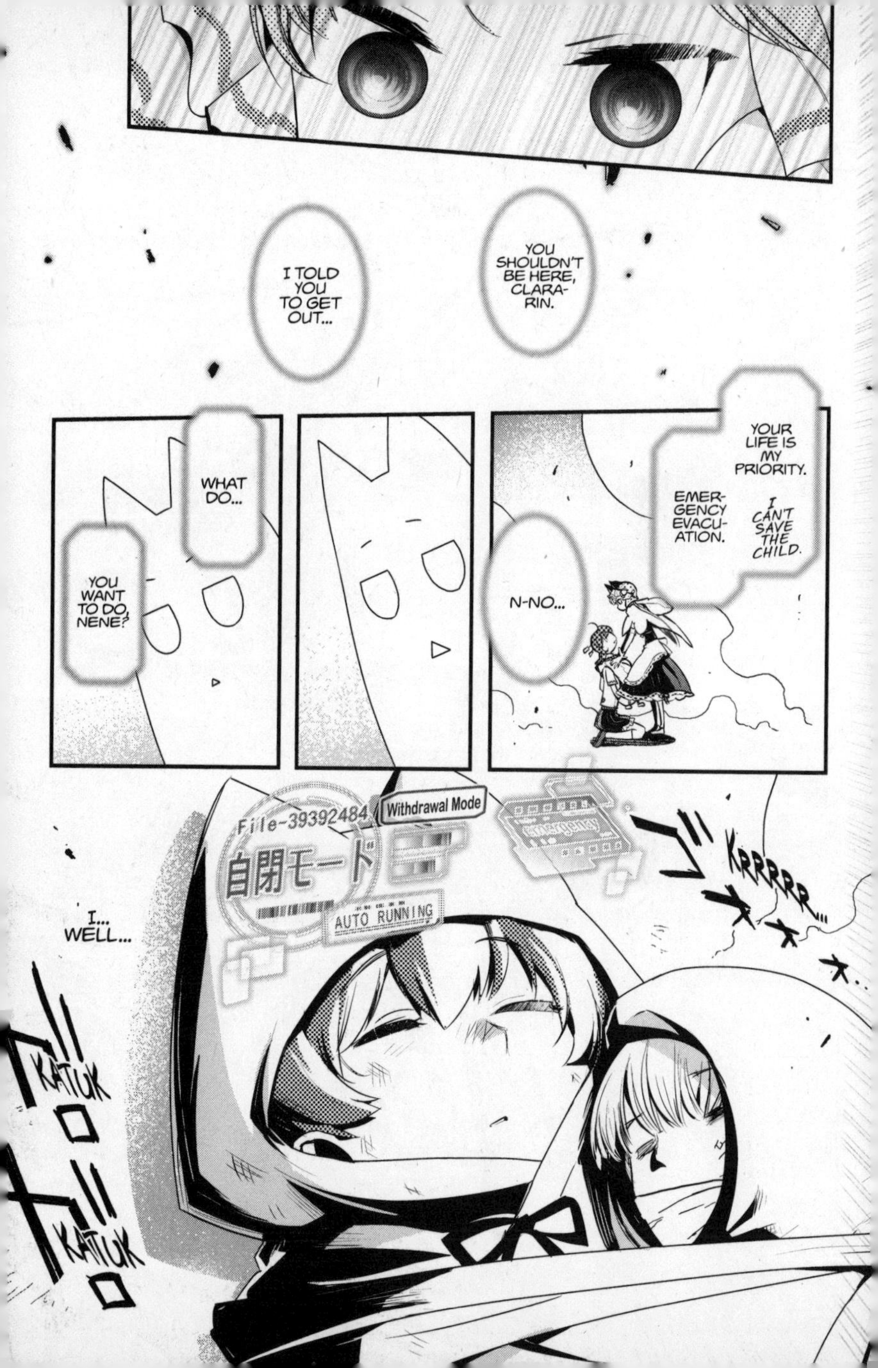
YOU SHOULDN'T BE HERE, CLARA-RIN.
I TOLD YOU TO GET OUT...
YOUR LIFE IS MY PRIORITY.
I CAN'T SAVE THE CHILD.
EMERGENCY EVACUATION.
N-NO...
WHAT DO...
YOU WANT TO DO, NENE?
KRRRRR...
File-39392484
Withdrawal Mode
自閉モード
AUTO RUNNING
I... WELL...
KATUK
KATUK

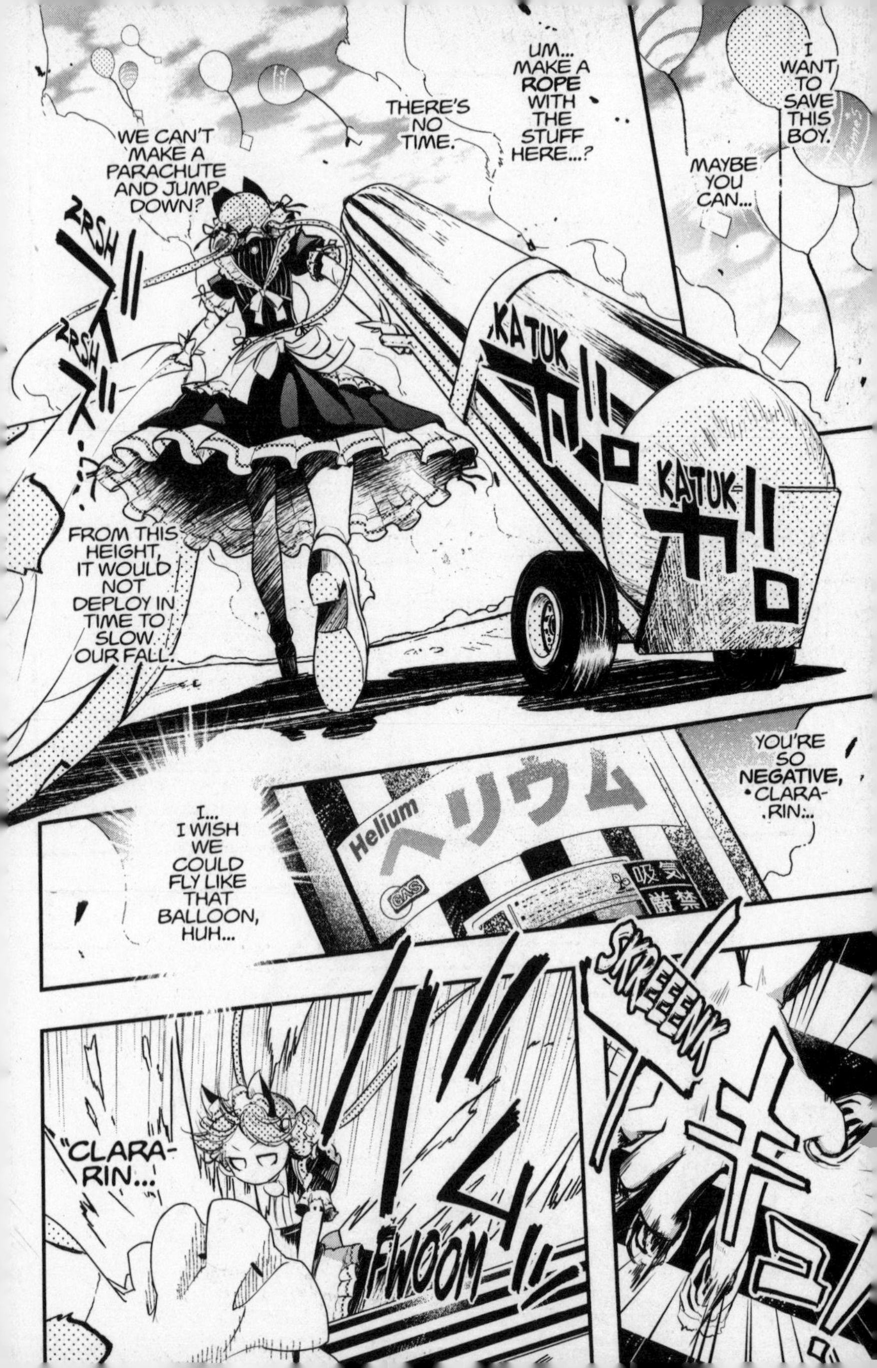
I WANT TO SAVE THIS BOY.
MAYBE YOU CAN...
UM... MAKE A ROPE WITH THE STUFF HERE...?
THERE'S NO TIME.
WE CAN'T MAKE A PARACHUTE AND JUMP DOWN?
ZRSH
ZRSH
KATUK
KATUK
FROM THIS HEIGHT, IT WOULD NOT DEPLOY IN TIME TO SLOW OUR FALL.
YOU'RE SO NEGATIVE, CLARA-RIN...
Helium
ヘリウム
GAS
I... I WISH WE COULD FLY LIKE THAT BALLOON, HUH...
SKREEEENK
FWOOM
"CLARA-RIN...!"

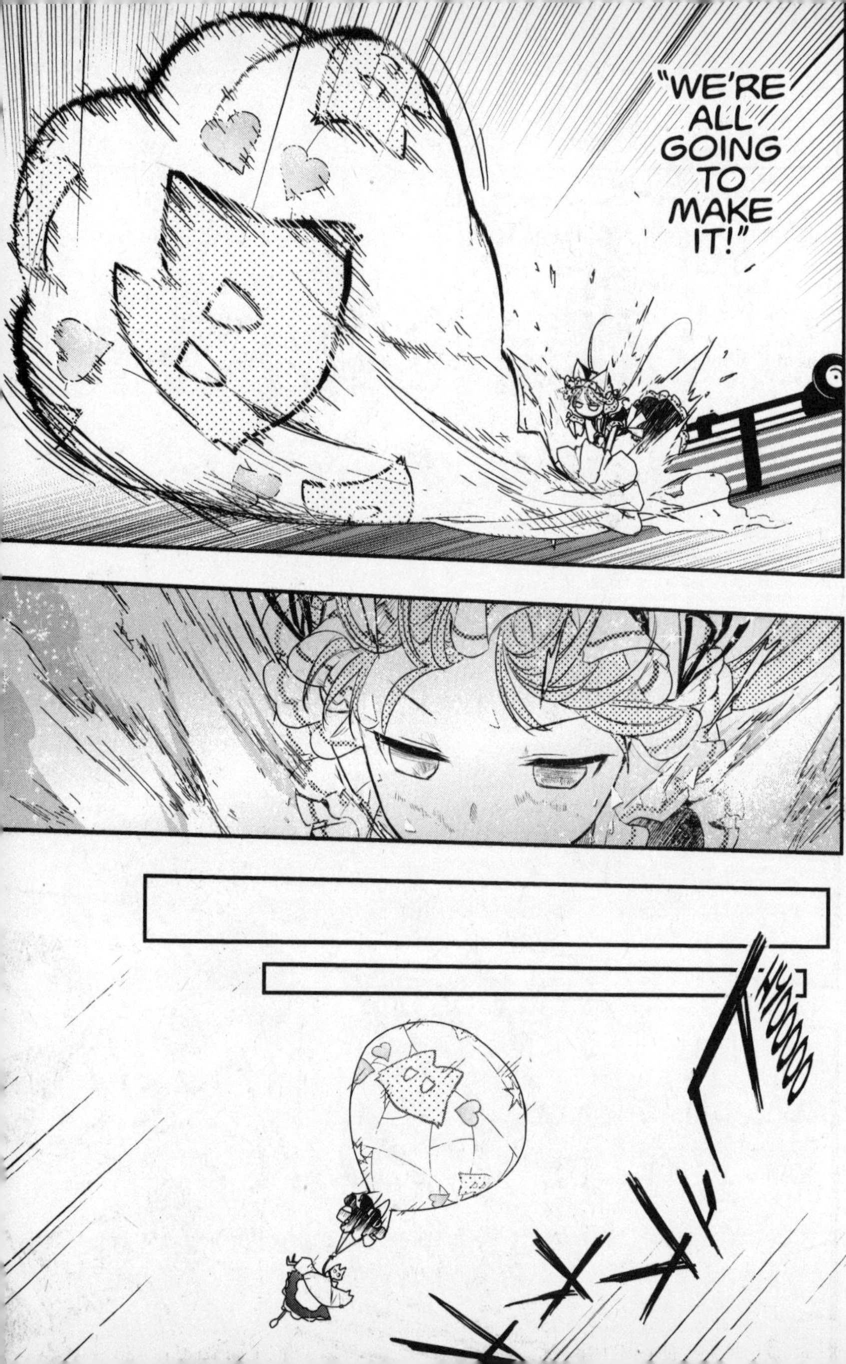
"WE'RE ALL GOING TO MAKE IT!"
HYOOOOO

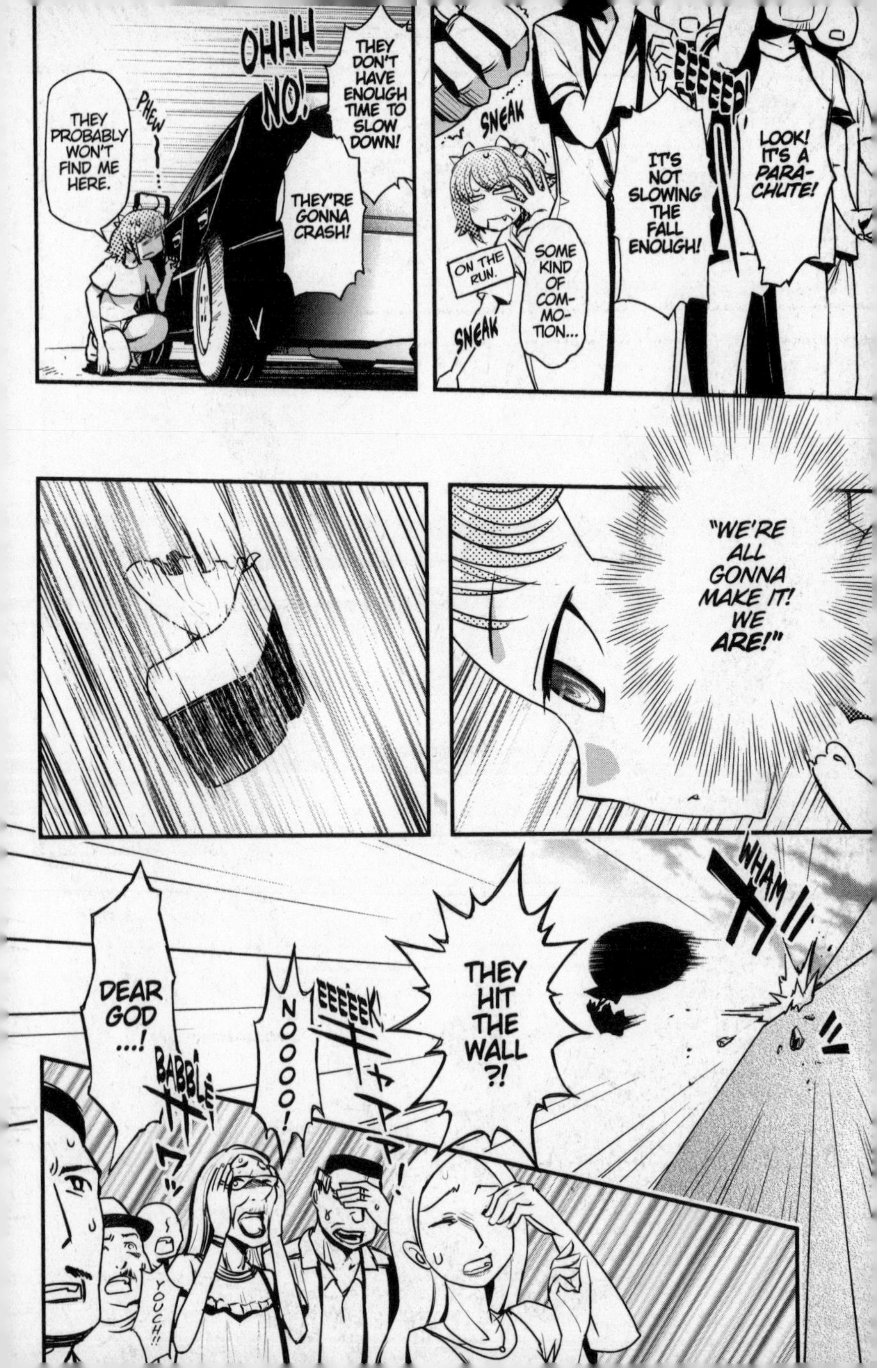
LOOK! IT'S A PARA-CHUTE!
EEEEEEP!
IT'S NOT SLOWING THE FALL ENOUGH!
SNEAK
SOME KIND OF COM-MO-TION...
ON THE RUN.
SNEAK
THEY DON'T HAVE ENOUGH TIME TO SLOW DOWN!
OHHH NO!
THEY'RE GONNA CRASH!
PHEW...
THEY PROBABLY WON'T FIND ME HERE.
"WE'RE ALL GONNA MAKE IT! WE ARE!"
WHAM!!
THEY HIT THE WALL?!
EEEEEK!
NOOOOO!
DEAR GOD ...!
BABBLE
YOUCH!!

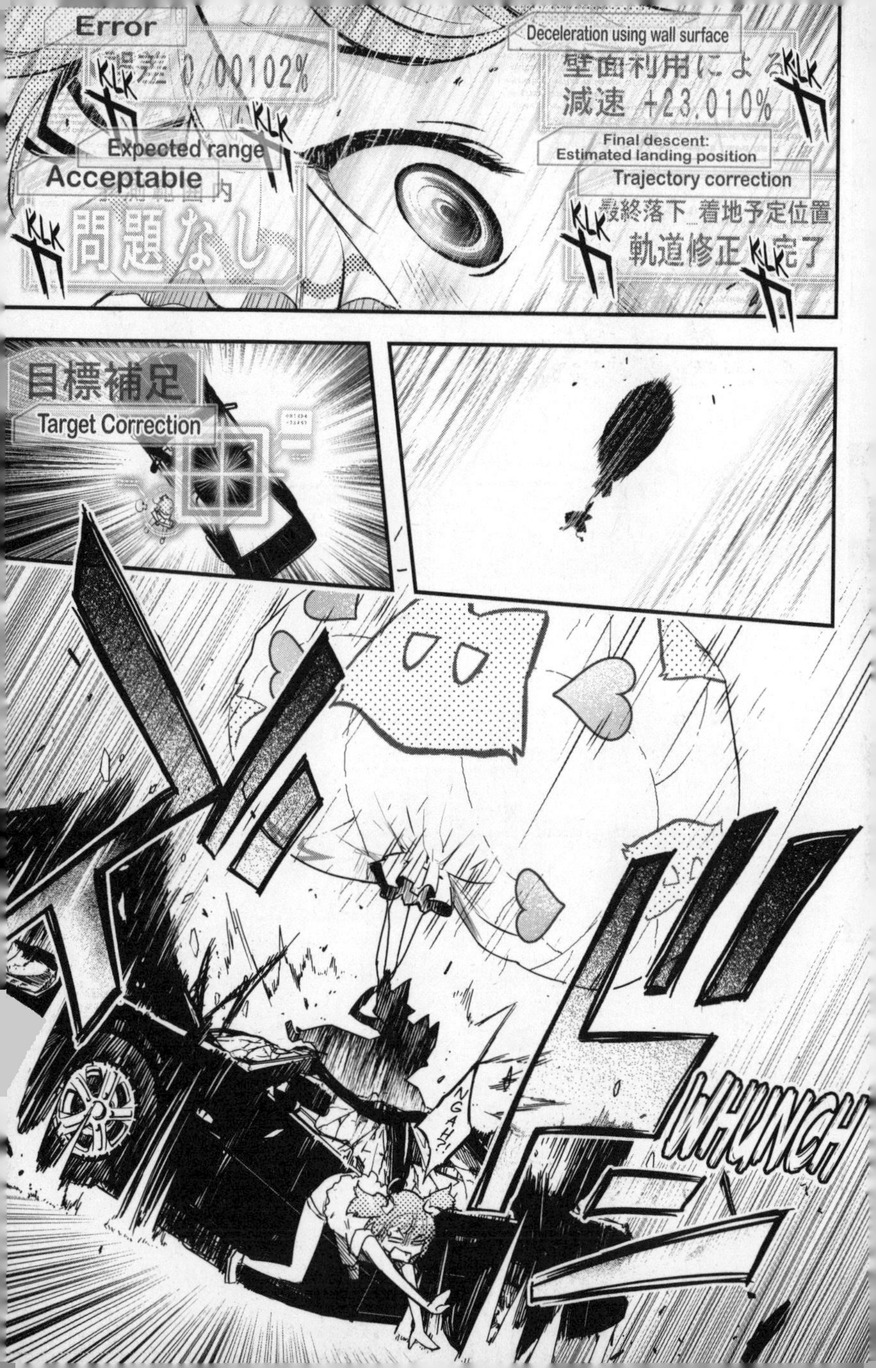
Deceleration using wall surface
壁面利用による減速 +23.010%
KLK
Final descent: Estimated landing position
Trajectory correction
KLK
最終落下 着地予定位置
軌道修正完了
KLK
Error
誤差 0.00102%
KLK
KLK
Expected range
Acceptable
KLK
問題なし
目標補足
Target Correction
NGAH!?
WHUNCH

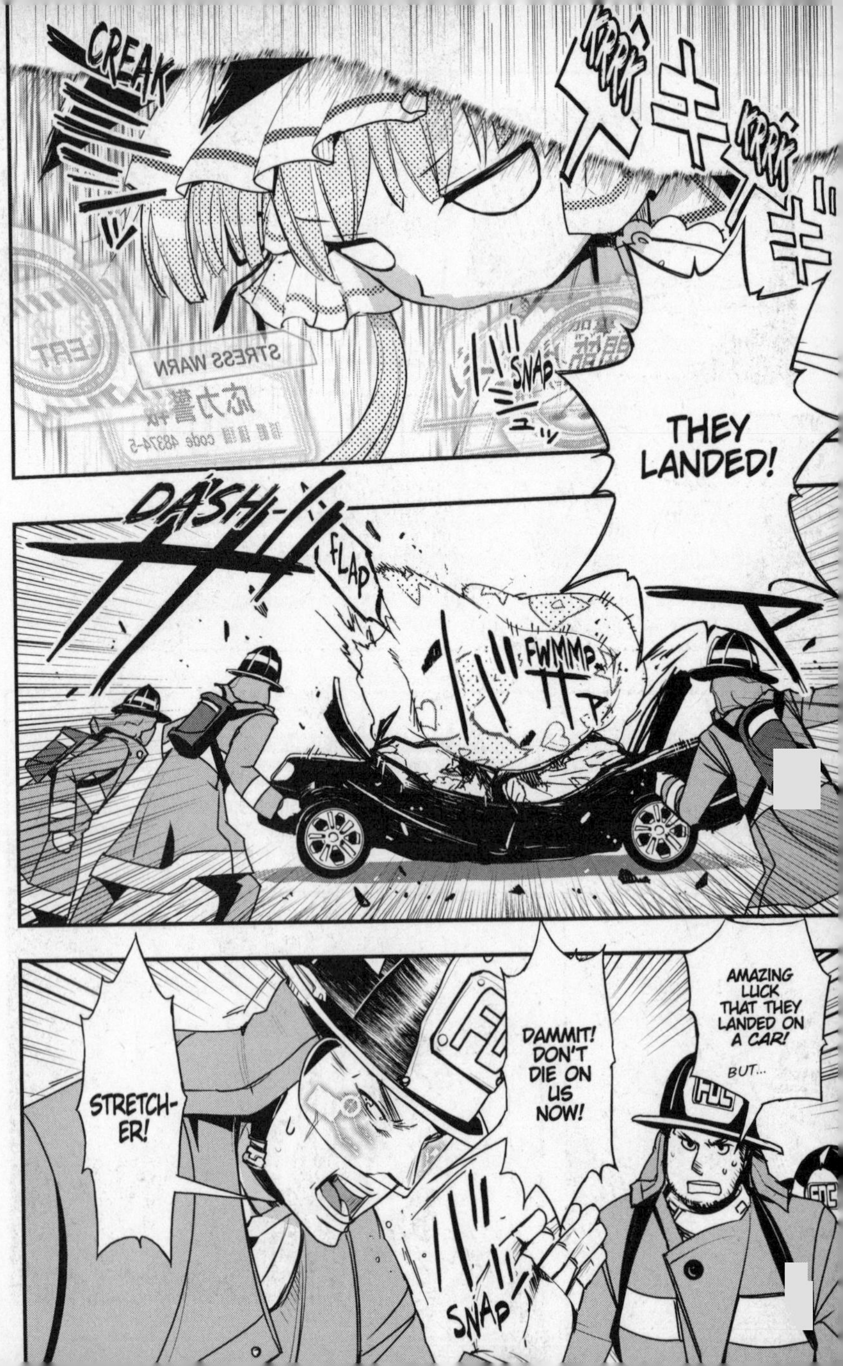
KRRRK
KRRRK
CREAK
STRESS WARN
SNAP
THEY LANDED!
DASH
FLAP
FWMMP
AMAZING LUCK THAT THEY LANDED ON A CAR!
BUT...
DAMMIT! DON'T DIE ON US NOW!
STRETCH-
ER!
SNAP

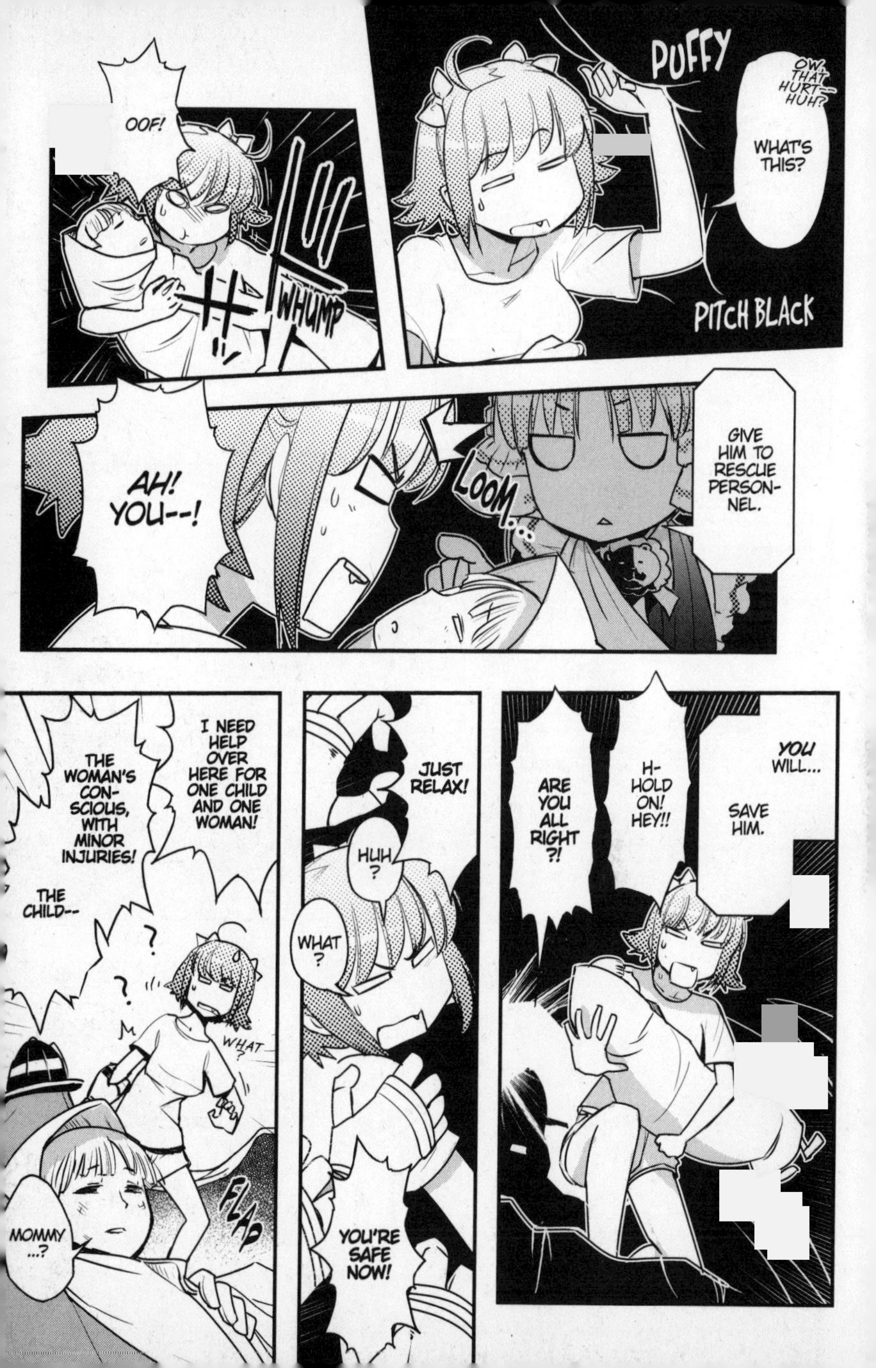
PUFFY
OW, THAT HURT— HUH?
WHAT'S THIS?
PITCH BLACK
OOF!
WHUMP
GIVE HIM TO RESCUE PERSON-NEL.
LOOM...
AH! YOU--!
YOU WILL...
SAVE HIM.
H-HOLD ON! HEY!!
ARE YOU ALL RIGHT?!
JUST RELAX!
HUH?
WHAT?
YOU'RE SAFE NOW!
I NEED HELP OVER HERE FOR ONE CHILD AND ONE WOMAN!
THE WOMAN'S CON-SCIOUS, WITH MINOR INJURIES!
THE CHILD--
WHAT?
FLAP
MOMMY ...?

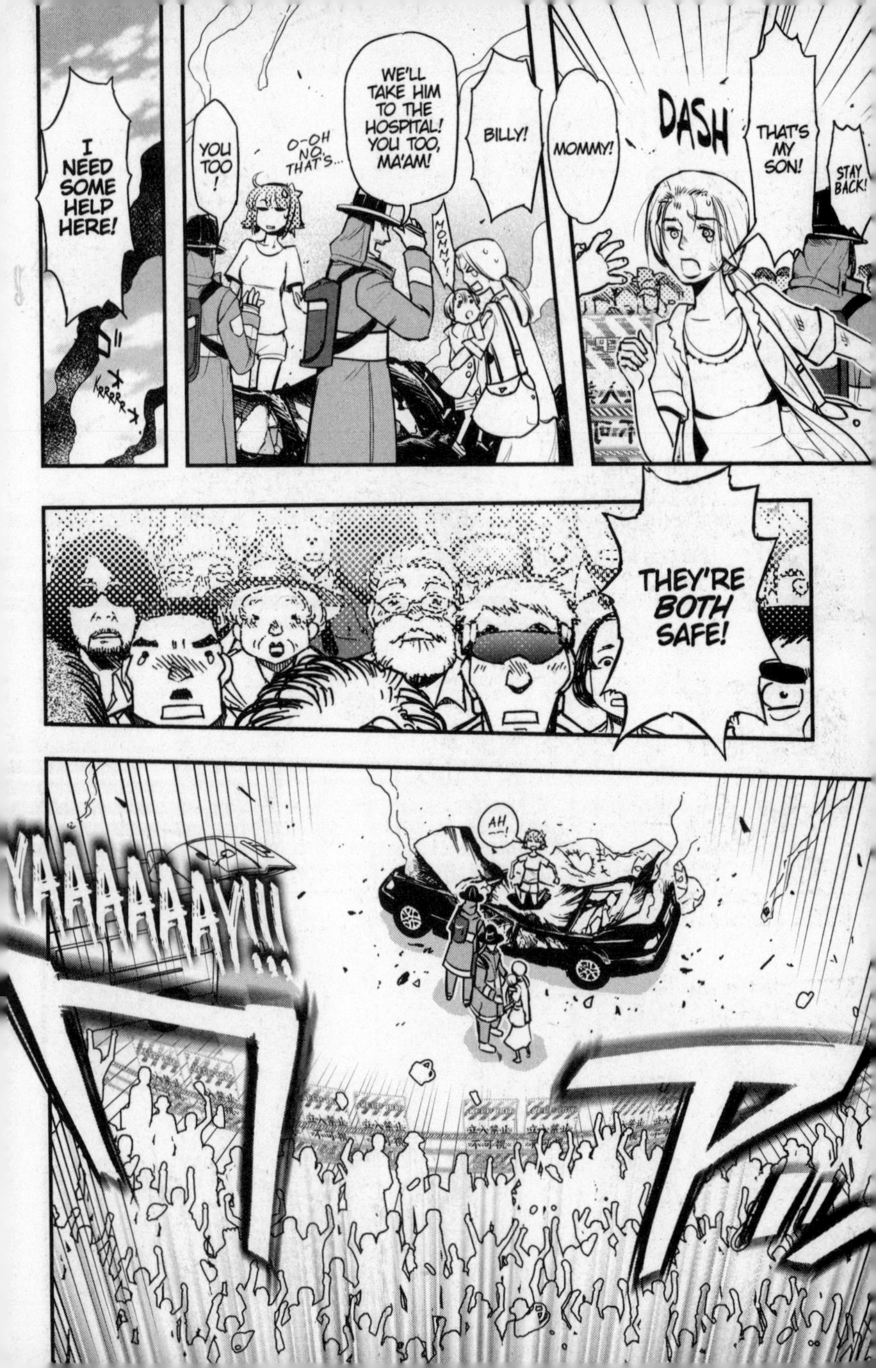
STAY BACK!
THAT'S MY SON!
DASH
MOMMY!
BILLY!
MOMMY!
WE'LL TAKE HIM TO THE HOSPITAL! YOU TOO, MA'AM!
O-OH NO, THAT'S...
YOU TOO!
I NEED SOME HELP HERE!
KRRRRR
THEY'RE BOTH SAFE!
AH!
YAAAAAAY!!!

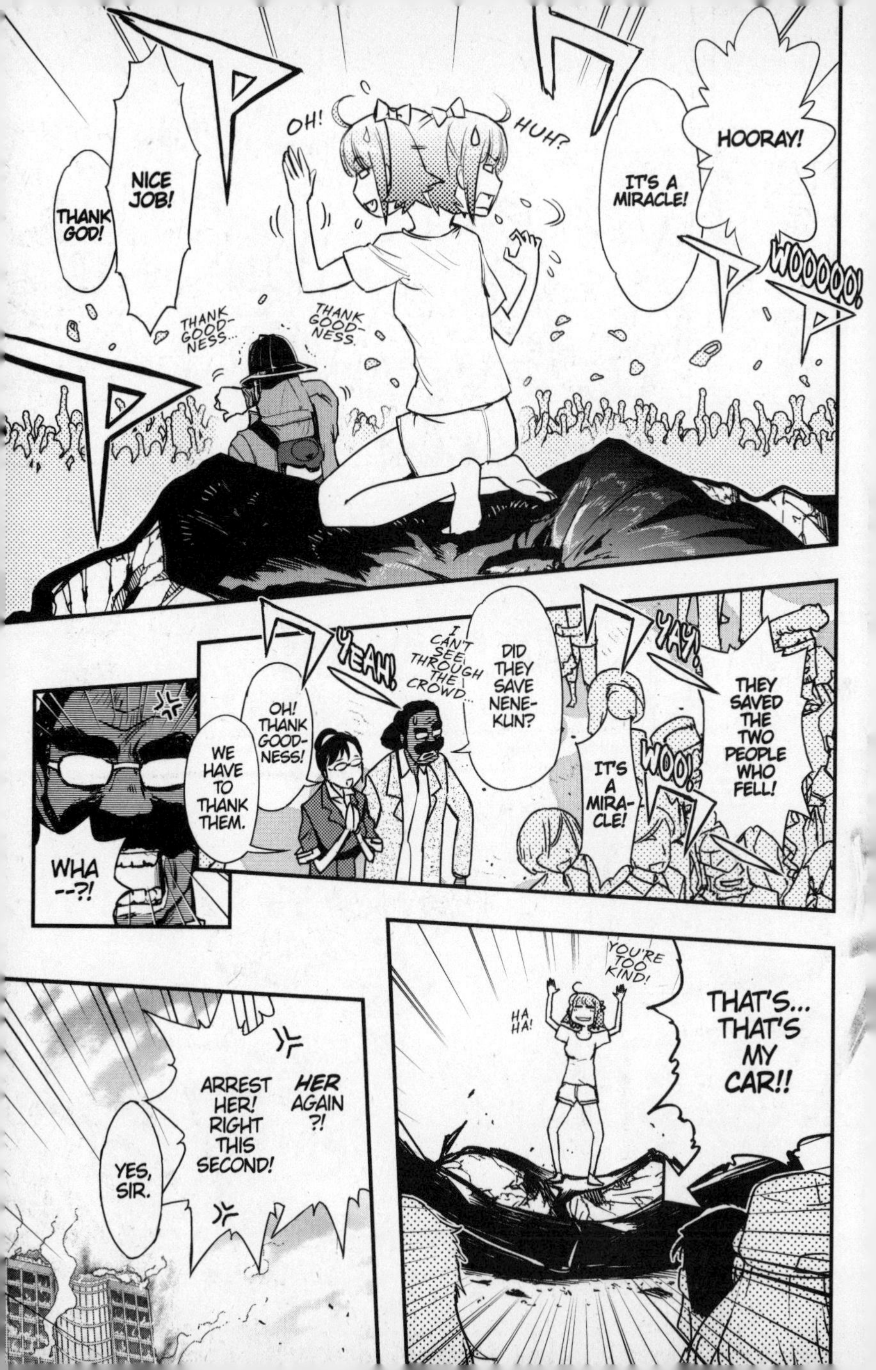
WOOOOO!
HOORAY!
IT'S A MIRACLE!
HUH?
OH!
THANK GOODNESS.
NICE JOB!
THANK GOD!
THANK GOODNESS...
YAY!
THEY SAVED THE TWO PEOPLE WHO FELL!
WOO!
IT'S A MIRACLE!
DID THEY SAVE NENE-KUN?
I CAN'T SEE THROUGH THE CROWD...
YEAH!
OH! THANK GOODNESS!
WE HAVE TO THANK THEM.
WHA--?!
THAT'S... THAT'S MY CAR!!
YOU'RE TOO KIND!
HA HA!
HER AGAIN?!
ARREST HER! RIGHT THIS SECOND!
YES, SIR.

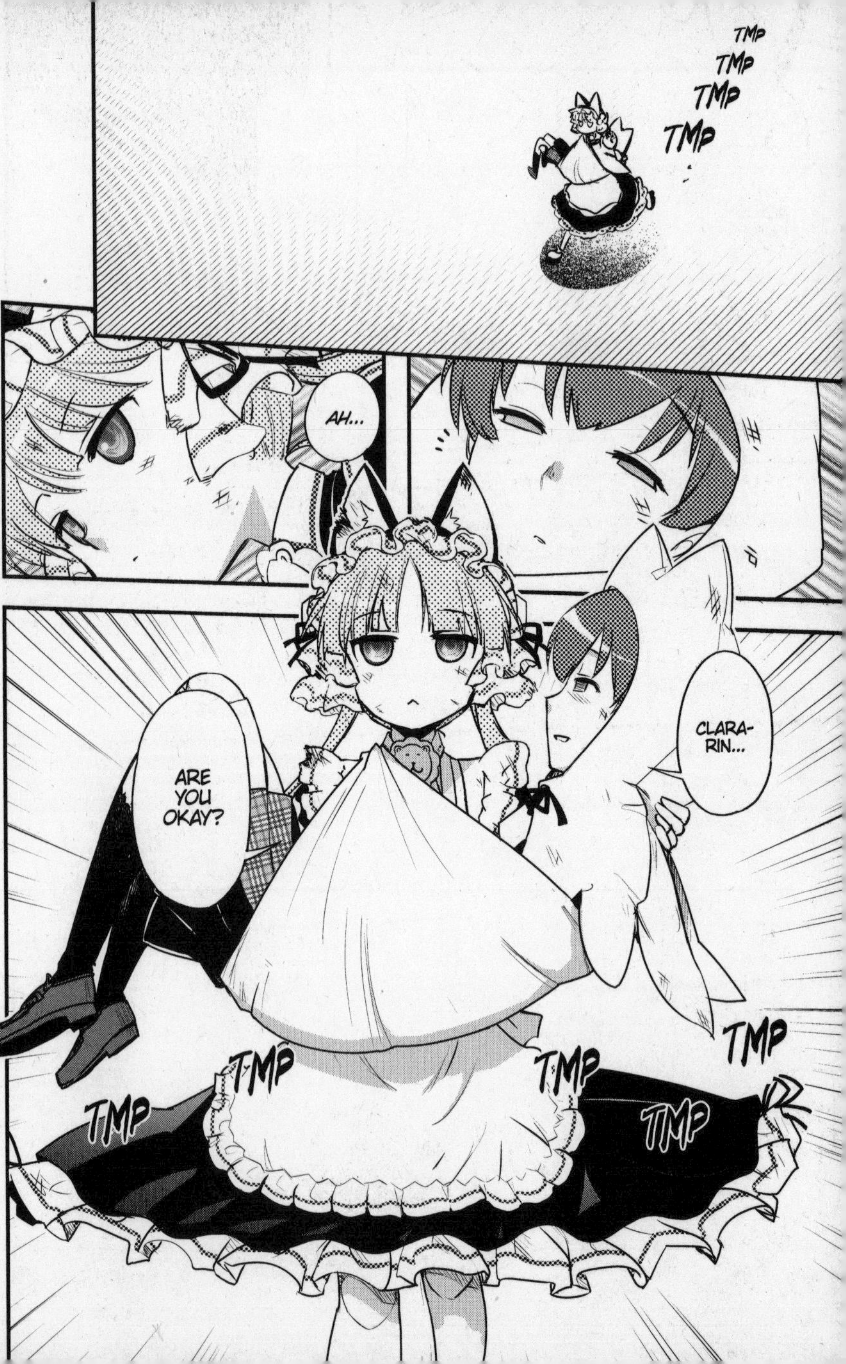
TMP
TMP
TMP
TMP
AH...
CLARA-RIN...
ARE YOU OKAY?
TMP
TMP
TMP
TMP
TMP

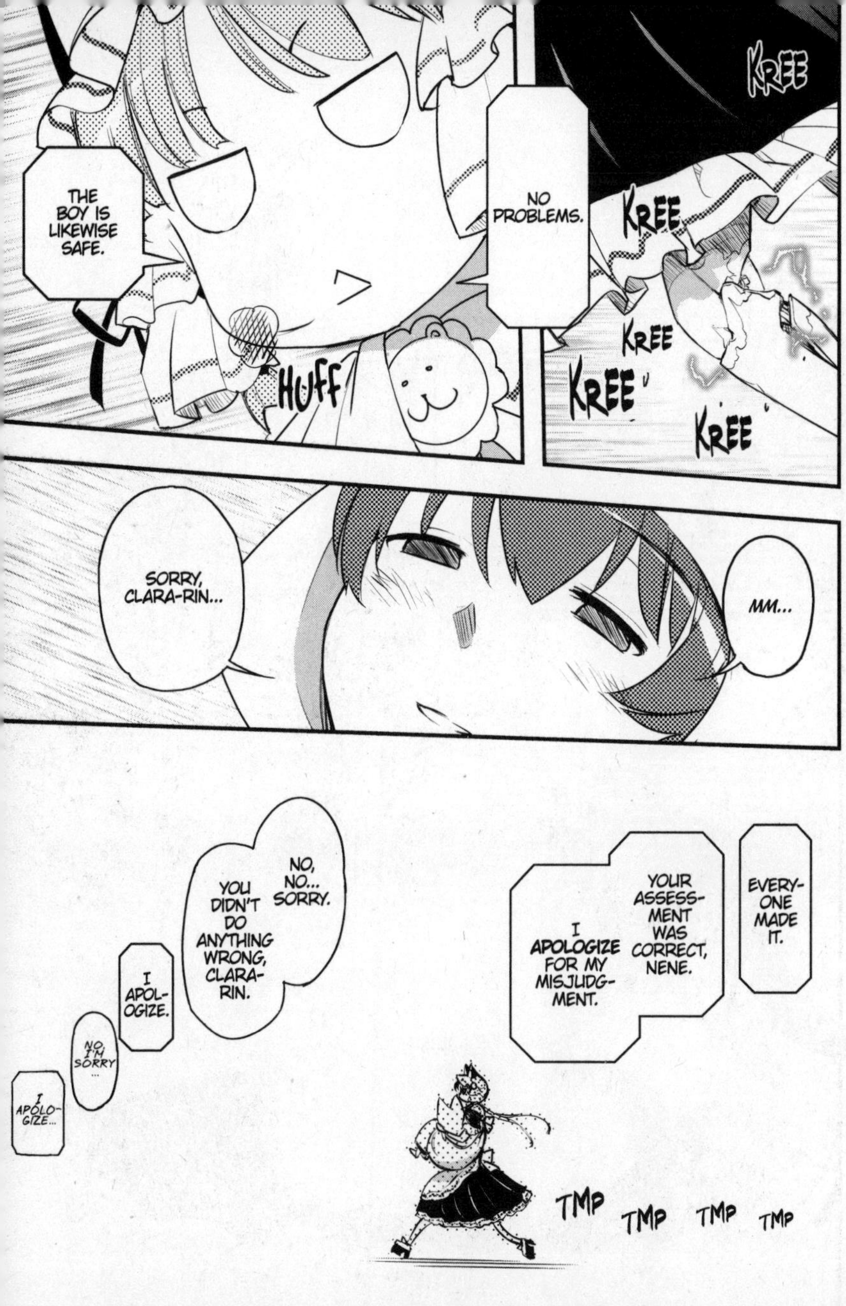
KREE
KREE
KREE
KREE
KREE
NO PROBLEMS.
THE BOY IS LIKEWISE SAFE.
HUFF
MM...
SORRY, CLARA-RIN...
EVERY-ONE MADE IT.
YOUR ASSESS-MENT WAS CORRECT, NENE.
I APOLOGIZE FOR MY MISJUDG-MENT.
NO, NO... SORRY.
YOU DIDN'T DO ANYTHING WRONG, CLARA-RIN.
I APOLO-GIZE.
NO, I'M SORRY...
I APOLO-GIZE...
TMP TMP TMP TMP

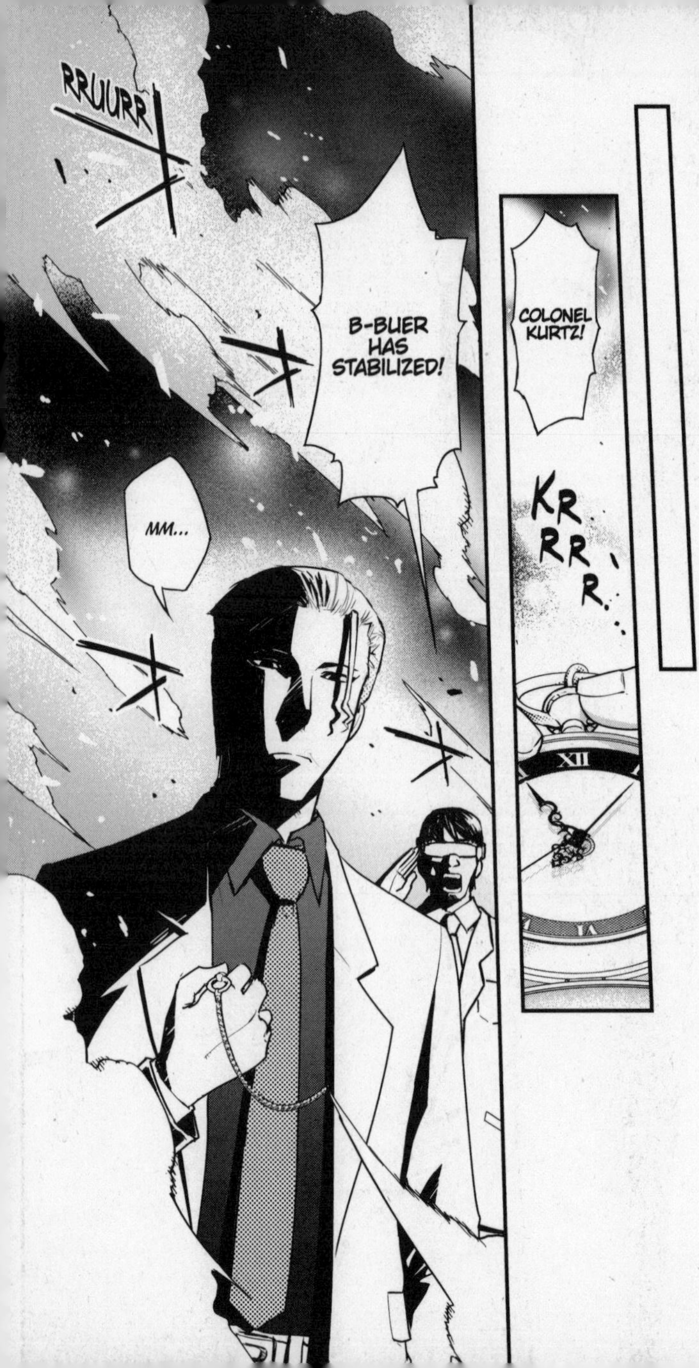
COLONEL KURTZ!
KRRRRR
B-BUER HAS STABILIZED!
RRUURR
MM...

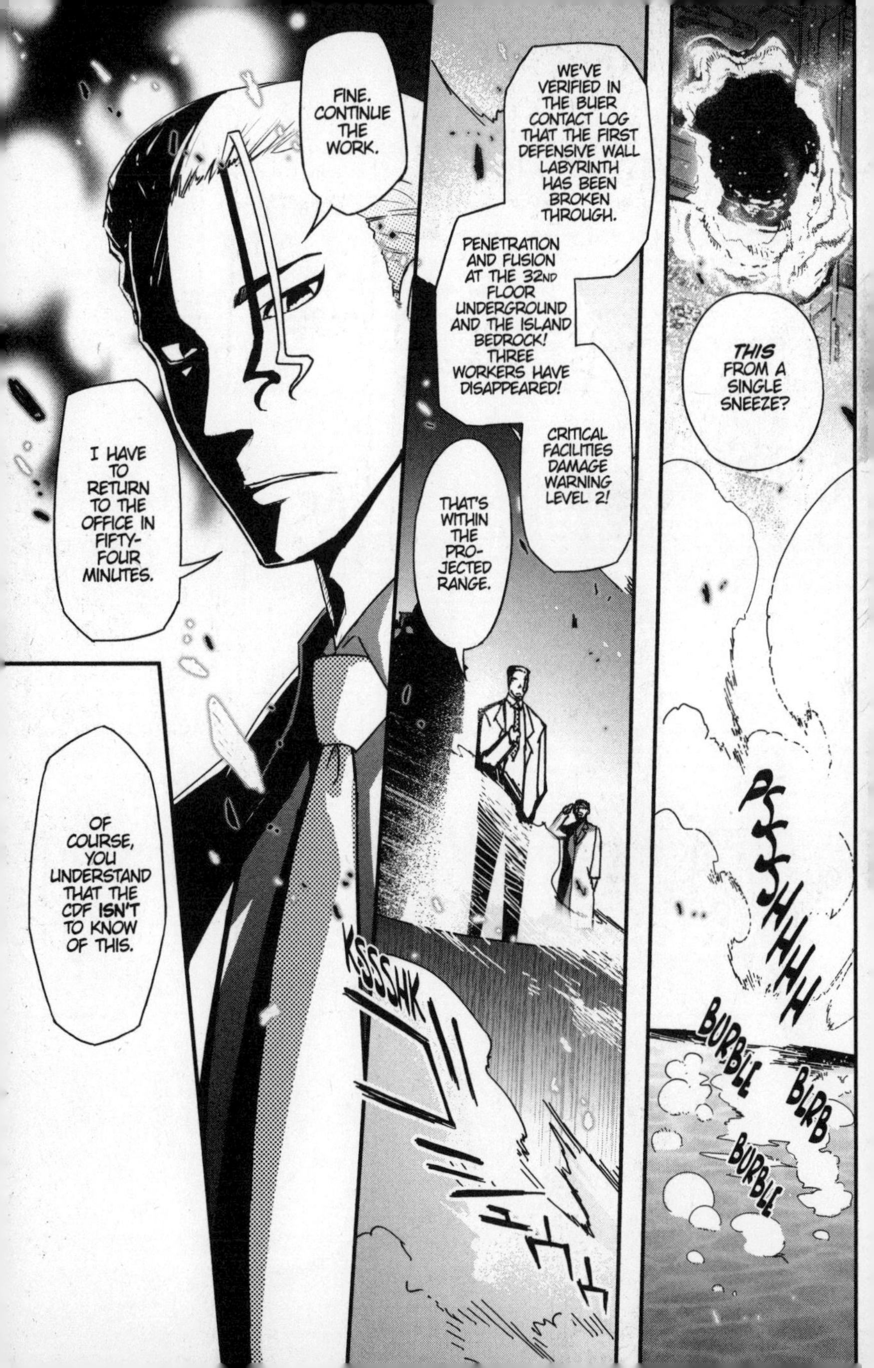
THIS FROM A SINGLE SNEEZE?
PSSHHHHH
BURBLE
BLRB
BURBLE
WE'VE VERIFIED IN THE BUER CONTACT LOG THAT THE FIRST DEFENSIVE WALL LABYRINTH HAS BEEN BROKEN THROUGH.
PENETRATION AND FUSION AT THE 32ND FLOOR UNDERGROUND AND THE ISLAND BEDROCK! THREE WORKERS HAVE DISAPPEARED!
CRITICAL FACILITIES DAMAGE WARNING LEVEL 2!
THAT'S WITHIN THE PRO-JECTED RANGE.
KSSSHK
FINE. CONTINUE THE WORK.
I HAVE TO RETURN TO THE OFFICE IN FIFTY-FOUR MINUTES.
OF COURSE, YOU UNDERSTAND THAT THE CDF ISN'T TO KNOW OF THIS.

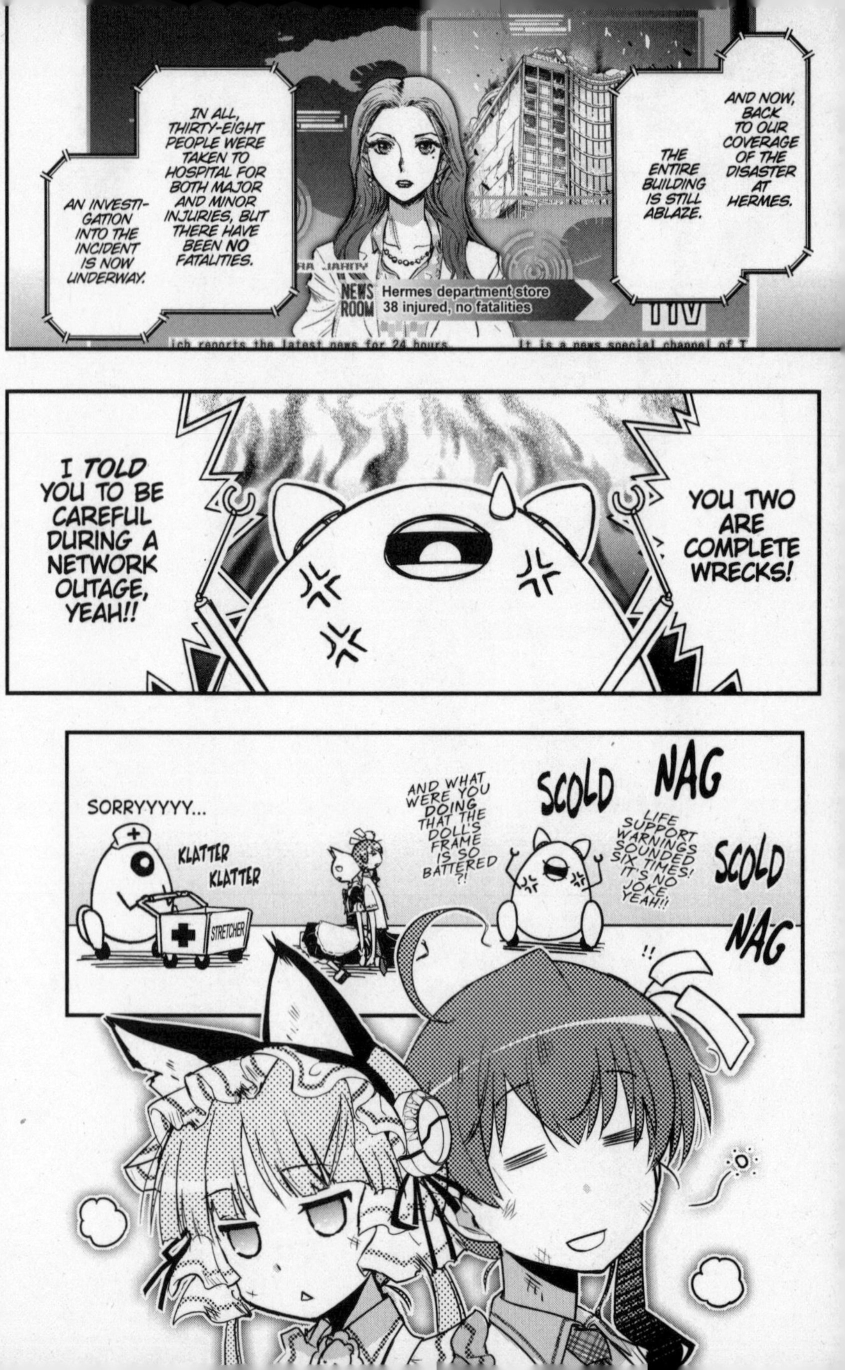
AND NOW, BACK TO OUR COVERAGE OF THE DISASTER AT HERMES.
THE ENTIRE BUILDING IS STILL ABLAZE.
IN ALL, THIRTY-EIGHT PEOPLE WERE TAKEN TO HOSPITAL FOR BOTH MAJOR AND MINOR INJURIES, BUT THERE HAVE BEEN NO FATALITIES.
AN INVESTIGATION INTO THE INCIDENT IS NOW UNDERWAY.
NEWS ROOM
Hermes department store
38 injured, no fatalities
ITV
ich reports the latest news for 24 hours.
It is a news special channel of T
YOU TWO ARE COMPLETE WRECKS!
I TOLD YOU TO BE CAREFUL DURING A NETWORK OUTAGE, YEAH!!
NAG
SCOLD
LIFE SUPPORT WARNINGS SOUNDED SIX TIMES! IT'S NO JOKE, YEAH!!
SCOLD
NAG
AND WHAT WERE YOU DOING THAT THE DOLL'S FRAME IS SO BATTERED?!
SORRYYYY...
KLATTER
KLATTER
STRETCHER
!!

···**TO BE CONTINUED**

TRANSMITTED SOMEHOW! PANDORADIO

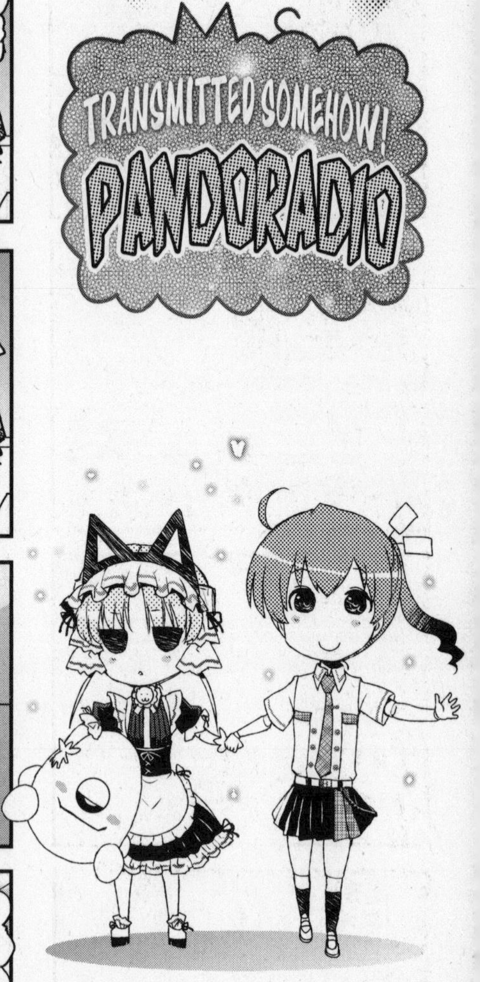

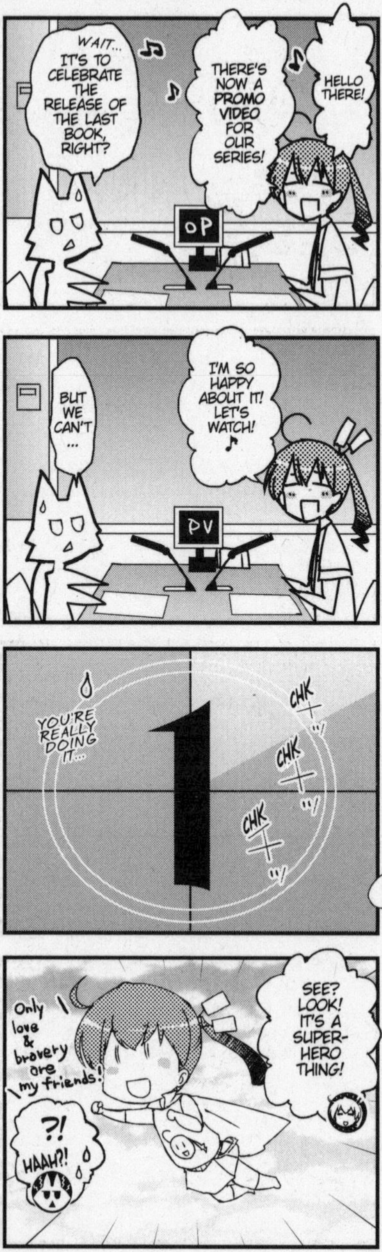
HELLO THERE!
THERE'S NOW A PROMO VIDEO FOR OUR SERIES!
WAIT... IT'S TO CELEBRATE THE RELEASE OF THE LAST BOOK, RIGHT?
OP
I'M SO HAPPY ABOUT IT! LET'S WATCH! ♪
BUT WE CAN'T ...
PV
CHK
CHK
CHK
YOU'RE REALLY DOING IT...
1
SEE? LOOK! IT'S A SUPER-HERO THING!
Only love & bravery are my friends!
?!
HAAH?!

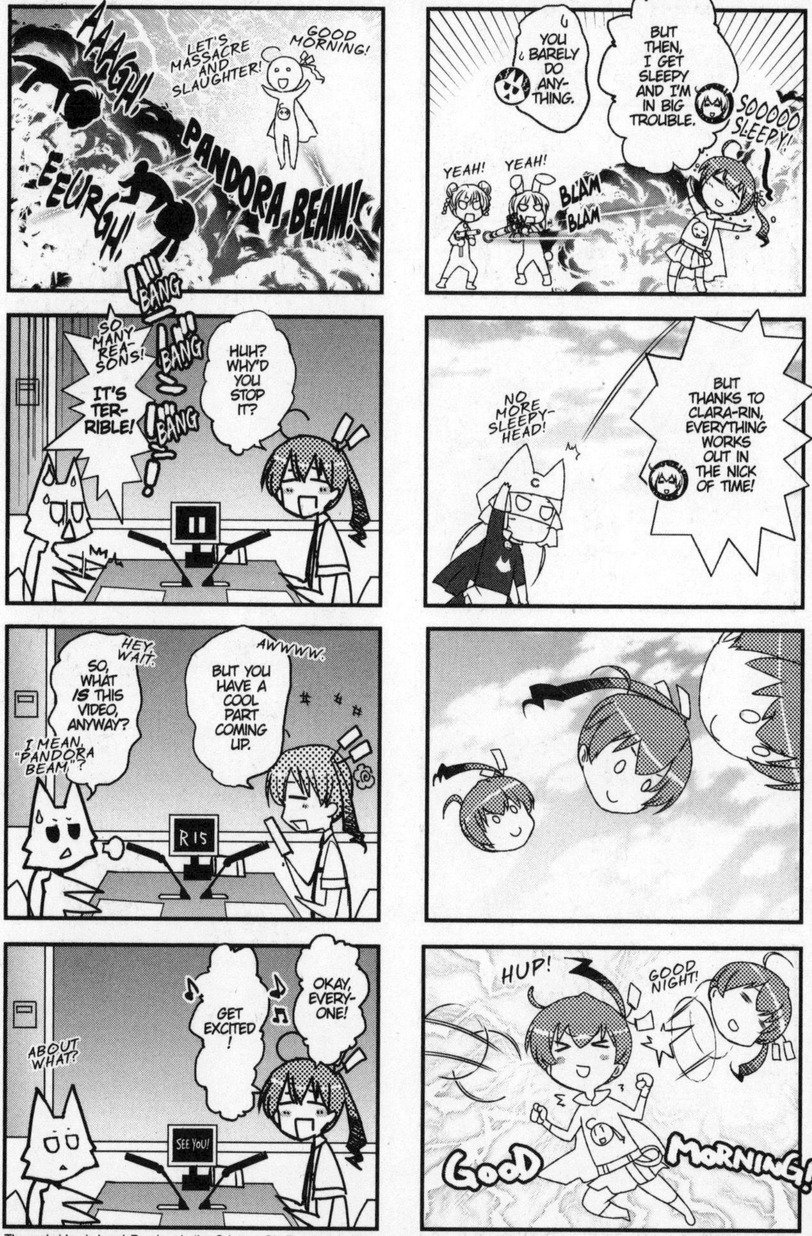
BUT THEN, I GET SLEEPY AND I'M IN BIG TROUBLE.
SOOOOO SLEEPY!
YOU BARELY DO ANYTHING.
BLAM
BLAM
YEAH!
YEAH!
BUT THANKS TO CLARA-RIN, EVERYTHING WORKS OUT IN THE NICK OF TIME!
NO MORE SLEEPYHEAD!
GOOD NIGHT!
HUP!
GOOD MORNING!
GOOD MORNING!
LET'S MASSACRE AND SLAUGHTER!
AAAGH!
PANDORA BEAM!
EEURGH!
BANG
HUH? WHY'D YOU STOP IT?
BANG
BANG
SO MANY REASONS! IT'S TERRIBLE!
AWWWW.
BUT YOU HAVE A COOL PART COMING UP.
HEY, WAIT.
SO, WHAT *IS* THIS VIDEO, ANYWAY?
I MEAN, "PANDORA BEAM"?
R15
OKAY, EVERYONE!
GET EXCITED!
ABOUT WHAT?
SEE YOU!

The real video is here! *Pandora in the Crimson Shell's* special site: http://kadokawa.co.jp/sp/pandora/

ORIGINAL CONCEPT DESIGN NOTES

Original Character Design Sketches

Originally, rather than there being only one Clarion, there were about twenty versions of her to do things like take care of the professor and perform all kinds of duties around the secret base. All but one of them would have been eliminated while taking countermeasures for Buer, and that last one would have been stuck working with Nene. Nene would have coincidentally found her way into the underground facility during a natural disaster, and the professor would have made her help bring materials in. Then the professor orders Clarion to obey Nene and live with (and monitor) her, and the rest is history.

Rikudou-shi used the concept of her teeth being like a shredder in a way that was in line with the design objectives (LOL), which I appreciate. Normally, no one would ever use a design like that.

She was also designed with a Plasma Cat Punch (LOL) and the same overheating function halt as Buer, but what happens with those is up to Rikudou-shi.

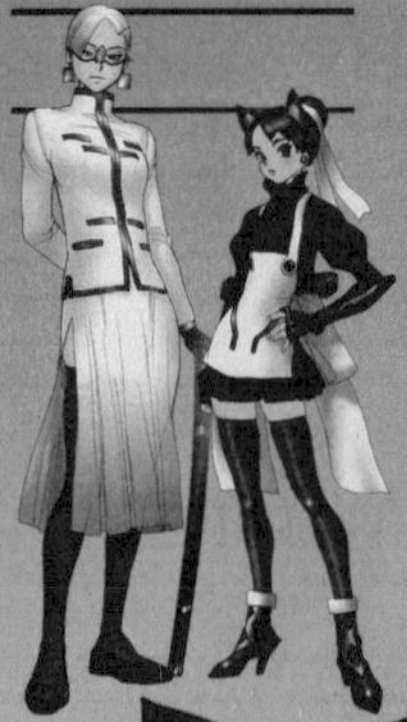

Always equipped with enhanced maid uniform Crow Black and invincible apron Snow Rabbit.

Fashion glasses are the professor's.

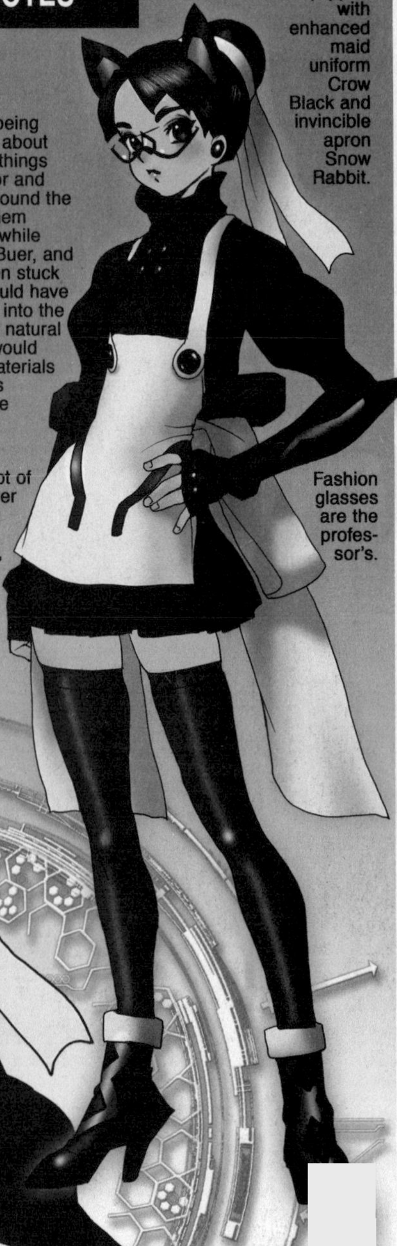

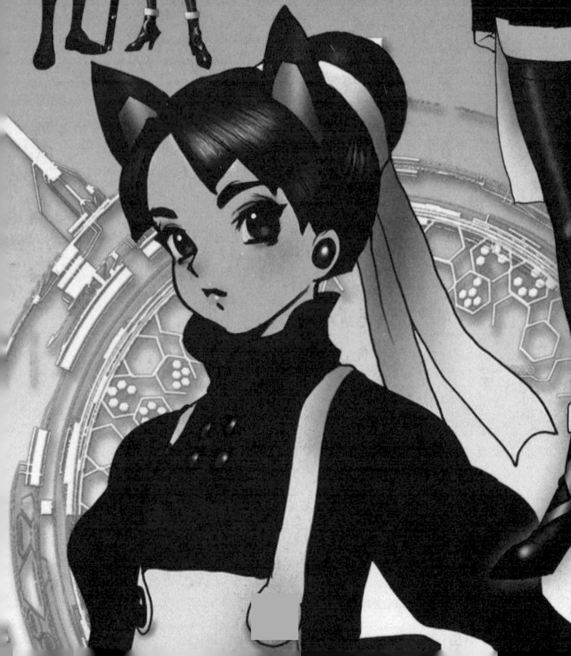

Original Character Design Sketches

Huh? What's the planning sketch for *Ghost in the Shell: Arise's* Kurtz doing here? Oh, right--she was originally designed for this project. *explodes*

In both works, I made changes to the appearance and other details, so they don't actually overlap, which mear there's really no problem. The original design may be th same, but the character is like an example of how differ- ent chefs can make very different dishes from the same ingredients. Or to put it another way, the Kurtz we see i this character design doesn't really exist anywhere.

In my original notes, I wrote "The colonel is petty and only thinks about her own benefit. Ultimately, she falls into one of her own traps." She's a member of the American CIA and supervisor of the self-proclaimed "Justice Organization."

But in fact, she plans to take a cut of the professor's action. She's a villain who persuades Nene to join the Justice Organization (the goals of which are the opposit of the name), intending to dispose of her once she has Clarion and Buer. But while she's trying to eliminate Nene, unforeseen things keep happening ***because*** of Nene. That was the idea, anyway, but...the overall proje took a very different turn, so these designs... *explodes*

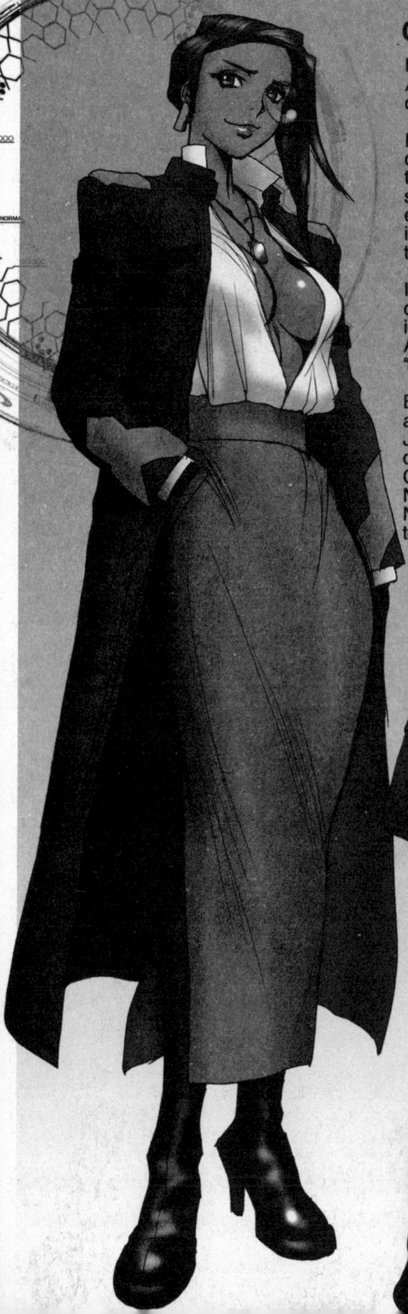

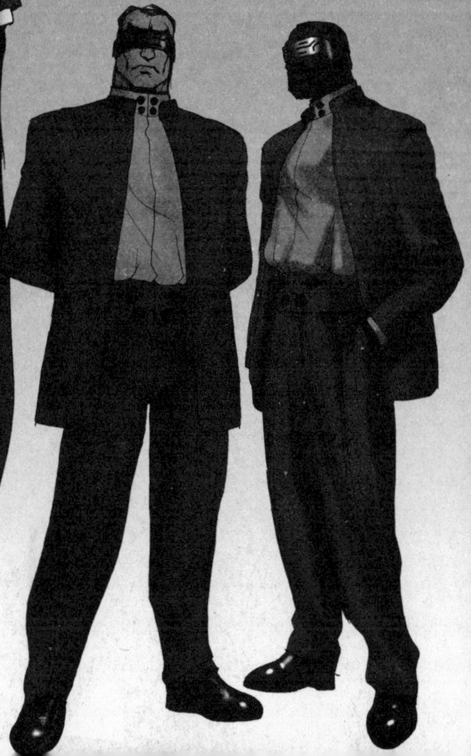

Greetings! (For the fourth time!)

On October 29, 2013, Rikudou-shi and I had a face-to-face meeting to get to know each other. At that time I gave him color printouts of the designs for the professor, Clarion, Auntie, and Vli--*whump* (as souvenirs, not instructions). So this time, when I was writing about the designs, I didn't include anything about how this was the first time Rikudou-shi was seeing them.

Naturally, the head editor would have taken a look at the initial text and pictures, but as we moved forward with this project, we took the approach of leaving everything related to the story--both the major and minor plot elements--and the characters' evolution up to Rikudou-shi, which meant he was responsible for all the critical elements of the manga. That left only the general worldview and overall structure.

At this point, I think things are going well--better than anyone who was originally involved imagined--thanks to Rikudou-shi. If (hypothetically) this were ever made into a movie down the line, it would all go perfectly smoothly without any involvement from my character images. The story has already shifted away from the initial booster rocket of my designs and is now under Rikudou-shi's supervision.

Possibly the fact that Rikudou-shi is able to have fun and really play around with the shell worldview and gadgets is ultimately why this work is interesting. And thus, *Ghost Urn*--a homeless concept since 2008--has happily been reborn as Pandora and given life. (I'm not the one who christened it *Pandora in the Crimson Shell*.)

I originally wanted to bring this into the world as the story of an amateur cyborg fighting and working as hard as she could, including many elements related to rescue efforts and saving lives. That was my goal before the Tohoku Earthquake disaster, but for whatever variety of reasons, that never came about. This is very different from my initial thoughts, but I'm glad it's been safely guided out of the nest. Now, all I can do is pray that this story about Nene and Clarion's adventures, crafted by Rikudou-shi, brings someone somewhere a moment of pleasure.

November 15, 2013
Shirow Masamune

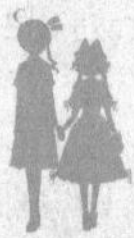

原案 》SHIROW MASAMUNE

04 STAFF

Original story	Shirow Masamune (in cooperation with Crossroad)
Production	Rikudou Koushi
Composition/ Art	Masahito Watari Rin Hitotose Rikudou Koushi
Art assistance	Takepon G Unamu Kibayashida
Editing	Koichiro Ochiai (Kadokawa)
Design	Noriyuki Jinguji (Zin Studio)
Special Thanks	Seishinsha Co., Ltd.

GHOST URN

SEVEN SEAS ENTERTAINMENT PRESENTS

PANDORA IN THE CRIMSON SHELL

GHOST URN vol. 04

story by **SHIROW MASAMUNE** / art by **RIKUDOU KOUSHI**

TRANSLATION
Jocelyne Allen

ADAPTATION
Ysabet Reinhardt MacFarlane

LETTERING
Roland Amago

LAYOUT
Bambi Eloriaga-Amago

COVER DESIGN
Nicky Lim

PROOFREADER
Shanti Whitesides

PRODUCTION MANAGER
Lissa Pattillo

EDITOR-IN-CHIEF
Adam Arnold

PUBLISHER
Jason DeAngelis

Edited by KADOKAWASHOTEN.
First published in Japan in 2014 by KADOKAWA CORPORATION, Tokyo.
English translation rights arranged with KADOKAWA CORPORATION, Tokyo, through TOHAN CORPORATION, Tokyo.

ISBN: 978-1-626922-60-0

Printed in Canada

First Printing: April 2016

10 9 8 7 6 5 4 3 2 1

FOLLOW US ONLINE: ***www.gomanga.com***

READING DIRECTIONS

This book reads from ***right to left***, Japanese style. If this is your first time reading manga, you start reading from the top right panel on each page and take it from there. If you get lost, just follow the numbered diagram here. It may seem backwards at first, but you'll get the hang of it! Have fun!!

1
2
3
4
5
6
7
8
9

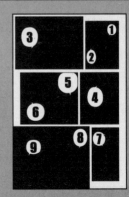